INTRODUCING

Child Psychology

H. RUDOLPH SCHAFFER

Blackwell
Publishing

BLACKWELL PUBLISHING
350 Main Street, Malden, MA 02148-5020, USA
9600 Garsington Road, Oxford OX4 2DQ, UK
550 Swanston Street, Carlton, Victoria 3053, Australia

First published 2004 by Blackwell Publishing Ltd

8   2010

Library of Congress Cataloging-in-Publication Data

Schaffer, H. Rudolph.
Introducing child psychology / H. Rudolph Schaffer.
p. cm.
Includes bibliographical references and index.
ISBN 978-0-631-21627-8 (hardcover); ISBN 978-0-631-21628-5 (pbk.)
1. Child psychology. 2. Child development. I. Title.

BF721.S349 2004
155.4–dc21   2003004192

A catalogue record for this title is available from the British Library.

Set in 10/12½ pt Baskerville
by Graphicraft Ltd, Hong Kong
Printed and bound in Singapore
by Markono Print Media Pte Ltd

For further information on
Blackwell Publishing, visit our website:
www.blackwellpublishing.com

Contents

Boxes

Figures

Tables

Preface

Children are fascinating; children are important – both very good reasons for wanting to find out more about them. They are fascinating because they are both like adults and yet different: on the one hand, they so clearly have the potential to develop the full range of all those human capacities that we value in mature individuals, and on the other hand, they have abilities and requirements of their own, specific to each age range, that we need to acknowledge and respect and that need to be catered for. Children are also fascinating because the essence of childhood is change, and to observe the way the newborn baby develops into a toddler who then successively becomes preschooler, schoolchild and adolescent, and to try to account for the mechanisms underlying this change, is something both intellectually intriguing and emotionally satisfying. Do experiences in the earliest years leave irreversible effects on the mind? To what extent are we shaped by our genetic endowment? Why do some children acquire language at earlier ages than others? What are the effects of divorce on children of different ages? Are there optimal ways of helping children to develop problem-solving skills? These and a great many other questions arise during the everyday business of caring for and educating children to which we would like answers, even if it is simply to satisfy our curiosity.

But children are also important, for the future of society depends on how we bring up and educate the next generation. Again, a great many questions arise. Are there certain 'right' ways of rearing children and helping them to achieve their potential? Are there risk factors that we need to know about and avoid? Is early aggressiveness a danger sign heralding later violence and delinquency? Can children make up for missing out on important experiences at the usual time, such as forming close relationships with parents in infancy or being exposed to print well before school age? Finding answers matters not only to the individuals responsible for children's upbringing; it matters also to those charged with formulating general policies in the fields of education, welfare, health and care, to enable them to design these policies with a view to furthering the best interests of children.

Child psychology aims to answer questions such as those above by setting up an information base derived from objective enquiry, in this way going beyond mere opinion to factually based conclusions about the nature of children's development. Although still a very young science, it has grown enormously over the last half-century or so, and to do full justice to all aspects is clearly impossible, indeed undesirable, in a relatively concise introduction to the subject. Rather than provide coverage in depth, the book aims to provide an overview of the main findings that have emerged, concentrating on those topics that have attracted most atten tion in recent years, and so give an account both of the nature of child psychology and of its achievements.

The book is for anyone wanting to find out what child psychology has to offer – either because they are setting out on psychology courses in school or university, or because the subject is relevant in professions such as teaching, social work, psychiatry and law, or because of sheer curiosity as to 'what makes children tick'. It is written at a level that assumes no previous knowledge, but, while attempting to avoid too many technicalities, some technical terms are occasionally necessary; these are printed in **bold** and are defined on their first use in the margin as well as in the Glossary at the end of the book. Also, at particular points throughout the book, boxes will be found that pick up certain specific matters raised in the text in order to consider them in somewhat more detail. At the end of each chapter a list of further reading is provided for anyone who wants to investigate the topics discussed there in greater depth – and a measure of the success of this book may well be the extent to which its readers do feel inspired to consult these sources and pursue the subject further.

Rudolph Schaffer
University of Strathclyde
Glasgow, Scotland

About the Author

Rudolph Schaffer was born in Germany, educated in England and has spent most of his working life in Scotland, where he is at present Professor Emeritus in the Psychology Department of the University of Strathclyde in Glasgow.

Initially he had intended to become an architect, and after leaving school he spent two years studying architecture at the University of Liverpool. However, as a result of working with deprived teenagers in his spare time in a hostel where he was living and helping out as a part-time warden, he decided that psychology was a much more interesting and rewarding subject, and accordingly moved to London where he studied part-time at Birkbeck College while working as a shipping clerk in an import-export business.

After graduating he was appointed as a research assistant in John Bowlby's research unit at the Tavistock Clinic, where he participated in work on maternal deprivation and separation and witnessed the early stages of Bowlby's formulation of attachment theory. Following a move to Glasgow on taking up a post as clinical psychologist in the Royal Hospital for Sick Children, he was able to continue research on these topics, resulting in a number of reports on the effects of hospitalization on babies and on the early development of attachment relationships. Working in a hospital context also gave him the opportunity of finding out about some of the complexities of translating research into practice while attempting to apply the lessons learned from psychological research to the care of children in hospitals and other public institutions.

At the University of Strathclyde, which he joined in 1964, he was able to build up an extensive research programme concerned with early social development, with particular reference to socialization processes and the formation of early relationships. The topics that he and the members of his research team investigated included the cognitive basis to social behaviour, the beginnings of non-verbal communication in infancy, the interpersonal context of language development and the nature of parental socialization techniques. At the same time, he continued his interest in drawing attention to the practical implications of such research by means of books and articles as well as talks to a range of professional audiences in many countries.

CHAPTER ONE

Finding Out about Children

Chapter Outline

What is child psychology and why do we need it? Let us turn to these elementary questions first, for there is little point in giving an account of the subject until we have spelled out what it is we are talking about and why.

What is Child Psychology?

Nature and aims

Child psychology is the *scientific* study of children's behaviour and development.

Note the emphasis on the word 'scientific', for it is this which distinguishes child psychology from other, more subjective ways of looking at children. Psychologists attempt to describe and explain children's behaviour and the way it changes over age, and do so in ways that do not depend on vague impressions, guesswork or armchair theorizing but on the careful, systematic collection of empirical data. Research on children need not involve formal settings like laboratories, although these can be useful for certain types of investigation; data can be collected just as systematically from such seemingly chaotic situations as playgrounds, discos or the family dinner table. But whatever the setting, the aim of child psychology is to assemble a knowledge base which can provide insight both into the nature of childhood generally and into the distinctive characteristics of individual children.

In this way, we should become able to answer three kinds of questions, i.e. *when, how* and *why* questions.

- *When.* These are perhaps the most obvious ones to ask, for they refer to the process of continuous change which is the hallmark of childhood and makes the tracking of individual children so fascinating. *Milestones of development* take many forms: some are obvious ones, such as the ages when children first become able to walk and talk; others are less obvious in that they refer to more subtle developments, e.g. the age when children become capable of make-believe play, of taking the perspective of another person or of understanding the meaning of print. In each case, the aim is to establish the age range when most children can be expected first to show the new ability, and by means of these norms we can then check on the progress of any one individual child.
- *How.* These are questions not about the timing but about the manner of children's behaviour. How do preschool children form themselves into groups – in intimate twos and threes or in much larger numbers? Always among the same friends or indiscriminately? In same-sex or in mixed-sex groups? Or, to take another example, how do children draw the human figure? In what way do they progress from scribbles to representation? Are 'tadpole figures' an inevitable part of this progression? How do they spatially organize the figure? And one more example, how do children judge various kinds of misdeeds? Do they have just some sort of partially developed moral sense, and if so,

what kind? Can they make subtle distinctions according to the nature of the
misdeed and its consequences? Do they take the wrongdoer's intentions into
account? With respect to all three of our examples, we require descriptive
information about how children, of particular ages and in particular circumstances, go about the business of tackling everyday life, and how that changes
as they grow older.

- *Why.* Giving an account of children's behaviour is, of course, not only a
  matter of systematic *description*; it also involves *explanation*. Why do some children develop at a slower rate than others? Why is it that certain children
  show highly developed abilities in one specific area yet not in other areas?
  Why are boys physically more aggressive than girls? Why do some children
  become antisocial? Why is parental punitiveness linked with child aggressiveness? Why . . . ? It seems almost as though these sorts of questions can
  go on indefinitely – partly because every aspect of children's development
  requires an explanation, but partly also because, admittedly, we are not anywhere near as far advanced with explanation as we are with description. The
  latter is, after all, a lot easier than the former; our knowledge of the timing
  and manner of children's behaviour is consequently rather more advanced
  than our ability to understand its causation.

In theory, questions can be asked about all aspects of child development. In
practice, at any given time psychologists tend to pursue only a fairly limited number
of problems. There are two main reasons for this. For one thing, there is pressure
from society to provide answers to certain kinds of questions that happen to be
important just then. The sharp increase of divorce over the last few decades, for
instance, has highlighted the need to study the consequences which this experience has for children. Can one expect emotional disturbance, at least in the short
term? Are there repercussions for learning and classroom behaviour? Might long-
term consequences occur which manifest themselves in adulthood, such as in the
individual's own marital history? Thus there are practical considerations, stemming
from the concerns of parents and professional workers as well as from politicians
and administrators, which determine the direction of research and prompt psychologists to undertake particular kinds of investigations. In the second place, psychologists also choose to study certain problems because they have become theoretically
meaningful at the time. Knowledge, that is, has advanced to a particular point;
its progress hitherto suggests certain new directions; and because it is natural to
want to extend knowledge for its own sake, additional studies are undertaken in
order to push the frontiers out still further. A study, for example, that has found
shyness to be a stable and well-established trait by mid-childhood is likely to give
rise to all sorts of further questions. How early in life can signs of shyness be
detected? Is this already a stable trait in infancy? Do genetic factors play a part
in its origins? Are extreme manifestations early on indicative of later pathology?
Research, that is, has an impetus of its own and the pursuit of knowledge is undertaken as a venture in its own right.

There are, however, limits to the questions that psychologists are able to tackle. For one thing, some questions demand value judgements rather than research data. Should parents have the right physically to punish their children? Research can provide answers regarding the effects of physical punishment on children; what it cannot do is decide what the rights of parents should be or, for that matter, what rights children should have. These are issues for society to resolve. Another limitation lies in the availability of adequate methodological tools, for there are some aspects of human behaviour which, as yet, are too subtle for proper description, let alone measurement. Advances in knowledge depend, at least in part, on the development of assessment techniques; thus, the concentration on intellectual development in the early stages of child psychology reflected largely the widespread use of cognitive tests: social and emotional characteristics were relatively neglected because they seemed just too slippery for objective study. Not till recently, with the greater availability of the relevant tools, have these aspects begun to receive the amounts of attention that they too deserve.

Methods

Psychologists obtain their findings from three main sources: observing, asking and experimenting.

- *Observation* may seem an easy technique to apply; in fact, its skilled use requires a great deal of practice and much planning. Decisions have to be made about what, whom, when and where to observe, and about which of a number of different observational techniques to employ. Observations can be of a participant or a non-participant nature; take the form of a continuous narrative or be confined to only certain episodes; involve time sampling or event sampling; focus on a range of different categories of behaviour or just on one; and be based on a single individual at a time or on the interactive behaviour of a number of individuals. As it is by no means easy for any human being to be completely objective in recording the behaviour of another human being, reliability checks must be carried out, usually based on the agreement of several observers (for further details about this and the other data-gathering techniques mentioned below, see S. A. Miller, 1998).
- *Asking* involves two main approaches: interviews and questionnaires. Their use with young children is obviously limited, and yet, when questions are embedded in natural conversations about meaningful topics, some most useful information can be elicited even from preschool children (e.g. Bartsch & Wellman, 1995; Dunn & Hughes, 1998). When applied to older children or to their parents and teachers, both interviews and questionnaires can take a great many forms: structured and unstructured, formal and informal, predetermined and open-ended. The choice among these will largely depend on the purpose to which they are to be put, for the precise form of questions

and the conditions under which they are administered is likely to have considerable implications for the information obtained.

- *Experimenting*, when applied to children, may conjure up ideas of something nasty and undesirable; in fact, it merely refers to procedures whereby the situation in which a child is placed is controlled and standardized as precisely as possible. In this way one can, first of all, ensure that the conditions are the same for all children included in the study, and, secondly, deliberately vary some of these conditions in order to see how children's behaviour changes. It will then become possible to test some particular hypothesis and obtain answers to specific questions. Let us take an example: can children working jointly in a group learn to solve problems more readily than when working alone? To obtain credible evidence one needs to assign children of a given age randomly to two conditions, one in which they work with a stated number of other children and one in which they work on their own, the two sets of children being comparable in all respects that might conceivably influence the outcome, such as intelligence and educational achievement. A particular task needs to be chosen for the children to work on, and a pretest administered to demonstrate that the task is initially beyond each child's capability. The two sets of children will then be asked to attempt to solve the problem under conditions that are identical in all respects other than in the number of children working on the task, after which a post-test (or a series of post-tests over a period of time) will be administered. One can then determine, first, what progress has been made by the children in comparison with their pre-test performance, and, secondly, whether the children working jointly with others showed greater advances than the children working on their own. The advantage of collaborative over individual learning (at least as found under the conditions employed by this particular experiment) can thus be ascertained, and, having obtained the findings under strictly controlled circumstances, one can be reasonably certain that any difference found in performance is indeed caused by the variation in number of children. Experimental methods thus make it possible to arrive at cause-and-effect conclusions – something that is only rarely possible with other methods.

Cross-sectional and longitudinal approaches

Our questions about children may involve just one specific age group: for instance, are 3-year-olds capable of experiencing shame? Or, can 8-year-olds understand abstract scientific principles? Alternatively, our interest may lie in developmental change: how do children's reactions to separation from their family change with age? Do 10-year-olds have a more sophisticated self-concept than 6-year-olds? Questions about change involve a tracing over age of some particular psychological function, enabling one to follow up that function from its beginnings to maturity and right through to decline and so determine whether, for example, the function changes

Cross-sectional research designs. Different groups of children varying in age are compared on some specific measure in order to assess how particular functions change in the course of development.

Longitudinal research designs. The same group of children is followed up and tested at different ages in order to trace change in the course of development.

its overt manifestation as the child grows older, whether its developmental course is affected by the same influences at all ages or not, whether groups differing in specified ways such as gender resemble each other in their developmental characteristics, and so forth. Comparison of different age groups is thus required.

There are two ways in which such comparison can be carried out: by adopting either **cross-sectional** or **longitudinal research designs**.

- *Cross-sectional* designs entail the study of different groups of children of varying age, but all assessed under the same conditions and with the same techniques. Such research has the practical advantage of being relatively quick, for the various age groups can all be investigated within the same time period. However, it has the disadvantage that one cannot be wholly certain that the groups differ in age alone, for however hard one tries to keep other possible influences such as social class, intelligence and health the same, there may still be various uncontrolled factors of personality and background that could be responsible for the results obtained.

- In *longitudinal* designs the *same* children are followed up and studied at all ages. Thus one can eliminate variation due to children's individuality and be reasonably certain that differences between age groups are indeed due to age. The disadvantage is, however, that such studies take a long time: they require that the investigation takes as long as the age range examined, and loss of participants during this time then becomes a real possibility.

There is no doubt that longitudinal research is preferable if one is to make statements about developmental change. Unfortunately, because of their duration, follow-up studies are expensive and are therefore much rarer than cross-sectional studies. Most of what we know about change over age is therefore derived from the latter type of research and thus needs to be treated with some degree of caution until replicated by longitudinal studies.

Why Do We Need Child Psychology?

Turning to the second question that we raised at the beginning, let us confront the frequently heard criticism that we already know about children and how to raise them without all this scientific hullabaloo, that such knowledge existed long before psychology ever came into being and that it is indeed an ingrained part of humanity, without which the survival of our species would hardly be possible. Child psychology, it is sometimes asserted, is just a lot of long words for something that everybody already knows and, when the need arises, is able to put into practice.

But let us take the sort of assertions that are commonly made about children and their upbringing:

'Only children are lonely children.'
'Girls are more sensitive than boys.'
'Too much television viewing retards intellectual development.'
'Single-parent families are responsible for juvenile delinquency.'
'Men are naturally less proficient as parents than women.'
'Children of working mothers are at risk for maladjustment.'

There are many who regard generalizations such as these as common sense – so obvious that they do not need to be defended, let alone verified. But one can also argue that what is labelled as common sense is not always a reliable guide and can sometimes turn out to be a shaky foundation for conclusions about human behaviour, and that accordingly more systematic evidence is required. Let us therefore distinguish between two ways of obtaining answers to our questions about children: the subjective and the objective way.

Answering questions: The subjective way

In everyday life, confronted by individual children and their immediate needs and requirements, we inevitably rely to a large extent on our own personal feelings as to what is the 'right' course to adopt. These feelings have various sources:

- The most common are simply *hunches*: knowing how to comfort a crying child, how to stimulate a bored one, how to curb an aggressive one. These hunches can be excellent guides to personal behaviour; they represent intuitive knowledge that helps a great many people successfully to rear their offspring without ever opening a book on the subject. And yet, even at this level, there is much uncertainty, as seen in the sometimes puzzled, sometimes desperate letters which parents send to women's magazines, or in the advice columns written in response by 'experts'; or in the popularity of television programmes aimed at all those responsible for children's care and education and intended to provide insight into everyday child phenomena; or in the moves by governments to create establishments such as parenting institutes, designed to support and improve practices that may seem natural but that nevertheless appear to bewilder a great many people. What is more, these unanalysed hunches can sometimes stem from deep-seated prejudices and preconceptions: arguments about the ability of gay or lesbian couples successfully to rear children can have more to do with personal hang-ups about sex than with any knowledge about the effects that such upbringing has on children.
- Another source lies in people's *personal experience*, particularly of events in their own childhood. Such experience is bound to influence one's judgement,

whether in a positive way by wanting the next generation to have the same benefits or, quite on the contrary, by doing one's best to protect children from what one went through oneself. But however natural such a tendency may be, it is not always a reliable guide for making decisions either about individual children or about children in general. For one thing, memories of one's own past often give rise to highly emotionally charged feelings that can readily distort judgement; and for another, the single case (oneself) that the judgement is based on may well be quite atypical and therefore inappropriate in dealing with other cases. 'It never did me any harm' as an answer to the problem of using physical punishment is certainly inadequate as a guide for policy decisions about children generally; it is also of little relevance to determining how to discipline any other particular child – even one's own. We may never be able entirely to escape our own childhood, but we cannot automatically generalize from that to the childhood of others.

- The third source is of a somewhat different order, for it refers to *experts' advice* and is thus rather more explicit and articulate than the other two sources. Let us take the best known of all the childrearing experts, Benjamin Spock, whose book *Baby and Child Care* (1948) played such an enormous part in determining how parents brought up their children in the 1950s and 1960s. There is no doubt that much of the advice Spock had to offer was shrewd and helpful, and that a great many parents found him a considerable source of comfort. And yet, if one closely examines Spock's writings in order to determine what that advice is based on, it soon becomes apparent that most of his pronouncements had no firmer base than a mixture of personal opinion, guesswork, folklore and experience with clinical, and therefore atypical, cases. The same applies to many other so-called experts, and under the circumstances it is no wonder that fluctuations and abrupt changes occur periodically in what these individuals regard as acceptable in the upbringing of children. In the 1930s, for instance, the emphasis was very much on strictness, largely due to the influence of Truby King (1924), a paediatrician who advised mothers to feed by the clock, start toilet training early and not respond to a baby's cries for attention. In the 1950s the pendulum swung to the opposite extreme as a result of Spock's emphasis on permissiveness; yet this too eventually changed when Spock, blamed by a later generation as directly responsible for the student troubles and other manifestations of youth unrest of the 1960s, retreated from his previous position. The eminence and considerable clinical experience of people such as Spock and Truby King no doubt played a large part in persuading parents to adopt their advice as the 'right' course: their wisdom was taken for granted and they were accordingly treated as authority figures. Only when one is prepared to examine the source of their assertions more closely does it become apparent that their advice is also often based on purely subjective considerations. As to conclusions based on clinical experience, these certainly have their uses: they may draw attention to particular phenomena that are clearly of importance in children's lives, and they may lead to hypotheses about the causation of various kinds of child behaviour that require investigation. However, for one thing, children requiring clinicians' help cannot be regarded as representative of children generally; for another, findings obtained in a clinical context can rarely be collected in any systematic, standardized way; and in addition there is usually no possibility of comparing the data so collected with those from non-clinical cases. Conclusions arrived at in the course of clinical work may be the first step in leading to significant insights, but on their own they do not constitute evidence. A surer guide is required than hypotheses and general impressions (for a detailed example of the contentious nature of experts' advice, see box 1.1).

Answering questions: The objective way

The aim of child psychology is to apply scientific methods to the investigation of human development. In this way an attempt is made to answer questions about children's behaviour and the way it changes over age in as systematic a manner as possible, and to minimize the influence of subjective factors such as opinion, guesswork and armchair theorizing. To this end, various safeguards are built into the research procedures employed – safeguards such as spelling out in detail all aspects of the methods used in obtaining the findings, making these aspects public and thus open to other people's scrutiny, subjecting results to statistical analysis to determine whether they are credible, and always insisting on replication by other investigators instead of merely relying on the conclusions of any one study. It is the application of means such as these that justifies the distinction between objective and subjective approaches.

To illustrate the way the distinction works in practice, let us consider the consequences for young children of having a working mother. This is not only an issue where a large number of individuals want information to help them make personal choices, but also one where governments and other policy-making organizations require guidance on such matters as the drafting of employment legislation and the provision of nursery facilities. How do psychologists set about the task of determining the effects on children of such an experience, and how does their approach differ from the more subjective approaches?

Psychological research, if it is to arrive at valid conclusions, must follow certain procedures. Among the more important of these are:

- *Precise description of the sample investigated,* so that one knows to what sort of children and their families the results can be applied. The meaning of maternal employment may be very different among poor families, where economic needs are paramount and where child care during the mother's absence from home is difficult to arrange, compared with well-off families, where the mother goes out to work primarily because of career aspirations and where professional carers can be engaged to look after the child in her absence. Findings from one

BOX 1.1

How much television should children watch?

In the course of 1999 the American Academy of Pediatrics, which has 55,000 members and is the main representative organization for paediatricians in the United States, issued a report on the impact of television on children. This report concluded with the following guidelines:

1 Children under 2 years should not be allowed to watch any television at all. Instead, their parents should play with them, as a child of this age has a critical need for social interaction which, if not fulfilled, will stunt healthy brain growth and thus impede the growth of intelligence.
2 Children over 2 years should be strictly limited to a maximum of 2 hours per day, regulated with a timer. No TV screens of any sort should be allowed in children's bedrooms, which (according to a spokesperson) 'should be a sanctuary, a place where kids can reflect on what happened that day'.

The report, not surprisingly, received considerable publicity in the media and a great deal of comment. Yet in no case were questions asked about the nature of the evidence on which the conclusions were based; its credibility, its replicability and the extent to which statements about such matters as stunted brain growth could actually be borne out by facts were not challenged. Instead, there was a general assumption that if such authority figures as the members of the American Academy of Pediatrics issued pronouncements of this nature, they must be taken seriously. How they came to reach their conclusions appeared to be irrelevant; the possibility that personal factors led to bias and misinterpretation of whatever data the paediatricians examined was not considered.

Equally significant was the popular reaction to the report, illustrated by two letters published in the London *Times* (10 August 1999). In one of these, the writer thoroughly approves of the recommendations because 'all our instincts' told her husband and herself that this was the proper way of bringing up her children. In the other letter a mother, on the contrary, pours scorn on the report because she found, by 'exercising my own common sense', that encouraging her child even before the age of 2 to watch television helped rather than hindered development. Each of these mothers was clearly convinced that her way of doing things was the 'right' way because her gut feelings told her so. Yet they reached diametrically opposed conclusions: common sense, it appears, is not all that common.

Parents will, of course, always follow their own feelings about such matters as television viewing. However, they do look for guidelines from people assumed to be experts, and it therefore behoves these experts to base their advice on proper evidence, just as it is essential for the media and all potential consumers of the advice to ask the all-important question, 'How do they know?'

of these groups may not apply to the other, and though ideally samples in research should be representative of all individuals affected and therefore involve large numbers, practical difficulties usually dictate the need to confine investigations to certain specific and relatively small groups. Specification of the characteristics of the group is therefore essential, so that one can determine how widely the findings from a particular study can be applied and what may account for any differences when compared with findings from other studies. Subjective approaches rarely take into account the specific characteristics of the individuals on whom their conclusions are based but tend to assume that one can simply generalize from one group to another.

- *Assessment that is based on valid and reliable methods.* **Validity** refers to the extent to which an assessment technique really does measure the characteristic it claims to measure; **reliability** is the consistency with which the same results are obtained by that technique on different occasions or as administered by different individuals. Thus, any conclusions about the effects of maternal employment on, say, children's emotional adjustment should be based on measures in which one can have faith: they must go beyond the vague impressions we tend to rely on in everyday life and which so often form the basis of conclusions arrived at by more subjective approaches.

  Validity. The extent to which a particular measuring instrument really reflects what it purports to measure. Usually assessed by comparing the result with other indices.

  Reliability. Refers to the confidence we can have in a measuring instrument. Usually assessed by comparing results obtained at different times or from different testers.

- *Precise description of all aspects of methodology.* Whatever findings one obtains from research are influenced by the methods used to acquire them. Different methods do not necessarily yield identical results: a child's emotional adjustment can be assessed by interviewing the mother, interviewing the child's carer, administering questionnaires to either of these individuals, or by direct observation carried out by a research worker. Which is chosen will contribute to some extent to the results obtained; it is therefore essential to be explicit about the particular methods used. Inability to spell out how conclusions are arrived at is one of the main problems about the use of hunches: it means that two individuals who have reached diametrically opposed conclusions cannot resolve their differences by inspecting the means whereby they have got to those positions and may thus be left with nothing but dogmatic assertion.

- *The use of control groups.* To find, say, that a certain percentage of children of employed mothers are emotionally maladjusted is, by itself, of little use. One needs also to determine the incidence of maladjustment among children of non-employed mothers and thus establish a baseline. However, such a control group is only of use if it is precisely matched to the maternal employment group on all other characteristics that might possibly influence the results obtained, such as the child's age, sex and social class, the family's structure and relationships, various pre-existing personality features, and so on. Only then will the comparison yield meaningful results that can be correctly interpreted.

- *Precautions taken against bias.* If, say, children of employed mothers are compared with children of non-employed mothers by means of observation, those
  collecting the data should be blind as to which group each of the children
  they are observing belongs to; if possible, they should also not know about
  any hypotheses and expectations guiding the investigation. There are many
  ways in which precaution can be taken against personal influence in psychological research; awareness of the role of such influences is perhaps the most
  important way in which subjective and objective approaches differ.

Applying procedures such as these justifies psychological research as a distinctive
way of finding out about children. But let us now confess that the difference between
subjective and objective approaches is not as absolute as we have so far pretended
for the sake of exposition. However great the effort, it can be extremely difficult
to eliminate all subjective influences on research, and especially so because such
influences can operate at an unconscious level. Take as an example the effects of
parental divorce on children. The early work on this topic was carried out at a time
when there was still widespread social disapproval of divorce, and as a result it was
inconceivable that such an experience could have anything but harmful consequences
for children. Given such a climate, it is perhaps not surprising that research workers
quite automatically looked for nothing but pathology in the children they investigated and that their inventories and questionnaires contained only items referring
to symptoms such as anxiety, aggression and regressive behaviour. The possibility
that there might actually be positive consequences was not considered. Only now,
when divorce has become so much more common and socially acceptable, are
investigators willing to concede that, whatever undesirable effects there may be,
positive effects (freedom from tension, greater independence, increased tolerance
of stress, etc.) might perhaps also be found in children and should therefore be
included as items in questionnaires. Value judgements, which we make without even
being aware of them, can thus affect such an apparently straightforward task as
the design of assessment tools and thereby produce distortions in the findings
obtained.

  One other note of caution: quite apart from the possible influence of subjective
factors, not all research is good research. Just because something appears in print
does not mean that one has to believe it: this would be just another version of a
naive faith in experts, with researchers assuming the position of authority figures
merely because they are researchers. Questions need to be asked about the way
the study was carried out. Was the sample such that one can generalize the findings
to other individuals? Were the procedures appropriate and reliable? Were controls
imposed so that one can rule out other interpretations? Most important of all, have
the findings been replicated by other studies? Ideally, however foolproof a study
may seem, there must always be some hesitation in accepting its findings until they
have been confirmed by other studies: advances in knowledge and any social
action that may result therefrom require a more solid data base than a single,
unconfirmed study.

Thus the research foundation on which child psychology is based is by no means as firm as ideally one would like it to be: not every study is perfectly designed and executed, and, despite the safeguards normally put in place, value judgements and personal expectations do sometimes creep in and affect the outcome. Subjective and objective approaches, we have to conclude, are not wholly distinct; rather, they differ in degree. Nevertheless, the advantage of the latter over the former is that in research there is at least an awareness of the dangers of unchecked assumptions, and a recognition that all possible attempts should be made to guard against them if dependable knowledge and action are to follow.

The role of theory

In everyday talk the word 'theory' tends to be used contemptuously: 'it's just theory', for instance, means it is merely guesswork and therefore to be dismissed. In science, however, theories are much more: they are used to make sense of isolated facts by relating them to more general principles; they order whatever information has already been obtained, and they guide the search for further information by generating new questions to be answered. They are thus an essential part of the scientific enterprise.

Research in child psychology has been greatly influenced by a number of theories: psychoanalysis, behaviourism, social learning theory, Piagetian theory, ethology. We shall refer to these in due course; more detailed accounts can be found elsewhere (e.g. Crain, 1999; P. H. Miller, 2002). Here let us make just two points. In the first place, theories vary greatly in what they cover: the aim of behaviourism, for instance, was to make sense of all aspects of overt behaviour, human and animal; Piaget, on the other hand, concerned himself only with the development of children's cognitive functions; whereas Freud's focus was primarily the emotional life of adults and its origins in the early years. For that matter, there are many mini-theories that are applied to just a limited set of phenomena such as the formation of children's peer groups or the acquisition of object names. It follows that theories are not necessarily contradictory: one does not have to align oneself with psycho-analysis *or* with Piaget, for the two dealt with different sets of psychological functions – both formulations can be recognized as useful and accepted simultaneously.

Our second point is to stress that a theory should be thought of as just a tool – a tool, that is, to enable one to think about the known and dig out the unknown. And, like all tools, theories have limited use, to be discarded when found wanting. Certain parts of psychoanalytic theory, for example, are no longer regarded as useful, either because they rely on concepts that are too vague and untestable (such as libido or death wish) or because they have been put to empirical test but not been confirmed (such as the theory of infantile trauma as a cause of all later psychological disturbance). When that happens, the theory needs to be replaced by something better – a new tool that will provide new insights and point in new directions, until it too gives way to something preferable.

Summary

Child psychology is not just a lot of factual information; it is also a particular way of obtaining such information. One cannot make proper use of the former without understanding the latter, and we therefore began by looking at the ways in which psychologists go about the task of finding answers to questions about children and their development.

The kind of questions psychologists ask about children are basically no different from those asked by others. They are about *when, how* and *why*, dealing respectively with matters of timing, manner and causation. Asking *when* and *how* questions involves the description of children's behaviour; *why* questions involves explanation of that behaviour.

Various methods are used to obtain the data required to answer these questions, but for the most part they fall into three categories: observing, asking and experimenting. Some of the questions we ask refer to children of just one particular age group, while others are about change from one age to another. To answer those about change, one can use either *cross-sectional* or *longitudinal* methods; the latter are preferable but practically more problematic.

In response to the charge that child psychology is not really needed because we know intuitively how to care for and rear children, we have contrasted two ways of obtaining such knowledge: *subjective* and *objective* approaches. The former rely on hunch, personal experience and the advice of 'experts'; while these have their uses, they are of limited help in providing reliable guidelines. The latter involve scientific research, the main advantages of which are that it is explicit, open to scrutiny and guards against subjective influences like personal bias and value judgements. The two kinds are not wholly distinct: research too can be affected by subjective factors, though it does attempt to place checks against them.

The formulation of *theories* is an essential part of any scientific enterprise. Their role is to organize factual information already obtained and to direct the search for new information. Theories are, however, only tools, to be discarded when no longer useful.

FURTHER READING

Miller, P. H. (2002). *Theories of Developmental Psychology* (4th edn). New York: W. H. Freeman. A comprehensive account of the various theories that have been put forward to explain children's psychological development. Includes a useful discussion of what is meant by a theory, what theories are for, and what the main issues are confronting developmental psychology.

Miller, S. A. (1998). *Developmental Research Methods* (2nd edn). Englewood Cliffs, NJ: Prentice-Hall. For the reader who wants a detailed, up-to-date account of all aspects of research into child psychology, including such topics as the design of studies, statistical analysis and ethical considerations.

Pettigrew, T. F. (1996). *How To Think Like A Social Scientist.* New York: HarperCollins. An excellent, well-written introduction to how social scientists (including child psychologists!)

go about their task. Contrasts the distinctive way social scientists think about problems requiring solutions with popular analyses as reflected in the media.

Robson, C. (2002). *Real World Research.* Oxford: Blackwell. Not specifically about child psychology topics, but useful in providing insight into the nature of research when applied to aspects of real-world social problems.

CHAPTER TWO

The Nature of Childhood

Chapter Outline

What is a Child?

At first sight this may seem a silly question, for surely the answer is obvious and known to all. More often than not, a child is seen as a smaller, weaker version of an adult – more dependent, less knowledgeable, less competent, less well socialized and emotionally less well controlled. The problem with this description is, of course, that it is all in negative terms, drawing attention to what a child lacks, with no mention of the vast potential for growth in future years. However, such a picture does at least have the advantage of also drawing attention to the role of adults responsible for the child, whose task it is to make up for the child's deficiencies with resources from their own make-up and, at the same time, to help the child acquire the missing qualities and take them over as personal characteristics.

Yet on further reflection, characterizing the nature of childhood turns out to be a much more complex business. The trouble is that we cannot simply define it in purely impersonal terms: we were all children ourselves, and how we see childhood inevitably expresses something about ourselves. To some, such as to Wordsworth when writing his *Ode: Intimations of Immortality*, those early years appear in retrospect to be a magical time:

> When meadow, grove, and stream
> The earth, and every common sight,
> To me did seem
> Apparelled in celestial light,
> The glory and the freshness of a dream.

To others, less fortunate, childhood evokes darker memories – of abuse, rejection and intense unhappiness, a time of bleakness rather than of golden glow. At a purely personal level, the notion of childhood is thus *constructed*: we see it in the light of our own experiences and interpret it to fit in with whatever world view we have developed.

The constructed nature of childhood becomes even more apparent when we contrast the concepts of childhood that prevailed at different historical periods or in different cultures: how children are viewed varies according to a great many social, economic, political and religious forces that exist at that time and in that place. The answer to our question 'What is a child?' cannot therefore just be given in terms of a bunch of inherent characteristics that necessarily constitute the make-up of children; it also depends on the nature of the particular society and its beliefs and customs in which that child is brought up.

Historical Perspective

Let us first go back and examine how our ancestors in the western world thought about childhood. Obviously, the further back we go, the more sparse and unreliable the information is likely to be, and historians are by no means unanimous in their interpretation of the material that has come to light. Nevertheless, some general trends are apparent: we may lack statistical data, but we are able to get some glimpses of how children were treated in past times and thus of the concepts of childhood underlying these practices.

The child as miniature adult

According to Philippe Ariès, whose book *Centuries of Childhood* (1962) constitutes a most detailed examination of the history of children, childhood is a relatively recent invention. As he put it:

> In mediaeval society the idea of childhood did not exist; this is not to suggest that children were neglected, forsaken or despised. The idea of childhood is not to be confused with affection for children; it corresponds to an awareness of the particular nature of childhood, that particular nature which distinguishes the child from the adult, even the young adult. In mediaeval society this awareness was lacking.

Children, that is, were regarded as adults, albeit as smaller versions, and as far as feasible were treated the same. In paintings surviving from the Middle Ages, for instance, children are depicted as miniature adults, body size being their only distinguishing mark. No allowance is made for differences in body proportion, and their clothes are simply scaled-down copies of what men and women wore. To quote Ariès again:

> Language did not give the word 'child' the restricted meaning we give it today: people said 'child' much as we say 'lad' in everyday speech. The absence of definition extended to every sort of social activity: games, crafts, arms. There is not a single collective picture of the times in which children are not to be found, nesting singly or in pairs in the *trousse* hung round women's necks, or urinating in a corner, or playing their part in a traditional festival, or as apprentices in a workshop, or as pages serving a knight, etc.

Children, that is, were not only made to look like adults; they were also expected to share in the same activities, whether in work or play. Chronological age was not a marker as it is now: the paucity of birth and other records would in any case have made this difficult; however, what mattered more at times of considerable economic need were the strength and abilities distinguishing individual children that enabled them to contribute to the survival of their family and the well-being of society.

One overriding consideration to bear in mind when examining past attitudes to children is the very high rate of infant mortality that prevailed in the Middle Ages. For a child to reach his or her first birthday was an achievement: between one and two out of every three children died in infancy (McLaughlin, 1974). This changed little till the eighteenth century; even then no really substantial improvement was seen until the beginnings of the twentieth century. A child's death was thus a common and recurring phenomenon, one which would normally play emotional havoc with mothers and also colour their attitude to their living children. According to some historians, the self-protective device which was generally adopted under these circumstances was maternal indifference: mothers simply did not allow themselves to become too fond of their children until their survival beyond the early years was assured. To us, seen from an age when mother love is regarded as an absolutely essential requisite for development, this may seem hardly credible, and direct evidence is indeed hard to come by. What is certain is that the practice, at least among the better-off, of sending their children away from home, to wet-nurses in infancy and to tutors and craft masters from mid-childhood on, was widespread and regarded as perfectly acceptable. Emotional and physical closeness, it appears, were not considered as necessary to the parent–child relationship as they are today.

According to Ariès, it was not until the seventeenth and eighteenth centuries that a change in the prevailing concept of childhood first appeared. Children began to be depicted *as* children in dress and appearance, though this was initially confined to boys: as Ariès put it, 'boys were the first specialized children'. In general, the change was a slow one, as seen in the reluctance to accept the idea that children's need for education must take precedence over adults' need to use them as workers. The Industrial Revolution at the end of the eighteenth century created an enormous demand for cheap labour; parents were often dependent on their children's wages, and unscrupulous employers did not hesitate to send children as young as 6 to work in factories, down mines and up chimneys under appalling conditions and for long hours. The Factory Acts, passed by the British Parliament at various points in the nineteenth century, only slowly created a childhood as we see it: the Act passed in 1833, for instance, provided that children aged 9 to 13 were not to work more than 48 hours a week and those from 13 to 18 not more than 68 hours a week – an advance over previous conditions but still leaving many children with little time for play or learning. Even these changes encountered much opposition from employers: as one mine-owner put it, for miners' children a practical education in the collieries was superior to a reading education (Kessen, 1965). Child labour remains a problem in many countries to this day; when harsh economic conditions prevail, the idea of childhood as a happy, free period of leisure and enlightenment is less likely to take root.

The child as victim

The history of childhood is a nightmare from which we have only recently begun to awaken. The further back in history one goes, the lower the level of child care, and the more likely children are to be killed, abandoned, beaten, terrorized and sexually abused.

With this statement Lloyd DeMause opened his book on *The History of Childhood* (1974), summarizing a theme that is borne out by many sources. In the absence of statistical records we cannot make precise quantitative comparisons, but it does seem that in ancient and medieval times the extent of maltreatment of children was far greater than that prevailing nowadays.

The notion that children have *rights* is of very recent origin. In ancient Rome, for example, children were the legal property of the father; it was he who had absolute control over their lives, and if he exercised this power to take away their life it was regarded as no one's business other than his own. The dividing line between state and parents concerning responsibility for children was drawn with great strictness: children belonged to the father; their upbringing, their discipline, and even matters concerning their life or death were left to him to determine. Inevitably, without external constraints, maltreatment occurred with considerable frequency: sexual abuse in particular, both in ancient Greece and in Rome, appeared to have been common; chastisement of children was sometimes of a savageness that would now be regarded as intolerable; and infanticide was a regular practice that continued with few checks throughout the first millennium, especially in the form of exposure of newborns and particularly of females and of infants with birth defects. The Tiber, it was said, was awash with the unwanted babies of Roman mothers.

There is, of course, no suggestion that parental affection was not the norm. It is rather in comparison with today's practices that the extent of maltreatment of children in past times strikes one as abnormal, as does its tolerance by society. But society as a whole tended to behave with harshness to children, as illustrated by the eighteenth-century German schoolmaster who openly boasted that, according to his reckoning, he had given his pupils 911,527 strokes with the stick, 124,000 lashes with the whip, 136,715 slaps with the hand, and 1,115,800 boxes on the ear (DeMause, 1974). Existence for adults in earlier centuries was often harsh too, but there was little concerted attempt to regard children as in need of special protection and to shield them from the brutalities of life.

At times, and especially so in the seventeenth and eighteenth centuries, the harsh treatment of children was justified on grounds of religious morality. According to the Puritans' doctrine of original sin, we are all conceived and born in a spirit of evil, and it is the task of parents and educators to curb that evil in the child's soul. Thus children, far from innocent, come into the world as little savages; uncurbed, their natural depravity would be a threat to society, and the primary purpose of childrearing is therefore to eradicate the base and negative nature with which each child is endowed. 'Breaking the will of children' thus became a central theme in the parental advice literature of the time. As Mrs Wesley, mother of the founder of Methodism, wrote in the eighteenth century:

> I insist upon conquering the wills of children betimes; because this is the only foundation for a religious education . . . Heaven or hell depends on this alone. So that the parent who studies to subdue self-will in his children works together with God in the saving of a soul: the parent who indulges it does the devil's work . . . Whatever pains it cost, conquer their stubbornness; break the will, if you would not damn the child.   (*Quoted in Newson & Newson, 1974*)

The naturally evil nature of children thus justified their harsh treatment; it was seen as the only way to spare them from eternal damnation.

Today's child

One overall theme arises from past accounts of childhood, namely, that children in previous times were regarded as adjuncts to the adult world rather than as beings in their own right. Children, that is, were viewed primarily in the light of the needs of society and their families; their treatment was justified by prevailing economic, moral and religious forces based on adult requirements, with little attempt made to define the needs and characteristics of children themselves. That children have a status of their own, and that adults should adapt to that status rather than vice versa, is an idea of recent origin.

Take the idea of children's rights. The very idea that children have rights was utterly alien to past centuries. Children existed to serve adults' requirements, and even when these took a perverted form in individual cases, society did little to protect the victims. The notion that children's helpless status calls for protection rather than exploitation has developed only slowly in the last 200 years or so, and it is really only in the second half of the twentieth century that this idea has become formally enshrined in national legislation and international agreement.

As an example of present attitudes, we can take the United Nations Convention on the Rights of the Child, agreed on in 1989. The Convention is significant because, first, it asserts that children do have rights; secondly, because it attempts to list these rights (see box 2.1); thirdly, because it asserts the obligation of all governments to enforce them; and finally, because it is based on a definite image of childhood that must have been in the minds of those responsible for drafting the Convention. The image is spelled out in the following quote from the declaration adopted by the World Summit for Children that took place after the United Nations' passing of the Convention:

> The children of the world are innocent, vulnerable and dependent. They are also curious, active and full of hope. Their time should be one of joy and peace, of playing, learning and growing. Their future should be shaped in harmony and cooperation. Their lives should mature, as they broaden their perspectives and gain new experiences.

BOX 2.1

The United Nations Convention on the Rights of the Child

The following is an abridged list of the rights of children, drawn up in the UN Convention on the Rights of the Child and adopted by the General Assembly of the United Nations in 1989:

- Children have the right to life; their survival and development should be ensured.
- Children have a right to a name and a nationality and to have their identity preserved.
- Any child separated from one or both parents has the right to maintain personal relations with them.
- Every child capable of forming his or her own views has the right to express those views freely in all matters affecting the child.
- Children have the right to freedom of expression.
- Children have the right to freedom of thought, conscience and religion.
- Children have the right freely to associate with others.
- Children have the right to privacy.
- Children have the right to enjoy the highest attainable standard of health.
- Disabled children have a right to receive special care.
- Every child has the right to a standard of living adequate for the child's physical, mental, spiritual, moral and social development.
- Children have the right to education.
- Children have the right of access to leisure activities and to engage in play and recreation appropriate to the age of the child.
- Children have the right to be protected from economic exploitation and from performing any work likely to be harmful to the child's development.

Such statements, however vague and sentimental they may strike some, have the overriding virtue that they express a definite awareness of the psychological needs of children, as well as a realization that society has an obligation to satisfy these needs. What is more, there is an explicit acknowledgement that children's needs and those of their adult caretakers do not always coincide: children are not merely an extension of their carers; they are separate beings with rights of their own. As the UN Convention also puts it:

In all actions concerning children, whether undertaken by public or private welfare institutions, courts of law, administrative authorities or legislative bodies, the best interest of the child shall be a primary consideration.

Such statements still represent more of an ideal than a reality. Nevertheless, we have come a long way from the child of ancient times: regarded as the father's property, possessing no rights as an individual and thus subject to neglect, cruelty and exploitation without check. Children then were viewed as serving the adult world; nowadays it is the adult world that is regarded as having obligations to children, whose separate yet dependent status it is expected to acknowledge.

Cultural Perspective

Variations in our images of childhood can be found not only by going back over time but also by travelling the world and comparing different cultures as they exist today. Admittedly, the world is getting smaller: improved methods of transportation and the spreading influence of the media have brought about a gradual westernization in even the remotest corners. And yet, as anthropological findings have shown, there are still many versions to be found of the answer to 'What is a child?' Such cross-cultural comparisons are useful because they make us aware that what we, in our part of the globe, regard as 'normal' may not be so elsewhere: each society has its own particular set of values and will view its children in the light of these values.

Variations in childrearing practices

Let us look at some examples to illustrate that our own view of the 'right' way of bringing up children is by no means shared by all societies.

- Observe a western mother with her baby on her knee, and you will see how utterly absorbed the two are in each other. The mother does her best to foster this often emotionally very intense interaction by cuddling, smiling, rocking, singing and talking, and so ensuring that she is very much the focus of the baby's attention. Now consider observations of Kaluli mothers and their babies (Schieffelin & Ochs, 1983). The Kaluli people are a small society living in the tropical rainforests of Papua New Guinea, and there mother–baby interaction takes a very different form. Babies are not treated as partners in one-to-one exchanges: thus, the two do not spend long periods gazing into each other's eyes but, on the contrary, mothers hold their babies so that they face outwards and can therefore be seen by and see others who are part of their social group. What is more, mothers rarely talk directly to their babies; instead, other people (mostly older children) talk to the baby and the mother then speaks in a high-pitched voice 'for' the baby. Thus from the beginning children are involved in multi-party exchanges. The reason for treating children in this way is to be found in the Kaluli living arrangements: communities there are composed of 60–90 individuals, all of whom live in one large longhouse with no internal walls. The mother–child unit and the family as we know it have less significance; from an early age on, children are therefore prepared to be aware of the social community as a whole – hence the practice of facing the child outward and not towards the mother, and hence the playing down of one-to-one interchange. Anything else would be considered 'abnormal' and not helpful to the child's development.

- Among the Gusii people of Kenya everything a mother does with her baby is aimed to avoid or dampen down any excitement the baby might normally experience in one-to-one interaction – to soothe, that is, rather than to arouse. Here too there is little face-to-face interaction: what there is tends to be slow and devoid of emotion. A mother's most common response to her baby's gaze or vocalizing is to look away. Instead, the emphasis is on holding and physical contact, even during sleep. The moment a baby cries he or she receives attention, whether by being offered the breast or by being rocked and cuddled – again, in order to avoid excitement. Once more, the mother is following a cultural agenda by means of these practices: at an early stage of the child's life, she must return to working in the fields, when the infant will be handed over to the care of older children and when he or she must therefore be sufficiently calm and manageable for them to be able to cope. The mothers' treatment of their infants is thus regarded as the 'right' way of accomplishing this culture-determined aim (LeVine et al., 1994).

- In western society considerable importance is attached to play, and mothers frequently join their children in order to foster their cognitive and educational skills thereby. Not so among low-income Mexican mothers, who regard play as of little importance and as having no role in furthering development. When specifically requested to join their children in play, these mothers find it a strange and embarrassing experience, and their contributions mainly take the form of explicit teaching rather than of actions designed to make it all a 'fun' experience. Given their economic circumstances, these mothers appear to operate on the basis of a 'work model': life is serious, play is a luxury, and the sooner children learn this lesson the better (Farver & Howes, 1993).

There are many such cross-cultural comparisons that can be quoted; a rather more detailed account, involving the childrearing practices in traditional Japanese society, is given in box 2.2. Together, these descriptions show how cautious we have to be in assuming that certain practices are universal and part and parcel of human nature just because we ourselves engage in them. To us, the practices of other societies such as those described above may seem aberrant; however, when seen against their particular cultural background they make sense, because they are

BOX 2.2

Japanese mothers and their children

In traditional Japanese society a very different concept of the nature of childhood prevails when compared with the West. The western mother sees her task as helping a highly dependent infant to achieve independence in the course of childhood, and from early on will adopt practices that foster both physical and psychological autonomy. Children are encouraged to explore new situations on their own, assertiveness is valued and emotional clinging is frowned upon. The Japanese mother, on the contrary, sees childhood as proceeding in the opposite direction, from independence to dependence. The newborn baby, that is, is viewed as a separate, autonomous being, whom the mother must socialize into becoming dependent on other members of the group. Her task therefore is to use childrearing techniques that bind the child increasingly to her and subsequently also to others.

Descriptions of Japanese mothers show how this is accomplished (e.g. Bornstein, Tal & Tamis-LeMonda, 1991; Shimizu & LeVine, 2001). In particular, physical closeness is maintained to a far greater extent than between a western mother and her child. For example, children sleep with their parents, and during the day too mothers are much more likely to stay in physical contact with their children throughout the preschool years – to an extent that family relationships in Japan have been described (by westerners, of course) as a 'skinship' system. Children are believed to have only limited ability to function on their own up to the age of 6 or 7; only then do they reach the stage of 'understanding'. In the earlier years mothers make few demands on them and tend to be generally permissive and indulgent, and overall show an intense emotional involvement in their children.

Observations of mother–child play sessions reveal the kind of strategies Japanese mothers employ to foster social bonds (Fernald & Morikawa, 1993). Whereas the western mother makes use of toys to draw the child's attention to their properties and functions and so encourages an orientation to the world of things, the Japanese mother is more likely to insert herself in the play and to stress routines that bind child to mother. Confronted by a car, for example, the western mother might say: 'That's a car. See the car? You like it? It's got nice wheels.' The Japanese mother would say: 'Here! It's a vroom vroom. I give it to you. Now give it to me. Yes! Thank you.' Teaching the child the object name or demonstrating its properties is of little importance; what matters is to teach the child the cultural norms for polite speech, and toys are merely a means of involving the child in social rituals that will bind mother and child more closely together. In the one case the mother's aim is to focus the child's attention on the toy; in the other case it is to focus it on interpersonal aspects.

Such different treatments naturally produce different results as far as children's personality development is concerned. Japanese children, for instance, are initially much more dependent on their parents and become far more distressed when separated from them. Moreover, their early experiences seem to have long-term consequences, as seen in a lifelong need to be a conforming member of a group. The need for close relationships developed in a family context is thus extended in later years to relationships with peers and colleagues.

adaptive in that specific society. Cultural differences and not cultural deficiencies is thus the key theme, the differences being a function of the kind of child the various societies wish to produce.

Individualistic and collectivistic orientations

Cultures come in many different forms and vary in all sorts of subtle ways. Nevertheless, it has been found useful to make one fundamental distinction, namely, between cultures that are basically **individualistic** and those that are primarily **collectivistic** (Triandis, 1995).

> **Individualistic cultures** are those societies where the independence of the individual is valued above all, and where children are therefore brought up to be self-reliant and self-assertive.

- *Individualistic* cultures are those that emphasize the independence of the individual. In such societies children are brought up from the beginning to stand on their own feet, to be socially assertive and to strive for personal achievement and self-reliance. Anyone who does not become self-sufficient is regarded as a socialization failure.
- *Collectivist* cultures, on the other hand, stress mutual dependence. According to this orientation, children should learn to value loyalty, trust and cooperation, and to put social conformity before individual goals. The aims of socialization are therefore to inculcate obedience, duty and group belongingness.

> **Collectivist cultures** are those societies which emphasize the mutual dependence of its members, and which accordingly bring up their children to value social conformity before individual goals.

The distinction between the two orientations is not an absolute one: both may be found in any one culture. Nevertheless, some emphasize a sense of individuality to a far greater extent than others: western countries, and especially the United States, are prime examples. In many Asian countries, on the other hand, and also in some African societies, it is a sense of connectedness that is of prime importance:

the group takes precedence over the individual, and all aspects of life, but especially the socialization of children, reflect this orientation.

As an example of the distinction, let us look at the words that parents belonging to two different cultural groups use to describe their children, i.e. those from a metropolitan community in America and those from a rural society in Kenya (Harkness & Super, 1992). When the American mothers were asked about their children they tended to concentrate on the children's cognitive abilities: words like 'intelligent', 'smart' and 'imaginative' were frequently used, as were phrases referring to the children's independence and self-reliance, such as 'can make choices', 'able to play by himself', and 'rebellious' or 'defiant' – characteristics which were clearly regarded as desirable, as were social qualities such as 'confident' and 'comfortable with others'. The African mothers, on the other hand, paid most attention to characteristics reflecting the children's obedience and helpfulness: 'good-hearted', 'respectful', 'trustworthy' and 'honest' were among the most frequent descriptive words found in their accounts of their children. Clearly, these mothers had different values from those of their American counterparts: their concept of a well-adjusted child reflected the importance attached to fitting in with the group and contributing to common needs, rather than wanting children whose characteristics would serve them in competition with others.

These differences make sense when one considers the socio-economic settings of the two groups. In the competitive West, 'getting ahead' matters: from the beginning children are taught to pit themselves against others and vie for praise and prizes. In a poor rural community in Africa, on the other hand, cooperating with others is essential: individuals cannot achieve much on their own and what matters therefore is the ability to contribute to the common good. Such social needs shape the way parents treat their children and, in turn, affect children's behaviour. As we can see from table 2.1, the amount of time that children from the two communities spend on various activities differs greatly. Thus in America play is considered by parents to assume a vital and increasingly significant role because it is viewed as a preparation for intellectual development; household chores, on the other hand, are thought of as quite inappropriate for such young children. In Kenya, on the other hand, the decrease in play and sharp increase in chores from the age of 2

Table 2.1 Child activities in two societies (in percentage of total time)

| | America | | Kenya | |
	2 years	4 years	2 years	4 years
Eating	23	18	14	9
Away from home	14	16	1	2
Play	36	42	42	28
Household chores	0	0	15	35

Source: Adapted from Harkness & Super (1992).

indicate the socialization pressures that parents there exert towards the early learning of responsibility and group participation. It is therefore not surprising that the two groups of children differed in the kinds of accomplishments they were found to have achieved: the American children were far more verbally competent and adept at imaginative play activities than the Kenyan children; the latter, on the other hand, were able at the age of 5 to take responsibility for supervising a baby and at the age of 8 could cook dinner for an entire family.

Cultural differences become very evident when children from different countries are observed in the same kind of setting such as a nursery school. Comparing practices in American, Japanese and Chinese nurseries, Tobin, Wu and Davidson (1989) have demonstrated vividly the extent to which the three cultures differ in terms of their individualist–collective orientation, with American practices at one extreme and Chinese at the other. In Chinese nurseries children did virtually every-thing in groups: play, for instance, was seen not as a basically individual activity as in American nurseries but as an opportunity to learn to do things together with others. 'Groupism' was the key distinguishing feature: the uniformity of action and the importance of subjugating individual needs to those of the group were thus taught from early on to these Chinese children. When American teachers were shown films of Chinese nursery schools they were horrified by the failure to do justice to children's individuality; by the same token, when Chinese teachers saw American nursery practices they deplored the way selfish attitudes were actively fostered and the sense of loneliness that then apparently ensues. Each set of teachers had no doubt as to who behaved correctly.

Personality development viewed cross-culturally

Cultural norms influence socializing practices; socializing practices in turn influence children's personality development. Thus the characteristics which each society values in its members are conveyed to children in the course of their upbring-ing: as we saw above in the comparison of American and Kenyan children, the kinds of competence the two groups develop – cognitive facilities in one case, domestic responsibilities in the other – are those that the nature of their societies demands and that their parents accordingly set out to foster.

The links between culture, socialization and personality development become most evident when we consider societies that differ radically from our own. Consider Margaret Mead's (1935) description of the Mundugumor people – a tribe in eastern New Guinea that once engaged in almost constant warfare with neighbouring tribes, glorified the killing of other people and practised cannibalism as well as headhunt-ing. In such a society there can be no place for the mild-mannered; aggressiveness above all is valued and children are therefore brought up to be combative, pug-nacious and unfeeling. They experience little in the way of mother love, for from birth on babies find themselves in a society that appears to have an intense dislike of children. That dislike is expressed in all the attitudes and rearing practices children encounter: in the quick and peremptory way they are suckled, in the sullen resentment with which mothers greet any sickness or accident that may befall them, and in the refusal of mothers to let their children cling to them when afraid or insecure. All signs of affection are stifled; instead, the hostile upbringing engenders a belligerent character that is precisely adapted to the lifestyle of that society.

The Mundugumor may be an extreme example, but the culture–rearing–personality linkage becomes evident from many other cross-cultural comparisons. Take the case of shyness – a personal attribute that is to some extent genetically based but that is also influenced by children's upbringing. In the West, an outgoing nature is by and large regarded as an asset; shyness, on the other hand, is seen as something of a social handicap and therefore undesirable. In its more extreme form shyness is regarded as a sign of psychological maladjustment, and, as research has shown, such children are more likely to be rejected by their peers, feel lonely and depressed and develop a poor self-image (K. Rubin, 1998). In Far Eastern countries such as China, Thailand, Indonesia and Korea, on the other hand, a very different attitude prevails: shyness is positively valued; extraverted, assertive behaviour is seen as socially disruptive; and children are therefore brought up to be restrained and reticent. Parents and teachers thus tend to praise and encourage such behaviour and to describe shy children as socially competent – a very different attitude from that shown by their western counterparts. What is more, shy children in Far Eastern cultures are also positively responded to by their peers, and so are more likely to develop a favourable image of their own self-worth than outgoing, uninhibited children (Chen, Hastings, Rubin, Chen, Cen & Stewart, 1998).

Thus one and the same personal characteristic has different meanings in different cultural settings. In the Far East, where a collective rather than an individualist orientation prevails and where the Confucian doctrine of filial piety calls for submissive behaviour of children to their elders, shyness is seen as a quality that contributes to maintaining the social order and is therefore encouraged. No wonder the incidence of shyness among Far Eastern children is considerably greater than among children in the West, where such an attribute is seen as undesirable and not in keeping with the social norms of assertiveness and independence.

Adults' Thinking about Children

Even within any one culture there are differences in the way people think about childhood. Let us emphasize that parents *do* think about being parents: they have certain preconceptions, often half-formed and unspoken, about the nature of children and the role parents play in their development, and these preconceptions may show interesting variations from one individual to another. At one time psychologists investigated the parent–child relationship entirely in terms of parents' *actions*; now it is appreciated that parental *beliefs* must also be taken into account if we are to understand children's development (see Sigel & McGillicuddy-DeLisi, 2002).

The nature of belief systems

Anyone responsible for children brings to the task a set of presuppositions – a 'naive psychology' that will influence how they interpret children's development and how they themselves behave towards children. As we have seen, there are temporal and cultural constraints to such theories, yet within these constraints people may still differ in their beliefs about a great range of issues. Take the way in which people might answer questions such as the following:

- Why are some children more intelligent than others?
- What causes emotional maladjustment?
- Are children born shy or made shy?
- Should there be differences in the way boys and girls are brought up?
- Do parents play a part in children's academic achievement?

Asked about issues such as these, it becomes apparent that adults often hold very different views about the nature of children and the reasons why they develop as they do. It also becomes apparent, however, that their views tend to be consistent across a range of topics, i.e. that they do not just approach each question anew but on the basis of more or less coherent belief systems.

Scales have been developed to assess these systems. Let us consider one of these as an example – a scale containing 30 items where questions such as the following are posed, together with alternative answers (Martin & Johnson, 1992):

Q: Why are children able to make up imaginative stories?
- Make-believe is a natural part of childhood.
- Teachers and parents encourage and foster the child's imagination.
- As children play with others and think about objects, their imagination develops.

The first response option represents a belief in the importance of maturation: children are bound to develop such skills because that is the way they are made. The second puts the onus on adults: development occurs because of the way in which the child is treated. The third emphasizes children's own role, in that it is their participation in the relevant activities that will bring about the appearance of new skills. Each person chooses the answer that appears to them the most convincing, and as there is a certain amount of consistency in the way people answer different questions, an impression can be gained of each individual's assumptions about the nature of child development.

One of the main ways in which belief systems vary is along the nature–nurture axis. Thus at one extreme we have those individuals who would consistently check answers such as the first one above, in that they are convinced that children are set from birth to develop certain characteristics at certain times, and that the role of adults in this progress is minimal. They therefore interpret their task as one of giving children opportunities to develop their innate potential; beyond that, however, they consider themselves to have no active part to play and indeed to be powerless when things go wrong. At the other extreme are those who believe a child at the start of life is a mere blob of clay that must be shaped by adult action. They will check answers such as the second one above, in the conviction that whatever characteristics children develop reflect the way they are brought up and the kinds of experiences they are exposed to. Parents, teachers, peers, television and other external influences are therefore to be blamed for developmental failures, just as they can claim credit for developmental success. In fact, relatively few people are to be found at either extreme of the nature–nurture continuum and most are ranged at points in between. Nevertheless, it is to be expected that childrearing practices will differ according to whatever preconceptions parents have as to whether the causes of children's development are to be found largely within the child or in outside influences.

Links to child development

Belief systems exist within people's heads: they are mental constructions and, as such, do not affect children directly. Instead, they affect people's *behaviour* towards children; their influence is thus an indirect one in that it is applied via childrearing practices, and it is these which act upon children's behaviour and, for that matter, upon the belief systems which children themselves come to develop (see figure 2.1).

As an example, let us consider a study of the effects of divorce on children (Holloway & Machida, 1992). There are great differences between children in the way they respond to such an experience, and while no doubt all sorts of influences account for such differences, one of these is the kind of environment the custodial parent creates for the child following the divorce, and that in turn is likely to be a function of the parent's belief in her ability to control events rather than be controlled by them. This is indeed what was found in this study. Some mothers believed that the child's behaviour was very much their responsibility, that it was up to them to offer protection against distress and guide the child towards maturity. These beliefs were then put into practice: such mothers ensured that household rules were enforced, that limits were set to children's behaviour and that routines were firmly established. The children of these mothers tended to be

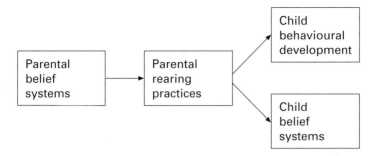

Figure 2.1   *The relationship of parental belief systems to rearing practices and children's development.*

the better adjusted: they had fewer psychological and health problems and reasonable self-esteem. Other mothers, however, saw themselves as unable to exert control in the situation in which they found themselves, feeling helpless and on the sidelines and therefore not able to protect their children from the negative effects of divorce. Their homes tended to be chaotic and their everyday lives disorganized, and, not surprisingly, their children were those who had most difficulty in adjusting to the new life they had to lead following their parents' divorce. The mother's view of herself as a parent thus leads her to adopt certain practices in arranging her child's life, which in turn result in the child coping or failing to cope with events.

However, the relationship between the several steps in the sequence is by no means a simple one. For example, the beliefs that people hold about childhood are only one of several determinants of how they actually behave towards children: in particular, all sorts of momentary considerations concerning the situation in which parent and child find themselves will also play a part, such as the immediate problem confronting them, the child's behaviour, the presence of others, and so forth. Indeed, the beliefs they express may then be a post hoc justification for their action: the arrow from belief to rearing practices can therefore go in the opposite direction too. And yet, the very fact that beliefs express certain overarching orientations can mean that they are more predictive of children's development than any specific parental action. If, for instance, it is part of a parent's philosophy that it is primarily up to adults to stimulate children's curiosity in the world around them, then that is not something that can be conveyed through single actions but only through a cumulative history of interaction with the child. If, on the contrary, the parent believes that children have their own inbuilt curiosity urges, or that it is up to professional people such as teachers to stimulate their children's interests, they will adopt an attitude that may have very different effects but is equally pervasive over time. It is at this level that belief systems exert their influence.

Summary

The answer to the question 'What is a child?' turns out to be far from straightforward. How we think about childhood depends on a range of historical, cultural and personal influences. Historically, there has been a gradual progression from an adult-centred to a child-centred view of childhood. In ancient times children were seen as miniature adults, with no distinctive requirements or characteristics of their own. The notion that a child is in need of protection and special treatment received little consideration; instead, children were regarded as adults' property and therefore more likely to be subjected to maltreatment. The idea that children have rights that adults must respect is of very recent origin, and as a result our current ideas of childhood differ drastically in many respects from those prevalent at one time.

Even today there are variations in our images of childhood when we compare different parts of the world with different cultural traditions. What is normal in one society may not be acceptable in another, and these differences are apparent in such routine rearing practices as how children are talked to, held or played with. Each society thus sets out to produce children with personality characteristics that fit in with its own values. This is seen in particular when comparing societies with individualistic and those with collectivistic orientations, i.e. where children are brought up respectively to value self-sufficiency as opposed to mutual dependence.

Even in any one society such as the western one, differences can be found in the way people think about childhood. Most adults have more or less developed belief systems about the nature of childhood and about their own role in a child's development. Thus some will stress the influence of the child's own potential, others the effect of adult rearing and teaching practices. Beliefs affect how adults behave towards children; such behaviour in turn helps to determine the course of the child's development.

FURTHER READING

Ariès, P. (1962). *Centuries of Childhood.* Harmondsworth: Penguin. A fascinating and scholarly, though controversial, account of how childhood was viewed throughout the ages. Puts forward the provocative idea that childhood, as a special period in its own right, is a comparatively recent invention.

DeLoache, J., & Gottlieb, A. (2000). *A World of Babies: Imagined Childcare Guides for Seven Societies.* Cambridge: Cambridge University Press. A delightful account of childrearing practices in seven cultures around the world, written as though by an 'expert' in each culture in the form of guidelines to new parents. Brings alive the great diversity of assumptions about the nature of children and the tasks of parents.

DeMause, L. (ed.) (1974). *The History of Childhood.* New York: Psychohistory Press. Contains chapters by different authors, each covering a particular period from Roman times to the nineteenth century. Especially interesting for its description of children's maltreatment during this time.

Harkness, S., & Super, C. M. (eds) (1996). *Parents' Cultural Belief Systems.* New York: Guilford Press. A wide-ranging collection of essays examining the nature, origins, manifestations and consequences of the beliefs parents hold about the nature of children. Examples provided by societies all over the world show how parents from different cultural backgrounds explain to themselves their children's behaviour and the meaning of parenthood.

Kessen, W. (1965). *The Child.* New York: Wiley. A most readable account of the development of our ideas about children, from the seventeenth century on. Based primarily on readings selected from texts written during this period, with comments linking these to present-day ideas.

CHAPTER THREE

Beginning Life

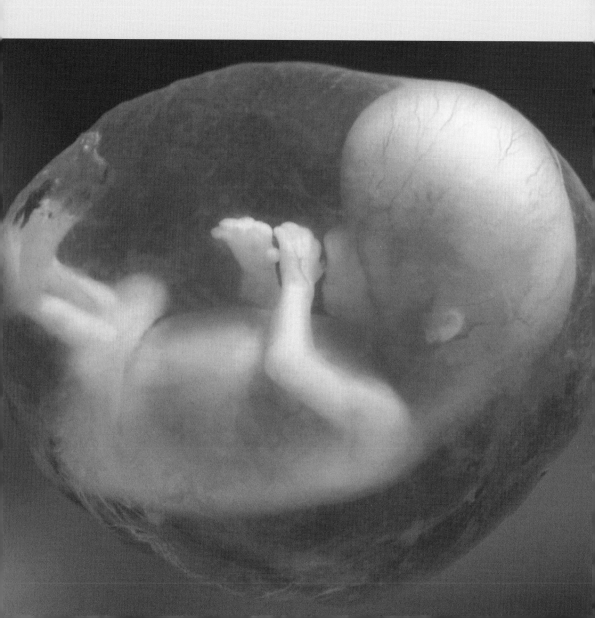

Chapter Outline

The story of child development does not start at birth but at conception. At birth a child is already 9 months old, and a great deal has happened in those months that is relevant to understanding the kind of being the child will become. From a parent's point of view, birth may seem like a beginning; seen from the child's point of view, however, what is significant is the *continuity* between prenatal and postnatal life. At conception children are provided with the genetic endowment that will form one of the great influences on their development; subsequently, during their life in the womb, much will take place that also has a bearing on their ensuing psychological growth. In the following pages, we shall therefore examine both genetic and prenatal influences on development.

Our Inheritance

The union of a female egg and a male sperm signals the arrival of a new and unique being. At that moment mother and father pass to this being the particular combination of genetic material that the individual will retain throughout life and that constitutes the foundation on which the child's personality will be built. It is only quite recently that we have begun to understand something of the nature of genes and the part they play in shaping behaviour, and to appreciate that quite a few of our ideas concerning nature and nurture are in fact misleading.

Chromosomes are tiny rod-shaped structures found in the nucleus of every cell in the body, housing the DNA of which the genes are composed.

Genes are the units of hereditary transmission. They are made up of DNA and are found in particular locations on **chromosomes**.

Sex cells (also known as gametes) are the eggs of a female and the sperm of a male that combine during fertilization. Unlike other cells, they contain only 23 chromosomes instead of 46.

Genetic transmission

The complexity of development from the moment of conception on is of truly awesome proportions. We begin life as a tiny single cell, yet within that cell is housed the individual's entire genetic endowment. We end up as adults with bodies composed of trillions of cells, but within each of these cells can be found the same set of genetic material, made up of **chromosomes** and **genes**. Cells provide their own motive power for development: whenever a new cell is required for growth or tissue replacement, an existing cell divides, producing a copy containing the same genetic material. In the earliest stages of growth following conception this process occurs very rapidly, the number of cells doubling every few hours. In time, the cells form themselves into groups, each assuming a special function: some as part of the nervous system, others to form muscles, still others to become bones, and so on. Eventually, a fully developed human being will emerge in this way.

The nucleus of each cell, with the one exception of the **sex cells**, contains an identical set of 46 chromosomes – rod-shaped structures arranged in pairs, one of each pair having been passed on by the mother and one by the father (figure 3.1). The sex cells (egg and sperm) differ in that they contain only 23 chromosomes; on conception, however, the two sets combine to provide the new individual with the full complement of 46 chromosomes. Strung along the chromosomes like beads on a necklace are the genes – chemical particles composed of DNA, which is a threadlike molecule shaped like a double helix. Genes, of which (according to the latest estimate) there are about 30,000 to 40,000 in the human body, are the basic units of hereditary transmission that contain the genetic code for each individual. Every gene is related to some specific aspect of a particular characteristic or developmental process – height, weight, eye colour, intelligence, schizophrenia, extraversion and so forth, though the relationship between gene and individual characteristic can be of greatly varying complexity. The inheritance of a physical feature such as eye colour, for example, is controlled by a single gene; psychological characteristics, on the other hand, mostly involve the joint action of several, often very many, genes: intelligence, for instance, is estimated to depend on at least 150 different genes. However, genes are concerned not just with static characteristics involving the individual's appearance or personality but also with the course of developmental change. Thus the emergence of particular skills and abilities, such as the onset of walking and talking or of puberty, is just as much a function of the genetic blueprint with which each one of us comes into the world. In so far as each gene is to be found on the same spot of a particular chromosome in all members of the species, locating the genes responsible for any given feature has now become feasible, and indeed an

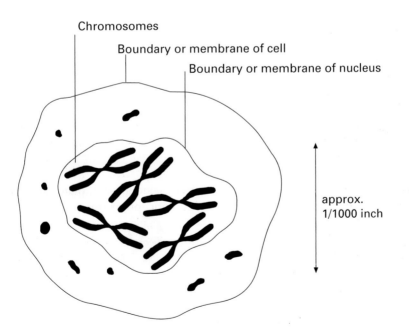

Figure 3.1 *Cell containing pairs of chromosomes (total size across approx. 1/1000 inch).*

Figure 3.2   *Sequence of motor developmental milestones (in Oates, 1994, p. 217, adapted from Shirley, 1933).*

enormously ambitious international effort, the Human Genome Project, has been devoted in recent years to specifying the location and function of all human genes. In due course this will result in great progress in our ability to diagnose inherited defects by means of prenatal screening and, even while the child is still in the womb, to carry out genetic modification techniques such as the replacement of defective genes. The elimination of many inherited diseases, including some forms of mental handicap, is thus a distinct possibility for the future.

Some of our genes refer to attributes that are common to all human beings: they ensure, for example, that each member of the species typically develops a body with two arms and legs, is provided with a particular kind of nervous system and becomes sexually mature within a certain age range. They also ensure that development takes place in given sequences: the motor development of infants, for example, carefully plotted by paediatricians and psychologists in the early part of the twentieth century, occurs in an orderly series of milestones marking the appearance of abilities such as head control, sitting up, crawling, standing, walking and so on (see figure 3.2), the predictability of this sequence being determined by a genetic programme found in all typically developing members of the human species. Other genetic messages, however, refer to those aspects that distinguish us as individuals and make each of us a unique person – aspects such as our physical appearance and psychological traits, and also characteristics like the speed with which any given child reaches the common milestones of motor development. This uniqueness is brought about by the incredibly large number of different ways whereby the 23 chromosomes from the father and the 23 from the mother, with all the genes that they carry, can combine, resulting in an enormous range of different con-figurations of characteristics. How they combine is purely a matter of chance – the *genetic lottery*, of which each of us is the end product.

Genetic disorders

Considering the complexity of genetic transmission, it is perhaps not surprising that mishaps occasionally occur during the process of forming genetic material. In addition, some disorders are directly inherited; the defective genes may be passed from parents to offspring even though the former show no overt sign of the disorder. The prevalence of these various problems can be difficult to determine; however, according to one estimate, as many as two out of every three conceptions are spontaneously aborted in the early weeks of pregnancy, the major cause being genetic or chromosomal abnormalities. Genetic disorders take many forms, something like 3,000 having been isolated so far, though some of these are to be found only in certain racial groups while others are sex-specific. Below are examples of some of the more common:

- *Down's syndrome.* This is one of the best-known congenital disorders, referred to at one time as Mongolism after the appearance of individuals so affected. Children with this disorder have learning disabilities of varying degrees, and also commonly show visual, hearing and heart problems. Down's syndrome is an example of a chromosomal abnormality, due to a chance mishap after conception in the formation of chromosomes, resulting in the presence of a third member on chromosome pair no. 21.
- *Klinefelter's syndrome.* This disorder is also due to an extra chromosome, but in this case involving the pair of sex chromosomes to which a third member has accidentally become attached. It occurs only in males, and becomes evid-ent after puberty when the individual fails to develop masculine characteristics and instead begins to show feminine features such as enlarging of the breasts and broadening of hips. Retardation in verbal intelligence is also often found.
- *Turner's syndrome.* Also a sex chromosome abnormality, but in this case involving only females and caused by a missing chromosome. As a result there is failure to develop secondary sexual characteristics and sterility. Here, as in cases of Klinefelter's syndrome, administration of the appropriate sex hormones at puberty will lead to a more typical appearance.
- *Phenylketonuria (or PKU).* A metabolic disorder in which the child from birth on is unable to process the amino acid phenylaline found in milk and in various other foods. If untreated, it results in mental retardation; screening procedures carried out after birth and followed by the administration of a phenylaline-free diet will prevent ill effects. PKU is an example of a

Recessive gene disorders appear when both parents supply the same recessive gene, with no dominant gene present to override its effects.

recessive gene disorder brought about by both parents being carriers of a defective gene that prevents the normal processing of the relevant foods.

- *Tay-Sachs disease.* A degenerative disease of the nervous system, resulting in the progressive loss of motor and mental functions and generally ending in death by the fifth birthday. It is found almost exclusively among Jewish children of Eastern European origin. This too is a recessive gene disorder, where the gene responsible for breaking down a toxic product into a non-toxic one in the neurons is missing.

- *Cystic fibrosis.* Also a recessive gene disorder, where affected children lack an enzyme that prevents mucus from obstructing the lungs and digestive tract. In the past, few who inherited the condition survived beyond adolescence; now, as a result of early diagnosis and improved treatment, life expectancy is considerably extended.

- *Colour blindness.* Involves an inability to distinguish red and green, and is found mainly in males. Its cause is a recessive gene found only on **X chromosomes**.

X and Y chromosomes are the bundles of DNA that determine an individual's sex.

As the pair of chromosomes that females carry are both of the X type, a deficient gene on one will be compensated for by the properly functioning other gene; only if both are deficient will colour blindness result. Males, on the other hand, having one X and one **Y chromosome**, are more vulnerable, in that no corresponding gene on the Y chromosome can counteract the effects of a deficient gene on the X chromosome.

- *Haemophilia.* Known as the 'bleeder's disease', because the child lacks the substance that causes blood to clot, as a result of which any cut or bruise can result in bleeding to death. Also sex-linked, in that it occurs almost exclusively in males, the genetic mechanisms explaining its origins are similar to those for colour blindness. The best-known example of this disorder was to be found among certain of the royal families of Europe in the nineteenth century, where the origin could be traced back to Queen Victoria and a spontaneously deficient gene she probably received from one of her parents. However, neither she nor any of her female descendants developed the disorder even though some of them were carriers; only her male descendants were vulnerable to becoming haemophiliacs.

Prevention and treatment of genetic disorders such as those above have made considerable advances since the mechanisms of transmission have come to be understood – partly as a result of genetic counselling of parents at risk for the birth of defective children, partly through improved methods of detecting carriers by such means as DNA analysis, and partly also by developing effective methods of treatment, as in the case of PKU. However, the biggest strides forward will be made once the location and identity of all genes are known and methods of gene therapy can ensure the elimination of all such disorders.

Nature *and* nurture

Attempts to explain human behaviour have always primarily revolved around the nature–nurture question. Are we creatures of our inheritance, destined from the beginning to behave according to some plan inherent in our make-up? Or are we shaped by whatever experiences we encounter after birth, and especially in our early years? There have been fashions in the extent to which one or the other, nature or nurture, has been stressed: thus, at the beginning of the twentieth century, *nativism* reigned supreme in psychological theories; from the early 1920s, on the other hand, *environmentalism* became the popular belief, in that child development was considered to be primarily, or even exclusively, a function of the rearing practices and attitudes of parents. There are certainly plenty of demonstrations that particular kinds of parents have particular kinds of children: punitive parents, for example, tend to have aggressive children, depressed mothers are likely to have depressed daughters, and sensitive parenting is associated with secure child personalities. The fact that parents provide not only the children's environment but also their genes was not taken into account. In any case, the argument was always in terms of nature *or* nurture, one *or* the other.

It is only in recent years that we have moved from guesswork and fashion to informed research and empirical facts. This is largely due to the advent of the science of **behavioural genetics**, the aim of which is to investigate genetic *and* environmental factors and the way these two sets of influences interact (for a more detailed account, see Plomin, DeFries, McClearn & Rutter, 1997). Let us stress, however, that behavioural genetics is equipped only to explain the *differences* among individuals, e.g. why one person is more intelligent than another or more sociable or more likely to become schizophrenic. It cannot answer questions about the *causes* of, say, intelligence in the human species as a whole, i.e. to what extent intelligence is a function of heredity as opposed to environment, nor can it answer the same question with respect to any one person. The focus of behavioural genetics is solely on individual variability and the reasons for human uniqueness.

> **Behavioural genetics** is the science investigating the hereditary basis of human and animal behaviour.

The two principal methods used by behavioural geneticists are twin studies and adoption studies:

- *Twin studies* involve the comparison of identical and non-identical twins. The former are also sometimes called monozygotic (MZ), because they stem from a single fertilized ovum or zygote and as a result have all their genes in common. Non-identical (or dizygotic, DZ) pairs, on the other hand, stem from two zygotes and thus are no more genetically alike than ordinary siblings, sharing on average 50 per cent of their genes. This provides one with an experiment of nature: on the one hand, identical and non-identical twins differ in the degree of genetic relatedness; on the other hand, both sets share the same environment from the moment of conception on: the

Table 3.1 Correlation coefficients for intelligence and extraversion measures from monozygotic (MZ) and dizygotic (DZ) twins reared together and reared apart

	MZ twins (together)	MZ twins (apart)	DZ twins (together)	DZ twins (apart)
Intelligence	0.80	0.78	0.32	0.23
Extraversion	0.55	0.38	0.11	–

Correlations are a measure of the closeness of a relationship between two variables, in this case the test scores of twins. The nearer to 1.00 the coefficient is, the closer is the relationship. Thus the scores of MZ twins above, whether reared together or apart, resemble each other more than is the case with scores of DZ twins.
Source: Adapted from Pederson et al. (1992) and Rowe (1993).

same womb, the same birth process, the same family. It follows that if a psychological characteristic is influenced by heredity, the resemblance between identical twins should be greater than between non-identical twins; if, however, heredity plays no part, identical twins should be no more similar than non-identical twins. If it is possible to study identical and non-identical twins separated at birth and brought up in different families, the role played by genetics and environmental factors respectively can be determined even more clearly. Some relevant findings are shown in table 3.1; these indicate that even when identical twins are reared apart, they resemble each other in psychological characteristics more than do non-identical twins in the same family. The importance of heredity is made very apparent thereby.

- *Adoption studies* make use of another natural experiment to tease out the respective influence of heredity and environment. The comparison here involves children and their adoptive as opposed to their biological parents. If children, adopted soon after birth, resemble their adoptive parents more than their biological parents, environmental factors are indicated as the primary influences on the way they have developed; if, on the other hand, the resemblance is greater to their biological parents, despite the fact that they have had virtually no contact with them, genetic factors are indicated. As seen in table 3.2, when this method is applied to the investigation of two personality traits, extraversion and neuroticism, the closer resemblance of children to their biological parents than to their adoptive parents is apparent. While the strength of genetic effects varies from one psychological characteristic to another, evidence from adoption studies confirms that parent–child similarities, usually ascribed in the past to socialization effects, are in fact largely a reflection of heredity.

Two major conclusions arise from the findings obtained by these two methods. The first is that virtually all psychological characteristics examined show evidence

Table 3.2 Correlation coefficients for extraversion and neuroticism measures obtained from biological and adoptive parent–child pairs

	Biological *parent–child pairs*	*Adoptive* *parent–child pairs*
Extraversion	0.16	0.01
Neuroticism	0.13	0.05

Source: Adapted from Rowe (1993).

of some genetic influence (see table 3.3 for further details). The extent of that influence varies from one characteristic to another: thus cognitive aspects such as general intelligence, spatial ability, literacy and dyslexia have generally been found to be more heritable than personality aspects such as extraversion and neuroticism. In addition, some unexpected sex differences have emerged: alcoholism, for example, shows moderate genetic influence in males but only negligible influence in females. And one further constraint: not all investigations emerge with the same findings; in particular, twin studies and adoption studies sometimes disagree, indicating the effect that methodological factors may have on research results. Nevertheless, the overall conclusion is clear: if we are to understand the course of children's development and the reasons why particular individuals become the people they are, we must take into account their hereditary make-up and appreciate the extent to which genetic factors play a part in determining behaviour.

Table 3.3 Psychological characteristics investigated for genetic influence

Cognition
General intelligence
Language ability
Literacy (reading, spelling)
Dyslexia
Spatial ability
    (For review see Plomin, 1990)

Antisocial behaviour
Delinquency
Criminality
Antisocial personality disorder
    (For review see Rutter, Giller & Hagel, 1999)

Personality
Extraversion
Neuroticism
Aggression
Risk taking
Conservatism
Self-esteem
    (For review see Loehlin, 1992)

Psychopathology
Schizophrenia
Autism
Hyperactivity
    (For review see Rutter, Silberg, O'Connor
    & Simonoff, 1999)

There is, however, a second conclusion that we need to bear in mind. In every instance where genetic factors have been implicated, they account for only part of individual variability and never for all of it. Even in such cases as general intelligence or schizophrenia, where heredity plays a substantial role, the pervasiveness of environmental influences is also apparent. It is therefore a matter of nature *and* nurture, not nature *or* nurture. The two sets of influences are not opposites, each working separately – on the contrary, the pair almost invariably interact and produce their effects jointly.

Let us consider some of the ways in which nature and nurture cooperate. One example is seen in the fact that a particular genetic endowment increases the likelihood that people in the environment will treat the individual in a particular way. An outgoing, sociable child will elicit far more positive responses from others than a quiet, solemn one: even in the earliest months of life active, smiling babies are more likely to receive attention than passive babies, and as a result the former will be encouraged but the latter discouraged from seeking out further social interaction. Thus the original tendency is strengthened by the kind of response it elicits from others. The notion that children are wholly shaped by their parents' treatment is clearly a simplistic one; to a considerable extent, children determine their own treatment by virtue of their inherent make-up. As any parent with more than one child will have found out, what worked with the first one did not necessarily work with the second one, for each is a different being and as a result requires different handling. Unwittingly, children elicit the particular kind of nurture that accords with their nature.

Another example is provided by the tendency of people actively to select those environments that fit in with their particular genetic make-up. Thus children born with a temperament that predisposes them to hyperactivity and aggressiveness will seek the company of like-minded peers, so that they have the opportunity to engage in congenial activities and act out their genetic tendencies. Similarly, children who are by nature shy and quiet will select settings and companions that are compatible with these characteristics, thereby reinforcing their original predisposition. We can readily appreciate that adults make determined efforts to choose congenial environments – their friends, their marriage partner, their job, and so forth; however, even quite young children are already actively engaged in what has been referred to as **niche-picking** in order to function in settings that are in harmony with their inherited motivational, intellectual and personality characteristics. Neither genes nor environments operate in isolation; the two function conjointly to affect development. As the example in box 3.1 shows, this applies even to the development of sexual identity.

Niche-picking. The process whereby individuals actively select those environments that fit in with their genetic predisposition.

A further point to bear in mind is that characteristics strongly influenced by heredity can nevertheless be much affected by changed environmental conditions. Height, for example, is one of the most genetically dependent of all human characteristics; nevertheless, as a result of improved nutrition, it has increased greatly in the course of the last 100 years or so. The same applies to age at onset of puberty:

BOX 3.1

Male or female? Developing a sexual identity

Our genetic sex is determined at conception and depends on whether the sperm contributes an X chromosome or a Y chromosome. If it is the former, the child will be a genetic female; if the latter, a male. The sex chromosome provided by the egg is always an X, thus females are characterized by an XX sex chromosome pair and males by an XY pair. Six weeks after conception sexual differentiation begins, in that messages encoded in the XY chromosome pair will set in motion the development of testes; after a further 6 weeks the XX pair will similarly ensure the development of ovaries. Whether we are male or female will thus depend on very early biological processes.

However, the sexual identity with which we end up can also be influenced by life experience, and in particular by parental treatment. This becomes especially obvious when one examines certain pathological cases where sexual development has gone tragically wrong. These abnormalities and their psychological implications have been described in detail by Money and Ehrhardt (1972). Particularly striking is a boy (one of identical male twins) who at the age of 7 months lost his penis as a result of surgical mishap during circumcision performed by means of electrocautery. After considerable agonizing, the parents decided to treat the child as a girl, and from 17 months on changed the child's name (John to Joan), clothing and hairstyle to that of a female. This was followed in due course by surgical changes and (at puberty) by hormone treatment in order to bring about the development of feminine characteristics.

As a result, Joan soon developed some distinctly feminine attributes and began to differ from her twin brother in many respects. According to Money and Ehrhardt, this was largely due to her treatment by the parents, who made a point of dressing her in frilly frocks, providing her with bracelets and hair ribbons and encouraging her to help with the housework. Unlike her brother, the girl became neat and tidy, interested in clothes, proud of her long hair and dainty in her appearance, and while her brother preferred 'masculine' toys like cars and guns she played with dolls and other such 'feminine' toys. And yet, feminization was far from complete. Joan was described as tomboyish, with the abundant physical energy and domineering behaviour in play with other children usually associated with males – presumably due to her prenatal exposure to male sex hormones. She increasingly rejected the clothes and toys she was offered, and especially from the age of 9 or 10 began to experience severe identity problems centred in the main on her somewhat masculine appearance and preference for masculine occupations. As later reports show (Diamond & Sigmundson, 1997), these problems in due course became so severe that it was eventually decided to undertake sexual reassignment, and by means of surgical and hormonal means the girl became a boy once more, reverting to the name John. In consequence, John became very much happier and at ease with himself, developing into an attractive muscular young man and, at the age of 25, marrying a somewhat older woman whose children he adopted.

There have been other such cases where sexual identity was assigned arbitrarily or counter to the child's genetic sex (see Golombok & Fivush, 1994). These include so-called *pseudo-hermaphrodites*, i.e. individuals born with ambiguous genitalia who may then be brought up as either male or female, depending on parental whim. While in most cases the children developed a psychological identity that accords with the sex assigned to them, generalizations about the respective roles of nature and nurture cannot easily be made. For one thing, assignment of sexual identity needs to be completed by 3 years of age; after that, it becomes increasingly difficult. And for another, parental upbringing as an influence is rarely found on its own but is usually accompanied by hormonal treatment, making it difficult to sort out the respective roles of psychological and biological factors. What one can conclude is that nature and nurture both play a part and that, under normal circumstances, the two sets of influences work in tandem to bring about the development of sexual identity.

this too is strongly influenced by genetic endowment and yet, probably also as a result of better nutrition, children reach this point at much earlier ages than they did at one time. Genetic influence, we can conclude, by no means rules out environmental influence.

Fact and fiction concerning genes

Scientific progress in understanding our genetic make-up has in recent years been extraordinarily impressive and is showing every sign of continuing its advances (Rutter, 2002). Among non-specialists, however, there remains a great deal of misunderstanding about both the nature and functioning of genes and the implications that our growing knowledge may have for understanding human development. We have already seen this in the belief that nature and nurture are separate influences, when in fact they invariably act jointly. There are, however, various other mistaken beliefs, so let us look at some of the most common of these fictions and at the corresponding facts that have now come to light.

- *Fiction*: Genes cause behaviour.
- *Fact*: The influence of genes on behaviour is never as direct as this statement would have it. Genes are chemical structures that have chemical effects on the body, and so influence behaviour through their effects on the body's response to the environment. Thus there are, for example, no genes *for* neuroticism, though there is plenty of evidence that this characteristic is genetically influenced: rather, genetic effects on neurotic behaviour may involve a nervous system that is particularly sensitive to stress. Similarly, there are no genes *for* alcoholism: instead, genetic factors may in some way affect the body's sensitivity to alcohol. Thus all relationships between genes and behaviour are of an indirect and not a direct nature.

- *Fiction*: Each psychological characteristic is associated with the operation of some particular gene.
- *Fact*: Other than certain single-gene disorders such as PKU, mentioned above, there is no known psychological characteristic that appears to be related to just one gene. On the contrary, such characteristics are so complex that they are more likely to depend on the actions of a great many genes functioning cooperatively in groups. What is more, any one gene may affect many different psychological aspects; the gene–behaviour link is thus by no means a simple one.

- *Fiction*: Genetic programmes control the appearance of developmental milestones in particular sequences and at particular ages.
- *Fact*: This is true only in part. For example, milestones such as those found in early motor development (head control, sitting, crawling, standing, walking and so on) are triggered by a genetic clock. However, the timing of that clock can be affected by environmental events: where, for example, the child is reared under conditions of gross deprivation, the milestones are reached at far later ages than they would be otherwise. The sequence in which milestones appear is also not an invariable one but can be interfered with by lack of environmental opportunities.

- *Fiction*: Genetically determined conditions cannot be modified.
- *Fact*: It is a misconception that anything inherited is fixed and impervious to change, while all acquired characteristics are open to modification. Neither part of this dichotomy is true: as the example of PKU shows, an inherited disorder can be treated and indeed completely cured, while some instances of phobias show that behaviour acquired during the life course can be extraordinarily resistant to extinction. The fatalistic concept, that heredity is something one cannot do anything about ('genes are destiny', as the popular saying has it) is thus not tenable.

- *Fiction*: Genetic characteristics manifest themselves similarly in successive generations.

- *Fact*: Conditions such as haemophilia run in families, but that does not mean that every generation is affected. Parents may be carriers and therefore pass the disorder on to their children, and yet be quite free of it themselves. Similarly, autism is a genetically determined condition, yet the parents of autistic children so rarely show any psychological abnormality that for a long time it was assumed that the cause of autism was to be found in the environment, such as in parental attitudes – an assumption now known to be mistaken.

- *Fiction*: Genetic influences diminish with age.
- *Fact*: The idea that hereditary factors exert their most potent influence early on in development and then become slowed down by the increasing impact of environmental factors is widely prevalent and yet untrue. For certain characteristics this may be so; for others, not. There is evidence, for example, that with increasing age genetic factors become *more* important in explaining differences in intelligence among children. In any case, some clearly genetically determined characteristics do not appear until relatively late in the course of development, age at puberty being an obvious example; similarly, certain genetic disorders do not manifest themselves until late childhood or adulthood.

- *Fiction*: Genetics is all about heredity and tells us nothing about the environment.
- *Fact*: Behavioural genetics is able to contribute a great deal to our knowledge about environmental influences. For one thing, it has shown the intimate interaction of nature and nurture; for another, it can make estimates of the relative contribution that the two make to development; and finally, it can analyse environmental influences into their component parts. The last in particular has attracted attention, in that behavioural geneticists have found it useful to distinguish between two kinds of environmental influences, *shared* and *non-shared*. The former are those that are common to all children in a given family, such as social class, neighbourhood, number of books in the home, etc.; the latter are unique to each child in the family, e.g. birth order, the parents' preference for one child over another, illnesses and accidents, and so on. The distinction matters because of indications that non-shared influences are every bit as potent in affecting the course of development as the shared ones which have received the bulk of attention in the past. Ironically, it seems that genetics has as much to say about the environment as about heredity.

From Conception to Birth

In China and Japan in former times children were considered to be 1 year old when born. In some respects this may be nearer the true state of affairs than our own way of reckoning age, for during the time a child spends in the womb an enormous amount goes on that shapes the child's development. Physically, the rate of change during this period is in many respects greater than at any other time; however, from a psychological point of view too, prenatal life is highly relevant to understanding developmental outcomes.

Just what goes on in the womb and in what way these events affect the unborn child has always been subject to a great deal of folklore. The position of the planets, the application of magic, the working of demons – these are some of the forces that have been evoked as influencing prenatal development. Nowadays some highly sophisticated techniques are available to provide rather more objective findings, as a result of which we can view still pictures of the foetus and even obtain films that show, for example, the extent to which the unborn child, in the later stages of pregnancy anyway, is capable of some quite advanced movement patterns: thumb sucking, stepping motions, emotional expressions, and so forth. Modern research can also demonstrate in what way the foetus is affected by events in the external environment, for here too folklore has generated all sorts of fantasies such as the notion that mothers who listen to lots of music during their pregnancy will produce musical prodigies. Thus nutrition, drugs, smoking, alcohol and (more controversially) stress experienced by the expectant mother are all now regarded as affecting the child's development – in some cases producing ill effects of a long-lasting or even permanent nature, as highlighted by the thalidomide tragedy and its consequences.

Such effects demonstrate that the womb is by no means a totally sheltered environment – a kind of fortress shielding the child from outside influences. It is true that these influences are transmitted by the mother, but such transmission demonstrates that even before the child's birth the mother plays a crucial role in determining the kind of individual her child will become. Let us bear in mind, however, that the influence is a mutual one: the mother affects the foetus but the foetus also affects the mother. As Hytten (1976) has put it so vividly:

> The fetus is an egoist, and by no means an endearing and helpless little dependant as his mother may fondly think. As soon as he has plugged himself into the uterine wall he sets out to make certain that his needs are served, regardless of any inconvenience he may cause. He does this by almost completely altering the mother's physiology, usually by fiddling the control mechanisms.

It seems that mutuality of influence between child and caretaker is as noteworthy during prenatal life as it will be subsequently.

Stages of prenatal development

For descriptive purposes the 9-month period of pregnancy is often simply divided into equal thirds or *trimesters*. However, from a developmental point of view, a more useful division is into three distinct stages of varying duration, referred to as the germinal, the embryonic and the foetal stage respectively.

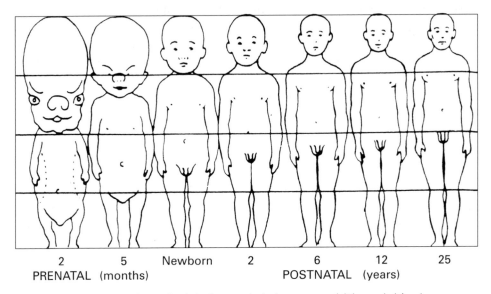

2	5	Newborn	2	6	12	25
PRENATAL (months)			POSTNATAL (years)			

Figure 3.3 *Proportional growth of the human body from prenatal life to adulthood.*

1 The germinal stage

This lasts for about 2 weeks, i.e. from conception until the ovum implants itself in the uterine wall. During this time the single cell that initially constitutes the indi-vidual splits in two, after which each of the new cells also splits – and so on. This multiplication process continues with extraordinary rapidity, thereby eventually trans-forming the one cell present at the beginning into a living being. At first the cells are undifferentiated, but before the end of the germinal stage they have begun to assume the particular roles they will subsequently play as parts of the body, forming organs, limbs and physiological systems.

2 The embryonic stage

This continues for about 6 weeks, during which more and more cells are formed, each serving a particular function and resulting in the formation of the spinal cord, the major sensory organs, arms and legs, and the beginnings of such organs as the heart and the brain. Even fingers and toes are present, as are such parts as mouth, tongue and eyelids. At the end of this stage the embryo is only about 1 inch long, but in its appearance it is already well on its way to becoming a recognizable human being. Only in its proportions is it very different from the being it will eventually become: the head in particular takes up a much larger part of the whole body than at later ages (figure 3.3). In addition, the organs have now assumed their various functions; thus the heart can beat, the stomach produce digestive juices and the kidneys filter blood. However, during this period of rapid formation of vital organs and bodily parts, the organism becomes increasingly vulnerable to harm from certain external agents; thus this is the danger period for German measles, which can result in irreplaceable damage to brain and eyes, causing mental handicap and blindness. It was also during this period that administration of the thalidomide drug, given to mothers to alleviate morning sickness, caused serious malformations to newly developing limbs, resulting in babies born without arms or legs.

3 The foetal stage

Lasting for 7 months, this period sees enormous gains in height (from about 1 inch to 21 inches) and in weight (from a few ounces to around 7 pounds). Most of the development that occurs is a matter of enlarging and refinement of the body parts and organs that emerged in the first 2 months; thus bones come to be formed, hair starts growing, sensory organs like eyes, ears and tastebuds develop to the full, and by about 28 weeks of conceptual age the nervous, circulatory and breathing systems are all capable of supporting independent existence should the baby be born prematurely. However, long before birth the baby has already made his existence felt, for from about 16 weeks the mother can feel the baby's movements inside her and soon he will become capable of administering some pretty vigorous kicks. These occur while the foetus is, as it were, exercising his limbs, for in the earlier months of the foetal stage he is capable of turning from front to back or even executing somersaults; only later on will the foetus become less active because he has grown too much to have sufficient room for movement in the confines of the womb. All such movements, which can be observed using ultrasound recordings, are spontaneous: they are a sign of the rapid development of the brain, which is now increasingly able to take over direction of the baby's actions.

Environmental influences on prenatal development

The period of most rapid brain development occurs during the early stages of the foetal period, and it is then that the unborn child is most susceptible to environmental influences transmitted by the mother. This becomes clear, often tragically so, by looking at the effects of **teratogens** – namely, substances ingested by the mother which cross the placenta and then adversely affect prenatal development, causing birth defects and persistent physical and psychological problems (*tera* is the Greek word for monster – an unfortunate association but one reflecting the horror with which such defects were greeted when they were still common and non-preventable and their cause subject to much superstition).

Teratogens are substances like alcohol or cocaine that cross the maternal placenta and interfere with the development of the foetus.

The most common teratogens fall under three headings: drugs, diseases and diet – the 'three Ds'.

1 Drugs

- *Alcohol.* The harmful effects of prenatal consumption of alcohol were brought into focus in the 1970s when a group of American scientists identified a set of physical and mental symptoms characteristic of children born to alcoholic mothers, and labelled them *foetal alcohol syndrome* (FAS). On the physical side, children born with FAS have small, narrow heads and a distinctive facial appearance, with widely spaced eyes, short nose and an underdeveloped jaw, and are mostly small in stature compared with age norms. Psychologically, the most prominent symptom is mental retardation, and though this is usually not of a severe degree FAS has become one of the more common causes of retardation. Various other signs of central nervous dysfunction are also often present, such as hyperactivity, short attention span, sleep disorders and defective reflex functioning. There is thus little doubt that alcohol, when consumed in large quantities during pregnancy, can cross the maternal placenta and produce markedly adverse and permanent effects on the growing foetus. While FAS is found in the children of women in the upper 5 or 10 per cent of alcohol consumption, the effects of lower levels of consumption ('social drinking') are more controversial. Yet even here there is some evidence that the unborn baby can be affected and that the effects, though mild, may still be found in late childhood (see box 3.2).
- *Tobacco.* The size of infants born to mothers who are heavy smokers is significantly lower than that of other infants. This is because nicotine constricts the blood flow to the placenta, thereby restricting the supply of nutrition to the foetus. Also, the more a mother smokes during the pregnancy, the greater the chances are that the baby will be born prematurely, and prematurity (as we shall see below) can lead to a variety of physical and behavioural problems. In comparison with alcohol, nicotine does not have

BOX 3.2

Does 'social drinking' during pregnancy have adverse effects?

The effects of heavy drinking on the unborn child have been firmly established, but there has been some reluctance to accept that even the odd drink taken socially can be harmful. The Seattle Longitudinal Prospective Study on Alcohol and Pregnancy, a large-scale and impressive investigation carried out in the United States, has come up with some convincing evidence to settle this matter (as published, for example, in Olson, Streissguth, Sampson, Barr, Bookstein & Thiede, 1997; Streissguth, Barr & Sampson, 1990).

A sample of about 500 pregnant women was interviewed in mid-pregnancy in order to establish their habitual consumption of alcohol, both before the pregnancy and during it. Fewer than 1 per cent of the women turned out to have a major drink problem, though 80 per cent readily admitted to some drinking in pregnancy. Questions were also asked about their use of tobacco, caffeine and drugs. Following birth, the children were evaluated during the first 2 days of life and then again at 8 and 18 months and at 4, 7 and 14 years. At each follow-up point, the children were assessed by means of a wide range of age-appropriate neurological and psychological tests.

Adverse effects of prenatal alcohol consumption, even at the low levels typical of the majority of mothers, were found from the beginning on. At birth the babies exposed to alcohol were more likely to show respiratory distress and to have less stable heart rate, and during the following 2 days they showed more sluggishness, weaker sucking and various signs of central nervous dysfunction. Subsequently in infancy, both motor and mental development were slightly retarded, and from 4 years on it became clear that children exposed prenatally to more than 1 ounce of alcohol per day (about two drinks) had somewhat lower intelligence test scores than the children of abstainers. The difference, approximately 7 IQ points, was not great, but it was persistent and 'dose-dependent', i.e. the extent of the deficit was directly related to the amount of alcohol consumed by the mother. From 7 years on a number of learning problems became evident, seen primarily in lower achievement in reading and arithmetic, and associated in particular with 'binge' patterns of drinking, i.e. the consumption of more than five drinks on any occasion during early pregnancy. It is likely that these various cognitive problems reflected the children's difficulties in maintaining attention, for vigilance tests indicated the presence of alcohol-related decrements in attending to and appropriately responding to signals – a problem already seen immediately after birth in the babies' reactions to lights and sounds and in the longer time they took to attach to the nipple. It is thus likely that the various school-age sequelae stem from a basic organic deficiency of the central nervous system.

It is perhaps particularly significant that even in adolescence a cluster of problems could still be found in children prenatally exposed to relatively low dosages of alcohol. Some of these problems were associated with slow or inefficient information processing and evident therefore in school achievement; others concerned such possibly indirect effects as poor self-image and antisocial behaviour. Of course, not every individual exposed to alcohol prenatally showed deficits; nevertheless, it is clear from this study that such exposure, even at levels well within the realm of social drinking, puts children's normal adaptive functioning at risk from birth on.

such drastic consequences, especially in the long term. However, some studies have found a somewhat greater incidence of behaviour problems and learning difficulties in children of mothers who smoked during the pregnancy, the effect increasing with amount of nicotine consumed.

- *Cocaine.* Infants born to cocaine users are at considerable risk for a variety of problems. These include stillbirth, prematurity, low birthweight, cot death and various neurological disabilities that lead on to subsequent attentional problems and learning difficulties. Such infants are often found to be difficult to care for from the early days on: they may be irritable and easily agitated, be hard to soothe, fail to establish regular sleep patterns and withdraw from social contact. For a mother to relate to such a child is no easy task: for example, a tendency for the infant to greet overtures from her with closed or averted eyes hardly encourages further interaction, and an inability to sustain positive play episodes similarly adds to a mother's frustration. A cycle of unsatisfactory mother–child interaction is thus set up as a secondary effect on top of all the other adverse consequences.

2 *Disease*

- *Rubella.* As we have already seen, rubella (or German measles) is most dangerous if transmitted during the first weeks of pregnancy. It can result in blindness, deafness, mental handicap, heart defects and other serious problems, and is thus one of the most dangerous agents the unborn child can encounter. Fortunately there is wide awareness of this danger, and by means of vaccination of females in childhood prevention is possible.
- *AIDS.* Women infected with the AIDS virus run a definite risk of passing the virus on to any child they may be carrying. The transmission rate has been variously estimated at between 12 and 30 per cent, though why some babies escape the infection and others do not is as yet unknown. Having a mother with AIDS makes prematurity and low birthweight more likely; also, these children are at risk of contracting serious infectious diseases like pneumonia in infancy. According to US statistics, AIDS is now the seventh leading cause of death of children from birth to 4 years of age.

3 *Diet*

- *Malnutrition.* The foetus is wholly dependent on the mother for his nourishment: her intake of food crucially determines growth and development. When the foetus does not obtain sufficient quantities of certain important nutrients, he will attempt to obtain these directly from the mother's body: if, for example, not enough calcium is made available through the mother's intake of food, the foetus will instead obtain it from the mother's bones. In cases of chronic malnutrition, the mother's personal nutritional supplies will become depleted and in turn cause problems for the foetus. This was vividly shown by an 'experiment of nature' that occurred in 1944 during the Second World War, when a severe famine was brought about by Nazi troops cutting off food supplies to the population of the Netherlands, thereby causing widespread malnourishment amounting to near-starvation. The effects of this experience were subsequently closely monitored, and showed that much depended on when in the pregnancy starvation occurred. If the worst was experienced in the first trimester, i.e. during the critical period of brain growth, foetuses were twice as likely as others to have defects of the central nervous system such as spina bifida and hydrocephalus, and to be stillborn. If starvation was at its most severe in the second and especially the third trimester, the babies were likely to be born underweight; yet once food supplies were rushed to the population following liberation, the babies caught up in weight and showed normal physical and mental growth. At age 19 the male offspring of the malnourished women were assessed for compulsory military service and found to be fit and normal: no long-term consequences of their prenatal experience could be detected. However, a curious and unexpected finding emerged subsequently: it appeared that the effect was passed on to the *third* generation, in that the babies of women who had been a foetus in the later trimesters of their mothers' pregnancy during the period of malnutrition were well below average in weight and height (see Diamond, 1990, for further details). The mechanisms responsible for such a three-generation effect are still to be understood. What we can conclude is that in certain respects human beings have remarkable resilience and capacity to recover; yet, as shown by the example of malnutrition in common with the other prenatal adversities mentioned, it is possible for certain kinds of injury experienced at certain times of development to have severe consequences that are not easily reversed.

There are many other environmental agents that are known to be health hazards to the unborn child – teratogens such as radiation, lead, mercury, amphetamine, genital herpes and smallpox, all of which can cross the maternal placenta and cause physical and, in the longer term, psychological damage. One other agent is worth mentioning if only because it has been the subject of much speculation, namely, maternal stress. It is natural that mothers who experience anxiety during the pregnancy, either continuously or as a suddenly encountered episode of acute stress, should be concerned about the effect on the baby. Convincing evidence, however, is hard to come by, for research into the effects of maternal stress is difficult to carry out. There have been quite a few studies of mothers pregnant at times of great trauma: war, disasters such as earthquakes or cyclones, incarceration in concentration camps and so on, but their results have been equivocal. Some have shown no increase in the incidence of abnormalities in these women's babies; in other cases any increase found could just as easily be attributed to such physical concomitants to the mental stress as torture, malnutrition or sickness. The mother's emotional state *after* giving birth must also be taken into account. It is true that the experience of intense stress results in the release of powerful hormones from the adrenal glands which can cross the placenta and affect the foetus. The nature and duration of that effect, however, have not been established.

The Newborn's Adjustment to the World

Having led an essentially aquatic and utterly dependent existence while in the womb, the baby is quite suddenly at the end of pregnancy thrust into a very different environment – one in which she is expected to breathe air, to regulate her own temperature and to obtain nutrition by wholly new means. No wonder there has been much speculation about the long-term effects of such an apparently traumatic and abrupt change.

Childbirth and its psychological consequences

A child's birth is not just a physiological event that can be described in terms of changes to the mother's and the baby's bodies. It is also an event which has immense social significance and which each culture views in a particular light. As Margaret Mead (Mead & Newton, 1967) put it,

> Childbirth may be experienced according to the phrasing given it by the culture as an experience that is dangerous and painful, interesting and engrossing, matter of fact and mildly hazardous, or accompanied by enormous supernatural hazards.

As a result, societies differ in the way they manage the birth process: in where it takes place, in who is present, in the help given to the mother and in how the baby is dealt with immediately after birth, and also in the extent to which childbirth is allowed to disrupt other aspects of the mother's life such as her work in office or fields. In our own society alone there have been considerable changes in management practices, as seen in the trend from home to hospital as the setting for the birth, in the encouragement now given to fathers to be present throughout labour and during the birth, and in the extent and kind of pain relief provided to mothers at the time. These variations, together with discussions about the use of caesarian rather than vaginal delivery or the application of techniques for handling mother and baby associated with such advocates as Dick-Read ('Childbirth without fear') and Leboyer ('Birth without violence'), give some indication of the complexity of this life event and of the many different forms it may take. Do these differences matter as far as the child's further development is concerned?

According to popular belief, the fact that birth marks the very first step the child takes in outside life should have considerable implications for the future. How easy and how natural the birth was, the mother's behaviour and even her thoughts and feelings at the time, the baby's position before delivery – these and other aspects of the whole process have been the target of all sorts of beliefs and assumptions that may have little grounding in evidence but that are nevertheless the subject of firm convictions as to their effects on the child in future years. Yet such irrationality is found among professionals too: the psychoanalyst Otto Rank (1929), for example, regarded birth as a highly traumatic event that lies at the root of all sorts of psychological problems found in future years. Thus the feelings aroused by being expelled from the totally protective environment of the womb into a tense and uncertain world would, according to Rank, resurface subsequently in the form of separation anxieties and other neurotic fears, and especially so when the birth had been long and complicated and particularly traumatic. Let us stress that no one has ever been able to confirm this theory; Freud for one found it implausible and disowned it.

There are, of course, some kinds of difficult births that give rise to psychological after-effects, but only where actual physical harm is done, in particular to the brain. The cells of the brain require a continuous supply of oxygen to be operative; in cases of **anoxia**, where the brain is deprived of oxygen for a prolonged period at birth, brain cells may be permanently destroyed and leave the child impaired by cerebral palsy, mental retardation, epilepsy or cognitive deficiencies of one kind or another. Newborns' mortality and morbidity rates have dropped sharply in recent times thanks to modern obstetric practices; nevertheless, given the difficulties of negotiating the narrow birth canal before the baby is born and the sudden need to adopt new modes of functioning immediately afterwards, birth is a crisis point even though only a small minority of babies (estimated at a fraction of 1 per cent) experience severe complications. It is therefore common practice straight after birth carefully to monitor the baby's condition and to record such vital signs as heart rate, muscle tone and breathing. The most common screening test used for this purpose yields an **Apgar score** (see table 3.4), which rates a baby on each of five criteria and results in a maximum score of 10. Less than 7 is regarded as a danger sign; less than 4 means the baby is in a critical condition.

Anoxia. The condition where the brain is deprived of essential supplies of oxygen, resulting in both physical and mental retardation if severe.

Apgar score. A measure of a newborn baby's condition, derived from a rating scale assessing a range of essential functions.

Table 3.4 The Apgar scale

Function evaluated	Score		
	0	*1*	*2*
Heart rate	Absent	Below 100	Above 100
Respiration	Absent	Slow, irregular	Regular, strong cry
Muscle tone	Flaccid	Weak	Well flexed
Colour	Blue; pale	Body pink; extremities blue	Pink
Reflex irritability	No response	Grimace	Full response

Extremely low Apgar scores tend to be associated with reduced oxygen supply to the brain and, if the baby survives, are predictive of permanent and usually severe disability. Apgar scores in the medium range (around 5–8), on the other hand, have little predictive power – at least not on their own, for the developmental outcome of these children depends not only on their original physical condition but also on the type of social and physical environment in which they are subsequently reared. Where that environment is a supportive one, the initial complications will be reduced and in due course disappear; where, however, it is inadequate, the child is more likely to be left with permanent disabilities.

Prematurely born children

The way in which physical and environmental conditions interact to produce a particular developmental outcome can also be seen in another group of children starting off life under a disadvantage, namely, those born prematurely and of low birthweight.

First, some facts:

- A premature baby is one born before the 37th week of pregnancy. The lowest age for survival is at present usually reckoned to be around 20 weeks.
- Premature babies are generally of low birthweight. However, low-birthweight babies constitute a separate classification, in that some full-term newborns are also below the definitional limit of 2,500 g ($5^1/2$ lb).
- About 5 per cent of all births occur prematurely, though the incidence varies greatly from one sector of the population to another. Social class differences in particular are pronounced: the lower the mother's socio-economic status is, the greater are the chances of prematurity. Premature births also occur disproportionately often among teenage mothers.
- The causes of prematurity are many, including drinking and smoking during pregnancy, drug abuse, illnesses such as diabetes and pre-eclampsia, abnormalities in the mother's reproductive system, and social conditions that affect the mother's general health such as poverty, malnutrition and inadequate medical care during the pregnancy.
- Premature babies are likely to suffer from a variety of conditions in the period following birth. These include jaundice, problems with breathing and temperature control, and difficulties in sucking and swallowing. The degree of risk varies greatly according to gestational age and birthweight: thus, babies who are marginally premature are unlikely to develop any serious complications, whereas those of greater prematurity may require assistance with vital bodily functions for prolonged periods in neonatal intensive-care nurseries.

In the short term premature babies are clearly at some disadvantage in coping with the outside world. But what of long-term consequences? There have been many studies which have followed up these children over the years, some into adolescence and even adulthood, yet the results produced have been inconsistent – at least in the case of those studies that focused exclusively on prematurity (or birthweight) as a developmental cause (for review see Lukeman & Melvin, 1993). As a group, premature children are more likely to be behind other children during the early years in perceptual and motor skills, language acquisition and play maturity; they have also been reported as showing more restlessness and inattention and greater difficulty in gaining emotional control. In later years IQs tend to be lower and the incidence of learning difficulties greater; according to some studies, social adjustment problems of one kind or another are also more evident. Yet such group results do not do justice to the considerable variability found among prematurely born children. Some children, mostly those placed at an extreme disadvantage at birth, continue to show disabilities throughout their later years, whereas many others catch up in both physical and psychological functioning. Whether children do catch up, and the extent to which they do so and how soon, depends in part on the severity of their condition at birth, in part on the medical care they get subsequently, and to a considerable extent also on the psychological support each child experiences in subsequent years as part of family life – a point convincingly argued by Sameroff and Chandler (1975) in a review of the consequences of various pre- and perinatal problems, including prematurity.

Prematurity, Sameroff and Chandler concede, is a risk factor, yet prematurity *per se* does not enable us to predict how well a child will function cognitively and socially in the years to come. It is only by taking into account the environment in which premature children are reared that prediction becomes possible: where parents provide the kind of experiences that offset potential ill effects, the outlook is favourable; where, on the other hand, they are unable to give adequate support or even offer adverse treatment, the ill effects are given full rein. The environment must therefore be taken into account in conjunction with the child's early condition if one is to understand the course of development. There are, of course, many aspects to that environment which may have a bearing on the child's future development, but the variable that Sameroff and Chandler found to provide the best summary explanation is social class. In socially advantaged families children who have suffered early complications show few residual effects in the long term; children with identical pathology reared in disadvantaged families, on the other hand, do show adverse effects. Social class is, of course, only an umbrella term that covers a great range of the specific conditions constituting the concrete experiences encountered by children: amount of toys and books in the home, linguistic input, educational encouragement, crowding, nutrition, adequacy of schooling, and so forth. The point is that it is these persistent experiences that interact with one-time perinatal events to determine long-term developmental outcomes.

The quality of care experienced by children is, of course, primarily the responsibility of parents. It is they who provide experiences such as language stimulation and educational encouragement, and if one is to understand how the environment can exert a compensatory effect on children starting life with disabilities such as

BOX 3.3

Interacting with a premature baby

Premature newborns have been described as behaviourally disorganized, less predictable in their reactions, less adaptable to changes of routine, over-reactive to some forms of stimulation and underreactive to others, and in addition less attractive in appearance – all characteristics that have profound implications for their caretakers and for the kinds of social interactions that develop between parent and child.

The circumstances under which social development gets off to a start differ for such infants in four main ways (Eckerman & Oehler, 1992):

1 Social interactions begin at a relatively much earlier point in development. The baby may consequently not be ready as yet to process the sights and sounds provided by parents.

2 Premature babies, especially those of very low birthweight, may not only be immature but also sick. In particular, they may be at risk for the development of neurological disorders that will cause further irregularities in their behaviour.

3 The period following birth may be one of great stress for the parents; their behaviour too will thus be altered.

4 Social interactions begin under quite different physical constraints, imposed by the intensive-care nursery in which such babies are initially reared. Parents have only limited contact with the baby; they are often intimidated by the equipment that forms a necessary part of such an environment; and they may also feel that their role is only a minor one, being of less significance than that of nurses and doctors.

It is thus not surprising that early parent–baby interactions, as observed for instance in face-to-face situations, take a different form compared with those involving full-term babies. Synchrony is more difficult to establish because of abnormally high or low thresholds to stimulation; the baby's attention cannot be easily elicited and maintained; and the parent's attempts to provide the baby with extra stimulation through talking and touching may result merely in greater irritability. Under such conditions, some parents may feel rejected and will withdraw; special efforts to coach them will then be required.

Yet even in the early weeks of life premature babies are already responsive to some forms of social stimulation: speech, for example, can maintain them in the awake and visually alert state that is presumed conducive to social interaction. Thus, whatever initial difficulties there may be, such infants do have the potential to be rewarding social partners, and indeed the great majority catch up within the first 3 to 6 months of postnatal life.

those associated with prematurity, it is necessary to investigate the nature of inter-action between parents and their premature infants. There is no doubt that the birth of a tiny and possibly sickly baby constitutes a considerable trauma for parents, and the greater the degree of prematurity, the more the formation of the initial relationship is likely to be affected by such aspects as the baby's confinement to an incubator that prevents any direct contact, the parents' feelings of helplessness while medical and nursing staff are in charge of the baby's care, and the uncertainty concerning the child's future which even experienced professionals may not be able to resolve. Add to that the effect that various adverse behavioural characteristics typical of premature babies may have on their parents (see box 3.3), and one must appreciate that the establishment of a satisfactory relationship is by no means an easy and straightforward task.

How the world looks to newborns

'A great blooming, buzzing confusion' – that is how the philosopher-cum-psychologist William James, writing at the end of the nineteenth century, characterized the mental state of newborn babies. Being a memorable phrase, it became one of the most widely quoted descriptions of early infancy – unfortunately so, because it gave a quite misleading picture of chaos and disorder in the early stages of psychological life, emphasizing infants' incompetence and suggesting that only maturity and experience would bring order to the developing mind.

As one example of this belief, it was assumed until fairly recently that the visual apparatus of newborn babies is initially incapable of functioning and that for the first few weeks babies are to all intents and purposes blind. The problem is, of course, that babies cannot tell you what they see. It therefore takes considerable ingenuity to find a way into their minds, and it was in fact not until the 1950s that a number of techniques were developed which made this possible and which replaced speculation with empirical data. The following are among the principal methods now available.

- *The preference technique.* As first pointed out by Robert Fantz (1956), babies may be motorically and linguistically immature, but they are able to inspect their surroundings visually and thereby can tell us something about their mental processes. By recording visual attention under controlled conditions (see figure 3.4), it is possible to ascertain not only *what* a baby looks at but also what she *prefers* to look at. In this way, it has been repeatedly demonstrated that from the very beginning of life babies have definite visual preferences: for patterned rather than plain surfaces, for solid rather than two-dimensional objects, for things that move rather than stationary things, for high-contrast rather than low-contrast contours, for curvilinear rather than rectilinear patterns and for symmetrical rather than asymmetrical stimuli.
- *Habituation technique.* When a baby is repeatedly shown a particular visual stimulus, she will, over successive trials, pay less and less attention (i.e. she

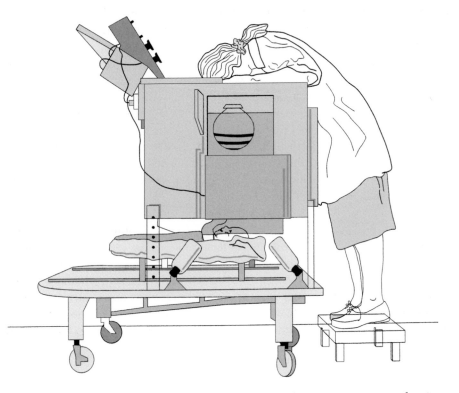

Figure 3.4   *Apparatus for recording babies' visual attention (from Oates, 1994, p. 98, fig. 6).*

will habituate). By then showing another visual stimulus differing in various respects from the first and ascertaining whether the baby renews her interest (i.e. dishabituates), it is possible to tell whether the two stimuli are perceived as different.

- *The non-nutritive sucking technique.* Babies can quickly be taught that they are able to produce some interesting sight or sound whenever they suck on a pressure-sensing dummy nipple. How hard they suck, or how long they persist, is another indication of the extent to which they can discriminate stimuli and prefer one to another.
- *Measures of heart rate and respiration.* These too vary according to the interest shown in particular features of the environment, and can therefore also be used to explore the perceptual abilities of quite young babies.

Techniques such as these have shown that the newborn, far from being functionally blind and visually disorganized, is a much more competent being than was thought at one time. It is true that, compared with older individuals, the visual system in the early months of life is still deficient in a number of ways: acuity, for example, is well below that of adults, as are colour vision and the ability to coordinate the two eyes. In addition, babies for the first few weeks can only see objects clearly when they are placed at a distance of about 8 inches from the eyes; those nearer or further away tend to be blurred. However, in the real world of infants these are probably not handicaps, for none of these apparent deficiencies interferes with development or with the kinds of tasks a child has to tackle in infancy. The distance of 8 inches for clear vision, for example, happens to be just about the gap between the mother's and the baby's face during most nursing and other routine social encounters, giving the baby plenty of opportunity to get to know the mother and learn to distinguish her from other people. Infants may not see as well as adults, but they see well enough to function effectively in their role *as infants* (Hainline, 1998).

In any case, whatever deficiencies initially exist in the visual system are soon made up as a result of visual experience. Looking, that is, is improved by looking. In part, obtaining such experience is due to what other people provide: the toys they offer, the funny faces they pull, the pictures on the wall they point to and so on. But it would be a grave mistake to think of babies as merely passive recipients of stimulation: from a very early age on they can be observed actively to explore their environment with their eyes, looking for interesting sights and in this way supplying their own stimulation. Eye movements occur already in the womb; they can also be found in the dark, and so are not just a reaction to being stimulated but a sign that babies are born prepared to explore their visual world. Such exploration is, moreover, not just a haphazard business; it appears to be governed by the following four 'rules' (Haith, 1980):

1   If awake and alert and the light is not too bright, open eyes.
2   If in darkness, maintain a controlled, detailed search.
3   If in light with no form, search for edges by relatively broad, jerky sweeps of the visual field.
4   If an edge is found, terminate the broad scan and stay in the general vicinity of that edge.

Thus babies come into the world equipped with particular strategies to get to know that world. As we saw just now, they have quite specific attentional preferences and, as a result, will scan their surroundings not at random but in an active search for those features of their visual world that are important to them. And there is no better example of that than their interest in the human face.

As has been repeatedly shown, particularly by means of the visual preference technique, infants attend more to face-like stimuli than to virtually any other stimulus. This is not surprising: the face, considered as a visual stimulus, contains nearly all the features that infants are innately equipped to find attention-worthy: it is complex, patterned, symmetrical, three-dimensional, mobile, and usually appears at an optimal distance for focusing. It is as though nature has ensured that babies are preadapted to attend to that aspect of their environment that is most important to their survival and welfare, namely, other people. For example, in one experiment babies, soon after birth, were shown the three stimuli in figure 3.5 and tested

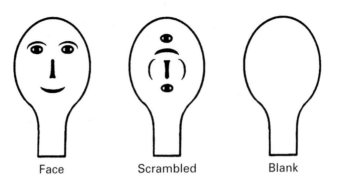

Face   Scrambled   Blank

Figure 3.5   *Stimuli used in experiments on face perception (from Johnson & Morton, 1991).*

for their ability visually to follow them. The newborns were found to be considerably more likely to track the 'face' than either of the other two stimuli, prompting the experimenters to suggest the existence of an innate face-detecting device which serves to direct the newborn infant's visual attention (Johnson & Morton, 1991). It is possible that such a device is tuned to nothing more than to three blobs in the location of eyes and mouth, but that at least brings the baby into contact with her caregivers and is thus one step along the road towards social bonding.

However, very young babies are still at an extremely early stage of being able to process faces effectively. One reason concerns the so-called *externality effect*, which refers to the tendency of babies in the first few weeks of life to attend mainly to external boundaries of stimuli and neglect the interior, except for such gross and salient features as the hairline and the region around the eyes. It is as though the baby's capacity to take in information is initially limited and the ability to attend to an increasing number of facial features only becomes possible with maturation and experience (see figure 3.6). This means that at first the baby will not be aware of those features that distinguish one person from another; visually at least, people are all alike to young babies. According to Johnson and Morton (1991), there are thus two stages in the development of face perception:

1   A reflex-like tendency, present from birth, to turn to and look at face-like patterns more than at any other stimuli. Though indiscriminate, the tendency ensures that young babies get maximum exposure to people's faces and so have the opportunity in time to learn to discriminate among them.
2   After several weeks of such exposure, babies develop the ability to recognize individual faces, largely by paying attention to internal features. Thus on the basis of a primitive, inborn perceptual preference babies gradually construct representations of specific faces after repeated experience of them. It is likely that the first stage is based on the lower, more primitive parts of the brain; the second, on the other hand, requires the higher functions of the cortex which clock in from 2 to 3 months on and thereafter increasingly take over control of the baby's visual orienting.

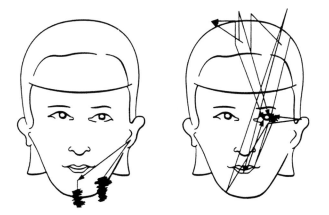

Figure 3.6   *Scan lines of a human face by 1- and 2-month-old infants (from Fogel & Melson, 1988).*

When we turn to babies' ability to make sense of their *auditory* world, we find that here too even very young babies are considerably more competent than they had once been given credit for (Aslin, Jusczyk & Pisconi, 1998). Again there is evidence for an inborn organization that propels the baby actively to attend to certain aspects of her environment, and here too these aspects refer above all to other people. At birth the auditory system is in many respects well advanced in its structural development compared to that of the visual system; indeed, it is already functional *in utero* from about the seventh month of conceptual age. However, it is also remarkable how well developed preferences for certain kinds of sounds are at birth or soon thereafter. These preferences are to be found at three levels:

1 At a general level, the type of sound most likely to elicit newborns' attention is the human voice. Testing for auditory preferences is mostly done by examining babies' orienting responses such as headturns or physiological measures like heart rate, and from these it is evident that even prematurely born infants are far more responsive to speech sounds than to any type of non-speech sound. Some degree of selective tuning to the human voice thus appears to be part of the neuronal organization with which the infant comes into the world, analogous to that shown by the visual system to the human face.

2 Among voices newborns prefer those of adult females. Young babies will orient to men who raise the pitch of their voice; however, the marked preference for the female voice may well be due to prenatal exposure to the mother's voice. The possibility of prenatal learning, and the consequent extremely early ability to recognize the mother's voice and distinguish it even from other female voices, is one of the more fascinating discoveries to have been made in recent years and is described in greater detail in box 3.4.

BOX 3.4

Newborns can recognize their mother's voice

The ability to recognize another person, whether by sight or sound, is a quite sophisticated psychological process, and until recently it was thought that infants in the early weeks of life were incapable of such an accomplishment. It is now apparent that, at least as far as voices are concerned, the ability is already present in the newborn period.

In a classic study performed by DeCasper and Fifer (1980), the non-nutritive sucking technique was used to assess whether babies within the first 3 days after birth could differentiate the mother's voice from that of another adult female when both read the same story. The babies readily found out that, by sucking on a blind nipple in two different ways, they could produce either one voice or the other, and having learned this demonstrated a definite preference for the mother's voice by consistently sucking so as to produce that rather than the stranger's voice. Clearly, these very young babies were well capable of distinguishing the two.

There are two possible explanations for this phenomenon. One is that the babies learned to recognize the mother's voice as a result of being exposed to it after birth. This would, however, have involved extremely rapid learning, as the babies were kept in a separate nursery and thus had only a few hours at most of contact with the mother. The other explanation involves prenatal learning. As we saw, babies become capable of hearing in the last trimester of pregnancy, and one of the most frequent sounds they hear would be the mother's voice. It is therefore at least conceivable that the very early appearance of the ability to differentiate voices is the result of a quite prolonged learning period, though mostly taking place before birth.

DeCasper and Fifer's study has been followed up by a number of other investigations, which have produced results such as the following:

- Newborns, aged 2–3 days, showed a definite preference for a story that the mother had read out aloud during the 6 weeks before birth to a story they had not heard before. The difference was found both when the mother read the story during testing and when another woman did so (DeCasper & Spence, 1986).
- Newborns preferred listening to a melody that the mother had repeatedly sung during pregnancy to an unfamiliar melody. When newborns, who had been exposed either to a sequence of classical music or a sequence of jazz (depending on the mother's own preference), heard both of these following birth, they preferred the familiar music (Lecanuet, 1998).

- At the age of 2 days babies born to English-speaking and to Spanish-speaking mothers heard samples of both languages. They preferred to listen to their 'native' language (Moon, Panneton-Cooper & Fifer, 1993).
- Newborns were found *not* to prefer their father's voice to that of another male, even after 4 to 10 hours of postnatal contact. It seems most likely that the difference between this finding and that concerning mothers' voices is due to the lesser prenatal exposure to the father's voice (DeCasper & Prescott, 1984).
- Two versions of their mother's voice were played to newborns: one an airborne (normal) version; the other a specially prepared one simulating the kind of sound heard while still in the womb. The babies showed a definite preference for the latter (Moon & Fifer, 1990).

These various studies not only demonstrate the remarkable ability of babies immediately after birth to make sophisticated distinctions among voices, but also suggest that the most likely explanation for such an early ability concerns learning while still in the womb. In certain respects at least, there is an intriguing continuity between prenatal and postnatal existence.

3 Still more specifically, the kind of maternal speech young babies prefer to listen to is **motherese** – the name given to the particular style adults tend to adopt quite automatically when talking to children, marked by such characteristics as exaggerated intonation, higher pitch and more rise and fall of the voice. For example, when in one experiment infants were taught to turn their heads to one side to switch on a voice speaking normally and to the other side to switch on motherese, all turned their heads more frequently to the latter. There are suggestions that motherese makes it easier for young children to acquire language; if this is so, we have another instance of the baby being equipped from the beginning with mechanisms that are biologically useful in coping with developmental tasks.

Motherese. A particular style of adult-to-child talk (hence also referred to as A-to-C talk), in which adults modify their usual speech in order to make it more comprehensible and attention-worthy to the child being addressed.

Action patterns and the brain

Babies are busy people. They do not just spend their time feeding, sleeping and crying, but show a great range of behaviour both in response to external stimulation and quite spontaneously. Much of that behaviour is of a fairly primitive form, yet reflexes such as breathing, sucking, blinking and urinating ensure that the newborn baby can already function independently in certain respects, while other reflexes like the palmar grasp and the rooting (headturning) response lead to more complex voluntary actions that will appear later on. Even the generalized squirming that babies seem to be engaged in for much of their time turns out on closer analysis to be far from random, consisting of rhythmical, stereotyped motor patterns that serve the all-important purpose of self-stimulation and, moreover, emphasize that from the start the baby can *initiate* behaviour and not merely be at the mercy of external stimulation.

REM sleep. This denotes the period of sleep when the brain is in a relatively active state, resulting in various bodily movements including rapid eye movements (REMs).

Non-REM sleep. The quiet and deepest periods of sleep when brain activity is at its lowest.

Much of the groundwork for all this activity is already laid during foetal life. As ultrasound recordings of foetuses show, from the gestational age of 36 weeks on it is possible to observe behaviour taking the form of sucking, breathing and crying, and though these serve no function until after birth they do indicate that the motor components of the baby's adaptive behaviour are in place well in time. From 26 weeks gestational age it becomes possible to discern distinct patterns of waking and sleeping states in the foetus – patterns that cycle about once every 40 minutes and that in the next few weeks become increasingly complex. By 32 weeks gestational age both **REM** (rapid eye movement, or active) sleep and **non-REM** (quiet) **sleep** can be observed, and in the next few weeks various other states such as drowsiness and quiet and active alertness emerge as distinct entities. Thus by the time they are born, babies are already well able to divide their time between different states of rest and activity, ranging from great excitement to deep sleep (see table 3.5).

These states, and the cyclical changes between them, form the background to the daily lives of both babies and their caregivers. Thus the state of alert inactivity is the time when the baby is most likely to attend to her surroundings; it is therefore optimal for social interaction and learning about the world. However, for parents the most important consideration is how much and when a baby sleeps. On average, newborns sleep 16 to 17 hours in every 24, though some sleep as little as 11 and others as much as 21 hours. In the first

Table 3.5   Sleep–wake states in newborn babies

State	Description
Quiet sleep (non-REM)	Eyes closed and still, regular breathing, full rest
Active sleep (REM)	Bursts of rapid eye movements, irregular breathing, spontaneous movements such as grimaces and startles
Periodic sleep	Slow breathing alternates with bouts of rapid, shallow breathing
Drowsiness	Eyes open and close, breathing variable, increased activity
Alert inactivity	Eyes bright and focused, breathing regular, body still
Active alert	Frequent diffuse movement, vocalizing, irregular breathing, less focus on environment
Distress	Crying, diffuse bodily movements

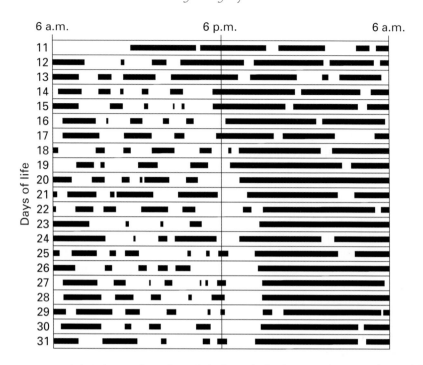

Figure 3.7 *One baby's sleep and awake periods, for each day between days 11 and 31: solid lines represent sleep (from Sander, Stechler, Burns, & Lee, 1979).*

weeks, sleep tends to occur in many short periods, distributed throughout the day and interspersed by periods of wakefulness that are even shorter. Very soon, however, both sleep and waking periods become longer and less randomly distributed within each 24-hour block; a regular daily pattern gradually emerges and in due course the baby becomes a more tolerable being for the weary parents to live with (see figure 3.7).

Such changes come about as a result of all sorts of environmental pressures on the baby, in particular those exerted by the parents to conform to their own preferences. In the same way, babies' feeding rhythms change from what is 'natural' to what is socially convenient as far as a particular mother is concerned or what a particular culture regards as 'right'. Babies arrive in the world with certain inborn characteristics – of feeding rhythms, of sleep–waking cycles and so forth, but these need to adapt to the demands of the outer world. Thankfully, these characteristics are relatively flexible, and the first steps in the child's socialization can therefore take place right at the start of life.

What a baby is able to do depends on the development of her brain. However, brain development in turn depends to a considerable extent on what and how much a baby does. Thus, on the one hand, the growth of the brain during foetal life and infancy takes place at a spectacular rate, enabling the baby to display an increasing range of activities, but, on the other hand, the feedback stimulation experienced as a result of engaging in activity plays an important part in promoting further brain growth. Babies brought up under conditions of gross deprivation will therefore become retarded in development because maturation alone is not sufficient for behavioural change; in the absence of opportunity to exercise their faculties, neurological development in these babies will become slowed and off course. Brain, experience and behaviour are thus intimately linked.

Let us summarize some of the known facts about early brain growth (for further details see van der Molen & Ridderinkoff, 1998):

- Already during foetal life the development of the brain outpaces that of all other parts of the body. For example, between 4 and 6 months of postconceptual age the weight of the brain increases fourfold. As a result, the baby's head at birth is disproportionately large in relation to the rest of the body (as shown in figure 3.3, p. 54).
- The increase in weight and volume in the foetal period reflects the increase in the sheer number of neurons (brain cells). Something like 250,000 neurons are thought to be produced each day, giving rise eventually to hundreds of billions in total.
- The growth spurt continues for the first few years of life (see figure 3.8). Thus at birth the baby's brain is about 25 per cent of the weight of the adult brain, and by 3 months it reaches about 40 per cent. By 6 months it has reached half its final mature weight – something that the body as a whole does not do until about the age of 10 years.
- The increase in weight and volume after birth is due not to any further increase in the number of neurons but entirely to the growth of connections

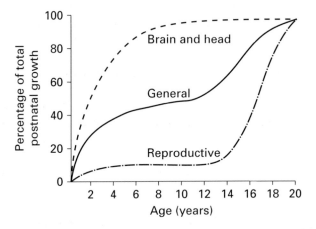

Figure 3.8   *Relative rates of growth of brain, reproductive organs and general body size (from Tanner, 1962).*

(synapses) between neurons. By the age of 2 years, any single neuron may have up to 10,000 different connections to other cells, creating a highly complex network which reflects the increasingly sophisticated mental activities of the young child.

- However, the number of synapses does not continue to increase in a straightforward manner with age. Around the age of 2, a 'pruning' process takes place, which eliminates those synapses that are not required by the individual and so reorganizes the pathways in the brain to fit in with the living patterns of the child.
- The development of the brain does not proceed evenly in all regions but occurs from the lower parts up. Subcortical structures, the 'old' parts that we share with other mammals, develop first, while the cerebral cortex, which controls the higher psychological functions, develops last and indeed continues to develop throughout childhood.
- Development is also uneven within the cortex. For example, the occipital cortex, dealing with vision, matures well before the prefrontal cortex, which is concerned with various executive functions such as attention and planning.

With structural developments come functional advances, in that cells become increasingly specialized in what they do. To understand this process, let us note a distinction that has been made between two different neural systems in the brains of newborns (Greenough, Black & Wallace, 1987):

1 The *experience-expectant system* refers to those neural pathways that are already established at birth to deal with the kinds of experiences and activities that are common to all human beings. They refer in the main to reflexes and functions essential to survival, such as sucking, breathing and temperature regulation. A baby has to have these available straight away; they are therefore 'pre-wired', and though some may require a certain amount of experience in order to function efficiently, they exist primarily as a result of genetic programming found in all members of the species and thus 'know' what to do from the beginning.

2 The *experience-dependent system* contains the neural pathways that have no specialized function at birth. What they will do depends entirely on the sensory input which the individual child is exposed to, and as a result of repeated experience of particular inputs specific neural connections come to be formed and strengthened. Children will acquire these connections slowly over time as a result of learning and experience, and whereas the experience-expectant system has to be ready early on, this system will continue to develop throughout life. In so far as different individuals have different experiences, the experience-dependent system will come to reflect the personal lifestyle of each person.

Thus some aspects of the brain's construction are genetically determined, whereas the development of others is tailored to the experiences of each individual – a point illustrated by the two-stage development of face perception mentioned on p. 68. Admittedly, the distinction between the two systems is not an absolute one but reflects more a tendency than a rigid difference in mode of operation. Learning and experience, for instance, do play some part in setting up the experience-expectant system; however, certain kinds of perceptions and actions will be acquired very quickly because the neural organization is already prepared for them, whereas in the case of the experience-dependent system the setting up of cell assemblies is a relatively slow affair and requires repeated exposure to the relevant sights and sounds. Any cell assemblies that are not so used and strengthened are likely to be discarded.

Yet even though the brain becomes increasingly organized in its structure–function relationships, a certain degree of *plasticity* is also found: different parts of the brain, that is, can take over particular functions previously served by other parts. This becomes extremely important when some parts of the brain are destroyed as a result of injury or are otherwise prevented from carrying out their normal function. However, plasticity depends to a considerable extent on age; the evidence (described in box 3.5) suggests that the younger the child, the more likely it is that other parts of the brain can compensate for damage sustained elsewhere. The young brain is not yet, as it were, too set in its ways to function in a manner it was not originally set up for.

BOX 3.5

Brain damage and brain plasticity

Damage to the brain can occur at any time: prenatally, as a result of harmful substances in the mother's body; perinatally, during a birth process that does not go ahead smoothly; and at any stage from infancy on as a consequence of accident, illness or abuse. Injury to such a vital organ needs to be taken very seriously; the cells in the brain cannot be renewed and the only hope therefore is that other parts of the brain can take over the function of the damaged part. To what extent is such plasticity possible?

Whether particular parts of the brain are dedicated to particular aspects of psychological functioning has been a matter of controversy for a long time and is still by no means resolved. There is no doubt that some degree of localization does occur: language, for example, depends principally on the left hemisphere of the cortex, spatial abilities on the right. So what happens to each of these functions if their particular cortical basis is destroyed? The answer, it appears, depends largely but not wholly on the child's age, in that recovery from brain damage tends to be better in younger than in older children. It depends also, however, on whether the damage is bilateral or unilateral and on what aspects of psychological functioning are implicated.

The following three developmental epochs can usefully be distinguished (Goodman, 1991):

1 *Prenatal life and early infancy.* At this time recovery even after bilateral damage can be remarkably good as far as specific abilities are concerned. Undamaged parts of the brain can take over functions they would not serve ordinarily; plasticity is at its greatest and major reorganization of neurons is still possible.

2 *Childhood up to puberty.* The prospects of recovery from unilateral damage are still fairly good, but this no longer applies to bilateral damage. Transfer of function from one hemisphere to the other is still possible; language functions, for example, can still be 'relearned' by the right hemisphere after injury to the left hemisphere.

3 *Adulthood.* Both unilateral and bilateral damage are now much more likely to produce permanent deficits, for neuronal organization is no longer as flexible as it had been in earlier years. Following damage to the left hemisphere, for example, most adults never fully recover the use of language – presumably because the right hemisphere is now too specialized to take over functions for which it was not originally designed. Yet some degree of recovery of functioning is still possible: even after adolescence the brain is by no means wholly set and is still capable of some degree of reorganization (C. Nelson & Bloom, 1997).

In general, age is the most important consideration as far as prognosis is concerned. However, much depends also on whether specific abilities such as language and visuo-spatial skills are involved or general intelligence. Whereas early localized brain damage is *less* likely to result in specific deficits such as aphasia than later brain damage, the situation is reversed with regard to the effects on general intellectual ability, where early damage is *more* likely to give rise to an overall lowering of intelligence, possibly because of the greater potential for misconnections and unhelpful rewiring of the brain during neuronal reorganization (Rutter & Rutter, 1993).

Thus the developing brain is both more resilient and more vulnerable than the adult brain to damage. Degree of recovery depends on a complex interaction of three factors, namely, the age when damage occurred, whether one or both hemispheres is affected, and the type of effect (specific skills or general intelligence) that is assessed.

Parental adjustment

Just as newborns have to adjust to such things in the outer world as parents, so parents have to adjust to their newborns. In the majority of cases this is a period of joy; nevertheless, many couples experience various kinds of stress and especially so when the child is a first-born. Stress can take the following forms (Sollie & Miller, 1980):

1 *Physical demands.* Interrupted sleep in particular is a drain, but all aspects of caring for a highly dependent being can result in fatigue, and especially so as the baby's care needs to be accommodated within the normal household routines that the parents continue to pursue.

2 *Emotional costs.* Joy and satisfaction at the child's arrival may be uppermost in the parents' minds; nevertheless, the knowledge that the child's well-being and indeed her life depend on them can represent a source of tension even more draining than the physical demands.

3 *Restrictions of other opportunities.* Inevitably, the child's dependence means that a new lifestyle must be adopted, with implications for both work and leisure. The mother may have to give up employment, with financial consequences for the family; both parents are less likely to engage in activities outside the home; and, in general, the day-to-day life the parents now lead involves a narrower set of routines than those to which they were previously accustomed.

4 *Strains in the marital relationship.* While in many cases a new baby brings parents more closely together, in some it changes (temporarily at least) the existing relationship for the worse. A pair has now become a threesome, and jealousy, disruption in sexual relationships and the stresses resulting from the three factors above may all play their part in reducing the previously existing closeness of husband and wife.

5 Couples vary greatly in the extent to which they successfully negotiate the transition to parenthood (Heinicke, 2002). A great many factors are implicated in producing these differences: the age and maturity of the parents, their relationship with their own parents, the amount of social support available to them, the level of marital satisfaction existing before the baby's arrival and any postnatal depression a mother may experience (see box 3.6). One other influence on the course of the parents' adaptation must also be taken into account, namely, the child herself. Where a newborn is 'difficult', whether due to inborn temperamental qualities or prematurity or sickness or handicap, the parents will not only experience the transition as more stressful but, in more vulnerable relationships, may drift further apart (Putnam, Sanson & Rothbart, 2002).

BOX 3.6

Postnatal depression and its effects on children

However much joy the newborn child brings to the mother, the 'baby blues' are a common reaction. Well over half of all new mothers experience some feelings of low mood and a 'could not care less' attitude in the days follow-ing the birth. In the majority, however, these symptoms are of short duration and are probably linked to fatigue. In about 10 to 15 per cent, on the other hand, postnatal depression is more persistent and takes a more severe form.

These women show all the signs of a clinical depression: feelings of hope-lessness and despair, irrational anxiety, continuous low mood, irritability, poor concentration and sleep disturbance. Mostly these symptoms gradually dis-appear 6 to 8 weeks after the child's birth; in some (estimated at around 1 to 2 per cent), they are still evident a year or more later and take the form of a full-blown mental disorder. In general, postnatal disorder tends to be more common among women who did not plan their pregnancy, do not have a supportive partner and had recently experienced some drastic life change such as loss of employment or the death of someone close. These are con-tributing factors; the cause itself of postnatal depression remains unknown, though hormonal changes as the mother's body returns to its normal state following the birth may well be implicated.

What about the effects on children? Given the above symptoms of depression, it is hardly surprising to find that there are often quite marked disturbances in the mother–child relationship (for reviews see Cummings & Davies, 1994a; Radke-Yarrow, 1998). As observations during infancy have shown, the women may be physically present but are psychologically absent: they tend to be with-drawn, are insensitive to the baby's state and unresponsive to his signals, lack emotional warmth and can sometimes be outright hostile. Babies react by mir-roring their mother's depression: they smile less and cry more, are withdrawn and lacking in energy, and show less interest in their surroundings and in play. The emotions they usually display tend to be negative ones like sadness or anger rather than positive ones like joy and interest. Such behaviour may be shown even when they are with people other than the mother, suggesting that they are in danger of developing an overall distorted style of social interaction.

Follow-up studies of these children, such as that undertaken by Lynn Murray and her colleagues (e.g. Murray, Hipwell, Hooper, Stein & Cooper, 1996; Murray, Sinclair, Cooper, Ducournau, Turner & Stein, 1999; Sinclair & Murray, 1998) show that some aspects of development may be vulnerable to long-term con-sequences, even when the mother's illness lasted only a few months. These effects are more likely to be seen in boys (who in general are more vulnerable during the early years to physical and psychological stresses than girls), and are mostly found in socio-emotional aspects of development rather than in cognitive functions. Thus Murray's children, observed in the course of their second year, were more likely to show a range of behaviour problems and more likely to have formed attachments to their mothers characterized by insecurity than children whose mothers had not been postnatally depressed. Assessed again at the age of 5, they showed diminished responsiveness in their relationship with the mother, a greater incidence of various behavioural disturbances, and tendency to engage in low-level physical play rather than in more creative activities. Also, according to their teachers, they were somewhat more immature and were more likely to be hyperactive and distractible. Yet in other respects these children were no different from their comparison group: their relationships with peers and with their teacher, for example, were like those of typical 5-year-olds, and though some other investigators had found evidence of cognitive deficits in such children, these were not observed in this sample.

These results suggest that postnatal depression, even when its duration is limited to the very early months of the child's life, can have long-term effects. These are more likely to occur in boys than in girls and to be found in some aspects of behaviour rather than in others. They indicate that these children are an at-risk group, in need of help long after the mother's own recovery.

Summary

A child's life begins at conception, not at birth. Prenatal and postnatal development are continuous: what happens before a child is born can have profound implications for later outcome.

This applies in particular to the individual's genetic endowment, which influences all aspects of psychological functioning. However, apart from some genetic disorders the relationship is usually of considerable complexity, in that in no known case are particular mental characteristics determined by just a single gene. What is more, in virtually all instances genetic endowment is just one influence; as the science of behaviour genetics has shown, it takes the combination of nature *and* nurture to affect the course of development.

Prenatal life is divided into the germinal, the embryonic and the foetal stages, during each of which particular kinds of development occur and the child is susceptible to particular kinds of harm. This is seen especially in the early parts of the foetal period, when brain development is most rapid and the child becomes highly susceptible to the effects of *teratogens*, i.e. noxious agents related to drugs, disease and diet that cross the placenta and can bring about long-term physical and psychological deficiencies. Thus the womb is by no means a totally sheltered environment; the unborn child is already influenced by external events, though it usually takes the mother to transmit these.

Childbirth takes many forms; there is, however, no evidence that the birth process has any long-term psychological consequences, other than in those cases where actual physical harm is done to the baby's brain. The development of children born pre-maturely, on the other hand, can be affected quite drastically in the early months of life, and when combined with social disadvantage may act as a risk factor even in later childhood.

While newborns were regarded at one time as completely incompetent and 'empty' psychologically, recent research has shown that they arrive in the world already equipped with an impressive range of abilities. Vision and hearing, for example, are sufficiently developed to allow the baby to orient to other people, and motor patterns such as those involved in sucking, breathing and crying can already be observed dur-ing the later stages of foetal life, indicating that the newborn's brain is by then sufficiently advanced to regulate a range of basic functions required for living in the external world. Thus the brain is not an empty box, waiting to be filled by experi-ence and functioning only when prodded by external stimulation. Brain development is rather an activity-dependent process: newborns actively seek experiences that fit in with the nature of their brain, and obtaining such experiences will in turn promote further brain development.

For the parents, the transition to parenthood is a major step that involves a realign-ment of family relationships and a drastic change in lifestyle. The majority of par-ents have little difficulty in making the necessary adjustment; in some, however, strains do develop, and in cases of postnatal depression there may be problems not only for the mother but also for the child.

FURTHER READING

Bateson, P., & Martin, P. (1999). *Design for a Life: How Behaviour Develops.* London: Vintage. Highly readable account of the way in which the many ingredients provided by both nature and nurture interact to produce unique individuals – a process that the authors describe on the basis of scientific evidence yet with plentiful use of literary quotes.

Ceci, S. J., & Williams, W. M. (eds) (1999). *The Nature–Nurture Debate: The Essential Readings.* Oxford: Blackwell. A collection of articles that raise a variety of important issues concerning the nature–nurture debate, indicating the many diverse implications this has for under-standing psychological development.

Kellman, P. J., & Arterberry, M. E. (1998). *The Cradle of Knowledge: Development of Perception in Infancy.* Boston: MIT Press. An account of what we have learned about the way in which children come to perceive the world and how such perceptions change over time to produce knowledge.

Plomin, R., DeFries, J. C., McClearn, G. E., & Rutter, M. (1997). *Behavioral Genetics* (3rd edn). New York: W. H. Freeman. Tells what we know about the role of genetics in psychology. Aims to introduce readers to the methods and findings of behavioural genetics. Not an easy read for beginners, yet a rewarding one.

van der Molen, M. W., & Ridderinkoff, K. R. (1998). The growing and aging brain: Life-span changes in brain and cognitive functioning. In A. Demetriou, W. Doise & C. F. M. van Lieshout (eds), *Life-span Developmental Psychology.* Chichester: Wiley. A concise over-view of brain development throughout the life span, providing an outline of central nervous structures and such functional aspects as brain plasticity, neuronal interactions and the effects of ageing from prenatal life to maturity.

CHAPTER FOUR

Forming Relationships

Chapter Outline

Growing up is a process that we can usefully think of as a series of developmental tasks, which appear in a particular sequence at various ages and which children need to confront with the help of their caregivers. Various lists of such tasks have been proposed; that given in table 4.1 is one example which concentrates on early childhood – a period when developmental tasks emerge more suddenly and succeed one another at a greater rate than at any subsequent time (Sroufe, 1979). Their appearance depends largely on genetic programming; their subsequent course, however, relies very much on the adults responsible for the child's care. All psychological functions develop in a social context: whatever strong genetic push may be responsible in the first place for the emergence of new capabilities and for the transition to new levels of functioning, a propensity cannot become reality unless the caregiver supports, maintains and furthers the child's efforts.

The establishment of relationships with other people is thus one of the most vital tasks of childhood and, as we see in table 4.1, one of the earliest. We have learned a lot in recent years about the way children develop their primary attachments, usually to their parents, and about the differences among children in the way these manifest themselves. Whether the nature of the earliest relationships formed exerts as profound an influence on all subsequent close relationships, even in adulthood, as Freud suggested long ago, remains a contentious issue. Whatever the answer, relationship formation remains a lifelong issue. Just consider all the relationships children establish – with parents, siblings, grandparents and other relatives, substitute carers in and out of the home, friends and other peers and also with teachers at all stages of schooling, as well as with members of the opposite sex from adolescence on, each relationship so rich, complex and subtle that we often lack the necessary vocabulary to describe it. What is certain is that relationships provide the context in which all of a child's psychological functions develop: it is there that children first encounter the outside world, learn what is significant and worth attending to, acquire labels and means of communicating and, in the process, develop

Table 4.1 Tasks in early development

Phase	Age in months	Tasks	Role for caregiver
1	0–3	Physiological regulation	Smooth routines
2	3–6	Management of tension	Sensitive, cooperative interaction
3	6–12	Establishing an effective attachment relationship	Responsive availability
4	12–18	Exploration and mastery	Secure base
5	18–30	Autonomy	Firm support
6	30–54	Management of impulses, sex-role identification, peer relationships	Clear roles and values, flexible self-control

Source: From Sroufe (1979).

ways of viewing themselves in relation to that world. What is also certain is that differences among children in the nature of their relationships with others can have profound implications for the particular developmental path that each child embarks upon. Understanding relationship formation is thus an essential part of understanding child development.

The Nature of Relationships

We all know about relationships from personal experience, and we all spend much time thinking about them. Failure to establish them, misunderstandings, conflicts, separations – all are a source of much misery, just as happy, successful relationships provide essential comfort and security. For professional people such as social workers, psychiatrists and clinical psychologists, relationships usually form a crucial focus in any action taken to help and support, and yet it is only lately that a start has been made to develop a science of relationships which would enable us actually to analyse objectively what goes on between people (Hinde, 1997). Let us summarize what we know:

- Relationships are not directly perceived but are inferred. What we are aware of are *interactions* between people: their touching, kissing, chatting, shouting, hitting and other visible and audible encounters. It is only when interactions form consistent sequences over time that we conclude that a particular kind of relationship exists. Thus a parent who repeatedly hits a child in the course of many contacts is said to have an abusive relationship with that child; it is the totality of these episodes that allows one to make the inference about the relationship and not any one episode. Interactions are thus here-and-now phenomena whereas relationships imply continuity over time. This is a basic distinction, though the two terms are often confused and used as though they are interchangeable.
- Even though relationships are inferred from interactions, a relationship is more than the sum of the interactions which gave rise to it: each has characteristics of its own that cannot be found in the other (Hinde, 1979). Take relationship qualities like faithfulness or intimacy or devotion: none would be appropriate to specific interactions. Similarly with interactive characteristics such as frequency or reciprocity or vigour, which in turn would be inappropriate to characterize a relationship. For descriptive purposes it therefore becomes essential to keep the two levels distinct.
- In any attempt to understand relationships the level of interactions is not the only one that is relevant. Figure 4.1 illustrates a scheme, drawn up by Hinde (1992), which shows relationships embedded in a range of levels, ascending in complexity from an individual's physiological processes up to society as a whole. The levels are all interconnected: what goes on at one has implications for any other. Ideally, therefore, if we are fully to understand a

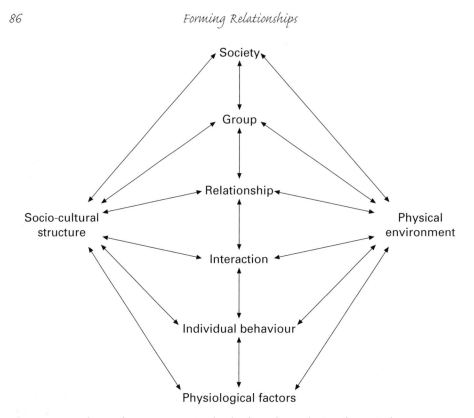

Figure 4.1 *Relations between successive levels of social complexity (from Hinde, 1992).*

relationship, we ought to pay attention to all other levels too – to the group or family that provides the immediate context of the relationship, the individuality of each of the participants, the society to which they belong, and also the physical environment and cultural structure that form the background to the relationship. In practice, all this is usually much too complex to take into account and we tend therefore to confine ourselves to the more immediately relevant aspects. What matters is that all the levels are seen as distinct – that, for example, interactions should not be seen as the sum of their participants' individual characteristics any more than interactions should be regarded as adding up to relationships.

- Relationships are two-way affairs. This may seem an obvious statement, yet somehow child psychologists managed to overlook it completely for a long time when writing about parent–child relationships. Instead, they portrayed the socialization of children as a one-way process going from parent to child – a kind of clay moulding where parents shape passive children into any form that they arbitrarily decide upon. It is now clear that any relationship or interaction involving even the youngest baby proceeds in both directions; that the effect children have on parents is as great, though different, as the effect parents have on children; and that socialization can only be understood if it is seen as a bilateral and not a unilateral process. Examining the characteristics of just one partner (albeit the older and more powerful one) is insufficient to explain the child's progress.

• Relationships do not exist in isolation from other relationships; each is connected with other relationships. We shall develop this point further in the following section when discussing the family. Here let us simply make the point that relationships tend to occur in networks: what happens between husband and wife has implications for the relationship each has with their children; what goes on between siblings will affect the relationship between the mother and any one of the siblings, and so forth. Similarly, studies of marital conflict have vividly shown that in such a situation the parent–child relationship also tends to suffer: what happens in one part of the network reverberates in other parts.

Families

Children's first experience of relationships generally occurs within the family. This small, intimate group is the basic setting within which most children are introduced to social living, where the rules of interpersonal behaviour are acquired and which will continue to serve them as a secure base when they encounter the often bewildering world outside. In view of the many social changes that have occurred in the last 50 years or so – divorce, single parenthood, employed mothers, role reversal among husband and wife, gay couples, step- and blended families – it has become clear that the family can no longer be as narrowly defined as was once assumed, and the implications that the variations of family form have for children's development have consequently become one major area of enquiry. We shall turn to this below, but first let us consider just how we can usefully think about families – whatever their form.

Families as systems

Take a family composed of two parents and one child, as portrayed in figure 4.2. Three aspects are involved: the individual members, the relationships between them and the family group as a whole. However, the family is more than the sum of its constituent parts: it is a dynamic entity in its own right. To do justice to such an entity, it is useful to apply the concept of **systems theory** in thinking about families.

Systems theory can be applied to complex organizations of all kinds, but has been found particularly useful with respect to families (Minushin, 1988). The theory is based on the following principles:

Systems theory is a particular way of describing organizations such as families. These are seen both as complex wholes and as made up of subsystems that, for certain purposes, can also be treated as independent units.

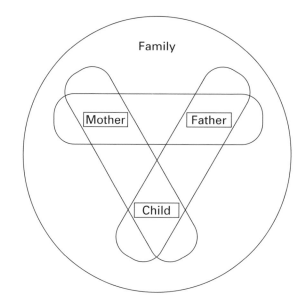

Figure 4.2   *The family and its subsystems.*

- *Wholeness.* A system is an organized whole that is greater than its parts. Its properties cannot therefore be understood by merely studying the individual components. Applied to the family, this means that one cannot consider the family as the sum of its component individuals or relationships: it has properties of its own such as cohesiveness or emotional atmosphere that are not applicable at the other levels. Knowing everything about the individuals and the relationships between them within a family group does not reveal anything about the group as such.
- *Integrity of subsystems.* Complex systems are composed of subsystems that are related to each other. Each such relationship may also be regarded as a subsystem and studied in its own right. Applied to the family, it follows that not only relationships can be regarded as systems, but also the relationships between relationships. The interconnectedness of the husband–wife relationship with the mother–child relationship, for example, is thus a topic in its own right.
- *Circularity of influence.* All components within a system are interdependent; change in one has implications for all others. Statements such as 'A causes B' are therefore inadequate because components affect each other in reciprocal fashion. Applied to the family, this has become one of the most important but also one of the most difficult conclusions to grasp. Simple causal statements, particularly as applied to the parent–child relationship, have been regarded almost as common sense, yet replacing such linear thinking with circular thinking has become essential in view of the repeated demonstration of *mutual* influence in all social interactions, including those of young children

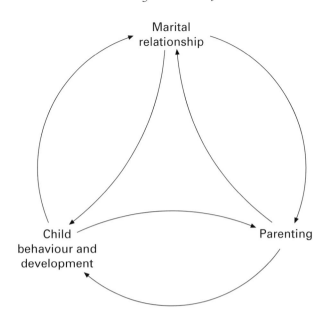

Figure 4.3 *Mutuality of family influences (Belsky, 1981).*

and adults. Figure 4.3 illustrates this mutuality with respect to some aspects
of family functioning: a child's behaviour is affected by, but also affects, parental
behaviour; further, it affects and is affected by the relationship between mother
and father; and that in turn affects and is affected by the nature of parenting
activities. Thus each aspect of the system is mutually involved with every other
aspect; to talk only of, say, the influence of parenting on child behaviour
would provide an incomplete picture.

- *Stability and change.* Systems like families and relationships are *open*, i.e. they
  can be affected by outside influences. Change in one component means change
  in all others and in the relationship between them. A sudden stress, such as
  a father's loss of employment or a child's accident, will have implications for
  all individual family members and for the relationships between them, and
  may well alter the equilibrium of the family as a whole.

Let us pick out two themes to illustrate the 'family as a system' approach. The
first refers to the interconnectedness of relationships: what goes on in one subsystem has implications for other subsystems within the family. Most attention has
been given to the way in which the quality of the parents' marriage is related to
the child's adjustment, on the assumption that a good marital relationship is likely
to be associated with a satisfactory parent–child relationship, this in turn leading
to optimal development in the child. When, on the other hand, parents do not
get on with each other, the relationship with the child can also be expected to
deteriorate. The evidence bears out these assumptions (see Cummings & Davies,

1994b): marital quality has been found to relate to such diverse aspects of children's development as security of attachment, effective learning strategies, impulse control and emotional maturity. Given such results, it is, of course, tempting to conclude that children develop satisfactorily *because* their parents get on well together, i.e. that parental behaviour is the cause and child development the effect. However, this is just the one-way linear kind of thinking that systems theory warns us against, for the path of influence may also be working in the opposite direction from child to parent and in a circular manner. Thus characteristics of the child, present from the beginning, may affect the kind of parenting provided and also the quality of the marital relationship – a situation most evident when the child is 'difficult' to rear by virtue of being handicapped. The strain of parenting such a child may in some cases then have negative repercussions on the marital relationship, which in turn will create a family atmosphere inimical to healthy child development. Straight cause-and-effect statements clearly fail to do justice to the complexity of influence processes in such a family situation (see box 4.1 for a more detailed illustration).

Other connections have also been shown to exist among various aspects of family functioning. One example is the link between the marital and the sibling relationship. As has been demonstrated in several studies (e.g. Dunn et al., 1999), the greater the hostility between husband and wife and the more dissatisfied the partners are with their marriage, the more likely it is that there will be sibling rivalry and conflict between the children of that couple. The quality of one relationship is thus closely associated with the quality of the other relationship. Again it is tempting to think in simple cause–effect terms, in that a hostile marital relationship may be regarded as responsible for engendering hostility among the siblings – either

---

BOX 4.1

Families with handicapped children

At one time psychological studies of handicapped children focused almost exclusively on the children's individual characteristics: their intelligence, their adjustment, their emotional control, and so forth. Subsequently, attention also began to be paid to the interactions and relationships formed by these children, with particular reference to mother–child interactions and the way these differ from interactions seen amongst the non-handicapped (Marfo, 1988). It is only of late that yet another approach has been adopted, where researchers make use of a family systems framework to understand their findings and to consider the implications for the family as a whole in order to throw light on handicapped children's development (for review see Hoddap, 2002).

That any form of handicap in a child has implications for other family members cannot be doubted. Mothers in particular are affected: the incidence of depression, for example, is generally found to be significantly greater than among mothers with non-handicapped children. The same applies to fathers, where the rate of depression as well as of such other symptoms as lack of self-esteem and lowered dominance exceeds the rates found in comparison groups. Other children in the family may also be affected, in that the risk of emotional disturbance and behaviour disorder among both older and younger siblings is greater than norms for comparable age groups.

Effects on family relationships and domestic roles have also been reported. According to some studies, the incidence of divorce in these families is greater and there is general agreement that marital difficulties are more likely to occur, especially when the parents react in different ways to the handicap, such as when the mother becomes overinvolved with the child while the father withdraws. Some fathers, however, also show increased involvement in the child's care, particularly when the handicap is such that the child remains in an infantile dependent state. And for that matter, the role siblings play in the family may also be affected, in that they may be asked to perform services on behalf of the handicapped child or, especially in the case of older daughters, take over some of the mother's domestic responsibilities. The nature and distribution of family roles as a whole is thus altered, and particularly so when the child's condition requires drastic changes in day-to-day routines, limiting social life outside the home and cutting down on opportunities for leisure activities and holidays.

The child's handicap is thus a matter for the family as a whole, and how the family reacts will affect the child's development in turn. However, let us note two additional points. In the first place, there are great variations among families in coping: not all are adversely affected, and the variability is only partly explained by the severity of the child's handicap. Other factors also play a part, such as the support available to the parents from others and the prior cohesiveness of the family, and one of the main questions now examined by researchers is therefore how families are able to meet the challenge posed by the handicapped child in a positive manner. The other point is to emphasize that families are far from passive in their reactions: on the contrary, parents actively set out to find a *meaning* to bringing a handicapped child into the world, and whatever meaning they assign to this experience will then influence how they conduct themselves. Thus, when parents' feelings of guilt and responsibility predominate, it is likely that their daily lifestyles will be accommodated in a very different way than when the handicap is seen in an objective, impersonal manner. In some cases, however, individual family members differ in the meanings they assign, and when these differences are substantial, difficulties may ensue in the way the family as a whole is able to function (Gallimore, Weisner, Kaufman & Bernheimer, 1989).

by setting an example, or by creating a family atmosphere of strain and unhappiness, or indirectly by changing the parents' relationships with the children and making them more neglectful or ill disposed. Such influences may well be at work, but the possibility of influences going in the opposite direction must also be considered, i.e. the notion that conflict between siblings is responsible for tension developing between mother and father, possibly brought about by disagreements as to how to handle the situation or by the general atmosphere of strife resulting from the siblings' behaviour. Let us not forget yet another possibility, namely, that genetic influences common to the various family members play a part, i.e. that similar dispositions bring about similar patterns of behaviour, irrespective of environmental influences. Clearly, teasing apart the role of each of these effects is a difficult task, and until we are able to do so it is perhaps safest to consider that all the effects mentioned may play some part in accounting for the links observed.

The second theme to illustrate the family-as-system approach concerns the implications for the family as a whole of an event which in the first place impinges on just one of its members. Take a father becoming unemployed – an experience that not only affects the individual but also has repercussions for the rest of the family, as seen in the way in which relationships become altered and the equilibrium of the group as a whole changed – all of which will then have further consequences for the father's reactions. This has been well illustrated in a classic study by Glen Elder (Elder, 1974; Elder & Caspi, 1988) of the effects of the Great Depression – the economic crisis that hit the United States in the early 1930s and which caused widespread unemployment and financial hardship. In analysing the reactions of family groups containing both parents and adolescent children, Elder traced the various shifts of economic and domestic roles that took place in these families as a result of the father's sudden income loss. The fathers themselves, being no longer breadwinners, became peripheral figures, not knowing what role to assume and increasingly suffering from loss of morale. Instead, responsibilities devolved to the mothers, and particularly so in those families where the mother was able to pick up a job and herself became the main breadwinner. However, as conditions worsened, the adolescent children also became more valuable, in that they too were required to help meet the increased work and domestic needs of these deprived households. Thus some of the sons managed to obtain paid jobs, albeit part-time and unskilled, while daughters took over many of the domestic duties from their employed mothers. As a result of taking on such extra responsibilities, these young people rapidly left the world of childhood behind, becoming more independent and more oriented to adult values than others of their age. In short, the family as a whole became a different organism, and the nature of the changes that occurred within it had further consequences for the father's emotional reaction to his traumatic experience.

It is customary, in trying to explain the behaviour of an individual or the course taken by a particular relationship, to focus on that alone and treat all other aspects of family functioning as extraneous. Systems theory, on the other hand, proposes that all these aspects are inextricably linked and need to be taken into account if a full understanding is to be reached. Thus it helps to view the family as a dynamic unit that is always seeking some kind of equilibrium. Any change that occurs – birth, death, illness, unemployment, departure for college or for work abroad – upsets the balance of the system and calls for new roles, relationships and internal patterns to be adopted. The system eventually readjusts and settles into a different equilibrium. The changes occur simultaneously at the level of individual, relationship and family, and it is their interconnection that provides insight into the adjustment of particular families.

Family variety and child development

What is a family? At one time the answer was simple: a family is a group of people composed of a man (the breadwinner) and a woman (the homemaker and care-giver) who were permanently tied in marriage, and the children that this particular couple had brought into the world. This traditional family was regarded as the bedrock of a stable society, and moreover assumed to be the essential context for bringing up well-adjusted children.

   The considerable social changes that have occurred from about the middle of the twentieth century on throughout western society have put paid to this tradi-tional ideal. Marriage is no longer regarded as an essential prerequisite to family life; the divorce rate has increased sharply; single parenthood is common; many children experience their parents' sequential marriages and live in stepfamilies; a large proportion of mothers are employed outside the home and shared care arrange-ments have therefore become part of many families' lives; fathers now participate in children's care and in some cases act as principal caregiver; and same-sex couples, male as well as female, are increasingly tolerated as 'proper' parents. These changes had a momentum of their own and occurred with astonishing rapidity; at the same time, they gave rise to considerable unease as to the implications for children's psychological development of being brought up in such unconventional households.

   A substantial body of research findings is now available to throw light on this problem. Let us summarize the main conclusions (see Golombok, 2000, for more details):

*   *Maternal employment* is, statistically speaking, the most common deviation from the traditional norm and has given rise to a great deal of controversy, especi-ally when very young children are involved. However, the evidence now available from a large number of studies indicates that conclusions about effects cannot be stated in clear-cut, 'good–bad' terms, because of the large number of conditions that exert some sort of moderating influence on the outcome – conditions such as the mother's ability to cope with role strain, the support available from father and relatives, the nature of the mother's motivation to work and the effect on her morale, and the quality and consistency of

substitute care arrangements made for the child. Thus a simple cause-and-effect model, where maternal employment is the cause and children's development the effect, is inappropriate: the mother's employment is embedded in a context of a great many other family variables which also need to be taken into account, producing its consequences not directly but through an altered pattern of relationships. What can be safely concluded is that, where conditions are optimal, children of employed mothers may actually benefit compared with those of non-employed mothers, largely as a result of extra experiences with other adults and with peers in day-care settings, and that, even in the early years, 24 hours a day mothering *per se* need not be regarded as a necessary prerequisite for healthy psychological development (Gottfried, Gottfried, & Bathurst, 2002).

- *Single-parent families* have increased many-fold in recent decades – largely because of the high divorce rate but also because marriage is no longer regarded as a *must* by many women. Are children living in homes with only one parent in any way handicapped thereby? Simply comparing such children with their two-parent counterparts would suggest so: the former tend to do worse on a wide range of measures, including emotional adjustment, social competence, self-concept and academic achievement. But does this necessarily follow from being part of a single-parent family structure as such? Single-parent households are not just distinguished by the absence of one of the parents; they also tend to be financially worse off, with children more likely to be materially deprived than their peers. Indeed, when the effects of low income are discounted, together with the concomitant stress on the mothers, the difference between one- and two-parent children disappears. As in the case of maternal employment, a range of other variables needs to be taken into account. As well as family income, these include the reason for single parenthood (children of widowed mothers do better than those of divorced mothers), the mother's age (teenage mothers tend to be less competent as parents and to have more problems), the amount of contact with the non-residential father or with some other father-figure, the social support available to the mother and the mother's personal ability to cope with stress. Single parenthood is thus embedded in a whole network of other social and personal conditions, and while it is true that the children of lone parents are at greater risk for developmental disabilities of one kind or another than other children, much of this has to do with facets other than single parenthood as such (Weinraub, Hornath & Gringlas, 2002).

- *Men as principal parents*, though still a minority phenomenon, is by no means as unusual as it was at one time. Fathers' participation in childrearing has certainly become much more common, and an increasing number of children are now living in father-headed families. In so far as women have for long been regarded as 'natural' parents, being biologically prepared for the part and thus supposedly endowed with a maternal instinct, any departure from the traditional division of labour has been greeted with suspicion, in the belief that men will provide inferior parenting to that provided by women. In fact, there is considerable variation among different cultures in the extent of fathers' involvement in child care, suggesting that whatever sex differences exist in this respect is a matter of social convention and not an immutably fixed part of being male or female. As to the consequences for children of being brought up by a man, the admittedly sparse evidence gives no indication that such children are in any way different from others in their development. Furthermore, direct observations of men in their fathering role has shown them to be as capable of as much warmth and sensitivity as women. In short, children's developmental outcome appears to be affected not by the parent's gender but by the kind of relationship existing within each individual parent–child couple (Parke, 2002).

- *Gay and lesbian couples as parents* have probably aroused more controversy than any other form of non-traditional family set-up, amid the fear that such an 'unnatural' context for development is bound to affect children's development adversely and in particular that it will give rise to confusion in the children's own sexual identity. While this is still a relatively new research topic, the studies that have been published are remarkably unanimous in their findings. Comparing children brought up in either lesbian or gay households with the children of heterosexual parents, no differences have emerged in any aspect of social, emotional or intellectual functioning. Also, when followed up into adulthood, there are no indications that their sexual identity or sexual orientation is affected by having two parents of the same sex. Moreover, studies of the parenting abilities of both gay and lesbian individuals indicate that these are as capable, warm and child-oriented as heterosexual parents – indeed, even more so according to some studies, presumably because of their higher motivation in the face of a sceptical world. The assertion that children require a parent of each sex for healthy development is thus challenged by these findings (Golombok, 2000).

There are other forms of non-traditional families that have also been investigated (box 4.2 gives details of one of the latest to appear, i.e. where children are brought into the world as a result of 'artificial' means, using the new reproductive techniques that are now available). Surveying all these studies on the influence of family characteristics on children's development, one conclusion emerges clearly from the accumulated evidence, namely, that *family structure plays a far less significant part than family functioning* (Schaffer, 1998). Structural variables such as the number of parents, their sex, their biological relatedness to the child and the roles they assume have repeatedly been found to exert little influence on children's psychological outcome: human nature is flexible and can satisfactorily develop in a wide range of family settings. Of far more importance is the quality of relationships prevailing among whatever individuals constitute the household – qualities such as warmth, commitment, mutual understanding and harmony, i.e. all those characteristics which indicate how well the group functions as a group (for a direct comparison of

BOX 4.2

Children brought into the world by means of the new reproductive techniques

As a result of advances in reproductive technologies, it has become possible for children to be conceived and born 'artificially' to parents who would otherwise remain childless. There are a variety of techniques employed to this end, namely: *in vitro* fertilization (IVF), where sperm and egg are provided by father and mother but the two sets of gametes are combined in the laboratory; artificial insemination by donor (AID), where the mother is impregnated by the sperm of a male other than her husband and where the child is therefore genetically related only to her; and egg donation, where the father's sperm fertilizes another woman's egg and the genetic relationship is thus only with him. In addition, the pregnancy may under some circumstances involve a surrogate arrangement, whereby another woman bears and gives birth to the child, who is then handed over to the couple acting as parents.

What about the effects on children brought into the world by such 'unnatural' means? There are various potential problems that they and the parents may encounter: the often stressful nature of prolonged fertility treatment; the secrecy surrounding the act of conception; the possibility of tension between the parents because one of them is infertile, as well as feelings of inadequacy or guilt on the part of that parent; the realization by children that they are somehow different; and the absence of a genetic link with one or both parents involved in some of the techniques employed. So far there have been only a limited number of studies that have followed up these children in order to assess their progress; however, those by Susan Golombok and her colleagues (Golombok, Cook, Bish & Murray, 1995; Golombok, Murray, Brinsden & Abdalla, 1999; Golombok, MacCallum & Goodman, 2001) provide some particularly useful and comprehensive information.

Golombok's research involves the investigation of several groups, namely, families with a child conceived by IVF, families where the child was conceived by egg donation, and families with a child conceived by donor insemination. They were compared with two control groups: one of naturally conceived children and another of children adopted at birth. All children were between 4 and 12 years of age at the time of the study. A wide range of measures was obtained to assess the children's socio-emotional development and cognitive competence; in addition, the parents were assessed with respect to their warmth and emotional involvement with the child and the amount of stress experienced in the course of parenting.

None of the findings gives support to the fear that the new reproductive technologies have negative consequences for either parents or children – a conclusion borne out by other studies of such families. The parents were as competent and the children as well adjusted as those in the control groups, and neither the lack of a genetic relationship nor the manner of the children's conception had any implications for the well-being of these families. In particular, together with studies of adopted children, they show that a 'blood bond' is not necessary for the development of sound parent–child relationships; this can be found even when the role of parenthood is fragmented between a biological and psychological parent. It is true that the techniques are still so new that children born by their means have not yet been followed up to maturity; nevertheless, there is nothing in the findings obtained so far to suggest that children who come into the world by unusual, assisted means are in any way psychologically handicapped thereby.

functional and structural variables see Chan, Raboy & Patterson, 1998, and McFarlane, Bellissimo & Norman, 1995). Any attempt to improve family life, whether at a general policy level or with respect to specific cases, ought therefore to focus on these functional aspects rather than try to impose some one specific type of structure to which all families are supposed to conform.

Divorce and its consequences

Families are in a constant state of change, but there is no greater change than the parents' separation and divorce. However, a mother left alone with her children is still a family, and the experience may well be one in a series of family reorganizations, as the mother remarries, a stepfamily is formed, new children are born, new living arrangements made and new roles assumed. Disequilibrium is followed by attempts to regain equilibrium, and for the sake of children involved in particular it is essential to search for new adjustments.

What are the effects on children of parental divorce? The large number of studies now available indicate the following conclusions (see Hetherington, 1999, for details):

- Divorce is not a specific event happening at one particular point in time. It is a long-drawn-out process that may impinge on children over a period of years, beginning with parental arguments and extending well beyond the departure from home of one of the spouses and the parents' legal separation. How children react can vary greatly over time, and care must be taken not to generalize findings obtained at one point of this process to other points.

- The majority of children experience problems in the months immediately following divorce. These take many different forms, depending largely on the child's age. No one age period is more vulnerable than any other: differences in reaction are qualitative rather than quantitative.
- Marked maladjustment is two or three times more likely in the children of divorced parents than in children of non-divorced parents. However, even among the former this is found in only a minority: 70 to 80 per cent do not show any severe or enduring problems.
- In the long term most children show considerable resilience; they are able to readjust to a large range of new family circumstances. In a few instances, however, problems that had disappeared re-emerge, especially in adolescence, or emerge in a new form such as delinquency.
- A whole configuration of factors influences the process of adjustment: the child's age, the child's sex, the nature of previous relationships with each of the parents, the arrangements made for parental responsibility, the quality of life in the single-parent family, the parents' remarriage, and so on. No wonder great variability in outcome can be found!
- As follow-up studies have shown (e.g. Chase-Lonsdale, Cherlin & Kiernan, 1995; O'Connor et al., 1999), in adulthood the children of divorced parents are more likely to experience psychological problems such as depression and are more likely themselves to divorce than are other individuals. Yet the risk factor is small, for only a minority of the total are thus affected. The fear that children are scarred for life by parental divorce is thus not justified as a generalization.

Just what is it about divorce that can bring about harmful consequences? Divorce *per se* is too global a term; it encompasses various aspects, of which three in particular have been singled out as possible explanations: the absence from home of one of the parents (usually the father); the socio-economic consequences of living in a single-parent family; and the conflict between the parents that the child witnessed before and sometimes also after the divorce.

There are indications that all three of these factors play a part in the emergence of psychological difficulties in children (Amato & Keith, 1991). Yet it has also become apparent that, of the three, it is *conflict* that has by far the most potent influence. For one thing, children who lose a father through death are considerably less likely to be disturbed in the long run than children who lose a father through divorce. It is thus not so much parental absence as such as the circumstances surrounding that absence which accounts for the child's reactions. For another, when one discounts the effects of lowered socio-economic status resulting from divorce, either by statistically removing the effects or by studying only families where the custodial parent remained well-off, the adverse consequences for the child's development are still apparent. And most of all, several follow-up studies of children have shown that children whose parents divorce are already showing signs of psychological upset as early as 8 to 12 years before the divorce (e.g. Amato & Booth, 1996). This, it is believed, is due to the deteriorating nature of the marital relationship and the atmosphere of conflict that characterizes such homes.

Marital conflict is probably one of the most pathogenic influences on children's psychological development that one can find (Cummings, 1994). It works in two ways, direct and indirect:

- *Direct* influences involve the child actually witnessing scenes of verbal and/or physical violence and discord. Children, from an early age on, are highly sensitive to other people's emotions; negative emotions such as displays of anger may well produce adverse effects, and particularly so when they become a constant feature of the psychological climate of the home. At a time when the child's own capacity for emotion regulation is still developing and in need of adult assistance, parental loss of control is likely to be a particularly frightening experience and, in failing to provide a model, prevent that development from taking place.
- *Indirect* influences occur in that husband–wife conflict will adversely affect the parenting ability of each partner, this in turn having unfavourable consequences for the child's adjustment. By analysing the results of 68 studies investigating the association between the husband–wife relationship and the parent–child relationship, Erel and Burman (1995) were able to show that this association takes a 'spill-over' form rather than a 'compensatory' form, i.e. that the greater the difficulties are between the two parents, the greater also are the problems each has in caring properly for the child, rather than that a parent compensates for an unsatisfactory marital relationship by being extra attentive and loving towards the child. The emotional tone of the parent–child relationship suffers even when the child is not exposed to direct influences.

Once again we must conclude that it is family functioning more than family structure that is responsible for children's adjustment. The drastic reorganization that takes place in a family following divorce may well produce some marked short-term effects, but it is the quality of the parenting environment that has the most decisive and enduring consequences. This explains, for example, why children exposed to parental conflict are more likely to become delinquent than other children even when the parents do not divorce, whereas children experiencing parental separation and divorce but without conflict are not at any greater risk (Fergusson, Horwood & Lynskey, 1992). Similarly, it accounts for the finding that parental death is not a risk factor for adult psychopathology, whereas parental divorce is – despite the fact that both result in separation from a parent (Rodgers, Power & Hope, 1997). Parental divorce must thus be seen in the wider context of children's experience of family relationships, for the nature of these can attenuate or exacerbate the consequences of that event.

Developing Attachments

The very first relationship a child forms (usually with the mother) is of particular significance in several respects. For one thing, it is more vital to the individual's well-being than any other subsequent relationship, in that it spells protection, love and security and so spreads itself over all of a child's physical and psychological functions. For another, it is generally an enduring bond that continues to play a central role throughout childhood and is a source of comfort even in adolescence and beyond. In addition, it is considered by many to be a prototype for all other close relationships that the individual forms subsequently, even in adulthood.

That a young baby is already capable of something as intricate as forming a relationship with another person is a remarkable accomplishment. Relationships are highly complex phenomena; they depend on the characteristics of both individuals involved, and thus require the meshing of these characteristics into one behavioural flow and the exchange and mutual management of the sometimes extremely intense emotions aroused by the interchange. All relationships, including the primary one between parent and child, involve a range of dimensions; it is the attachment dimension, however, that has been given by far the most attention in the last few decades and about which we have learned the most. This is largely thanks to the writings of John Bowlby (1969/1982, 1973, 1980), whose attachment theory has become the dominant approach to understanding early social development and given rise to a great surge of empirical research into the formation of children's close relationships.

The nature and functions of attachments

An attachment can be defined as *a long-enduring, emotional tie to a specific individual*. Such ties are characterized by the following features:

- They are *selective*, i.e. they are focused on specific individuals who elicit attachment behaviour in a manner and to an extent that is not found in interaction with other people.
- They involve *physical proximity seeking*, i.e. an effort is made to maintain closeness to the object of attachment.
- They provide *comfort and security*, these being the result of achieving proximity.
- They produce *separation upset* when the tie is severed and proximity cannot be obtained.

According to Bowlby, such ties have an evolutionary basis and a biological function. They came into being because in humanity's distant past, at a time when predators spelled real danger, a mechanism was required whereby offspring could keep close to their caregivers and so obtain protection and thereby enhance their chances of survival. As a result of evolutionary selection, babies are thus equipped with means of attracting the attention of their parents (such as crying), maintaining their attention and interest (such as smiling and vocalizing), and gaining or maintaining their proximity (such as following or clinging). Babies, that is, are genetically 'wired' to stay close to individuals likely to protect them and to signal for their attention and help at times of distress. The various attachment behaviours used for this purpose are in the baby's response repertoire from the early months on; they function in an automatic, stereotyped fashion to begin with and are elicited initially by a wide range of adults, but in the course of the first year become focused on just one or two individuals and organized into much more flexible and sophisticated behaviour systems subject to purposeful planning. The *biological* function of attachment is thus survival; the *psychological* function is to gain security. This would only work, of course, if the parent reciprocates the child's behaviour, hence the development of a parental attachment system that emerged in complementary fashion in the course of evolution and ensures that parents for their part are programmed to respond to the child's signals.

An attachment, according to Bowlby, functions like a control system, i.e. rather like a thermostat. It is geared to maintain a particular steady state, namely, to stay within proximity of the parent. When that state is attained, attachment behaviour is quiescent: the child has no need to cry or cling and can pursue other goals such as play and exploration. When the state is threatened, say by the mother's disappearance from view or by a stranger's approach, attachment responses are mobilized and the child makes active efforts to regain the status quo. The way in which the child sets about this task will change with age and increasing cognitive and behavioural competence: where the 6-month-old will merely cry, the 3-year-old will also call for the mother, follow her and search in particular places. It will also change according to the child's condition: if ill or tired, attachment responses are activated much sooner as the need for the mother's proximity is greater. Similarly, it changes according to the external situation: in familiar surroundings the child's tolerance for the mother's absence is greater than it is in a strange environment. However it is expressed, though, the attachment is made up of a network of actions, cognitions and emotions, the aim of which is to promote the most basic need of humanity, namely, survival.

Developmental course

Establishing a relationship with another person is a highly complex skill, and it is hardly surprising that it takes a large part of the first year for the baby's attachment relationships to emerge. Paying selective attention to human faces and voices, the ability to recognize a familiar individual, responding to others with a smile or crying until some discomfort is dealt with by a feed or a cuddle – these are the building blocks of an attachment bond but should not be taken as the bond itself. Even when it appears, it does so in a somewhat unsophisticated form that

Table 4.2 Phases of attachment development

Phase	Age range (months)	Principal features
Pre-attachment	0–2	Indiscriminate social responsiveness
Attachment-in-the-making	2–7	Learning the basic rules of interaction
Clear-cut attachment	7–24	Separation protest; wariness of strangers; intentional communication
Goal-corrected partnership	24 on	Relationships more two-sided; children understand parents' needs

will take a good many years to reach maturity. A four-stage framework has been proposed by Bowlby for this development, showing how the nature of attachments gradually develops as behaviour becomes increasingly organized, flexible and intentional. The four stages (summarized in table 4.2) are described below.

In phase 1, *Pre-attachment*, babies give clear evidence that in many respects they arrive in the world already equipped to interact with other people. Such social preadaptation takes two forms:

- *Perceptual selectivity*, referring to the visual and auditory biases that predispose babies from birth on to attend to other human beings.
- *Signalling behaviour*, namely, devices like crying and smiling whereby babies can attract and maintain other people's attention.

Though crude and indiscriminate in the early weeks of life, these mechanisms ensure that the baby is brought into contact with other people at a time of great dependence and that survival is thus ensured.

In phase 2, *Attachment-in-the-making*, from 2 to 7 months, babies acquire the basic rules of interacting with others. These involve above all the mutual regulation of attention and responsiveness, which are needed especially in the face-to-face interactions that are the joy of mothers and babies alike. For an interaction to be 'smooth', the behaviour of the partners needs to be synchronized, and it is the art of meshing their responses with those of the other person that babies have to master. Consider turn-taking, a vital requirement for certain kinds of interaction such as conversations, which can already be found in the preverbal exchanges of mothers and babies. At first, this is brought about almost entirely by the mother: she listens to the baby's bursts of vocalizations and then skilfully inserts her contributions in the pauses between bursts. It is she, that is, who takes responsibility for an alternating pattern being established, but by doing so gives the baby the opportunity to find out how such an interaction is to be conducted. In time, therefore, the baby learns that there are times to vocalize and times to listen, making mutual exchanges possible that are the *joint* responsibility of both partners.

In phase 3, *Clear-cut attachment*, lasting up to about 2 years, unequivocal indications are found that the baby's individual interactions have become organized into lasting relationships. Above all, from about 7 or 8 months on babies become capable of missing their mothers: whereas previously a baby would show little orientation to the absent mother when separated from her and would willingly accept other people's attention instead, now separation upset and reluctance to make contact with strangers show that a bond has been established which no longer depends on the actual presence of the mother but is of an *enduring* nature. People are no longer interchangeable; the baby rejects the stranger because he or she remains oriented to the mother even in her absence. An attachment, focused on a particular individual, has now come into existence. This is an extremely important milestone of development, and it is significant that it occurs at about the same age in a wide variety of cultural settings, apparently irrespective of childrearing practices. Whether it has to be formed at that age, or whether it can be delayed and, if so, how much, has become an important issue in relation to children spending their early years under conditions of deprivation and so having no opportunity to form an attachment to specific parent-figures at the normal time. Observations of late-adopted children are now available which suggest a considerable amount of flexibility in this respect (see box 4.3 for further details).

In phase 4, *Goal-corrected partnership*, from 2 years on, the attachment relationship undergoes a number of profound changes. In particular, children's behaviour towards other people becomes increasingly intentional. Take crying: when the 3-month-old has a pain, she will cry as a reaction to that pain; the 2-year-old, on the other hand, will cry in order to summon the mother to come and deal with the pain. The younger child has no anticipation of any possible outcome of her behaviour; the older child

BOX 4.3

Can the formation of the primary attachment be delayed?

Children typically form their first lasting and emotionally meaningful relationship in the second half of the first year. But what if they are unable to do so because they lack the opportunity, as happens when they are brought up in an impersonal institution where no consistent, personally committed parent-figure is available? Are there critical periods beyond which this ability atrophies, making it impossible for the child ever again to form permanent relationships? John Bowlby believed so, declaring that 'even good mothering is almost useless if delayed until after the age of two and a half years'. If such a delay does occur, the child is condemned to develop what Bowlby referred to as an *affectionless character*, marked by an inability to form attachments to anyone.

Two investigations have put this to the test, both by examining the attachment abilities of children socially deprived in their early years and adopted subsequent to the cut-off point of $2^{1}/_{2}$ years. One, carried out by Tizard (1977; Hodges & Tizard, 1989), concerned a group of children who had been reared in various children's homes from the early weeks on, where they were looked after impersonally by a constantly changing staff and thus had virtually no opportunity to establish an attachment to anyone. They were subsequently adopted at ages well beyond infancy, some as late as 7 years, and assessed when they were 8 years old and again at age 16. In some respects the children showed undesirable characteristics: for example, they were overfriendly with strangers and at school tended to be aggressive and unpopular with other children. Nevertheless, relationships in the adoptive family were good in the majority of cases: the children soon began to show real affection for their new parents and this developed into close attachment bonds. Even in adolescence none resembled the stereotype of the ex-institutional child described by Bowlby; none showed signs that a delay of several years had resulted in a complete inability to form close attachments.

The second report (by Chisholm, Carter, Ames & Morison, 1995; Chisholm, 1998) concerns a group of Romanian orphans, who had also spent their early years in highly deprived institutions and who were subsequently adopted at ages between 8 months and $5^{1}/_{2}$ years. Here too there was no indication that their early experience had resulted in a complete inability to form attachment relationships with their adoptive parents: even those who did not experience normal family life until age 4 or 5 were still able to develop emotional bonds. On the other hand, the nature of these bonds did give rise to some concern, in that they lacked the feeling of security that a typically attached child would show with his or her parents; the children also tended not to be easily comforted when distressed. What is more, like Tizard's sample, these children too were inclined to be overfriendly with strangers.

Both studies indicate that there are no 'critical periods' confined to the first 2 or 3 years when children *must* form attachments if such an ability is to develop. It appears that primary attachments can still be formed well beyond the usual age, even after a delay of several years. Not that the children emerge entirely unscathed from their early experience: behaviour with peers, strangers and even with the adoptive parents themselves shows a number of worrying features. Nevertheless, the notion that development must occur according to a fixed timetable and that children who have missed out on certain experiences cannot make up subsequently receives no support from the available evidence.

can envisage that outcome and will therefore cry deliberately to obtain help. What is more, the older child can adjust his crying according to circumstances: for instance, the further the mother is, the louder he will cry. If crying does not work, other attachment responses can be used to obtain the same goal, such as shouting or following. At the same time, children are beginning to understand other people's goals and feelings and take these into account in planning their behaviour. In short, children become increasingly able to plan their actions in the light of goals, both their own and those of other people, and in this way take part in what Bowlby referred to as **goal-corrected partnerships**. Thus, whereas attachment in the initial stages was primarily a matter of external responses activated and terminated by particular conditions, later on it becomes increasingly guided by internal feelings and expectations – a development which Bowlby ascribed to the formation of **internal working models**. These are mental structures which embody the interactions and emotions experienced day by day with attachment figures; once formed, they act to guide the child's behaviour in the context of all future close relationships. We shall discuss these in greater detail below.

Goal-corrected partnerships is the term used in John Bowlby's attachment theory to denote mature relationships. They are characterized by the ability of both partners to plan their actions in the light of their own goals and simultaneously to take account of the goals of the other person.

Internal working models are the mental structures which John Bowlby hypothesized as carrying forward into adulthood the attachment-related experiences encountered in early childhood.

Security–insecurity

If children's experiences of early interpersonal relationships are crucial to their psychological development, we need to ascertain just how different experiences produce different outcomes. Attachments are multifaceted and can affect children in various ways; however, one aspect above all has been singled out for attention, namely, the way in which children obtain a sense of security from that relationship. This is largely due to the work of Mary Ainsworth and her colleagues (1978), who devised both a way of assessing attachment security and a classification scheme for describing different patterns of security.

Assessment is based on a procedure known as the **Strange Situation**, which consists of a series of brief, standardized episodes that take place in a laboratory observation room unfamiliar to the child and which include being with the mother, being confronted by a strange adult, being left with the stranger by the mother, being left entirely alone and being reunited with the mother. The stresses inherent in such a situation activate children's attachment behaviour and, according to Ainsworth, will thereby reveal what use they make of the mother as a source of security. It can therefore be employed as a standardized instrument for evaluating the essential nature of early attachments and highlight the ways in which young children differ in the type of attachment they have formed with the mother.

Strange Situation is the procedure whereby the quality of young children's attachment is assessed. It consists of a series of episodes stressful enough to activate attachment behaviour, and is used to assign children to various categories denoting the security of their attachments.

Table 4.3 Types of attachment

Type	Behaviour in Strange Situation
Securely attached	Child shows moderate level of proximity seeking to mother; upset by her departure; greets her positively on reunion
Insecurely attached: avoidant	Child avoids contact with mother, especially at reunion after separation; not greatly upset when left with stranger
Insecurely attached: resistant	Child greatly upset by separation from mother; on her return difficult to console, both seeks comfort and resists it
Disorganized	Child manifests no coherent system of coping with stress; shows contradictory behaviour to mother such as proximity seeking followed by avoidance, indicating confusion and fear about the relationship

These differences have been classified in terms of four basic attachment patterns (see table 4.3 for details). They are considered to represent fundamental differences in the way in which social relationships are first established, and indicate the degree of security inherent in the internal working model formed of the primary bond. Most children fall into the *Securely attached* category; as a result of their initial positive experiences, they can be expected to form confident relationships with adults and peers alike and will consequently also develop an assured self-image which, in turn, stands them in good stead in coping with cognitive tasks such as those encountered in school or at play. The *Insecurely attached* groups do not have that advantage: their subsequent relationships are put in jeopardy and their adjustment in many spheres of life is not as soundly based as that of the secure group. The small number falling into the *Disorganized* group in particular are thought to be at risk for developing psychopathology in later life. If such predictions are true, the classification of early attachment patterns is indeed of considerable significance.

How confident can we be that the Strange Situation really does reveal so much? The procedure has met with some vigorous criticism (e.g. from Clarke-Stewart, Goossens & Allhusen, 2001); its shortcomings include its applicability to only a very narrow age range (about 12 to 18 months), its artificial nature, the small sample of behaviour it provides and the even smaller sample of behaviour on which categorization is primarily based (i.e. the child's reactions when reunited with the mother after separation), and its doubtful utility with certain kinds of children such as those in day care and children used to rearing practices different from conventional western ones. The very large body of research now available still does not provide a conclusive answer, though it has thrown light on some of the questions asked about the Strange Situation. These include the following (see Goldberg, 2000, for details):

- *How stable are classifications from one age to another?* Much of the importance ascribed to early attachment patterns rests on the assumption that once a particular pattern is established, it is self-perpetuating. As is now apparent (Thompson, 2000), short-term stability over periods of, say, 6 months is high; longer-term stability is less impressive. It is true that comparing infants with older children involves switching to different methods of assessment for age groups too old for the Strange Situation, and this introduces a complicating factor. Nevertheless, it is clear that the longer the gap between assessments, the more children will be found to have changed classification status. The internal working models on which attachment behaviour is based appear to possess some degree of continuity, but they are by no means impervious to change – as seen in particular when the nature of parental treatment for some reason undergoes drastic change, or when the child's family environment is altered as a result of stresses such as illness, divorce or abuse (Waters, Merrick, Treboux, Crowell & Albersheim, 2000). Under such circumstances, stability is very much less likely.

- *How comparable are attachments to mothers with those to fathers?* Much of the earlier research was carried out with mothers only, in keeping with the general belief at the time in the relative insignificance of fathers. Now that the focus has been widened, the results from quite a number of studies are available which enable us to compare mother attachment with father attachment. These indicate that more often than not there is consistency in classification status, presumably reflecting consistency of treatment by the two parents. However, different patterns with different caregivers do occur, indicating that the classification is a function of particular relationships and not something inherent in the child.

- *What accounts for differences among children in attachment classification?* According to Ainsworth, the main reason why children are secure or insecure lies in the mother's sensitive responsiveness to them in the early months of life. Mothers, that is, who respond to their babies in a sensitive manner in situations such as feeding, play or distress convey to them a caring and interested attitude, giving rise to confidence in the mother's availability as a source of security; mothers who fail to provide such sensitivity, on the other hand, are likely to have children in whom early security is not established. The link between maternal sensitivity and child security is, however, not as firm as Ainsworth had suggested: reviews of studies investigating the association (e.g. DeWolff & van IJzendoorn, 1997) have shown that sensitivity is an important but by no means an exclusive condition for attachment security, and that other parenting qualities also play an equally important part. For that matter, even extreme deviations of parental behaviour, such as occur in cases of abuse, do not necessarily give rise to deviant forms of attachment in all children subjected to such treatment (see box 4.4).

- *Do early attachment differences lead to later psychological differences?* This is an especially important question – one that seeks to establish whether experiences in

BOX 4.4

Attachment formation in parentally maltreated children

The basic function of attachment concerns protection, which young children require from their caregivers while still in a relatively helpless and dependent state. But what happens if the caregivers fail to provide this requirement, as seen in physical abuse, emotional abuse, neglect and various other forms of maltreatment? What effects are there on children's attachment formation?

A number of studies have investigated such children and assessed their capacity for forming relationships, both in infancy and in later years (e.g. Barnett, Ganiban & Cicchetti, 1999; Cicchetti & Barnett, 1991; Crittenden, 1988). It is hardly surprising to find that most children with a history of maltreatment show markedly disturbed patterns of relationships, which are evident from early on and tend to persist. Assessed in the Strange Situation, maltreated children, in comparison with other children, are far less likely to be classified as secure in their attachments (approximately 15 per cent as opposed to 65 per cent), the majority being placed in the disorganized pattern (about 80 per cent as opposed to 12 per cent). The disorganized pattern is perhaps the most worrying of the various insecure categories, in that it highlights a markedly disturbed way of relating to caregivers. Such children do not seem to have developed any consistent strategy of relating, in that they show proximity seeking to the parent one moment and avoidance and resistance the next, mixed up with signs of fear, confusion and lack of any positive emotion. Assessment of attachment to the parent at later ages suggests that the relationship disorder persists in many cases, and that it may well generalize to other relationships. Interaction with peers, for example, is often marked by a 'fight or flight' pattern, i.e. either high levels of aggressiveness or avoidance and withdrawal. Of special concern is the finding that abused children are likely to become abusing adults, passing on the relationship disorder from one generation to the next. In addition, there are various indications that early maltreatment leads to later psychopathology, in that conditions such as depression, stress disorder, conduct disturbance and delinquency are more common than among those who have not suffered maltreatment.

Maltreated children are clearly a group at risk. More than anything else, the fear aroused by the abusing parent and the subsequent lack of basic trust rob the child of a sense of security, and make it difficult to develop means of emotion regulation and those social skills that are needed for establishing subsequent relationships. The element of fear, moreover, is reinforced when (as frequently happens in cases of child abuse) other relationships in the family such as that between the parents are also characterized by violence. In so far as these families are also often marked by such other problems as poverty, alcoholism and psychiatric illness, the dice seem indeed loaded against such children.

Yet among all this gloom there are two, perhaps surprising, positive features. In the first place, maltreated children usually do show some signs of attachment to their abusing parents. They may do so in a confused and disorganized manner, but it appears that the attachment system is so powerful that even in the absence of consistent love and emotional warmth children still persist in attempts to attach themselves to their parents. In the second place, in all groups investigated, there are always some children (admittedly a small minority) who follow a typical development pattern. In about 15 per cent secure attachments emerge; some children can form good relationships with peers and other people in later years; and by no means all abused children become abusing adults. Not much is as yet known about these exceptions, but an understanding of the reasons for their escape from the fate of the majority should eventually be of use in helping the rest.

infancy have significance for long-term development. Considerable claims have been made, in that children classified as secure in infancy have been said to be more competent and mature in subsequent years in a great range of psychological functions, cognitive as well as socio-emotional, than children assigned to any of the other three categories. There are indeed certain suggestive findings, particularly linking early attachment security with later social competence: secure infants, for instance, are more likely to develop into children popular with their peers. However, the link (especially with cognitive functions) is by no means firmly established – in part because of some children's change of classification in the intervening years, in part because of different classifications with different caregivers, but largely also because the various outcomes that have been examined (e.g. maturity of play, independence, self-esteem, antisocial behaviour and so forth) are also determined by a range of other influences, all of which must be taken into account. Where prediction has been possible, it has usually taken place under conditions of family and child-care stability, where the kind of parenting the children receive in infancy is likely to be more or less the same as that received in later years, and where consequently the more economical explanation is that it is *current* rather than early relationship patterns that account for a child's behaviour. A great deal more evidence is required before we truly understand the extent to which and in what way the earliest relationships can provide a base for subsequent development.

Internal working models

For a long time the development of the Strange Situation as an assessment tool focused attention almost exclusively on the behavioural manifestations of attachments in young children. It is only much more recently that new methods of assessment have made it possible to extend this focus to older ages, including adults, and as a result one of Bowlby's most promising concepts has attained prominence, namely, the notion of internal working models.

As we have already mentioned, Bowlby suggested that such models are mental structures, based on the child's previous experiences with attachment figures. By their means the child can internally represent the pertinent attributes of each attachment figure and the kind of relationship developed with that person. From the end of the first year on, children become increasingly able to represent the world mentally in symbolic form, i.e. they can think about their attachment figures, about themselves, and about the relationship between themselves and the other person. The very fact that they are able to cry for an *absent* mother means that their behaviour is now guided by an internal model of the mother, and in time these models exert an ever greater influence over the child's actions. Thus, experience of a warm and accepting mother will give rise to an internal working model in the child that depicts her as a source of security and support; as a result the child will have confidence in her availability at all times of need and make use of her as a haven of safety. What is more, the child's model of himself will reflect the relationship built up with the mother: if the relationship is experienced as a satisfying one, the child will feel secure and accepted and so be more likely to form a positive self-image; an abusive relationship, on the other hand, will give rise to a negative self-image that may then have further adverse repercussions for the child's behaviour. The initial models formed might then generalize to other people and other relationships: children viewing themselves as lovable are likely to expect positive interactions with others; those who see themselves as rejected will probably approach any new relationship with negative expectations. Thus, on the one hand, internal working models are representations of the past; on the other hand, they are used to guide behaviour in the context of future close relationships. The models are by no means inflexible and impervious to change as a result of new experience; however, Bowlby believed that the earliest models formed are most likely to persist, largely because they tend to exist outside consciousness and so are not readily accessible. A summary of the most salient characteristics of internal working models is given in table 4.4.

These models emphasize the fact that attachment is a lifelong phenomenon and not merely confined to the earliest years. However, while external manifestations of attachments can readily be observed, access to such internal phenomena is more difficult. Various attempts have been made to develop techniques appropriate for different age groups, especially so for adults (see Crowell & Treboux, 1995), and

Table 4.4   Characteristics of internal working models

- Internal working models are mental representations that are not just 'pictures' of the other person and the relationship; they also refer to the feelings aroused by the relationship.
- Once formed, the models exist for the most part outside consciousness.
- Their development is shaped by the child's proximity-seeking experiences and how these are met.
- Basic differences in the nature of working models exist between individuals whose proximity-seeking attempts in infancy were consistently accepted and those whose proximity seeking was blocked or inconsistently accepted.
- In the course of development, working models become stable but are by no means impervious to the influence of further relationship experiences.
- The function of these models is to provide rules for the individual to guide both behaviour and feeling in relation to significant others. They make it possible to forecast and interpret the other person's behaviour and so plan one's own behaviour in response.

Source: After Main, Kaplan & Cassidy (1985).

of these the **Adult Attachment Interview** (AAI) is now the most widely used. This consists of a series of questions put in the course of a semi-structured interview, designed to elicit the individual's experiences of attachment relationships in early childhood and the way that person considers these experiences to affect later development and present functioning. It is in fact not so much the content of these recollections as the manner in which they are conveyed that is regarded as significant, with particular reference to their coherence and emotional openness. By means of a series of ratings a classification is arrived at, summarizing the individual's state of mind with respect to attachment. The classification contains the following four categories:

> **Adult Attachment Interview** (AAI) is a semi-structured procedure for eliciting adults' childhood experiences with attachment figures. It is used to assign individuals to various categories summarizing their state of mind with respect to close relationships.

- *Autonomous*: individuals so classified discuss their childhood experiences frankly and coherently, acknowledging both positive and negative events and emotions. They can thus be regarded as secure, unlike the further three groups.
- *Dismissing*: such individuals seem cut off from the emotional nature of their childhood, denying especially their negative experiences or dismissing their significance.
- *Preoccupied*: these individuals are overinvolved with what they recollect, appearing so overwhelmed that they become incoherent and confused in the interview.

- *Unresolved*: adults are so classified when they indicate that they have not succeeded in reorganizing their mental life after painful experiences in childhood involving loss and trauma.

Preliminary evidence suggests that these four categories are linked, respectively, to the secure, avoidant, resistant and disorganized categories found appropriate for young children's attachment relationships. Mothers, that is, falling into particular categories are likely to have children falling into the corresponding category. If this is indeed the case, it means that the internal working model that the mother builds up during her childhood will affect the way she interacts with her child, as a result of which the child will then form a particular kind of attachment with her. Intergenerational continuity is thereby provided. There are even indications that some degree of continuity is maintained across three generations, i.e. grandmothers, mothers and children (Benoit & Parker, 1994).

Relationships among Peers

As children get older they come to form an increasingly varied array of interpersonal relationships. Among these the bonds formed with age-mates play a particularly significant role in children's lives. The old assumption that only parents (or even only the mother) matter in psychological development cannot be sustained: in all cultures children spend a great deal of time in the company of their peers; what is more, from quite an early age on they are more often to be found with child

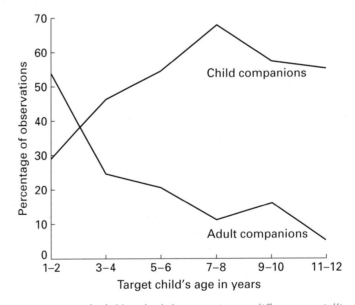

Figure 4.4   *Time spent with child and adult companions at different ages (Ellis, Rogoff & Cromer, 1981).*

companions than with adult companions (see figure 4.4). That alone suggests that peer relationships can have a noteworthy influence on forms of behaviour and thought – indeed some writers, such as Judith Harris (1998) and Steven Pinker (2002), have put forward the provocative notion that socialization takes place primarily in the peer group and that the influence of parents has been grossly exaggerated. This may well be an overstatement; a more likely conclusion is that parents and peers fulfil different functions and that each has a distinctive role to play in meeting certain needs in children's lives.

Horizontal and vertical relationships

It is useful to think of relationships as falling into two categories (Hartup, 1989):

- *Vertical relationships* are those formed with someone who has greater know-ledge and power than possessed by the child, and therefore mostly involve an older person such as a parent or a teacher. The interactions on which they are based tend to be of a complementary nature: the adult controls, the child submits; the child seeks help, the adult provides it. The main function of vertical relationships is to provide children with security and protection and to enable them to gain knowledge and acquire skills.
- *Horizontal relationships* are those between individuals with the same social powers; they are egalitarian in nature and the interactions on which they are based tend to be reciprocal rather than complementary: one child hides, the other seeks; one throws a ball, the other catches it. The roles can be reversed, for the partners have similar abilities. The function of horizontal relationships is to acquire skills that can only be learned among equals, such as those involving cooperation and competition.

In some respects horizontal relationships are more difficult to sustain than vertical relationships. Parents tend to 'carry' interactions with their young children: they may let the child set the topic of conversation, they complete the child's utter-ances, they interpret the child's wishes even when these are not explicitly spelled out. Such courtesies are not to be found in peer interaction; there each child has his or her own agenda, and though with age these agendas can increasingly overlap, the pressure on the child to acquire the necessary skills for joint interaction is in many respects much greater. Thus children learn in each other's company what they would not learn in the company of adults: leadership qualities, conflict reso-lution skills, the role of sharing, the uses of conformity, how to cope with hostility and bullying, and so on. Moreover, children's groups, once formed, quickly develop their own values and customs – from matters of appearance such as clothes and hairstyles to ideas about how the world should be run. Thus children socialize each other, and do so in ways that can be quite distinct from parental socialization.

Yet however different family and peer group are in the experiences they offer, the two sets of relationships are by no means unconnected. What occurs in one arena can have implications for the other, as seen in the two kinds of influence that parent–child relationships bring to bear on peer relationships (Ladd, 1992):

- *Direct influences* refer to parents acting as 'designers' of their children's social lives. They do so by, for example, choosing to live in a particular neigh-bourhood that provides safe environments for play or potential playmates of a particular social group; they invite children to their home whom they regard as 'suitable'; and they may take a direct hand in the activities of the peer group in order to ensure that their child has the 'right' kind of experiences. Such actions occur more with younger than with older children, though even at preschool ages there are indications that a high degree of intrusiveness on the part of the parent will have the opposite effect intended and result in a less socially skilled child.
- *Indirect influences*, on the other hand, are not deliberate actions but refer to the effects of children's family experiences on their conduct with peers. For example, attachment security is said to promote social competence gen-erally and to have positive consequences for peer relationships in particular. Also, certain kinds of childrearing styles are associated with the quality of peer relationships: thus cold and rejecting parents are more likely to have aggressive children than parents who are warm and supportive; highly author-itarian parents tend to have children whose repertoire of social skills is deficient; indulgent parents who do not set limits tend to have children who are under-controlled in their behaviour with others; and accepting, sensitive parents will convey to their children a feeling of confidence about relationships that will help them to participate in social activities outside the home as well. In all these instances the assumption is that what happens in one environment will carry over to the other, and in so far as the home is the child's primary setting, the influence is mainly from that to the world of peers.

We can summarize the chain of influences suggested by this account by looking at the solid arrows in figure 4.5. The parents' personality determines the kinds of childrearing techniques they adopt; these in turn will affect the child's personality characteristics, which will then play a part in the kinds of relationships formed with other children. The broken arrows, however, indicate that a one-way causal

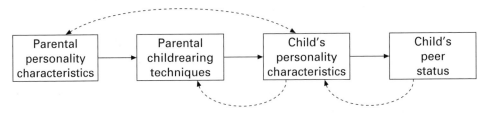

Figure 4.5   *Links between family and peer systems.*

account would be oversimplified: children's experiences with peers have implications for their self-concept and thus the personality characteristics they develop; these characteristics will affect their parents' treatment of the children; and parental and child characteristics are interlinked in many ways, not least through their common genetic endowment, which is thus also implicated in the kind of peer relationships that emerge. Family relationships and peer relationships are no doubt linked, but the kind of linkage is far from simple and straightforward (Parke & Ladd, 1992; K. Rubin, 1994).

Contribution of peer relationships to development

Even young babies are interested in other babies, though initially there is little more than staring, touching and the occasional snatching of a toy. From the toddler period on, however, interactions become more and more sophisticated: in particular, children become capable of playing *together* and not just alongside one another. Thus sequences of linked behaviour become longer and more frequent; cooperative and reciprocal play appears; and in addition children become more selective in their choice of partner. This is seen in the increasingly marked gender segregation of children's groups: from about 3 years on boys prefer to play with boys and girls with girls – a tendency that continues right through childhood (Maccoby, 1998). It is also seen in children's preferences for specific individuals: friendship becomes something highly meaningful and treasured, and children thus come to associate primarily with individuals whom they like and value and whose company they actively seek. Much of the use to which peer relationships are put thus comes from deliberately selected children who may form an increasingly influential feature of the child's daily life.

The contributions which peer relationships make to children's development take two forms, namely, social and intellectual. As to the former, one of the basic tasks of childhood is to establish a sense of identity – an attempt, that is, to find an answer to that all-important question: 'Who am I?' (a theme to which we shall return in chapter 10). A sense of self is constructed primarily in the context of relationships – initially with parents, subsequently more and more with peers. What other children think about the individual and how they behave towards that child matter hugely from the preschool years right into adolescence. That is why friendship counts for so much in childhood: it connotes being appreciated and accepted and therefore helps in forming a positive sense of self ('They like me, therefore I am good'). Within the peer group the child also discovers just what kind of social role is the appropriate one for that individual to adopt – as leader or as follower, as bully or as victim, as clown, as strategist, as financial benefactor or as any of the many other possible identities that groups quite naturally come to bestow on their members. In addition, the very fact that a child belongs to a peer group means that certain norms of appearance and behaviour and, eventually, of moral values come to be incorporated in that child's sense of self, dictating what is acceptable and what is not. Children's groups usually adopt certain routines and customs to which members are expected to conform: they may have their own ways of greeting and dressing, their private jokes and verbal play routines, their particular preferences for certain pop groups, their agreed opinions about teachers or public figures, and their common values of what is 'right' and what is 'wrong' in everyday life. In this way a peer culture develops that may well differ from the culture shared with adults, one with which children are highly motivated to identify and that can powerfully affect the way children come to think of themselves and of others. Thus, on the one hand, peers help to assign a distinctive individuality to each child, and, on the other hand, they make their members similar to one another by means of pressure to conform to group norms.

Peer influences on children's intellectual development are also notable. The assumption that children acquire knowledge solely from adults, that education is wholly a matter of parents and teachers passing on whatever they know to those who don't know it, is a gross oversimplification. Take the research on *peer collabora- tion*: there are now many demonstrations to indicate that naive children tackling a problem together will advance more in their understanding of it than they do when working alone. These involve the development of skills in areas as diverse as mathematics, musical composition, physics, moral reasoning and computing, and refer to a wide range of ages and abilities. Confront two children, equally ignor- ant, with an intellectual problem they need to solve. No teacher is present to instruct them; the relationship is based on mutual interest rather than on authority. Yet by active discussion and exchange of ideas, and by sharing their own partial and incomplete perspectives, the children eventually reach a solution when neither would have been able to do so alone. Learning is thus a matter of joint discovery: two heads, it seems, are better than one. Having to interact with someone who has a different view of the problem challenges children to examine their own ideas, and as a result a new approach emerges which is more appropriate as a solution than the children's individual conceptions. Just why peer collaboration can, under certain circumstances at least, be so effective a tool for learning, whether the essen- tial process involves the children's cooperation or, on the contrary, the conflict of their different ideas, is not yet established. What is certain is that relatively free- wheeling discussion among equally ignorant children of the problem facing them and the various solutions they might adopt generates new insights and promotes learning in the individual participants. Collaboration with peers, it seems, can advance cognitive as well as social development (Howe, 1993).

Status within peer groups

Children can be assessed as individuals, in terms of such characteristics as intellig- ence, anxiety or artistic ability. They can also be assessed as group members, i.e. with respect to their standing among peers. Popular or not? Leader or follower? Accepted or rejected? Sought after or friendless? These qualities matter a lot to children, given the importance they attach to their peers' opinions, but what has also become apparent is that such characteristics can tell us something about the likely course of psychological adjustment and behaviour in future years.

A variety of tests for assessing children's social status are now available, of which **sociometric techniques** are the most widely used. To ascertain popularity, for example, children may be given a list of classmates' names and asked 'Who would you most like to play with?' and 'Who would you not want to play with?' Alternatively, they may be asked questions about each individual classmate, such as 'How much would you like to be with this child?', thus producing ratings for each individual on a like–dislike scale. These peer nominations can then be used to ascertain the degree of any given child's popularity. Another possibility is to observe children, say in a playground, and note who interacts with whom and how often each child's company is sought out by others. In this way a picture of the social structure of the group is built up, giving indications as to the popularity or rejection of particular individuals.

> **Sociometric techniques** take a variety of forms, all designed to provide quantitative indices of individuals' standing within a group (e.g. their popularity).

By such means five *sociometric status types* have been established, namely, popular, rejected, neglected, controversial and average children, according to whether they are high or low on positive and negative peer nominations. The first three categories are of most interest; controversial children are simply those who are liked by some and not by others, while average children fall into the mid-range of peer ratings in that they arouse no strong feelings in others. As summarized in table 4.5, popular, rejected and neglected children are very different kinds of individuals. Popular children are outgoing and friendly and tend to be natural leaders. Rejected children are disliked because they are often disruptive and aggressive and their overtures to others are therefore resisted. Neglected children tend to be inept socially; being shy and unassertive, they usually play on their own or on the fringes of large groups.

As follow-up studies have shown, early peer status is linked to subsequent adjustment. Children's judgements of their peers, that is, can tell us something about the likely developmental outcome of these peers. Popular children, in subsequent years, tend to show the highest level of sociability and greater cognitive ability compared with other groups; they will also be lowest on aggressiveness and on social withdrawal. Neglected children (surprisingly perhaps) are also not at risk for later adjustment difficulties – in part because, unlike the other groups, their peer sociometric status is not very stable, depending more on the particular group of which they happen to be a member at the time. They tend to become less sociable individuals and possibly some-what passive, but these characteristics are rarely of any pathological extent.

It is rejected children, on the other hand, who must give rise to greatest concern, and it is they who have been investigated most intensively. For predictive purposes it is in fact useful to distinguish between two subgroups: those who are rejected by their peers because of their aggressive and disruptive behaviour (the majority) and those who are rejected because of their tendency to social withdrawal and extreme inhibition. Both must be considered to be at risk for later psychological disorders: the rejected/aggressive children for **externalizing problems**

> **Externalizing problems** refer to 'acting out' behaviour disorders, such as aggression, violence and delinquency.

Table 4.5   Personality characteristics of popular, rejected and neglected children

Popular children
- Positive, happy disposition
- Physically attractive
- Lots of dyadic interaction
- High levels of cooperative play
- Willing to share
- Able to sustain an interaction
- Seen as good leaders
- Little aggression

Rejected children
- Much disruptive behaviour
- Argumentative and antisocial
- Extremely active
- Talkative
- Frequent attempts at social approaches
- Little cooperative play, unwilling to share
- Much solitary activity
- Inappropriate behaviour

Neglected children
- Shy
- Rarely aggressive; withdraw in face of others' aggression
- Little antisocial behaviour
- Not assertive
- Lots of solitary activity
- Avoid dyadic interaction, more time with larger groups

Internalizing problems are disorders manifested through inward-turned symptoms, such as anxiety and depression.

and the rejected/withdrawn children for **internalizing problems**. Externalizing problems include such traits as interpersonal hostility, disruptiveness, lack of impulse control and delinquency; children so characterized will engage in a range of rough and antisocial activities, may become bullies and truants, and are likely to show various adjustment difficulties in school including underperformance and early drop-out. In their adult years too they may continue to show signs of acting out to a pathological degree. Internalizing problems include anxiety, loneliness, depression and fearfulness; such children become easily victimized and will develop into individuals who are socially isolated, with few ties to others and little skill in establishing relationships. Both sets of rejected children thus stand a greater chance than others of developing psychosocial difficulties in their later years and must therefore be considered to be a group of children at risk. We can conclude that the kinds of relationships which children form with their peers can tell us something about the coping mechanisms employed to deal with the social world generally; these mechanisms appear to have some stability over the years and can thus help in foretelling the likely development of later adjustment problems (K. Rubin, Bukowski & Parker, 1998; Slee & Rigby, 1998).

As with attachments formed in infancy, so with peer relationships in later years: in both cases the nature of relationships formed can provide some interesting insights into the future. Admittedly, predictions need to be made with caution; subsequent experiences may well alter the expected course of development, and prediction is always easiest under conditions of environmental stability. However, just as insecurely attached infants are thought to be at risk for later social difficulties, so peer-rejected children are also at risk. Let us emphasize that 'at risk' does not involve certainty; it only indicates that such individuals are statistically *more likely* to develop in ways different from other children. For that matter, the connection that has been proposed between attachment classification and peer relationship status also falls into this category: the admittedly limited evidence indicates that insecurely attached individuals are *more likely* to have difficulties in forming peer relationships, in that they are less popular, have fewer friends and are less self-confident in group situations than those who had been classified as securely attached in infancy (Sroufe, Egeland & Carlson, 1999). Establishing continuity over age is methodologically an extraordinarily difficult undertaking; nevertheless, there is enough evidence to indicate that the quality of an individual's relationships, at whatever age, is one of the best means of predicting adjustment in later life.

Summary

Children's development occurs in the context of interpersonal relationships, and relationships are encountered primarily in the context of families.

Families take many forms over and above the traditional form of a married couple and their children, but there are no indications that children are in any way adversely affected by being part of a non-traditional family group. Research suggests that it is family functioning, i.e. the quality of interpersonal relationships, that determines adjustment rather than family structure. For all types of families, a 'systems' view is most appropriate, whereby the family is seen as a dynamic entity with component parts at the level of individual members and of their interpersonal relationships. The three levels are interdependent: what happens in one part has repercussions in other parts. Divorce, for example, not only affects the equilibrium of the family as a whole but has implications also at the other two levels. However, as far as the effects on children are concerned, the most damaging aspect of divorce is parental conflict; this can be pathogenic even without divorce taking place.

From birth on children are preadapted to develop relationships with other people. Attachment relationships emerge in infancy, developing in the next few years from reflex-like behaviour patterns to highly selective, planned and flexible response systems. With the development of 'internal working models' of the relationship, children become capable of tolerating gradually lengthening periods of separation from the parent; increasingly also they are able to take into account other people's intentions, as a result of which their relationships become more balanced and flexible.

There are noteworthy differences among children in the nature of the attachments they form. This is seen particularly in the security–insecurity of the bond, as revealed by the Ainsworth 'Strange Situation'. Classification of children into four groupings on the basis of their behaviour in this situation in infancy is said to predict a wide range of psychological functions in future years, including the children's social competence, their self-image and various aspects of emotional development. The link, however, is not a firm one: early experiences may lay a foundation, but subsequent events can change the course of development.

Relationships formed with peers also have a noteworthy influence, distinct from that of parents. Associating with other children helps in the acquisition of a variety of social skills and in the formation of the child's social identity; peer collaboration also furthers intellectual development. A classification of children's peer status, based on categories such as popular, neglected and rejected, has been found to predict subsequent adjustment; rejected children in particular are at risk for the development of later psychological problems.

FURTHER READING

Dunn, J. (1993). *Young Children's Close Relationships.* London: Sage. A very readable account of the relationships children form with parents, siblings, friends and other children. Concerned in particular with the individual differences in the nature of these relationships and their meaning.

Goldberg, S. (2000). *Attachment and Development.* London: Arnold. A comprehensive account of research on the nature and development of attachments. Both theory and empirical findings are described, with special attention given to the factors that shape early attachment, the development of internal working models and the effects of different attachment types on mental and physical health.

Hetherington, E. M. (ed.) (1999). *Coping with Divorce, Single Parenting and Remarriage: A Risk and Resiliency Perspective.* Mahwah, NJ: Erlbaum. Contains chapters by leading researchers on a variety of topics related to family functioning and dysfunctioning. Special attention is given to children's adjustment to divorce, step-parenting and living in different kinds of family settings, and to the reasons for the great diversity of resilience and vulnerability found in both parents and children.

Hinde, R. A., & Stevenson-Hinde, J. (eds) (1988). *Relationships Within Families: Mutual Influences.* Oxford: Clarendon Press. A collection of chapters dealing with different aspects of family relationships, all stressing the interconnectedness of these relationships and how they affect children's development. Themes covered include the application of systems theory to families, the mutual influence of marital and parent–child relationships, the effects on families of a new child, the coherence of behaviour across generations, and the consequences for families of conflict and divorce.

Schaffer, H. R. (1998). *Making Decisions about Children: Psychological Questions and Answers* (2nd edn). Oxford: Blackwell. Provides information about a number of areas where research can give guidance on practical issues concerning families. These include, for example, the effects of maternal employment and of divorce, the implications of different family types, and the comparative fitness of men and women as parents.

Slee, P. T., & Rigby, K. (eds) (1998). *Children's Peer Relations.* London: Routledge. A collection of research reports on current issues in the study of peer relationships. Included are sections concerning the cultural, family and parental influences on children's social competence; the impact of gender and ethnicity on the nature of peer relationships; the implications of disability and illness; and the efficacy of interventions to promote harmonious relationships with other children.

CHAPTER FIVE

Emotional Development

Chapter Outline

Children learn about emotions mainly in the context of relationships. Close interpersonal relationships are invariably emotional affairs – full of love and hate, pride and shame, sadness and happiness – and it is while interacting with others that children are given the opportunity to observe not only how other people handle their feelings and emotions, but also how their own emotional behaviour affects others. For the sake of social adjustment and mental health, these are some of the most vital experiences from which a child should be able to profit.

So in more precise terms, just what is there to learn? Let us pick out the following three aspects as the most important:

- *Awareness of one's own emotional state.* Children need to learn that under certain circumstances they become angry (or afraid, or embarrassed, etc.), what these circumstances are, how each emotion feels inside and how it is expressed outside, and what label to give it in order to talk about it. All this involves a degree of self-awareness, that is, an ability to stand apart and monitor one's own feelings and behaviour – a sophisticated achievement in its fully developed form, though its beginnings can already be found at a very early age.

- *Controlling the overt expression of one's emotions.* All societies have their rules as to what is acceptable in the way emotional feelings are expressed. This applies most obviously to aggression, which needs to be inhibited or channelled in ways that are not disruptive to social life. Yet this also applies to positive emotions such as joy and pride: in some cultures, too overt an expression of such feelings is frowned upon and discouraged. Children must therefore learn to dissociate inner feelings from their overt expression, and finding out how to do so forms an important part of their socialization.

- *Recognizing emotions in other people.* The ability to 'read' others' inner feelings from their outer behaviour is an essential part of social relationships. Identifying an emotion from its overt expression and understanding how somebody else feels who behaves in a particular way enables children to take appropriate action in response. Thus, as a result of sometimes bitter experience, they formulate certain rules: father home from work frowning, mouth turned down, silent and avoiding eye contact signifies anger and frustration and requires 'steer clear' action; mother smiling, relaxed and talking gently means she is happy and can be approached for comfort, help and goodies. Lessons learned in the family can then be applied to other settings, and though some adjustment will need to be made to the idiosyncrasies of others' emotional style, the range of expression within any one society is fairly limited.

Emotional competence is the term used to designate individuals' abilities to cope both with their own emotions and with those of other people. It is the emotional equivalent of 'intelligence' as used for cognitive functions.

We shall say something about all these aspects, and in particular we shall consider the nature of emotional development in the course of early childhood and the influences, biological and social, that direct the course of that development. In due course, children are expected to acquire **emotional competence** – a concept employed to denote children's skill in handling their own emotions and in recognizing and coping with others' emotions. Failure to acquire such competence can sometimes lead to disastrous consequences, which is yet another urgent reason for needing to investigate and understand how emotional development occurs.

What are Emotions?

We are so intimately acquainted with emotions that it seems almost ridiculous to ask this question. Emotions are a constant accompaniment of our everyday experience, yet science has been slow in putting them under the microscope. In part this is because in the past our view of emotions was a wholly negative one: emotions, it was believed, are disruptive, disorganizing mental events that interfere with the efficient cognitive operations that were considered to be the hallmark of human beings. While cognitive functions are based on the central nervous system, emotions primarily involve the autonomous nervous system – a more primitive part of our make-up which brings us nearer to animal species and does not set us apart as the highest evolved species. It is only recently that a more positive view has come to prevail, which sees emotions not just as noise in the system but as having a definite part to play in promoting development and adjustment. Children's emotional development is now a very lively research area, and as a result our knowledge of its nature is rapidly increasing (see Denham, 1998; Saarni, 1999; Sroufe, 1996).

Nature and functions

Despite their familiarity, emotions are such vague phenomena that it will be best to start with a definition:

> Emotion is a subjective reaction to a salient event, characterized by physiological, experiential and overt behavioural change. (***Sroufe, 1996***)

This is one of many definitions, reflecting the uncertainty of how best to get to grips with the nature of emotions. However, it has the advantage of drawing attention to the fact that any one emotional episode is made up of a number of components, i.e.:

- *The eliciting event*, which is always specific to each emotion. Surprise, for example, is evoked by something mildly unexpected; anger by interference with a goal; fear by a threatening situation; shame by a blow to one's self-esteem, and so on.

- *Physiological components*, such as altered heart rate and pulse, faster respiration, sweating, skin conductance and other functions controlled by the autonomous nervous system.
- *Experiential components*, i.e. the actual feelings aroused inside us. This is the aspect with which we are most familiar from personal experience. In part it is the awareness of arousal produced by the physiological changes, in part it is linked to our cognitive appraisal of the eliciting situation and the way it affects us. One of the more important age changes that occurs in childhood is that cognitive aspects come to play an increasingly significant role: the frightened infant simply responds with all the signs of fear; the older child resorts to a plan of action such as running away, and so not just expresses but controls the fear.
- *Overt behavioural change* is what other people are mostly aware of in witnessing someone's emotional state. The most obvious signs are facial expressions, and, as we shall see below, these have formed a major focus for research on emotional manifestation and recognition. Vocal changes (e.g. the high-pitched voice associated with terror) and particular gestures (e.g. fist shaking when angry) are other overt signs, all of which enable other people not only to realize that the individual is emotionally aroused, but also to identify the particular emotion experienced.

Let us repeat and emphasize a remark made earlier: emotions have positive functions, they are not just noise in the system. Take fear of strangers – a phenomenon which surfaces in the second half of the first year when children become increasingly discriminative in their reactions to other people (Schaffer, 1974). As a result, any overture from an unfamiliar person is responded to with signs of anxiety and agitation, varying in intensity according to the behaviour of the stranger and the child's temperament. Such an emotional reaction is clearly useful: it is linked to adaptive responses such as resistance, withdrawing and turning to the familiar parent; in addition the child's crying acts as a communicative device that will alert the mother so that she can take whatever action is appropriate. By means of emotional responses and signals children can thus inform others of their needs and requirements long before they are capable of expressing these in words. The pattern of fear therefore ensures that the child remains with trustworthy people rather than go off with anyone, and so has the survival value that no doubt was originally responsible for including this response pattern in the innate repertoire of our species. All emotions have some kind of survival value, and all serve useful intrapersonal and interpersonal regulatory functions.

Biological basis

Children do not have to be taught to be angry or afraid or joyful. Such emotions are expressed naturally; they are part of our heritage. This does not mean, of course, that the baby arrives in the world with a full complement of emotions. Fear of strangers, as we saw just now, does not clock in till later on in the first year; complex emotions like pride and shame appear later still. Yet there is no evidence that children require particular experiences to bring these into being; it appears rather that a genetically set programme ensures that various emotions appear at various ages, and that these take the same form in all human beings, irrespective of social and cultural background.

That was certainly Charles Darwin's belief. His book *The Expression of the Emotions in Man and Animals*, published in 1872, was in many respects the first attempt scientifically to record emotional behaviour in children and to explain its origins. Much of the empirical data were derived from Darwin's painstaking observations of his own son, Doddy. Here, for example, is what Darwin recorded of Doddy's first displays of anger:

> It was difficult to decide at how early an age anger was felt; on his eighth day he frowned and wrinkled the skin round his eyes before a crying fit, but this may have been due to pain or distress, not anger. When about ten weeks old he was given some rather cold milk and he kept a slight frown on his forehead all the time that he was sucking, so that he looked like a grown-up person made cross from being compelled to do something which he did not like. When nearly four months old, and perhaps much earlier, there could be no doubt, from the manner in which the blood gushed into his whole face and scalp, that he easily got into a violent passion.   (***Darwin, 1872***)

As this example shows, Darwin placed great emphasis on the facial expressions of emotions, and it is these in particular that he considered to be part of our inheritance, having evolved from response patterns useful in the struggle for survival and having much in common with those shown by other primates. Thus 'some expressions, such as the bristling of the hair under the influence of extreme terror, or the uncovering of the teeth under that of furious rage, can hardly be understood, except under the belief that man once existed in a much lower and animal-like condition' (Darwin, 1872).

There have been many attempts to plot the course of emotional growth and, in particular, to determine the basic emotions which can be seen even in newborns. Emotional expressions tend to be fleeting phenomena, and much of the earlier work relied merely on impressions. However, in more recent years some highly sophisticated techniques have become available for describing facial expressions objectively, reliably and in great detail (see Ekman & Friesen, 1978, with respect to the Facial Action Coding System, or FACS, and Izard, 1979, regarding the Maximally Discriminative Facial Movement Coding System, or MAX), and though there is still no general agreement as to the precise way in which emotions emerge in the early weeks of life, there are six that are regarded by many experts as the primary emotions that can be identified even in newborn babies, namely, *anger, fear, surprise, disgust, joy* and *sadness*. Each of these is linked to a particular neural basis; each is expressed in a particular way and in each case that expression has a

Table 5.1   Six basic emotions and their expression

Emotion	Facial expression	Physiological reaction	Adaptive function
Anger	Brows lowered and pulled together; mouth open and square *or* lips pressed together	Increased heart rate and skin temperature; facial flushing	Overcome obstacle; attain goal
Fear	Brows raised; eyes wide and tense, rigidly fixated on stimulus	High, stable heart rate; low skin temperature; gasping respiration	Learn about threatening agent; avoid danger
Disgust	Brows lowered; nose wrinkled; raised cheeks and upper lip	Low heart rate and skin temperature; increased skin resistance	Avoid harmful source
Sadness	Inner corners of brows up; corners of mouth pulled down and middle of chin pulled up	Low heart rate; low skin temperature; low skin conductance	Encourage others to give comfort
Joy	Corners of mouth up and back; cheeks raised; eyes narrow	Increased heart rate; irregular breathing; elevated skin conductance	Signals readiness for friendly interaction
Surprise	Eyes wide, eyebrows raised; mouth open; continued orienting to stimulus	Heart rate slowed; breathing briefly suspended; general loss of muscle tone	Prepare to assimilate a new experience; enlarge visual field

particular adaptive function (see table 5.1). It is the behavioural expression, of course, that gives other people a clue as to what the child is feeling. When in one experiment (Lewis, Alessandri & Sullivan, 1990) 2-month-old babies were sat in an infant chair and had a string attached to their arm, they quickly learned that each arm pull turned on a short burst of music – something that they greeted with every sign of pleasure: opening of mouth, widening of eyes, smiling. When the experimenters switched off the music and arm pulling no longer had the desired effect, the babies' expression clearly showed all the signs of anger: clenched and bared teeth, square mouth, knit brow. Invariably, the behavioural manifestation of each emotion has some particular adaptive value: for example, babies given a bad-tasting substance will make a disgust expression, as part of which they try to expel the substance while their crying will alert caregivers to take appropriate action.

If emotional expressions are biologically determined they should be universal, and accordingly Darwin set out to collect relevant material from other cultures in order to find out whether people the world over express their emotions in similar manner. Since his days a great deal more material has become available from a wide range of societies such as, in particular, preliterate societies with little contact with outsiders (see box 5.1 for an example), and from this evidence we have learned that there is indeed great similarity in the way people all over the world express emotions facially and also by voice and movement (for review see Mesquita & Frijda, 1992). Asked, for example, to pose the expression appropriate to receiving news of someone's death, or to being confronted by a dangerous animal, or to being provoked by another person's derogatory remarks, identical expressions are assumed by all. This also means that the ability to recognize emotions in other people is universal: when shown photographs of posed expressions, members of various cultures, including preliterate ones, have little difficulty in identifying which emotion is expressed (see table 5.2). Indeed, children as young as 3 months appear to recognize at least some of other people's emotions, in that they respond differentially to faces bearing happy, neutral and angry expressions.

Table 5.2 Agreement (in percentages) among members of various cultures in identifying emotions on photographed faces

Emotion	United States	Japan	Brazil	Scotland	New Guinea
Happiness	97	87	87	98	92
Sadness	73	74	82	86	79
Anger	69	63	82	84	84
Disgust	82	82	86	79	81
Surprise	91	87	82	88	68
Fear	88	71	77	86	80

Source: Adapted from Ekman (1980) and Fridlund (1994).

Admittedly, universality does not necessarily indicate an innate origin: the reason for common behaviour patterns could be common species-typical learning experiences. It is therefore all the more significant to find that children cut off from such experiences by being born both blind and deaf also show emotional expressions in the same way as other individuals (Eibl-Eibesfeldt, 1973). From the beginning they laugh, smile, frown, startle and cry in the same way and under the same circumstances; thus, when angry they clench their fists and when sad their shoulders sag, and vocal accompaniments too are appropriate and 'correct' even though the child has never heard these from other people. An innate origin of our emotional repertoire is thus a virtual certainty, even though (as we shall see below) social influences do make themselves felt in the course of childhood by establishing norms for the extent and circumstances of emotional expression.

BOX 5.1

Studying emotions in a neolithic society

Are emotional expressions innate or learned? If the former, they should be identical in all human beings whatever their cultural background, even in those who have led an isolated existence and not been exposed to western influences.

The most thorough cross-cultural investigation to examine this problem was undertaken by Paul Ekman (1980; Ekman, Sorenson & Friesen, 1969). The society which he and his colleagues studied was the Fore people, a neolithic tribe living in a remote area of New Guinea that, until just before Ekman's visit, had been totally cut off from all outsiders. Various methods were used in the investigations. For example, individuals were told stories (translated into their own language) about such events as meeting a wild pig when alone, or about friends having arrived, and for each story they were asked to pick out the appropriate emotional expression from a set of photographs of western faces displaying a variety of emotions. In most instances they were successful: for happiness, for example, they were correct in 92 per cent, for anger 84 per cent, for disgust 81 per cent and for sadness 79 per cent. Fore children performed similarly. Another method was to show the Fore a photograph which had been judged by people in both western and eastern literate cultures to represent a particular emotion and ask each person to make up a story about that face, describing what was happening now, what had happened before and what would happen subsequently. This was a more difficult task for these people, but once again there was evidence that the photos conveyed the same emotions to them as to members of other cultures. Yet another technique was to ask Fore individuals to show how they would look if, say, they were angry enough to fight or happy because friends had come. When videotapes of these expressions were subsequently analysed, it was found that they moved the same facial muscles as do people in other cultures when feeling or trying to simulate these emotions. Moreover, when these tapes were shown to people in the West, they were for the most part correctly interpreted.

Ekman had no doubt that the results of his studies demonstrated that certain emotional expressions are universal. He identified happiness, surprise, sadness, anger, fear and disgust as belonging to a common, culture-free repertoire, and subsequently added contempt to this list. Not everyone has agreed with his conclusions (e.g. Russell, 1994) – in part because the methods he used were not foolproof and in part because other theoretical interpretations could be applied. Yet, taken in conjunction with other evidence, the belief that nature has equipped all members of the human species with a particular set of fixed action patterns to express basic emotions is still the most plausible.

Developmental course

In the course of development, emotions change as a result both of maturation and of socialization. New emotions appear: in the second and third years, for example, children begin to show signs of guilt, pride, shame and embarrassment. Emotions become blended: fear and anger may be shown at the same time. The basic emotions, of course, remain part of the repertoire for the rest of the individual's life; the circumstances under which they are evoked, however, will change with age. In particular, from the second year on symbolic representations of situations can elicit emotional feelings and not just the situations themselves: a child can be consumed with fear while sitting safely in a chair at home but listening to or even just remembering a horror tale. One other noteworthy developmental change: emotions come to be expressed in increasingly more subtle ways as the child gains control over behaviour and learns to react in socially approved ways. Thus, feeling and its overt manifestation will gradually become detached as the child learns 'manners': not to be angry when another child gets the coveted first prize; not to show disappointment when a present turns out to be something quite unwanted; and even to mask feelings by showing a more 'polite' emotion than the one really felt.

Emotional development goes hand in hand with cognitive development. This is well illustrated by the emergence of what have been called the *self-conscious* emotions, such as pride, shame, guilt and embarrassment, which are not usually found before the end of the second year. For children to be able to experience such emotions they must first have a sense of self – something which emerges at about 18 months of age. Emotions like fear and anger do not require this and so appear early on. However, when a child feels proud or ashamed, it is a matter of 'the self evaluating the self' (Lewis, 1992): the individual, that is, must possess some degree of objective self-awareness in order to judge him- or herself, and this is a relatively sophisticated cognitive capacity that is not present in infancy (see chapter 10 for a more detailed discussion). Thus, not until children are cognitively equipped to take an objective look at themselves can they evaluate their own behaviour, compare it against some standard set either by others or by themselves, conclude 'I have done something great (or awful)', and accordingly feel satisfied or dissatisfied with their performance (for some details of research on pride and shame see box 5.2).

Children's Conception of Emotion

Once children become able to talk, emotional development assumes a whole new dimension. Emotions can now become a subject for reflection: by being able to label the feelings they experience, children can stand apart from them, think about them and in this way objectify whatever is going on inside them. Having words for emotions, children can also enter into discussion about them: on the one hand, they can convey to others how they themselves feel, and, on the other hand, they can listen to other people give an account of the feelings that they experience. Emotions can thus be shared, and learning about their nature – their causes and consequences and how to handle them – becomes so much easier once they can be dealt with at a verbal level.

BOX 5.2

Investigating pride and shame

Basic emotions such as anger and fear are easily discernible in young children: their overt manifestations are clearly expressed and take more or less the same form in all. This is not the case with the later-appearing self-conscious emotions such as pride and shame, which do not give rise to unique facial indicators; to study such phenomena, investigators therefore had first to grapple with the problem of measurement (see Lewis, 1992; Stipek, Recchia & McClintic, 1992).

Both pride and shame are 'all-body' emotions: they may not be characterized by specific facial expressions but they do show themselves in the general stance of the individual, and especially so in young children, who have no inhibition about expressing them overtly and to the full. By putting children into situations where they are likely to encounter success or, alternatively, failure, observers have accumulated the signs of pride and shame that can be used to code these two emotions. Thus, it has been agreed that pride is essentially a matter of the body 'expanding': the child adopts an open, erect posture, with shoulders back, head up and/or arms open and up, eyes raised, accompanied by a smile and sometimes such positive verbalizations as 'I did it!' or just 'ahh!'. In shame, on the other hand, the body 'collapses': shoulders are hunched, hands are down and close to the body or placed in front of the face as though hiding, the corners of the mouth are downward, eyes are lowered, activity ceases, and there may also be negative verbal comments such as 'I'm no good at this'. Using such indices, observers can generally get good agreement on what a child is feeling, thus making it possible objectively to investigate these phenomena.

Take a study by Lewis, Alessandri and Sullivan (1992) as an example. Boys and girls aged 3 were given easy and difficult tasks to carry out (e.g. assembling a 4-piece or a 25-piece puzzle; copying a straight line or a triangle) and their emotional responses of pride and shame recorded from videotapes. The interest lay in the extent to which the children's reactions of pride and shame varied according to the difficulty of the task, and whether there are gender differences in children's behaviour. The results showed clearly that these children manifested pride and shame differentially and appropriately: no child showed pride on failing and no child showed shame on succeeding. The children did, however, assess their performance quite realistically according to the difficulty of the task: more showed shame when failing on the easy task than they did on the difficult task, and more pride was shown when they succeeded on the difficult than on the easy task. Simple success or failure was not sufficient to account for the children's reactions: even at age 3 they could evaluate their performance in relation to the objective to be achieved. As to gender differences, boys and girls did not differ in their manifestation of pride; however, in situations of failure, and particularly so on easy tasks, girls showed significantly more shame than boys – a finding that parallels similar observations for adult females and males.

The emergence of emotion language

Children first begin to use words referring to inner feelings in the latter half of the second year – words like happy, sad, angry and afraid (Bretherton & Beeghly, 1982; Dunn, Bretherton & Munn, 1987). The most common themes then are pleasure and pain; the most common function of such talk is simply to comment on how the child feels ('I fraid'; 'me glad'). In the course of the third year, usage of emotion terms increases rapidly in quantity and in range, and by age 6 the majority of children habitually refer to words like excited, upset, annoyed, glad, unhappy, relaxed, disappointed, worried, nervous and cheerful. What is more, while initially children talk almost entirely about their own feelings, by about $2^1/_2$ years of age they also refer to those of other people. By recording children's spontaneous talk in naturally occurring situations, remarks such as the following can be heard:

'It's dark. I'm scared.'
'Katie not happy face. Katie sad.'
'I give a hug. Baby be pleased.'

The significance of such remarks is that they show how very early children are able to make inferences about inner states. Already by the third year, instead of talking merely about external behaviour ('cry', 'kiss', 'laugh', etc.), they have shifted to a psychological level and are able to refer not only to their own but to other people's internal feelings. Moreover, the inferences they make are generally correct: show 3-year-olds pictures of faces displaying various emotions; ask them to state how these people feel; and for the basic emotions at least they will have little problem in identifying the appropriate feelings. Remarks such as 'Her eyes are crying; her sad' illustrate well the kinds of inferences made.

During the preschool period emotion talk rapidly gains in accuracy, clarity and complexity and, most significantly, in reference to the possible causes of people's feelings. Thus remarks like 'It's dark. I'm scared', 'Grandma mad; me wrote on wall' and 'I scared of Hulk. I close my eyes' show clearly that emotions are not merely treated as isolated events. These young children are already busily speculating about the reasons why people feel as they do: they construct plausible theories as to what brings about the emotional displays they witness, relate these displays to interpersonal events such as parents quarrelling or a mother scolding her child, and in addition talk about ways of coping with emotions ('I'm mad at you, Daddy. I'm going away. Good bye'). Once they have understood how emotions are brought about, they can start trying to manipulate the feelings of others ('If you are angry, Daddy, I'll tell Mummy').

Being able to talk about emotions means that children can take an objective view of feelings – their own as well as other people's. This ability increases throughout the middle years of childhood, enabling children to discuss past emotional incidents and anticipate future events, analyse these in terms of causes and consequences, appreciate how mood may affect behaviour and make allowance for differences among individuals in the nature of their emotional responsiveness. Thus, being able to think about inner feelings and discuss them with others means that, on the one hand, children can try to understand their own emotions and, on the other hand, listen to other people's accounts of their feelings and learn how they interpret various situations. Emotional talk, that is, has considerable implications for emotional development and greatly increases the opportunity for children to gain insight into interpersonal relationships.

Conversations about emotions

Children's interest in and understanding of emotions develop in the course of social interaction, as revealed by the conversations they hold with parents (see Dunn et al., 1987; Dunn & Brown, 1994). From these it becomes very apparent that it is often the children themselves who take the initiative in finding out about emotions: even at an age when their ability to talk explicitly about feelings is still limited, they will show great curiosity about the reason why people behave as they do. Take the following example, reported by Dunn (1988), of a $2\frac{1}{2}$-year-old boy who had overheard his mother talking about a dead mouse:

CHILD: 'What's that frighten you, Mum?'
MOTHER: 'Nothing.'

CHILD: 'What's that frighten you?'
MOTHER: 'Nothing.'
CHILD: 'What is it? What's down there, Mummy? That frighten you?'
MOTHER: 'Nothing.'
CHILD: 'That not frighten you?'
MOTHER: 'No. Didn't frighten me.'
CHILD: 'What that there?'

Here we have a child convinced that there must be some definite reason for his mother's emotional behaviour and so persisting in getting to the bottom of what caused her state. The child is not content merely to note the mother's overt behaviour: he wants to explain it in terms of the underlying emotion and find out about the conditions that brought about that emotion.

Initially, conversations about emotions serve mainly to help children understand their own feelings and to obtain comfort. This is seen in the following example of a 2-year-old who had been shown a book with pictures of monsters (from Dunn et al., 1987):

CHILD: 'Mummy, Mummy.'
MOTHER: 'What's wrong?'
CHILD: 'Frighten.'
MOTHER: 'The book?'
CHILD: 'Yes.'
MOTHER: 'It's not frightening you!'
CHILD: 'Yes!'
MOTHER: 'It did, did it?'
CHILD: 'Yes.'

Conversations serve a variety of functions:

- they enable children to face their own emotions;
- they help to explain other people's behaviour;
- they further children's understanding of an increasing range of feelings;
- they provide an insight into the nature and circumstances of interpersonal relationships; and
- they make it possible for children to share emotional experiences with others and incorporate these into the relationship.

The frequency of such conversations between children and their parents increases greatly during the early years, in keeping with children's growing verbal skills and their capacity for understanding. As seen in table 5.3, a marked advance in the incidence of children's references to feelings occurs in the course of the second and third years of life. However, what also advances is the incidence of mothers' talk to children about feelings. Indeed, mothers' talk develops in parallel with chil-

Table 5.3 Frequency of reference to feelings by $1^1/_2$- to $2^1/_2$-year-old children and their mothers

	$1^1/_2$ years	2 years	$2^1/_2$ years
Children	0.8	4.7	12.4
Mothers	7.1	11.1	17.4

Source: From Dunn et al. (1987).

dren's: thus at first they refer only to the child's own emotions and only subsequently will they mention other people's too; also, the number and variety of emotions mentioned match those of the child's, increasing as the child gets older; and similarly, just like their children, mothers discuss more and more the causes of emotions and their consequences. Do mothers thereby *cause* their children's growth of emotion talk? Or, alternatively, do they merely keep pace with the children's increasing ability to express and comprehend such talk? We do not know the answer, but it would not be surprising if both explanations hold – each partner, that is, affects the other one.

A similar cause-and-effect problem arises with regard to sex differences. As Dunn et al. (1987) found, mother–daughter conversations are characterized by more references to feelings than mother–son conversations. For one thing, girls talk more about emotional aspects than boys – a difference evident as early as age 2; for another, the mothers of girls refer more to emotions than the mothers of boys. Were the mothers responding to inherent, sex-linked inclinations in these children, or did they bring about the difference? The fact that Dunn and her colleagues found older siblings also talked more about feelings to girls than to boys may suggest the former explanation, but is by no means decisive.

The extent to which families mention emotion varies enormously. When Dunn, Brown and Beardall (1991) recorded naturally occurring conversations of families with 3-year-old children, they found some families to have as few as two and others as many as 25 conversations per hour that made reference to people's feelings. The frequency with which children are involved in emotion talk appears to have long-term consequences: as Dunn showed by following up the children to age 6, those who had been most exposed to such talk developed considerably greater skill in various aspects of emotional understanding than those who had experienced less exposure. It is as though frequent reference to people's feelings helps from the early years on to draw children's attention to that particular aspect of human behaviour, thus developing sensitivity to the different shades of emotional expressiveness and enabling children in due course to formulate a coherent body of knowledge about the causes and consequences of emotional behaviour.

Thinking about emotions

Children do not only *experience* emotions; as they grow older, they increasingly *think* about them as well. They try to understand what it means, for them and for other people, to be involved in emotional episodes, and accordingly they will construct theories about the nature and causes of the feelings they encounter.

The theories are at first rather primitive, and yet soon they begin to assume a more sophisticated form. We see this in children's appreciation that emotions are more than their outer manifestation and involve inner feeling states too. Take the little girl who commented about a picture shown to her: 'Her eyes are crying; her sad'. Not only is she aware of the relevant behavioural cues; she also uses these to make inferences about the internal mental state giving rise to that behaviour. To some extent a shift from behaviouristic to mentalistic conceptions takes place in children's thinking as they grow older; yet very early on children start to realize that emotions are part of people's inner life and that there is more to them than external responses to external situations. They then become much more accurate in assessing emotions and understanding what brought them about.

We can see this in the way in which children explain other children's emotional expressions. In a study by Fabes, Eisenberg, Nyman and Michaelieu (1991), observations were carried out on 3- to 5-year-olds in a nursery school, and note made whenever some emotional episode (a struggle over a toy, an argument about turns, a reaction to a hurtful comment, etc.) took place. On each occasion the observers not only noted how the children involved in these episodes reacted, but also asked a child who had witnessed the incident from nearby to describe what emotion had been shown and what had caused it. The results (summarized in table 5.4) show that even 3-year-olds are fairly accurate in labelling emotions correctly, as assessed by the proportion of agreements with the observer, and especially so with respect to negative emotions such as anger and sadness. They also show that even the younger children were also able to identify many of the specific causes that triggered the episodes. When analysing the *kinds* of explanations given, it was found that the younger children tended to focus more on external causes ('he's angry because she took his toy away'; 'she is mad because he hit her'), whereas older children

Table 5.4 Children's accuracy in identifying the nature and causes of emotions (accuracy defined as percentage of agreement with adult observer)

	Age group			Emotion	
	3 years	*4 years*	*5 years*	*Positive*	*Negative*
Nature of emotion	69	72	83	66	83
Cause of emotion	67	71	85	85	64

Source: Adapted from Fabes et al. (1991).

increasingly also referred to internal states ('she is sad because she misses her Mum'; 'she is annoyed because she thought it was her turn'). Internal explanations were especially likely for intense emotions and occurred more often for negative than for positive emotions. Thus with increasing age children move from visible to invisible causes and, by making inferences as to what motivates others to behave as they do, gradually obtain an increasingly complex understanding of other people's internal world.

For a true appreciation of that internal world, children must understand that it is of a distinctive nature in each one of us, and not assume we all feel as the child does. Again, there are indications that preschool children are already becoming capable of such insight. In a study by Dunn and Hughes (1998), 4-year-olds were interviewed about the everyday causes of happiness, anger, sadness and fear in themselves, in their friends and in their mothers. The accounts which these children gave were not only coherent and plausible, but also differed considerably according to the identity of the individual described. Asked, for example, what makes their mother happy, they would mention such causes as 'A cup of tea', 'A good sleep – my Mummy never has a good sleep, so that would make her happy', and 'Perfume, my Mum loves perfume'. These are very different causes from those offered when asked about their own feelings of happiness, and though their accounts for self and friend were more similar, the children gave sufficient indication that each individual was considered in his or her own right. Emotions, that is, were explained in terms of the needs and requirements of the person discussed and not merely generalized from the child's own experience.

Theory of mind (ToM) is the knowledge acquired in childhood that other people have an internal world of thoughts and feelings and that these are independent of one's own mental states.

We have here an early indication of the development in children of a **theory of mind** – the realization that other people have an internal world and the ability to depict that world as distinctive to each individual. We shall have more to say about this later on; here our concern is with the implications this has for understanding people's emotions. As Paul Harris (1989) has pointed out, that understanding develops greatly during the preschool period because children become increasingly more proficient in generating theories that help them predict other people's feelings. These theories get progressively more complex as children realize that the emotional impact of a situation on any one individual depends not so much on the objective characteristics of that situation as on the way the individual appraises it in the light of his or her wishes and expectations. Very young children assume that all situations have the same meaning for everybody – a meaning depending on the child's own reaction to it. In the course of the preschool period, however, children gradually come to realize that it is not the situation as such that brings about the emotional reaction but the mental characteristics each individual brings to it, and that therefore what is frightening to one person is not so to another, and that what causes pleasant surprise to one may well cause disappointment to another. Thus children become proficient at predicting others' emotional reactions once they are able to take into account the specific characteristics these individuals bring to the situation – a proficiency they attain by becoming able to set aside their own perspective and, by means of an imaginative leap, enter into the mind of others. By telling children stories about imaginary characters and asking them for their comments (see box 5.3 for an example), Harris was able to demonstrate that by the age of 6 at the latest, children have acquired the ability to understand another person's mental state: by then they realize that how people feel will depend on the desires and beliefs that they bring to the situation and with which each one of them appraises it. They can then correctly anticipate how that individual will be affected by the situation. By that age at least, children are therefore well capable of developing hypotheses about what sets other people's emotions going, how these reactions are likely to manifest themselves and what may in due course terminate them. Their skills in *mindreading*, that is, have improved markedly by the end of the preschool period.

BOX 5.3

The emotional life of Ellie the elephant

Investigating the ability of young children to understand other people's feelings requires the use of techniques meaningful to such children and tailored to their abilities to comprehend and respond. Thus, when Paul Harris (1989) set out to investigate how and when children develop the capacity for taking another person's perspective, he devised a series of stories with imaginary animal characters and asked the children he was testing to comment on the situations in which these characters found themselves.

For example, preschool children were told about an elephant called Ellie who was very fussy about what she was given to drink. Some children were told she only liked milk, others that she only liked Coke. When out for a walk one day, Ellie got very thirsty and longed for her favourite drink on her return. Unfortunately, a mischievous monkey called Mickey was at work during Ellie's absence and changed drinks over: for example, she poured all of Ellie's hoped-for Coke away, substituted milk and then offered Ellie the Coke can containing the disliked milk. The children were then asked how Ellie would have felt when she found out the real contents on taking a drink from the can.

The children, younger and older, were able to take into account Ellie's preferences in predicting her feelings. If Ellie liked Coke, they said, she would be happy to find Coke in the can; if she liked milk she would be sad to discover Coke. Thus from about 3 years on these children could base their prediction on others' *pre-existing desires*: they were able to put themselves in another person's place and judge how that person would feel when their desire was either satisfied or frustrated. Moreover, they could do so irrespective of what their own feelings and desires might be.

However, the younger children's understanding was still limited to some extent, as seen when the children were asked how Ellie would feel when she first saw the can before actually tasting its contents. What would be her reaction, for example, if she liked Coke but was given a can in which Mickey had secretly substituted milk? The older children answered correctly: they appreciated that Ellie's *pre-existing belief* that the can contained Coke would make her feel pleased about the drink she was about to receive, though sad when she actually tasted the contents. The younger children, on the other hand, could not make allowance for Ellie's mistaken belief: they themselves knew what was really in the can and therefore assumed that Ellie would have exactly the same knowledge.

There is thus a difference between understanding other people's *desires* and their *beliefs* as causes of their emotions. Even the younger children Harris tested could allow for Ellie's desire, i.e. they realized that her preference for a particular drink would influence her reaction to getting either that drink or another. On the other hand, these children could not shift away from their own personal beliefs: whatever they knew they considered would be known by other people too. Initially, understanding of emotion is therefore a somewhat egocentric business; gradually, in the course of the preschool years, it becomes a more mature ability that makes it possible for children to put themselves in other people's place.

Socialization of Emotions

Emotional development is based on common biological foundations; its subsequent course, however, is shaped by varied social experience. As a result, the way in which emotions are expressed may differ radically from one society to another. Take the following cultural norms and compare them with western customs:

- The people of Ifaluk, an island in the Western Pacific, disapprove of expressing happiness, believing that it is immoral and will lead to the neglect of duties. They therefore bring up their children to avoid any excitement associated with showing such feelings, convinced that it will give rise to misbehaviour and disruption. Instead, they are urged always to be gentle, quiet and calm (Lutz, 1987).
- The Yanomamo are a group of Indians living on the border of Venezuela and Brazil, who value fierceness above all other qualities in their interpersonal

relationships. They are almost constantly engaged in warfare with neighbours, aimed at killing men and abducting women, and amongst themselves settle all disagreements violently. Children are brought up with little affection, and both boys and girls are taught to conduct themselves aggressively in all dealings with other children (Chagnon, 1968).

- The Balinese are convinced that any form of emotional eruption is malign and must be avoided. Instances have been cited, for example, where people have fallen asleep with the sole aim of avoiding fear. From the beginning children's upbringing is therefore almost devoid of any but the mildest form of overt emotion (Bateson & Mead, 1940).

Each society (including our own!) has evolved certain socially approved ways of coping with emotion, and an important part of its distinctiveness lies in the set of implicit and explicit directions that the members are expected to follow when expressing their feelings. Conveying these directions to children is thus a major aspect of socialization. As the more detailed example in box 5.4 shows, the norms followed by other societies can sometimes look quite extraordinary to our western eyes.

BOX 5.4

'Never in anger': The Utku Eskimos' way of life

Jean Briggs, an anthropologist, spent 17 months among the Utku, an Eskimo group living near the Arctic Circle, where she was 'adopted' by a family that took her into their igloo and allowed her to observe them as well as their neighbours at close quarters. Her observations were reported in a book entitled *Never in Anger* (1970).

What makes the Utku so remarkable is the almost complete absence of any sign of aggression in their interpersonal relationships. The Utku disapprove of all displays of anger: the ideal person for them is someone who is always warm, protective and even-tempered in his or her dealings with others, and who will never express any hostility whatever in overt behaviour. The most that is permitted are such minor acts as teasing, gossiping and coolness towards others, and while anger can be expressed when handling dogs, even then it is defended as 'discipline'. Anger is disapproved of because it is incompatible with the highest values of Utku society, namely, affection and nurturance towards others; if someone does display such emotion, it is regarded as a sign of loss of reason and the person considered to be behaving like a very young child. The Utku even deny having angry thoughts, refusing to acknowledge them not only to others but also to themselves, in that they are convinced such thoughts would be capable of killing the person who harbours them. All disagreements must therefore be settled by peaceful means – an aim that they seem to be remarkably successful in achieving.

For the first 2 or 3 years of their lives children are allowed to express feelings of rage and anger, but from then on parents make it increasingly clear that such displays are not approved of. Much of their socialization efforts are devoted to channelling children's negative emotions in other directions, in order to help them acquire the Utku virtues of patience and self-subordination. Parents do so not by shouting or threats but by quietly conveying their disapproval with words or looks. Compliance to demands is not enforced, and while obedience is valued parents rarely insist on it. Children are never physically punished; all along, however, they are quite consistently taught that any overt indication of temper, anger and hostility is viewed disapprovingly.

Learning such a lesson is, of course, hard, and Briggs describes movingly how the young girl in the family with whom she lived coped with the hostile emotions aroused by sibling rivalry. At first she expressed her feelings surreptitiously – pinching her little sister when the adults' back was turned, or snatching a toy from her when they were alone. Mostly she reacted to adult demands with sullenness – complying with a set, expressionless face or turning to face a wall and quietly weeping. Thus, in response to some unwelcome request by a parent to give way to her sister, she would silently stare ahead with tears pouring down her face, but with no overt sign of any anger. As a result of such treatment Utku children, compared with those in the West, show strikingly little indication of aggressiveness, and from a quite early age hostility in peer groups is an astonishingly rare phenomenon.

Acquiring display rules

Display rules refer to the cultural norms for the overt expression of emotion, including both the kind of emotions displayed and the circumstances under which they can be displayed.

The concept of **display rules** is used to designate the conventions that govern the overt expression of emotion in any given social group – be it a particular culture or family or peer group. By means of such rules people become predictable to one another: all those brought up to share a specific set of conventions know what any one specific display of feeling signifies, thus facilitating communication among the members of that group. To appreciate the point, one need only put oneself in the place of a visitor to any one of the above-listed societies: the bewilderment and misunderstanding would be such that all efforts at communication would be bound to break down, however well the visitor could speak the local language. Thus children need to learn, from as early an age as is feasible, the set of display rules prevailing in their social environment, so that they know what emotional displays are appropriate in particular situations. Under some circumstances the 'natural' expression may be acceptable, but under many others even quite young children are expected to hold in check what comes naturally and even substitute the expression corresponding to an emotion different from that which they actually feel.

Let us illustrate. A common display rule is 'look pleased when someone gives you something they expect you to like – even if you don't like it'. Carolyn Saarni (1984) observed children aged between 6 and 10 in order to determine the extent to which children have learned this rule, i.e. that under certain circumstances it is necessary to hide one's disappointment and pretend to feel pleasure instead. Each child was asked to help an adult with a task evaluating school books and, on completion, was thanked and given an attractive gift. On a second occasion some days later, the children were asked to help again but this time were presented with a drab and unimaginative toy more suitable for a baby. Their facial expressions as they unwrapped the toys were video-recorded each time, as were their vocal and other bodily reactions.

In response to the first gift the children showed all the usual signs of pleasure: smiles, looks at the adult, an enthusiastic 'thank you' and so forth. When given the drab gift the older children managed well to hide their disappointment and show at least some signs of apparent pleasure; the younger children, on the other hand, were far less successful in hiding their true feelings and instead openly expressed their disappointment, though even amongst them there were some children, mostly girls, who did make an effort to follow convention and pretend to be pleased. Thus the older children had definitely mastered the need to dissociate outer expression from inner feeling; at younger ages, however, it appeared that the children were only just beginning to learn about this particular display rule.

Display rules fall under four headings:

- *Minimization* rules, i.e. those instances where an emotional expression is reduced in intensity in relation to what is really felt. The behaviour of the Utku Eskimos, quoted above, when experiencing anger is an example of such a strategy.
- *Maximization* rules, which refer mainly to the way in which positive emotions are expressed. It may well be that some of Saarni's older children, when receiving their first gift, smiled rather more enthusiastically than the gift actually warranted – because they regarded this as the done thing.
- *Masking* rules, when a neutral expression (a 'poker face') is thought to be appropriate. Our example of the Ifaluk illustrates that kind of behaviour.
- *Substitution* rules, when the individual is expected to replace one emotion with a quite different one, usually its opposite. The children who show overt pleasure instead of inner disappointment on being given a baby toy had clearly acquired this type of rule.

It appears that minimization and especially maximization are easier to acquire and are found at somewhat earlier ages than the other two strategies. Certainly, the 2-year-old who exaggerates his cries in order to get sympathy from his mother shows that he has already mastered the latter rule. However, let us distinguish between being able to *use* display rules and *knowing* that one is doing so. When Paul Harris (1989) interviewed preschool children who had successfully hidden their feeling of disappointment behind signs of pleasure about their understanding of this sub-stitution strategy, he found little conscious awareness that what they felt and what they showed could actually differ. The children, it seemed, were able to act in a socially appropriate manner without any insight into what they were doing. Only from about 6 years on was the distinction between real and apparent emotion firmly grasped, in that only then could children explicitly appreciate that feelings and behaviour need not correspond and that it is quite acceptable to deceive another person for the sake of social convention.

Parental influences

Children first learn about emotions in the family. How others interact with them even in infancy conveys messages about how to express emotion, the circumstances under which emotions can be shown and the kinds of action to be taken in coping with emotion-arousing situations. The kind of relationships they have with these others may therefore well determine the way and the extent to which emotional socialization takes place – as seems likely from examining the association of children's emotional development with their attachment style (Cassidy, 1994).

Attachment is usually defined as an *emotional* bond, i.e. a relationship where children encounter some of the most intense emotional experiences of their early years. The manner whereby these experiences are conveyed by parents, and how the parents respond to the child's displays of feeling, are therefore decisive influences on the course of further development. As we saw in the last chapter, maternal sensitivity in handling a child's emotional expressions is thought to foster attach-ment security; insensitivity, on the other hand, gives rise to insecurity. Children brought up by sensitive parents and developing secure attachments to them are thus likely to develop different strategies of emotion regulation from those who have insensitive parents and develop insecure attachments, and there is indeed evidence that the three main attachment classifications are associated with the following patterns (Goldberg, 2000):

- *Secure* children have learned that expressing emotions, whether positive or negative, is acceptable to their parents, and as a result feel free to display them directly and openly. They know, for example, that signs of distress will alert their parents and elicit help and comfort, and as a result do not hesitate to show anxiety and grief. Similarly, they have learned that signs of joy and happiness will be reciprocated and will therefore feel free to express these too. In turn, the children will be responsive to a wide range of emotions in other people.

- *Avoidant* children tend to have a history of repeated rejections of their emotional expressions. This applies in particular to negative emotions, to which the mothers are least responsive. As a result, the children develop a strategy of hiding any sign of distress, even though they may experience it as much as other children, in order to avoid being ignored or rebuffed. Positive emotions are also restrained, because they signal that the child wants to interact with someone who may not wish to reciprocate.
- *Resistant* children have learned that their emotional expressions are responded to inconsistently and that the effects they produce are therefore unpredictable. Consequently, they develop a strategy of exaggerated expression, particularly of negative emotions, because these are most likely to provoke their parents' attention.

Emotionality is thus influenced by the kind of relationship that develops between parent and child, in that the various types of attachment are associated with distinctive messages parents convey to their children about the acceptability of emotion. The lessons so learned are then carried forward to later years and generalized to other relationships, to become part of each individual's affective style.

There are three main ways in which these messages are conveyed by parents and other adults:

- *Coaching.* This refers to the direct instructions parents give: 'Boys don't cry'; 'Smile when granny gives you a present'; 'There is no need to be frightened of the dog'.
- *Modelling.* Children inevitably imitate parents and other role models, and will therefore learn from them through observation about the 'proper' way of behaving. How adults show or do not show emotion is a rich source of information and will thus influence the children's own modes of expression.
- *Contingency learning.* This is probably the most effective source of social influence. By examining in precise detail the to-and-fro that already in infancy is characteristic of sequences of parent–child communications, *emotional dialogues* become evident, when facial, gestural and other affective signals are exchanged, whether accompanied by words or not (Malatesta, Culver, Tesman & Shepard, 1989). At first these are largely determined by mothers responding to their children's emotional signals in a non-random manner: particular expressions, that is, are usually followed by particular matching expressions. Happiness in the child, for example, is followed by happiness in the mother; fear, on the other hand, by tenderness. The child thus learns that the other person's behaviour is predictable ('if I do X she will do Y'): for example, when a particular emotional expression is attended to and followed by some posit-

ive response, the child is likely to repeat that expression; however, when that expression is either not attended to or greeted with a negative response, the child will be discouraged from behaving in that manner in future. Just how quickly such discouragement can set in is shown by studies of unexpressive mothers, for example those who are suffering from a depressive illness or who have deliberately adopted a 'still-face' for experimental purposes (see box 5.5 for further detail).

However marked the influence of parents is on children's emotional development, other people play a part too. This is especially noteworthy when considering the pressures that peer groups exert, in particular to ensure that boys will be boys and girls will be girls. Thus boys are expected to be tough, girls tender – and for boys this means playing up anger and aggressiveness and finding ways of expressing these effectively, while at the same time minimizing softer emotions; girls, on the other hand, are meant to dampen signs of overt conflict, giving emphasis to cooperation and agreement instead and becoming sensitive to others' feelings and adept at expressing their own. Like all stereotypes, these are generalizations that do not hold for all times and all places; nevertheless, they serve to remind us that all peer groups have emotional climates just as families do, and that they too expect their members to conform to ways of preserving these climates. This applies to how much emotion is expressed, what emotions are tolerated, and also who is allowed to be emotional to whom. Peer groups often have strict pecking orders, and to show anger to some-one further up the order is just asking for trouble. Also, as we saw in our discussion of peer relationships in the previous chapter, children's groups have definite ideas about what emotions are acceptable under what circumstances: boys who are over-aggressive are likely to be rejected, though totally unassertive boys too will find it hard to gain acceptance among their peers. Thus, from preschool age on, the different kinds of interaction that a child gets involved in will foster different emotional skills, and membership of both family and peer group will accordingly help to widen the range of skills that become available to children.

BOX 5.5

Cutting off the emotional flow

A dialogue can be conducted even in the absence of words – a fact vividly illustrated by the face-to-face exchanges of mothers and babies, which give all the impressions of a conversation even though their components are facial expressions, gestures, glances and vocalizations rather than verbalizations. They give this appearance because of the way in which the components are woven together in a to-and-fro exchange of the two partners, in that what one 'says' is closely followed by what the other 'says' – an interchange where the baby soon learns that her emotional signals are of interest to the partner and are responded to contingently and predictably. As a result, young children have the opportunity to acquire some of the basic rules of social interaction; they are also able to obtain help in expressing their emotional expressions and modulating them in accordance with others' expectations.

Just how important such learning opportunities are can best be appreciated by deliberately interfering with the interactive flow. This has been done by means of the 'still-face' paradigm – a procedure conducted under laboratory conditions in which a mother is asked first to interact as usual with her baby, thus setting up an expectation of normal communication, and then to become silent and unresponsive for several minutes on end. By recording the baby's behaviour and comparing it in the two conditions, one can then determine the effects of such perturbation (see Cohn & Tronick, 1983; Tronick, Als, Adamson, Wise & Brazelton, 1978, for details). These are notable from 2 months on: babies are clearly puzzled and then increasingly upset by their failure to obtain the usual interest and responsiveness from the mother. They first make active attempts to engage the mother, looking and smiling at her; when these fail they cease to smile, while such other emotional expressions as crying, frowning and grimacing increase in frequency. Looks at the mother gradually become briefer until eventually the baby turns away altogether, as though the sight of the mother is too painful to bear. The baby then looks self-absorbed and 'depressed' – a condition which may continue for some little while when the mother resumes her normal behaviour.

It is apparent from these observations that the mother's emotional unavailability is a highly distressing event – more so even than the mother's temporary physical unavailability, as seen when reactions to the still-face condition were compared with behaviour during the mother's departure from the room (Field, 1994). In the first year of life children are old enough to have established definite expectations about the kind of responsiveness provided by mothers, but still too young to do without their support and be able to regulate their emotional behaviour independently. The mother needs to be available in order to offer optimal levels of stimulation, modulate the child's level of arousal and shape the course of the child's further emotional development by the way she reciprocates the child's affective responses. If she is not – and this is likely to happen on a much more prolonged basis when the mother suffers from depression – the course of the child's emotional development may well be at risk (see box 3.6).

Emotional Competence

The idea that people differ in intelligence is universally accepted, but the notion that one can similarly assess individuals' adequacy of emotional functioning has been much slower in gaining recognition. This is largely because emotions seem to be so much more vague and woolly than cognitive characteristics, and the idea that one can actually measure emotional functioning and determine that one individual is coping better than another has only lately been given serious consideration. However, we are now at last beginning to appreciate that emotional competence ought to be regarded as an aspect of our psychological make-up that is as important as intellectual competence: thus, when Daniel Goleman published his book *Emotional Intelligence* in 1995, it aroused widespread popular interest with its emphasis on the need to develop 'emotional literacy' and its warnings about the dire consequences of emotional malfunctioning. We have now accumulated sufficient research findings to understand something of the nature and determinants of the individual differences which make up competence in this aspect of human behaviour, and in particular we can justify the assertion that these differences have their roots in early childhood and in the influences that are at work then.

What is emotional competence?

Answering this question is complicated by the fact that emotional development refers to so many diverse aspects. Table 5.5 lists eight principal components that

Table 5.5 Components of emotional competence

---

1 Awareness of one's own emotional state.

2 Ability to discern others' emotions.

3 Ability to use the vocabulary of emotion commonly available in one's (sub)culture.

4 Capacity for sympathetic involvement in others' emotional experiences.

5 Ability to realize that inner emotional state need not correspond to outer expression, both in oneself and in others.

6 Capacity for adaptive coping with aversive or distressing emotions.

7 Awareness that relationships are largely defined by how emotions are communicated and by the reciprocity of emotions within the relationship.

8 Capacity for emotional self-efficacy, i.e. feeling in control of and accepting one's own emotional experiences.

Source: From Saarni (1999).

make up emotional competence, each one representing a skill that children need to master on the road to maturity. These eight components do not necessarily come in one unitary package: being proficient in one does not guarantee being proficient in any other, let alone all of them. To express emotional competence by one IQ-like index would therefore be meaningless; a profile that describes the various strengths and weaknesses of an individual across the principal constituents may be more useful, though a formal assessment tool for such a purpose has yet to be developed.

What can be regarded as competent must, of course, always be judged in relation to the individual's age. A 4-year-old may be well advanced in comparison with other children of that age, yet be quite immature in relation to a 10-year-old. Just as with intelligence so with emotional competence: both must always be tied to particular age periods. Judgements of competence need also to take into account the individual's cultural background: as we have mentioned before, what is regarded as 'mature' behaviour in one social setting may not be so in another. Compare the Utku Eskimos with the Yanomamo Indians (pp. 141–2 and 140–1 above): the very different values attached to the role of aggression in social inter-action ensures that each society pictures the emotionally competent individual in very different terms. Similarly, comparing Thailand with the United States, for exam-ple, the emotionally inhibited, shy individual valued amongst the Thai would be regarded as incompetent in the more freely expressive American society (see p. 32). Every culture makes demands on its members to conform to certain partic-ular standards, but in every case it is also possible to differentiate those who are emotionally competent from those who are incompetent.

Emotional competence is closely linked to social competence, and especially so because skill in dealing with one's own and others' emotions is central in social interactions (Halberstadt, Denham & Dunsmore, 2001). This becomes particularly obvious with respect to peer interaction, where popularity and friendship depend to a considerable extent on the success with which a child can sensitively link his or her own emotions to those of others. Here are some examples from research findings (e.g. Calkins, Gill, Johnson & Smith, 1999; Fabes & Eisenberg, 1992; Murphy & Eisenberg, 1997):

- Children who have developed constructive ways of managing their emotional experiences (e.g. keeping their temper; checking their tears) are more successful generally in their relationships with peers.
- Children adept at clearly signalling their emotional states to others are regarded as more likeable by other children.
- Children more accurate in choosing appropriate emotional messages tend to be more popular.
- Children who are more positively expressive have better peer relationships than children who are more negatively expressive.
- Children who interpret others' emotional messages accurately score highest in social approval.

- Children who can cope with anger in a non-aggressive way are better liked, more successful as leaders and generally more socially competent.

These are some of the examples which show how close the connections are between children's emotional behaviour and their interpersonal relationships. Whether children are popular or unpopular, whether they have friends or not, whether they have a constructive or destructive influence on group functioning – these and other aspects of social interaction are influenced by how children manage their emotions. Children characterized by intense emotionality and by poor control over its expression tend to have a disruptive influence: they are more likely to stir up conflict and are at greater risk of being rejected by the peer group than children who have developed the ability to manage their own emotional reactions. Emotional competence and social competence are thus overlapping concepts; indeed, some writers regard them as one entity more appropriately referred to as *affective social competence* (see Halberstadt et al., 2001).

From other-control to self-control

In the graphic words of Frijda (1986), people not only *have* emotions, they also *handle* them. Let us therefore single out one aspect of emotional competence, namely, the ability to inhibit or modulate one's emotions in a socially acceptable manner. Being able to regulate, control, redirect and modify one's impulses in conformity with the norms of society is essential if society is to run smoothly, as seen in particular with respect to aggressive impulses. Individuals incapable of checking these and giving vent to violence directed at others must be regarded as an example of extreme emotional incompetence, in that they have failed to progress along the route that children are normally expected to take, i.e. from a reliance on external to a reliance on internal controls.

The transfer of emotional control from caregiver to child is a major developmental task, which takes the whole of childhood and is really never wholly achieved, for even as adults we are not totally self-sufficient but, especially at times of crisis, remain dependent on those close to us. However, in the course of childhood we gradually accumulate a range of strategies for regulating our emotional feelings and expressions (see table 5.6 for some of the main ones), and the wider the range and the more flexible the individual becomes in using them, the more successful social adaptation is likely to be. Just when various strategies become available will depend on sensorimotor and cognitive development, and the following four-period outline presents a summary of this developmental course (for further details see Cole, Michel & Teti, 1994).

1 *Infancy (0–1 years).* Initially babies are very much dependent on adults for coping with distress: their cries are a signal for caregivers to soothe and comfort. Yet surprisingly early on, babies begin to make use of self-regulating

Table 5.6 Strategies for the self-regulation of emotions

Strategy	Behavioural expression	Age at appearance
Attention redirection	Looking away from source of emotional arousal	Around 3 months
Self-comforting	Finger sucking, hair twirling, rocking	First year
Seeking out adult	Clinging, following, calling for and other attachment behaviours used for security	Second half of first year
Use of transitional object	Clutching soft toy, cloth or other comforting inanimate object	Second half of first year
Physical avoidance	Walking away from emotionally distressing situation	Beginning of second year
Fantasy play	Expressing emotions safely in make-believe play	Second to third year
Verbal control	Talking about emotions with others, thinking about them	Preschool period
Suppression of emotional feeling	Deliberately switching thoughts away from source of distress	Preschool period
Conceptualizing emotions	Reflecting on emotional experiences and verbalizing ideas in an abstract way	Mid-childhood
Cognitive distancing	Self-conscious awareness of how emotions are generated and managed	Mid-childhood

techniques – first perhaps come across fortuitously, such as when a thumb strays into the mouth and produces the desired calming effect; subsequently employed as part of the regular behaviour repertoire. A particularly effective technique is seen even in very young babies: when some event is too arousing they look away, as found, for instance, during face-to-face interaction when an adult overstimulates the baby. At first this is a purely automatic process, but subsequently it will evolve into quite deliberate actions such as covering of eyes or ears.

2   *Toddlerhood (1–3 years)*. Once children are able to walk they can physically remove themselves from undesirable situations. In addition they can actively seek out the adults to whom they are attached and, by clinging to them or at least remaining physically close to them, they can take the initiative in obtain-

ing comfort from them. Processes of emotion regulation now move to a more symbolic level as children gradually become capable of thinking about events. Thus, they can use make-believe play as an outlet for their feelings, start talking about their experiences and, most important, develop a sense of themselves as autonomous agents who can take control of events. At the same time, caregivers remain essential to help them cope with all but the milder sources of arousal.

3   *Preschool period (3–5 years).* Children become increasingly capable of using language and thought for considering emotions, thereby objectifying these phenomena and putting a distance between them and themselves. Thus they can find different ways of interpreting events in attempts to make them harmless; similarly, by discussing them with others, they can share their feelings and hear others' interpretations. Their ability to mimic emotion in play increases, and they become more capable of masking or minimizing the feelings they experience.

4   *Later childhood (5 years on).* Cognitive ability enables children to take an increasingly abstract attitude to emotions and reflect upon them in a more impersonal way. They can show self-conscious awareness of how emotions are managed, and so ask themselves 'How can I best cope with my fear/anger/shame/etc.?' They also now develop ways of regulating emotions in others, e.g. by finding ways of lessening another child's anger, thereby also controlling the extent to which they themselves are exposed to emotion-arousing stimulation. Thus the range of regulating strategies increases, and differences between children in the kinds of strategies they employ and their success in using them become more and more obvious.

The above scheme is an ideal, and many children do not attain it. Maladaptive ways of managing emotions can emerge during any of the above periods, and in so far as emotional malfunctioning is a basic feature of most forms of psychopathology in later life, it is clearly essential to investigate the reasons for its emergence in childhood.

Why do children differ in emotional competence?

There are many possible reasons why some children become more competent than others; for simplicity's sake, let us group these under the three headings of biological, interpersonal and ecological influences.

*   *Biological influences.* Temperamental differences of primarily genetic origin are to a large extent responsible for variations in emotional behaviour. Characteristics such as the intensity of emotional responsiveness, the threshold of responsiveness, the ability to inhibit impulses and the ease of soothability when aroused have been mentioned as forming constitutionally based and relatively stable aspects of our individuality, with considerable implica-

tions for the ability to gain control over emotional impulses. This becomes particularly evident in cases of pathology: Down's syndrome children, for instance, are said to have problems with emotion regulation due, in part, to delayed maturation of those tracts in the brain that exert inhibitory influences over behaviour, and in part to their low physiological reactivity (Cicchetti, Ganiban & Barnett, 1991). As a result, such children tend to be hard to arouse yet, once aroused, have difficulty in controlling their feelings.

- *Interpersonal influences.* Whatever part biological factors play, they must interact with numerous external factors to produce the end result (Calkins, 1994). A child's capacity to cope with distress, for example, depends in the first place on inborn temperamental qualities; however, these qualities are affected by the kind of support the child receives from the parents. Where this support is lacking, as in cases of maltreatment (Cicchetti et al., 1991), children are put at risk of not being able to develop the necessary mechanisms for emotional self-control. Similarly, in a family riven by conflict, where they witness repeated displays of emotional outbursts, children will experience little encouragement to control their own emotions; also, in families where parents suffer from psychiatric disorders involving their affective functions such as depression, children are likely to be at risk of irregularities in their own emotional development. As we saw earlier, attachment history has been used to throw light on individual differences in outcome, and as a result links can be traced between variations in emotional competence and the type of relationship formed with the parent in infancy.
- *Ecological influences.* The wider environment in which a child is brought up by his or her family can also account for variations in emotional competence. Take the effects of poverty (Garner, Jones & Miner, 1994; Garner & Spears, 2000): the stresses associated with low income can have deleterious effects on the emotional lives of parents and constitute a definite risk factor for children's socio-emotional functioning. The effect may come about in various ways: such concomitants of poverty as financial worries, overcrowding and ill health may result in less responsive and warm parenting and so produce insecure attachments; tired, overworked and anxious mothers may have less time to talk with their children and thus be unable to discuss emotionally meaningful experiences with them; and anger and aggression tend to be disproportionally prevalent among low-income families on account of their stressful lives, and children will therefore be more exposed to conflict. By no means all children brought up under such circumstances are at an emotional disadvantage; nevertheless, poverty provides us with one example of the need to consider the child's wider environment if we are to understand individual differences in emotional competence.

In all, there is a wide range of different influences at work accounting for variations in emotional competence, and explaining any one child's standing generally requires a range of interacting factors. For example, physically abused children are at risk of emotional development that is deviant in various respects: they are more likely to be unresponsive to the distress of others, they tend to exhibit more anger and fear, they are emotionally more volatile, and their reactions to emotionally arousing situations are often inappropriate and non-adaptive (see Denham, 1998). Yet not all abused children develop in this way; some are remarkably resilient and cope well. Why the difference? The answer may well lie in the sheer number of risk factors the child is exposed to. For example, to parental maltreatment let us add a vulnerable temperament that predisposes the child to react intensely to stress; add furthermore the kind of poverty-stricken environment that makes stressful experiences highly likely, and the odds become much greater that emotional development will take a deviant route. There are, of course, some conditions which exercise such a powerful influence on their own that there is no escape; this applies in particular to certain biological states where impairment in neurophysiological functioning is a direct cause of psychological pathology. Autism is one such example; as detailed in box 5.6, children so afflicted are characterized by emotional malfunctioning as one of the main features of their disorder. In the majority of cases, however, emotional incompetence is a matter of several factors, usually drawn from all of the above three groups, which interact to produce the developmental failure.

BOX 5.6

The pathology of emotion in autistic children

Autism is a relatively rare condition, but one that received an enormous amount of attention on account of its intriguing and (so far) mysterious nature. First thought to be due to 'refrigerator parents', i.e. cold, unfeeling parental treatment, it is now regarded as almost certainly an inborn organic condition, possibly of genetic origin. No treatment is yet available, though children with milder versions can be helped to function reasonably well in society.

From the early years on, autistic children show three main kinds of psychological problems: (1) a failure to develop normal social relationships; (2) abnormalities and retardation in language development; (3) ritualistic and repetitive behaviour patterns. A large number of research studies in recent years have thrown some light on the specific processes underlying these general deficits. Autistic children's language problems, for example, are thought to be linked to deficits in the cognitive skills of sequencing, abstraction and organizing; while their difficulties in forming relationships are said to stem from lacking 'theory of mind' skills, in that these children appear to be unable to appreciate what others are thinking, and indeed even to realize that other people are thinking beings, i.e. that they have a 'mind'.

Such social problems are reflected in the emotional deficits typical of this disorder. Autistic children have repeatedly been found to lack the capacity for empathy with others: in experiments where an adult feigned distress such as pain or fear, autistic children, unlike typically developing children, would pay little attention to the adult's face and instead examine the object allegedly responsible for this reaction. Thus they make little use of emotional messages sent by others, or at least do so in a detached way, suggesting that they are not very interested in other people and in their feelings. For that matter, autistic children have problems in simply differentiating other people's emotions – not surprisingly perhaps, for they rarely establish eye contact with anyone. When typically developing, mentally handicapped and autistic children were asked in one study to sort photos of people's faces, both the former groups did so on the basis of facial expression; autistic children, on the other hand, sorted by type of hat worn.

Other areas of emotional functioning are also implicated, such as the children's own emotional displays. Thus they show less positive affect such as pleasure and joy when interacting with parents or peers; they also tend to express their emotions under inappropriate circumstances: sad when they ought to be pleased, pleased when they ought to be sad. As a result they fail to coordinate their emotional displays with those of others and so disrupt the smooth functioning of a peer group, resulting in unpopularity and rejection. Some autistic children are intellectually very bright and have little difficulty mastering cognitive tasks at the appropriate age, such as grasping the idea of physical causality. Yet while they can understand that kicking a ball will propel it in a certain direction, they cannot understand problems involving psychological causality, for example that disappointment may lead to another person feeling sad.

Such emotional deficits are bound to be closely linked to deficits in social functioning. If children cannot recognize the meaning of others' emotional signals, whether conveyed by facial expression, gesture or vocalization, they will have great difficulty in participating in interpersonal exchanges. And if they cannot even differentiate one emotion from another, they will behave inappropriately with other people and so compound the difficulties they experience already (Denham, 1998; P. Harris, 1989; Rutter, 1999).

Summary

At one time emotions were thought of entirely in negative terms – as disruptive, alien processes that merely interfere with people's efficient functioning. It is only fairly recently that a much more positive view has come to prevail, according to which emotions are seen as helpful to the task of adaptation and, above all, to play an essential part in interpersonal relationships.

Emotions are biologically based, being part of the inborn equipment of all human beings. A number of basic emotions can be discerned from the early weeks on, whereas others appear subsequently at given points in the course of development because they require more complex cognitive functions, such as a sense of self, that are not found until after infancy. A biological basis means that all human beings share the same emotions; this is confirmed by anthropological evidence from isolated, preliterate societies and from observations of children born blind and deaf. Subsequently, however, the way we show our emotions and the circumstances under which we do so will vary according to upbringing and experience.

Children do not only experience emotions; they think about them. Once they are able to talk they can label them, reflect upon them and discuss them with others. Also from the third year on they can make inferences about other people's inner states, and become increasingly capable of understanding the causes of others' emotions and of anticipating their consequences. This in turn makes it possible in due course to construct sophisticated theories as to why people behave as they do, and thus to acquire more and more complex skills in 'mindreading'.

This process is greatly furthered by children's conversations about emotions, first with parents and then with other children. These show that even quite young children have great curiosity about the reasons for their own feelings and those of others, and in families where such conversations occur frequently children tend to be more advanced in their emotional understanding than in other families. Emotional development thus becomes shaped by social experience, and this is seen most clearly when comparing the 'display rules' which children in different cultures are expected to acquire, i.e. the norms for expressing particular emotions under particular circumstances.

Just as individuals differ in intellectual competence, so they differ in emotional competence. There are many reasons for these differences: biological, referring to temperamental and other inborn characteristics; interpersonal, i.e. the way in which the child is brought up; and ecological, such as poverty. A particularly important component refers to the ability to regulate and control one's own emotions, for failure to acquire such a skill can have disastrous social consequences. Development of this ability is a matter of transfer of control from caregiver to child – a process that takes the whole of childhood and involves the acquisition of a variety of strategies for regulating our feelings and expressions.

FURTHER READING

Denham, S. (1998). *Emotional Development in Young Children.* New York: Guilford Press. A warm-hearted account, with plenty of case illustrations. Referring primarily to development in the preschool period, the book provides an informative outline of information gathered from recent research.

Fox, N. A. (ed.) (1994). The development of emotion regulation: Biological and behavioral considerations. *Monographs of the Society for Research in Child Development,* 59 (2–3, Serial No. 240). Specifically about the topic of emotion regulation, this monograph contains chapters on a wide range of physiological, behavioural and interpersonal aspects, giving an insight into the kinds of questions asked by research workers and the methods used to find answers.

Oatley, K., & Jenkins, J. M. (1996). *Understanding Emotions.* Oxford: Blackwell. An excellent introduction to the study of emotion, including a chapter on developmental aspects. Presents emotions in their evolutionary and cultural contexts, and pays special attention to psychopathological aspects.

Saarni, C. (1999). *The Development of Emotional Competence.* New York: Guilford Press. A lucid explanation of emotional competence and of the various components that make up this concept. Strongly influenced by the author's clinical experience, in that it pays special attention to developmental failures and malfunctioning.

CHAPTER SIX

The Child as Scientist: Piaget's Theory of Cognitive Development

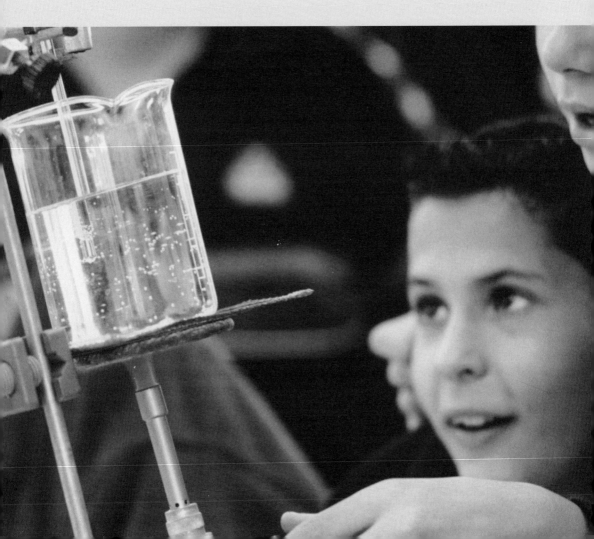

Chapter Outline

Cognition refers to knowing, and cognitive development to the acquisition of know-ledge in childhood. Included here are such processes as understanding, reasoning, thinking, problem solving, learning, conceptualizing, classifying and remembering – in short, all those aspects of human intelligence that we use to adapt to and make sense of the world.

Traditionally, in contrast to the 'hot' topic of emotional development, that of cognitive development has been treated as 'cold', in that it is concerned with purely intellectual functions that supposedly can be studied separately from socio-emotional functions. In this chapter we shall describe an immensely influential and in many respects highly productive theory that takes such a 'cold' view of cognitive develop-ment, namely, that put forward by Jean Piaget, who produced what is still the most comprehensive account of the way children come to understand the world. We shall also see, however, that in some respects his account was a little too cold, and in the following chapter we shall therefore turn to another view of cognitive development, that put forward by Lev Vygotsky, who to some extent attempted to redress the balance and relate intellectual to socio-emotional aspects of human behaviour.

Overview

Jean Piaget was the dominant voice in child psychology for a large part of the twentieth century. A Swiss by birth, his enormous output of theoretical propositions and empirical observations during a long lifetime (1896–1980) transformed our ways of thinking about children and their intellectual development. It is perhaps ironic that Piaget never held any formal qualifications in psychology, having origin-ally specialized in biology – a subject in which he published his first paper (an obser-vation on an albino sparrow) at the age of 11. However, in his adolescence Piaget also became keenly interested in epistemology, i.e. that branch of philosophy which is concerned with the origins of knowledge, and this remained his abiding interest throughout his life. To investigate this topic, however, Piaget decided to take a develop-mental approach and, by psychological methods, trace the way in which children acquire the basic tools of knowledge and come to develop these into sophisticated means of adapting to their environment.

Piaget published over 50 books, with titles such as *Judgment and Reasoning in the Child* (1926), *The Child's Conception of the World* (1929), *Play, Dreams and Imitation in Childhood* (1951) and *The Construction of Reality in the Child* (1954). Yet at first his influence was slow to spread – in part because he published in French and the Anglo-American world did not become acquainted with his books until, many years later, they were translated into English; in part also because his methodological approach and theoretical concepts were very different in many respects from those prevalent at the time. In due course, however, Piagetian theory aroused worldwide interest and inspired a large number of other investigators – first to replicate Piaget's findings with other samples, then to fill in gaps and extend his work to related topics, and eventually to modify and in certain respects replace his conclusions.

Aims and methods

Early on in his career Piaget worked for a time with Binet, the father of the IQ, on the standardization of intelligence tests, a task that involved scoring children's answers to questions as 'correct' or 'incorrect'. However, Piaget soon realized that what really interested him was not whether children succeeded or failed but *how* they arrived at the answer given, whatever it was. In other words, it was the mental processes underlying children's answers that he wanted to uncover: what they tell us about the child's conception of the world, how these processes change with age, and how the child thus becomes increasingly able to cope with reality. Unlike Binet, he was little concerned with individual differences and intellectual performance as an indicator of mental age; it was the general character of intelligence rather than its manifestation in specific individuals that he set out to investigate. As a result, he paid little attention to questions of sampling when selecting children for study – indeed, some of his most influential work was based on just three children, namely, his own. Norms of development were left to Binet and his colleagues to establish; Piaget's aim was to investigate the *nature* of development – an aim he hoped to achieve by tracing the way in which children become progressively more capable of adapting to their environment.

Piaget's work went through two main phases:

1 Initially, he investigated how children develop an understanding of certain specific concepts – such as time, space, velocity, class, relation and causality – that are the basic categories of knowledge and are fundamental to our grasp of reality. Most of these studies involved children in the 3- to 10-year range, from whom he obtained the relevant information through interviews aimed at elucidating each child's view of some particular phenomenon: 'What makes clouds move?', 'Where do dreams come from?', 'Why do rivers flow?' The interviews were entirely unstandardized, in that each question depended on the child's previous answer and proceeded until Piaget felt he had grasped how that child thought of that phenomenon (see box 6.1 for an example). As Piaget put it: 'I engage my subjects in conversation patterned after psychiatric questioning, with the aim of discovering something about the reasoning underlying their right but especially their wrong answers.' By interviewing children of different ages, Piaget traced the development of understanding of each concept, and it was this which first convinced him that changes in thinking occur in stepwise manner and not gradually, and that development is therefore most appropriately described in terms of stages. Take the example given in table 6.1 from Piaget's investigation of children's conception of causality. By asking a series of questions such as 'What makes clouds move?', Piaget obtained answers that convinced him that qualitatively different ways of thinking are typical of different age ranges, and that the development of understanding this particular concept could best be described as

a three-stage sequence proceeding from 'magical' to 'animistic' to 'logical' comprehension.

Table 6.1   Stages in the understanding of causality

Sample question: What makes clouds move?

Type of thinking	Illustrative answers
1 Magical (up to 3 years), i.e. child can influence external objects through thought or action	'We make them move by walking'
2 Animistic (3–7 years), i.e. child attributes own characteristics to objects	'They move themselves because they are alive'
3 Logical (8 years on), i.e. child understands the world in impersonal terms	'The wind moves them'

2   In the second phase of his work Piaget moved over to a much more global view of intellectual development. Instead of examining separate aspects of children's understanding, he combined these into an all-embracing scheme referring to the totality of cognitive growth from birth to maturity, and instead of putting forward developmental stages for individual concepts he proposed a four-stage sequential scheme to explain intellectual growth as a whole. We shall describe these four stages in detail below; here let us note that the downward extension of the age range investigated to infancy meant that Piaget could no longer rely exclusively on interviews and that observation of both spontaneous behaviour and reactions to specifically set-up situations played a very much more important role. For example, in order to find out about children's ability to classify things, Piaget would give them a set of carefully selected objects or pictures (houses, people, toys, animals, etc.) and ask them to put into groups those that 'go together' or that 'are similar'. In this way he would determine when children first understand the notion of classification and be able to investigate the criteria according to which they put things together – such as perceptual features like size or colour, as commonly found at younger ages, or more abstract characteristics such as type of object (e.g. toys vs. clothes) or usage (e.g. edible or not). As before, Piaget was not so much interested in the right or wrong of children's performance as in the manner in which they set about tackling tasks and what this revealed about the child's mental organization at that time, and for this purpose he kept detailed protocols of behaviour and of verbal responses, liberally quoting from these in all of his books (box 6.1 provides an example).

BOX 6.1

Piaget's data-gathering techniques

To illustrate the methods Piaget used to obtain information from the children he investigated, we quote two protocols below. The first is an example of the clinical interview method – an open-ended conversation designed to throw light on the way in which a child thinks about and explains some particular phenomenon. In this case the phenomenon being investigated is the nature of dreams; the child being interviewed is aged 5 years 9 months.

> Piaget: 'Where does the dream come from?' Child: 'I think you sleep so well that you dream.' P: 'Does it come from us or from outside?' C: 'From outside.' P: 'What do we dream with?' C: 'I don't know.' P: 'With the hands? With nothing?' C: 'Yes, with nothing.' P: 'When you are in bed and you dream, where is the dream?' C: 'In my bed, under the blanket. I don't really know. If it was in my stomach the bones would be in the way and I shouldn't see it.' P: 'Is the dream there when you sleep?' C: 'Yes, it is in the bed beside me.' P: 'Is the dream in your head?' C: 'It is I that am in the dream; it isn't in my head. When you dream you don't know you are in the bed. You know you are walking. You are in the dream. You are in the bed, but you don't know you are.' . . . P: 'When the dream is in the room, is it near you?' C: 'Yes, there!' (pointing to 30 cm in front of his eyes).

This excerpt comes from a book, published in 1929, entitled *The Child's Conception of the World*, which includes an account of Piaget's investigation of children's understanding of mental phenomena such as thought and dreams. While it demonstrates Piaget's skill and persistence in posing a great variety of detailed, relevant questions, it also shows that there can be some danger of putting ideas into the child's mind that were not there before – a consideration which was one of the reasons for Piaget's relying rather less on interview techniques in his later work. Nevertheless, it is apparent that the child quoted here has some difficulty in conceiving of mental phenomena such as dreams as *mental*, seeing them rather in physical terms, i.e. as things with substance. Piaget referred to this tendency as *realism*, seen as well in the identification of thought with the act of speaking which he also uncovered in his interviews with young children around the age of 4 or 5.

Our second example comes from Piaget's later work (it is taken from a book published in 1954, entitled *The Construction of Reality in the Child*) and illustrates the use of observation of a very young child's behaviour. The child was Piaget's own daughter Jacqueline, who was 18 months at the time.

Jacqueline is sitting on a green rug and playing with a potato which interests her very much (it is a new object for her). She says 'po-terre' and amuses herself by putting it into an empty box and taking it out again. . . . I then take the potato and put it in the box while Jacqueline watches. Then I place the box under the rug and turn it upside down, thus leaving the object hidden by the rug without letting the child see my manoeuvre, and I bring out the empty box. I say to Jacqueline, who has not stopped looking at the rug and who has realised that I was doing something under it: 'Give Papa the potato.' She searches for the object in the box, looks at me, again looks at the box minutely, looks at the rug, etc., but it does not occur to her to raise the rug in order to find the potato underneath.

Many of Piaget's observations are of children's wholly spontaneous behaviour, but as in this case he also made use of semi-experiments in which he tested children's reactions to various specifically set-up situations – the observational equivalent of assessing their mental processes by means of interview questions. The present instance is part of Piaget's investigation of children's ability to conceive of objects as permanent entities – a development which, as we shall see, forms an extremely important part of intellectual growth in the first 2 years of life.

Basic features of theory

Nature or nurture? For cognitive development, as with other aspects of behaviour, this question has generated persistent controversy. On the one hand, there are those who believe that the environment merely supplies content for already existing mental structures and that it is these innate structures that are the primary foundations of cognitive growth. On the other hand, there is the view that all aspects of development are explicable in terms of environmental stimulation and that it is therefore the child's learning experiences that need to be investigated if one is to understand the acquisition of knowledge.

The essence of Piaget's developmental theory is that intellectual development can only be accounted for by considering the dynamic and continuous *interaction* of child and environment. To give priority to the child's nature or to environmental influences is meaningless; instead, if we are to understand how children acquire knowledge, we need to plot in detail how, throughout the years, the child acts upon the environment and the environment upon the child. This was the task that Piaget set himself. He did not believe that the young baby, newly arrived in the world, is an empty vessel passively to be filled by experience, but is rather a being already equipped with a certain psychological organization, however primitive, which predisposes her to make use of whatever information she encounters in quite specific

Table 6.2 Definitions of some Piagetian terms

Term	Definition
Intelligence	According to Piaget, 'intelligence is a particular instance of biological adaptation'. It refers to the mental processes whereby such adaptation is brought about and not to the differences between individuals in their cognitive competence.
Adaptation	The inborn tendency found in all biological organisms to adjust to the demands of the environment.
Schema	The basic cognitive structure founded on sensorimotor action or thought which individuals use to make sense of their experience.
Assimilation	The mental process whereby an individual incorporates new experiences into existing schemas, thus transforming incoming information to fit previous ways of thinking.
Accommodation	The mental process whereby the individual modifies existing schemas to fit new experiences, thus adapting previous modes of thought to incoming information.
Equilibrium	The state of affairs when the individual's schemas are in balance with the environment. When there is disequilibrium, a restructuring of schemas needs to occur.

ways. At all stages of development children are capable of selecting, interpreting, transforming and recreating experience in order to fit it in with their existing mental structures. Initially these structures are very simple, based primarily on reflex activities such as sucking. Give a 2-month-old baby a doll and she will attempt to suck it rather than play with it in any of the diverse ways seen in a 2-year-old. As Piaget put it, the baby *assimilates* the doll to her sucking scheme because sucking is predominant at the time and will thus determine how children of that age make use of the objects they come upon. At the same time, however, the baby learns from such an encounter that the doll has other possibilities, as a result of which new ways of acting on it will come into being: stroking, cuddling, bending, shaking, etc. The baby, that is, *accommodates* herself to the nature of the object. The twin processes of **assimilation** and **accommodation** represent, according to Piaget, the basic mechanisms of cognitive change: on the one hand, children incorporate external reality into their own psychological structures; on the other hand, they are also thereby impelled to modify and extend their repertoire of actions to suit the demands of the environment (see table 6.2 for a definition of some Piagetian terms).

This simple example illustrates some of the most basic features of Piagetian theory:

Assimilation is Piaget's term for the taking in of information by using already existing mental structures.

Accommodation is the term used in Piaget's theory for the modification of mental structures to incorporate new information.

- Intelligence does not begin with the relatively sophisticated mental processes that that word normally conjures up, but rather with the primitive reflex-like action patterns present at birth. However, these action patterns are modifiable: they will change, adapt, combine and become more elaborate as a consequence of encounters with things in the external world.

- Knowledge is *constructed* through child–environment interaction. It is neither innately organized nor supplied by experience alone, but arises from the child's active exploration of things and (later) of ideas. Acquiring knowledge is thus action based, and never a process of passively accumulating information. This applies to all ages: just as the baby has to act upon the doll to discover its properties, so the school-age child has to act upon and manipulate mental ideas in order to find out their possibilities.

- The growth of intelligence is to be conceived of as a course of ever more precise and complex adaptation to the environment. All biological organisms strive successfully to adapt to their environment, and this is achieved through the twin processes of assimilation and accommodation – making use of external objects to 'feed' existing mental structures on the one hand, and being modified in the process by such experience on the other.

- Whenever a child encounters a new experience that does not correspond to her existing mental structures, she is in **disequilibrium**. Children, driven by their curiosity, constantly encounter such experiences and are then impelled to make sense of them, i.e. to seek **equilibrium**. This, according to Piaget, constitutes the motive force for intellectual growth; it will only occur, however, if the event is not too discrepant from what the child is already familiar with – hence the importance for parents and teachers of providing the child with new experiences that are at an optimal level of familiarity–unfamiliarity.

Disequilibrium. In Piagetian theory the mental state when the individual encounters new information for which no mental structures exist as yet.

Equilibrium. In Piagetian theory this is the state reached through **assimilation** and **accommodation** when the individual has absorbed and made sense of new information.

We can now appreciate why Piaget liked to refer to children as 'little scientists'. Just as scientists, confronted with some new problem, try to make sense of their observations by first fitting them into their existing theories and then, if not successful, extending these theories or creating new ones, so children will initially try out familiar ways of assimilating an unfamiliar event and then accommodate their existing mental and action patterns to fit the new experience. In both cases the individual is actively involved in looking for a solution, experimenting (perhaps on a trial-and-error basis) with different ways of achieving understanding, and eventually, by means of a creative act, responding to the challenge and so producing a satisfactory match between observation and comprehension. Consider the following observation reported by Piaget of his 10-month-old son:

Laurent is lying on his back . . . He grasps in succession a celluloid swan, a box, etc., stretches out his arm and lets them fall. He distinctly varies the positions of the fall. Sometimes he stretches out his arm vertically, sometimes he holds it out obliquely, in front of or behind his eyes, etc. When the object falls in a new position . . . he lets it fall two or three more times in the same place, as though to study the spatial relation; then he modifies the situation. At a certain moment the swan falls near his mouth; now he does not suck it (even though this object habitually serves this purpose), but drops it three times more while merely making the gesture of opening his mouth. (***Piaget, 1953***)

Here is a child busily making discoveries, driven by curiosity to investigate whatever potential new experiences he can uncover, wanting to learn all about these by active exploration, and in the process uncovering something of importance to him about the properties of objects and their behaviour in space. He may have made the discovery in the first place by chance, but just like a scientist his inquisitiveness leads him to explore the new phenomenon in all sorts of different ways, determinedly pursuing various possibilities and then carefully noting the consequences. The boundaries of knowledge, for the child as for the scientist, become progressively extended thereby.

Stages of Cognitive Development

An essential part of Piaget's theory is his belief in the stage-like progression of development. Piaget did not consider that cognitive development could simply be regarded as the quantitative accretion of knowledge: he saw it as a series of steps rather than as a continuous line, where each step represents a way of thinking about the world that is *qualitatively different* from the stage before and the stage after. Piaget concluded from his observations that wholly new strategies of understanding emerge periodically in the course of childhood, and while initially he confined himself to describing these for various individual mental concepts such as described above for causality, he eventually put all these together in one encompassing scheme involving four major stages. There are thus three points in childhood (around the end of the second year, at about 6 or 7 years and at roughly 11 or 12 years) when major mental reorganization takes place – a reorganization that Piaget believed to be profound and to apply to all aspects of understanding. Children vary in the age when they reach these points, and not all individuals achieve the final stage; the sequence, however, is invariant in that a child cannot function at a higher stage without having gone through the previous stages. Each of the stages represents an increasingly complex and adaptive way of making sense of the environment; each results in a qualitatively different way of understanding. The characteristics of the four stages are described below; table 6.3 provides a brief outline.

Table 6.3 Piaget's stages of cognitive development

Stage	Distinguishing features
Sensorimotor (birth to 2 years)	Babies depend on sensory and motor means of learning about and understanding their environment. Cognitive structures are action based, becoming increasingly complex and coordinated. Only in the latter parts of this period will actions be internalized to form the first representational symbols.
Preoperational (2–7 years)	Children are capable of using symbols (words, mental images) in their efforts to understand the world. Imaginative play becomes possible, with children able clearly to distinguish fantasy from reality. Thinking is primarily egocentric, and not until the latter part of this period will children become capable of taking into account the viewpoint of others.
Concrete operations (7–11 years)	Children acquire a variety of mental operations such as multiple classification, reversibility, seriation and conservation whereby they can mentally manipulate symbols in different ways. Logical thought appears, but problem solving is still mainly tied to concrete events rather than abstract concepts.
Formal operations (11 years on)	Children are now capable of mental operations involving abstractions and logical reasoning. They can consider a variety of possible solutions to a problem without having to act them out, in that they are able to deal with entirely hypothetical situations. Thinking is increasingly about ideas rather than objects.

Sensorimotor stage

This period extends approximately over the first 2 years, and derives its name from its principal characteristic, namely, the fact that children initially come to know the world in terms of the actions they perform upon their environment. Knowledge, that is, is obtained through sucking, grasping, watching, stroking, biting and other such overt responses performed on the objects in the child's world, and is not yet derived from the internal thought processes that enable children later on to manipulate objects mentally. However, Piaget believed that the initial action-based stage is an essential prelude to the development of thinking; mental operations, according to him, are internalized actions.

While sensorimotor activity is children's dominant way of relating to the environment in the first 2 years or so, development within the stage is by no means static and can, according to Piaget, be described as a series of substages. Let us pick out the most important general trends in this sequence:

- *From rigid to flexible action patterns.* Children are born with a number of response patterns that enable them from the beginning to come into contact with their environment. These patterns are initially able to cope with only certain quite specific stimuli: sucking, for example, is present from birth but is at first elicited in a reflex-like manner only by the nipple; all other objects with which the lips come into contact are rejected. However, based on very detailed observations of his own three children, Piaget describes how, in the course of the early months, rigidity gives way to flexibility as the baby gradually becomes able to adapt his behaviour to an ever larger range of stimuli. At the age of 9 days, for instance, Laurent, his son, accidentally comes into contact with his hand, which he tries to suck but then immediately relinquishes; he then tries to suck his quilt but with the same result. Nothing but the maternal breast will do. Yet only a week or two later the baby began to suck his thumb at length; gradually he also accepted a diversity of other objects such as the previously rejected quilt, his father's finger and toys of various shapes and texture. Moreover, whereas at first sucking only occurred when the object came into contact with the lips, the baby gradually learned to associate the appearance of the object with the act: thus at 4 months Jacqueline, Piaget's daughter, opened her mouth as soon as she was shown the bottle, and at 7 months she opened her mouth differently according to whether she was offered a bottle or a spoon. It is adaptations such as these that constitute, in Piaget's view, the beginnings of intelligence.

- *From isolated to coordinated action patterns.* Initially objects are there to be looked at, or grasped, or sucked. Only subsequently will babies learn that a series of different actions can be performed simultaneously or in coordinated sequence upon the same object. For example, a very young baby will grasp an object only if his hand comes into contact with it; no attempt is then made to bring the object up to his eyes in order visually to examine it. This is a subsequent development, though initially it will occur only if object and hand are in the same visual field. Eventually the baby will reach for objects he is looking at and look at objects he is grasping; later, moreover, he will coordinate this new visual-motor pattern with sucking by bringing the object to his mouth or (as with a rattle) by shaking it, so producing a sound and thus bringing listening into the picture too. As a result the child's action repertoire becomes greatly more complex, more coordinated and more effective.

- *From reactive to intentional behaviour.* Though the baby is active from the beginning, his activity is at first in no sense intentional and planned. The effects of his actions on the environment are accidentally produced: for example, when a young baby strikes the beads strung across his pram, making them jump up and down and producing a jingling sound, he has no awareness of the connection between action and effect and will therefore make no attempt deliberately to repeat the act. Not until the end of the first year will truly intentional behaviour become evident. Piaget demonstrated this by recording how his three children behaved when confronted by an obstacle while trying to attain some attractive object. Consider the following observation:

> I present Laurent [aged 6 months] with a match box, extending my other hand
> laterally to make an obstacle to his prehension. Laurent tries to pass over my
> hand or to the side, but he does not attempt to displace it. . . . [At $7^1/2$ months,
> however,] Laurent reacts quite differently. I present a box above my obstacle
> hand, but behind it, so that he cannot reach the matches without setting the
> obstacle aside. After trying to take no notice of it Laurent suddenly hits my
> obstacle hand as though to remove it or lower it. I let him, and he grasps
> the box. [When confronted by a cushion instead of the hand] Laurent tries
> to reach the box, and bothered by the obstacle he at once strikes it, definitely
> lowering it until the way is clear.   (**Piaget, 1953**)

Intuitively there is usually no problem of distinguishing intentional from
unintentional behaviour: thus Laurent's dogged determination to attain the
box is very evident. The progression to such forward-looking, planned
behaviour is one of the more important steps in infancy and gives the child's
behaviour a very different, more mature flavour.

- *From overt actions to mental representations.* While sensorimotor activities predominate in infancy, signs of mental processes gradually emerge towards the end
  of this period. Initially, there is no indication that children make use of images,
  symbols, thoughts or any other internal devices. Piaget illustrates this by noting
  behaviour in problem-solving situations such as when a toy is out of reach but
  could be attained by using a nearby stick. For most of the first year babies
  cannot see the connection between the two objects, even when they accidentally
  move the toy while manipulating the stick. Problem solving, at best, is still a
  matter of trial and error; only in the course of the second year will children
  work out *mentally* that the stick can be used as a means to attaining the desired
  end. Initially, children will need to see the stick near the toy to appreciate its
  significance; subsequently, they understand that in such a situation a stick is
  required and, in its absence, go and look for one. When that occurs the child's
  behaviour becomes much more versatile; what is more, the development of
  language at that time makes it easier for children to represent objects and
  people symbolically, so that they can now manipulate these mentally and plan
  their activities around them without actually having to carry out any actions.
  Use of mental representations is still rather primitive and inefficient, yet this
  is a hugely important step towards the mature functioning of human beings.

Object permanence
is Piaget's term for the
realization that objects
are independent
entities that continue
to exist even when the
individual is not aware
of them.

One highly significant development during the sensorimotor stage
deserves special mention, namely, the child's discovery of **object
permanence**. This is the understanding that the world is made up of
external objects that are independent entities which exist whether
we happen to be aware of them or not – an assumption that is so natural to us as adults that we find it difficult to conceive of any other
view. It is a mark of Piaget's genius to have realized that young babies
see the world quite differently from the way adults see it, namely,
entirely in terms of fleeting sensory impressions, and that objects are

merely tied to the baby's own awareness of them. Everything – rattle, thumb, mother, bottle, teddy or anything else the baby comes into contact with – is something that owes its existence to the child looking at it, listening to it or handling it. The moment the baby is no longer in contact with the object, that object ceases to exist: *out of sight, out of mind.* For that matter the baby has no sense of self either, for this too requires an ability to connect different impressions over time, and that is something that children are not capable of in the first year or so.

To bolster his argument Piaget used a hiding test. He would show his participants some attractive toy, and just as they were about to reach for it he would cover the toy with a cloth, concealing it from their sight. Younger babies would immediately act as though out of sight is out of mind: they would stop reaching for the toy, turn their attention elsewhere and behave as though the toy had ceased to exist. Older babies, on the other hand, would continue their attempts to obtain the toy, even though it is now hidden: they would stare at the cover, reach for it and lift it and then search for the toy underneath. Their continuing orientation to the missing object was taken by Piaget as evidence that an idea of the toy remained in their mind and that their knowledge of objects had, so to speak, solidified.

This new conception of objects as permanent entities does not, however, come suddenly, in full-blown, mature form. Piaget traced its development with his usual patient, detailed observations right through infancy, playing hiding games with his children at all sorts of ages and increasing the complexity of the task as the children got older. While the first indications of object permanence appeared some time towards the end of the first year, it was not until almost a year later that Piaget considered the child capable of realizing, in a mature and adult-like way, that things have a continuous existence whether the child is aware of them at the time or not. Object permanence, that is, is an idea that has to be *constructed* by the child: like such other concepts as space and time, Piaget believed that it cannot be taken for granted at the beginning of life but must be given the chance to develop. As detailed in box 6.2, such development tends to be protracted, spanning a major part of the sensorimotor period.

Preoperational stage

The change that occurs in children's cognitive abilities at the end of the second year is a massive one, for now children become able to engage in symbolic thought and are no longer tied to here-and-now reality. A *symbol* is a word or an image that stands for something else, as seen in the following observation by Piaget:

> At 21 months Jacqueline saw a shell and said 'cup'. After saying this she picked it up and pretended to drink. . . . The next day, seeing the same shell, she said 'glass', then 'cup', then 'hat', and finally 'boat in the water'. Three days later she took an empty box and moved it to and fro saying 'motycar'.
> (***Piaget, 1953***)

BOX 6.2

Searching for hidden objects

Throughout their infancy Piaget's three children were confronted with hiding games – to their entertainment no doubt and certainly to their father's and our edification. It was the way in which they responded to these games at different ages by searching or not searching that inspired the idea of *object permanence* and illustrated the developmental course of this concept over the first 2 years.

Piaget described this development in terms of a number of steps. Initially, in the first 4 months or so, babies make no attempt to search for a vanished object. They may briefly stare at the spot where the object (or person) disappeared, but this is no more than a continuation of an ongoing response. Thereafter, up to about 9 or 10 months, babies begin to show a much more active interest in what happens to a vanished object: instead of just passively looking at the last place where the object was seen, they will now visually search for it in a new location. Thus Piaget notes that when Laurent, at the age of 6 months, drops a box while lying down, he will immediately look for it in the right direction. As he continues:

> I then grasp the box and drop it myself, vertically and too fast for him to follow the trajectory. His eyes search for it at once on the sofa where he is lying. I manage to eliminate any sound or shock and I perform the experiment at his right and at his left; the result is always positive.

At this age the baby can anticipate the future position of a moving object by extrapolating from the trajectory, and visual search is now possible. Searching behind a screen, however, is still beyond the baby's ability, as seen in this excerpt:

> Jacqueline [aged almost 8 months] tries to grasp a celluloid duck on top of her quilt. [However, the duck slides away and] falls very close to her hand but behind a fold in the sheet. Jacqueline's eyes have followed the movement, she has even followed it with her outstretched hand. But as soon as the duck has disappeared – nothing more! I then take the duck from its hiding place and place it near her hand three times. All three times she tries to grasp it, but when she is about to touch it I replace it very obviously under the sheet. Jacqueline immediately withdraws her hand and gives up.

Here we see a very clear example of the 'out of sight, out of mind' mentality, in that the child fails to retrieve the object even though she is perfectly capable of carrying out the necessary movements.

From 9 or 10 months on children begin to search for hidden objects and are able to retrieve them from under covers or behind screens. However, their search is still limited, as seen by Jacqueline's behaviour at 10 months of age:

> Jacqueline is seated on a mattress without anything to disturb or distract her. . . . I take her parrot from her hands and hide it twice in succession under the mattress, on her left, in [position] A. Both times Jacqueline looks for the object immediately and grabs it. Then I take it from her hands and move it very slowly before her eyes to the corresponding place on her right, under the mattress in [position] B. Jacqueline watches this movement very attentively, but at the moment when the parrot disappears in B she turns to her left and looks where it was before, in A.

Thus Jacqueline's newly developed ability to find a hidden object is not the end of it all. The concept of object permanence is still constrained: despite the fact that she witnessed the toy being hidden in a new position, B, Jacqueline merely repeats her previous response and again searches in A – the so-called 'A/B error'. The child merely repeats what worked before; the object remains tied to her own behaviour and is not yet seen as a truly independent entity.

This occurs subsequently, in the course of the second year, though even then not all at once but in two steps. First of all, the child becomes capable of finding the object in position B but only if the displacement is visible, i.e. if the child actually sees it being moved from A to B. An invisible displacement is still beyond the child's capacity: if, say, one moves a small object in one's *closed* hand to the new location, the child continues to search in A. It is as though the child cannot yet mentally manipulate the object to work out in thought its possible trajectory and new location. An *inferred* displacement will be understood only later:

> Jacqueline [aged 1½ years] is seated opposite three screens, A, B, and C (a beret, a handkerchief and her jacket). I hide a small pencil in my hand, saying 'Coucou, the pencil.' I hold out my closed hand to her, put it under A, then under B, then under C (leaving the pencil under C); at each step I again extend my closed hand, repeating 'Coucou, the pencil.' Jacqueline then searches for the pencil directly in C, finds it and laughs.

Jacqueline thus shows that she believes the object continued to exist in her father's hand during the whole sequence of invisible displacements, and that she is thus able to work out where it has ended up *on the basis of a mental image* of the object. It is only this last step that Piaget regards as providing clear evidence of true object permanence.

By observing sequences of play, Piaget was able to demonstrate that towards the end of the second year a shift to a qualitatively quite new kind of psychological functioning occurs. Instead of engaging only in sensorimotor activities with toys – shaking, banging, sucking, throwing – children now begin to engage in imaginative play: dolls are given a drink out of an empty cup, a piece of paper becomes a bedcover and a cloth a royal cloak. Thus the child can now engage in representational thought, where images can be mentally manipulated, words used to stand for objects and people, and a fantasy world created that can be as different from the real one as the child likes. Instead of *direct* interaction with the environment, the child can now use *mental representations* of the environment and interact with these.

Operation in Piagetian theory is any procedure for mentally acting on objects.

Yet in many respects children's thinking at this age is still very different from that of adults. Piaget signified this by his choice of 'preoperational' as the name for this stage. An **operation**, according to Piaget, is an internalized action whereby information from the environment can be arranged as the individual chooses. For example, adding 3 things to 5 things is a mental operation; ordering a number of objects according to size is another; and so is classifying such diverse creatures as flies, elephants, dogs and cats under the one heading of animals. Piaget saw intellectual development as dependent on the acquisition of operations, but whereas the ability to think at a symbolic level is a necessary step to such a development, the child at the preoperational stage remains handicapped in the use of mental operations by a number of features characterizing thought, namely, egocentrism, animism, rigidity and prelogical reasoning. We can illustrate each of these characteristics by reference to Piaget's observations and experiments.

Egocentrism

This refers to the tendency to perceive the world solely in terms of one's own perspective. As used by Piaget, it is not a derogatory term and has nothing to do with selfishness; it connotes rather the natural inability of young children to realize that other people may see things from a different point of view. Piaget illustrated this with his classic *three-mountains landscape* (see figure 6.1), in which children are seated in front of a cardboard model of a landscape with three mountains of different size and shape. They are then shown a set of photos of the model taken from different angles and asked to choose the one that corresponds to the way they see it – something preschoolers can usually do without difficulty. A doll is then placed at one of the other sides of the display, and the child is asked to choose the photo corresponding to the doll's viewpoint. Most preschool children will then again point to the photo depicting their *own* way of seeing the scene.

According to Piaget, this is a clear demonstration of egocentrism, i.e. the inability of young children to shift focus from their own perspective and realize that other people can view the same scene in different ways. As we shall see below, other

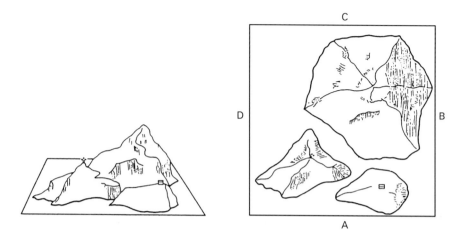

Figure 6.1 *Piaget's three-mountains landscape.*

investigators have not entirely confirmed these findings; for Piaget, however, ego-centrism is an all-pervasive tendency that can be seen in many spheres of young children's behaviour. For example, ask a young child whether he has a brother and he will say 'Yes'; then ask him whether his brother has a brother and he may very well say 'No'. Once again, we see an inability to shift focus from the child's own perspective, with adverse effects on the ability to reason about relationships. The same tendency is seen in young children's conversations: these often take the form of *collective monologues*, in which Child A will make a statement, followed by a statement from Child B that concerns a quite different topic and is in no sense a reply, and so forth. There is thus no true communication because neither child can shift focus, as a result of which both speak only in soliloquies.

Animism

As part of his investigation of children's conception of the physical world, Piaget set out to determine which objects are seen as animate and which as inanimate. Thus he would ask questions such as 'If I pull off this button, will it feel it?' 'Does the sun know it is giving off light?' and 'Does the chair mind being sat on?' From their answers Piaget concluded that in the preschool years children are not as yet able to make a clear distinction between what is alive and what is inanimate; instead, they tend to attribute the characteristics of living organisms to inanimate objects – a tendency referred to as *animism* and illustrated by the following exchange:

> *PIAGET*: 'What does the sun do when there are clouds and it rains?'
> *CHILD*: 'It goes away because it is bad weather.'
> *PIAGET*: 'Why?'
> *CHILD*: 'Because it doesn't want to be rained on.'

Only gradually, in the course of the preoperational period, will children begin to make the distinction between the animate and the inanimate. Initially, any object is regarded as potentially conscious – a stone, for example, 'knows' it is being moved. Then, only moving things are seen as alive – a bicycle, for instance, or leaves blown in the wind. Subsequently, life is confined to spontaneously moving things, such as a stream; and finally, the child realizes that life is to be found only in animals and human beings and that a fundamental distinction therefore exists in nature between the animate and the inanimate.

Rigidity of thought

This manifests itself in various ways; let us select two to illustrate. The first is *irreversibility*, i.e. the tendency to think of objects or events in the order in which they were originally experienced. Preschool children are unable *mentally* to reverse sequences; their thinking is as rigid as their perceptions. One of the great advantages of mature thought is that, by an act of imagination, one can rearrange symbols in any way one likes, in a manner not always possible with real things. Thus, it is only when children become capable of reversible thought that they can master addition and subtraction; only then will they understand that if 3 plus 4 equals 7, then 7 minus 4 must equal 3. Subtraction is the inverse of addition, and until children can comprehend this principle they will not grasp the fundamentals of arithmetic.

Rigidity of thought is also seen in children's inability to adjust to changes in the overt appearance of things. Take the following experiment: preschool children were shown a dog and asked to identify the animal. They all correctly labelled it as a dog. The experimenter then produced a cat's mask and, while the children watched, put it on the dog. Asked again to identify the animal, most of the children referred to it as a cat. Each time the mask was put on or taken off, the children changed the label accordingly. It appears that their thinking was dominated by a perceptual feature that was in fact irrelevant to the identity of the animal but that they nevertheless were unable to disregard.

Prelogical reasoning

Compared with adults, preschool children's reasoning ability is markedly deficient. Such children are not yet capable of either inductive or deductive thought, i.e. proceeding either from the particular to the general or from the general to the particular; instead they show a type of reasoning that Piaget referred to as *transductive*. For example: on missing her usual afternoon nap, Piaget's daughter Lucienne announced: 'I haven't had my nap so it isn't afternoon.' Lucienne is showing here a kind of reasoning that proceeds from one particular (the nap) to another (the afternoon), arriving at the conclusion that the one determined the other. Transductive reasoning thus sees a causal relationship between two concrete items where there is none, just because the two events occur together. Alternatively, children may invert cause and effect, such as is seen in one preschooler's statement: 'The man fell from his bicycle because he broke his arm.' Once again, we see here a failure, typical at this age, to understand the notion of cause-and-effect sequences. However, as with all aspects of young children's thinking, Piaget was not content to dismiss this merely as a sign of ignorance or stupidity; instead he regarded such efforts as a lawful step towards mature thinking. Children, he concluded, are not so much *illogical* as *prelogical*; the logical processes that are an essential part of systematic thinking are not yet in place at this age but will naturally grow out of the child's more primitive efforts.

Concrete operations stage

Somewhere around the age of 6 or 7 years of age another qualitative shift takes place in children's intellectual development. They now become capable of forming mental operations – in other words, they begin to reason systematically, try to work out problems logically and at last free themselves of the egocentrism that Piaget attributed to their earlier psychological outlook on the world. The change is seen especially in children's new-found ability mentally to reverse their thoughts, juggle them about in any manner they decide and no longer be bound to the way things happen in external reality. As a result, thinking becomes more flexible and more effective; it remains, however, still constrained in one important respect, in that children require concrete objects and events to support their mental operations – hence the name which Piaget applied to this stage. Thinking about purely hypothetical and abstract notions is still beyond children's capability.

Let us consider some of the new achievements that take place during the concrete operations stage.

- *Seriation.* One of the hallmarks of operational thinking is the ability mentally to arrange items along some dimension such as height, weight, time or speed. A child in the stage of concrete operations can, for example, think about his friends in terms of their *relative* height instead of, as before, seeing them only one at a time as individuals. This in turn leads to the ability to make *transitive inferences*, i.e. to work out problems such as 'If James can run faster than Harry and Harry can run faster than Sam, who is faster – James or Sam?' This requires the coordination of information about three items and two relationships, and has implications for the teaching of numbers and measurement. Piaget believed that this kind of understanding is not possible till the age of 6 or 7 (an assertion, however, challenged by subsequent work that has found considerably younger children to solve such problems).
- *Classification.* Children's ability to sort objects into groups according to some criterion and to see the relationship between groups advances markedly during this stage. Take the phenomenon of *class inclusion*, i.e. the understanding

of whole/part relationships. Piaget illustrated this by showing children a necklace of 10 wooden beads, of which 7 were brown and 3 white. When asked if there were more brown beads or more wooden beads, preoperational children would usually answer that there are more brown beads, reflecting their inability to think simultaneously about a whole class (wooden beads) and a subclass (brown beads). Concrete operations children, on the other hand, can see the relationship between part and whole: they are able to free themselves from some perceptual characteristic (such as the colour brown) and understand that two different characteristics are involved, one of which is subordinate to the other.

- *Number concepts.* The abilities to seriate and classify, according to Piaget, help to bring about an understanding of number. Quite young children may be able to count, but this is an exercise that can be carried out by rote with no real comprehension of the underlying concepts. At first children tend to think of each number as though it were a name assigned to that object, so that the particular number becomes the 'property' of that object. It is only at the start of the concrete operations stage that children acquire a more mature conception: they realize that numbering is an arbitrary procedure and that numbers are therefore exchangeable; they come to appreciate that numbers can be arranged in classes and subclasses (e.g. that 3 and 4 make up 7, in the same way that white and brown beads make up 'beads'); and they develop the notion of *invariance of number,* i.e. that (for example) the total number of coins in a row remains the same whether the coins are spread out or are pushed together, and that only adding more coins or taking some away can alter the total.

Conservation is Piaget's name for the understanding that certain basic characteristics of an object, such as its weight and volume, remain constant even when its appearance is perceptually transformed.

By far the most attention has been given to another development that occurs in the concrete operations stage – one which Piaget was the first to uncover and which highlights the most noteworthy advances in children's thinking at this time. This is the **conservation** phenomenon, i.e. the realization that the basic nature of objects is not altered by changes in their superficial appearance. Let us illustrate (see figure 6.2). A child is asked to pour equal amounts of water into

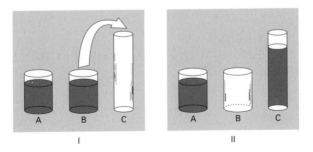

Figure 6.2   *Experiment to test conservation of volume.*

two identical beakers, A and B, and to confirm that the beakers indeed contain the same amounts. The contents of beaker B is then poured into another beaker, C, which is taller and thinner, as a result of which the water level will be higher than that in beaker A. When asked whether A and C contain the same amount of water, preschool children will deny this, asserting that C contains more water. It is only when they get to the concrete operations stage that they will be able to give the correct answer, i.e. that A and C are the same. In Piagetian language, they are now able to conserve volume.

Why is this simple experiment so significant? It is in fact one in a series of demonstrations by Piaget, illustrating that conservation applies to a whole range of object qualities such as length, number, mass, weight and area as well as volume (box 6.3 gives further details). All show that the child's thinking about the world has now moved (as Piaget put it) from a reliance on perception to a reliance on logic. Take our example above: when the water is poured into beaker C, the preschool child's judgement is dominated by one prominent feature of that beaker's perceptual appearance, namely, its height, as a result of which the water level will rise on transfer from B and lead to the conclusion that there is now more water. Young children cannot as yet simultaneously take into account two features, height and width, and will therefore be unable to understand that a change in the one is compensated for by a change in the other. Equally, the preschool child cannot imagine reversing the procedure and so realize that pouring the water back from C into B will restore the water level to its original height. This involves operational thinking, which develops only after the preschool stage and enables children to work out problems logically rather than on the basis of some salient but irrelevant perceptual feature.

Let us stress once again that the shift to a more mature level of thinking is not a matter of previously ignorant children being given the necessary information and so learning how to solve problems correctly. It has, for example, been shown that trying to train children to conserve has little effect if they are still at the preoperational stage. It is rather a matter of such children still lacking the mental processes necessary for the more advanced level, and no amount of training will put those into place.

BOX 6.3

Investigating children's understanding of conservation

Piaget invented a range of tasks to demonstrate the nature of children's thinking, and among these his conservation experiments are probably the best known. In each case he set out to show that preschool children's conception of objects is dominated by overt perceptual characteristics and that they are therefore easily swayed by changes to their superficial appearance, whereas older children in the concrete operations stage realize that these changes are irrelevant to the fundamental nature of objects, and as a result are able to conserve their basic qualities. And in each case his procedures were basically the same: he got children to agree that two objects were identical in some respect; he then made some change to the appearance of one of the objects and asked if the objects were still the same in that respect.

Take the conservation of *number* (see figure 6.3). The child is shown two rows of buttons, lined up so that it is obvious they contain the same number. The buttons in one row are then spread out while the child is watching and asked whether there are still the same number of buttons in each row. Preschool children will say that there are now more buttons in the longer row. If the buttons in one row are moved together so that it becomes shorter, they will say that there are now fewer buttons in that row.

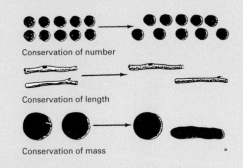

Conservation of number

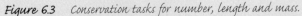

Conservation of length

Conservation of mass

Figure 6.3   Conservation tasks for number, length and mass.

To investigate conservation of *length*, two sticks are placed exactly one above the other and the child agrees that they are equally long. One stick is then moved so that it protrudes beyond the other and the child is again asked if they are of the same length. Preschool children will be swayed by the protrusion and state that that stick is now longer.

One more example concerns the conservation of *mass*. Two identical balls of clay are put in front of the child, who agrees that there is indeed the same amount of clay in each. One ball is then rolled into a sausage while the child is watching. When asked whether the two shapes still contain the same amount of clay, preschool children will say that the longer shape now has more clay in it than the other.

Questioned about the reasons for their answer, preoperational children have no hesitation in pointing out the perceptual changes made. Thus they will point to the sausage and say 'It is longer now', or 'You made it stick out further'. The explanations of the concrete operations child, on the other hand, will emphasize that the change made is irrelevant, e.g. 'You didn't take any clay away, so it must still be the same', 'It is longer now but it is also thinner', or 'You can roll it back into a ball and then it will still have the same amount'.

These last three explanations illustrate the various operations required for an understanding of conservation. The first concentrates on the essential *identity* of objects when nothing has been added or subtracted. The second refers to *compensation*, i.e. the knowledge that a change in one dimension can be compensated for by a change in the other. And the third illustrates the older child's *reversibility* of thought, for the child can imagine what would happen if the sausage is rolled back into a ball and thus conclude that the amount of clay is not affected by the change in appearance.

Formal operations stage

Around the age of 11 or 12 children reach the most advanced level of thinking. We need to bear in mind, however, that there are great individual differences among children in this respect; let us also note that not everyone reaches the highest level but that there are those who remain stuck at stages lower down. For that matter, even the most mature thinker does not function at that level all the time but will occasionally resort to more primitive ways of thought.

Formal operations differ from concrete operations in several ways:

- *Reasoning about abstractions.* Children can now reason about things they have never directly experienced. Thought is no longer tied to actual objects and events: children can cope with purely hypothetical and abstract notions. Thus they are able to think about the future, including their own, and consider all sorts of possibilities and plan accordingly. They realize that the reality around them need not be the only reality: there are other possible worlds they can conceive of and, if they so wish, attempt to put into place. The adolescent can thus become an idealist, who can strive for political, moral and religious principles other than those currently in place.

- *Applying logic.* Deductive reasoning now becomes a possibility, in that children can take some general proposition and work out the consequences along 'if-then' lines. This means, among other things, that they can make rapid progress in scientific understanding, for science is full of deductive propositions whereby specific observations are deduced from a general theory. Thus children come to appreciate that it is possible to foresee something that will happen at some point in the future because it follows as a matter of necessity from a general theoretical statement, e.g. that a star can be discovered not just by random searching of the sky but because it follows from mathematical propositions that the star should exist in a certain place.

• *Advanced problem solving.* Piaget demonstrated the kind of progress found in adolescents' thinking by setting his participants various tasks, typically drawn from physics or chemistry, and then noting how they set about solving the problem. He asked them, for instance, to discover how a pendulum operates, giving them objects of various weights and strings of varying lengths in order to see whether they can work out the principles underlying a solution. Unlike children in the concrete operations stage, those capable of formal operations would set about the task systematically, varying factors such as weight, height and force one at a time and so building up a picture of the processes in an organized and coherent manner. Their strategy in tackling such problems was thus very different from that of children at the concrete operations level: instead of haphazard trial-and-error attempts, formal operations youngsters can construct hypotheses, mentally work out different outcomes and so have various possible solutions to hand before eventually putting them to the test. At their best, that is, these adolescents are able to adopt a hypothetico-deductive approach to solving problems.

The formal operations stage is the highest level that children can reach, having passed through each of the previous three stages. Thinking has now become rational, systematic and abstract, and though there are further developments in adulthood, these concern primarily the range of knowledge and not its basic nature.

Pros and Cons of Piagetian Theory

Piaget's account of child development has been hugely influential. Long the dominant model of the way in which children acquire knowledge, it stimulated a large amount of research worldwide aimed at replicating and extending the various facets of the theory. As a result we can now more easily evaluate the theory and recognize both its many contributions to our understanding of children and the various shortcomings that have also become apparent.

Contributions

One of the strengths of Piaget's approach is that he was no armchair theorist. There is a solid observational basis to all his ideas, and it is thus both the empirical material he produced and the theoretical explanations for that material which help us to understand how children view the world at different ages and how their conception changes in the course of development. We can single out the following as the most significant aspects of his contribution:

- *Children's thinking is qualitatively different from that of adults.* Intellectual development is not just a matter of giving children more information and so adding to their store of knowledge. As Piaget spelled out in great detail, children think *differently*; the nature of these differences changes from one developmental period to another; and while children's attempts to understand and solve problems may sometimes seem foolish from an adult point of view, in fact they reflect a legitimate progression through the various stages the child must pass through on the way to maturity.
- *Intellectual development is continuous from birth on.* Piaget's account was very much a developmental one: he argued that the newborn's adjustment to the nipple and the school-age child's attempts to solve classroom problems are based on some of the same mechanisms, that the former as much as the latter indicate intellectual functioning, and that any attempt to understand the development of intelligence must start at birth. There is thus a basic continuity despite the changes that occur as the child progresses from one stage to another.
- *Children are active learners.* Acquiring knowledge is not a matter of passively absorbing information. Again and again Piaget emphasized children's intense curiosity in the world which drives them to explore and experiment. The observations he recorded of his own children make this point particularly well: these children are not willing merely to wait for stimulation to be provided by others but set out to play the role of the 'little scientist' from the early months on.
- *A diversity of phenomena can be found that open the way into the child's mind.* Object permanence, egocentrism, class inclusion, conservation – these and other examples were used by Piaget to illustrate the nature of children's understanding. Not only did he draw our attention to such phenomena, he also devised ways of investigating them, thereby enabling others to follow up his work.

Given the nature of Piaget's theory, it is no wonder that it has aroused considerable interest among teachers. The proposition that children are *active* learners is not a new one, but Piaget spelled out in greater detail than anyone had ever done before just how children's natural curiosity impels them to explore and experiment and so discover *for themselves* the way the world works. The idea of children sitting at desks, passively listening to a teacher transmitting knowledge, was anathema to Piaget: children must be actively involved and the younger the child, the more important it is that he or she has the opportunity to learn by doing. This provides the rationale for discovery-based teaching, where the job of the teacher is to create environments that lend themselves to children constructing knowledge for themselves. Such knowledge is meaningful; imparted knowledge on its own is not.

It follows that careful thought needs to be given to individual children's capacities to handle particular experiences. It is here that Piaget's contribution is of greatest relevance to education, and especially so in the teaching of mathematics and science. Children's thinking, as we have seen, is qualitatively different from that of adults; its nature, moreover, changes from one cognitive stage to the next.

One cannot assume that children's understanding of problems is identical to that of an adult – hence the need for child-centred teaching, where the tasks set are adapted as precisely as possible to the child's cognitive level. The preoperational child, for instance, requires play materials that make it possible to learn about their functions and properties from handling, touching and manipulating them, for at this stage knowledge is acquired through direct interaction with the environment. Similarly, children in the concrete stage, though now capable of mental operations, need real objects to support their problem solving; giving them such assistance will enable them to tackle tasks that would be beyond them if based on abstractions. Thus successful teaching requires, first, specification of the individual child's cognitive capacities; second, analysis of the demands that particular tasks make; and third, a matching of child and tasks so that the latter are tailored to the former. Piaget's detailed analysis of children's capacities at different ages has made such matching a lot easier.

Shortcomings

Most of the criticisms that have been raised as a result of further research concern two aspects, relating to questions about ages and stages respectively.

First, *did Piaget underestimate children's abilities?* A great many subsequent studies have found that the ages Piaget gave for first achieving particular cognitive milestones are misleadingly high, suggesting that he was much too pessimistic about what young children are capable of. It is true that Piaget cared little about age norms and was more interested in the sequencing of abilities – an aspect that has by and large been confirmed by further work. Nevertheless, the age discrepancy is often so great that an explanation is required. Take object permanence – a concept which Piaget believed children do not acquire until the end of the first year. He demonstrated this by means of his object-hiding experiments which, when applied by others, generally yielded the same results. However, when different techniques were used, it was found that much younger babies already display some understanding that objects continue to exist when they disappear from view. For example, Bower (1974) showed 3-month-old babies an attractive toy that was then hidden from view by a screen. In one condition, when the screen was subsequently removed, the toy had disappeared; in another condition it was still there (see figure 6.4). By measuring the babies' heart rate (as an indication of surprise or upset), Bower showed that even at this very young age heart rate showed greater change when the toy was no longer there than when it was still present – an apparent indication that these babies had expected the toy to remain in place even when it had disappeared for a short period. Similarly, when a different object was substituted, the babies again showed greater 'surprise' than when the same toy was revealed. Thus, by employing a less demanding task which relied on visual rather than manual search, it was possible to reveal the existence of object permanence at a much younger age than that suggested by Piaget's object-hiding test.

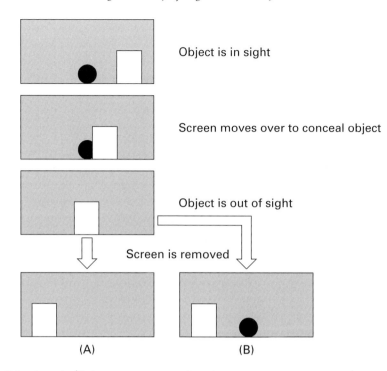

Object is in sight

Screen moves over to conceal object

Object is out of sight

Screen is removed

(A)   (B)

Figure 6.4   *Bower's object permanence experiment.*

Let us quote one further example to illustrate that changes in procedure may yield different results. According to Piaget, conservation cannot be achieved by children until they reach the concrete operations stage. Thus (as we saw in box 6.3, pp. 179–81), when one of two rows containing the same number of buttons is pushed together by the experimenter, so shortening it, children below the age of 6 will assert that there are now fewer buttons in it than in the other row, thereby indicating an inability to conserve. McGarrigle and Donaldson (1974) repeated the procedure, but introduced a 'naughty teddy' who swooped down on the buttons and accidentally displaced one row, thereby shortening it. Whereas few of the preschool children were able to conserve number when the experimenter displaced the buttons, the majority were successful when the naughty teddy did so. Thus even 4-year-old children could conserve number in one condition but not the other. Why the difference? According to McGarrigle and Donaldson, the explanation lies in the way the child interprets the situation. When the adult moves one row of buttons and asks the child to compare the numbers, preschool children believe that a real change must have taken place, as otherwise there is no point in asking the question. This is not the case when the 'naughty teddy' accidentally alters the appearance of one row, making it easier for children to display whatever conservation abilities they have developed.

BOX 6.4

Cultural influences on Piagetian task performance

Piaget set forth his account of knowledge acquisition as though the findings obtained by him from samples of Swiss children were of universal significance. The impression is thus given that the manner of passing through the stages outlined by Piaget is an inevitable consequence of being human, and that external influences stemming from the child's social environment play no part in this development.

But is this so? A considerable body of evidence is now available on the way in which children from many different cultural backgrounds perform on Piagetian tasks (see Dasen, 1977, for examples). Thus conservation experiments have been administered to such diverse samples as Eskimo and Aboriginal children, African children in locations such as Senegal and Rwanda, children in Hong Kong and in Papua New Guinea, as well as those from a great many other settings differing sharply from one another in a large range of childrearing and educational experiences that might be relevant to the course of cognitive development. How such children perform on a task originally designed for European samples will, of course, depend on the familiarity of the material used, the way the instructions are communicated and the child's grasp of 'being tested'. Nevertheless, certain conclusions have become evident.

In the first place, children from non-western societies often show a considerable lag in acquiring operational thinking. For example, Aboriginal children living in Central Australia and having only minimal contact with white culture do not succeed on conservation tasks till several years later than their European counterparts; some indeed are still not capable of concrete operational thinking in late adolescence or even as adults (Dasen, 1974). Yet Aboriginal children living in white communities and attending schools there solve such tasks within the same age range as Piaget's children, presumably because schooling provides the spur for the concepts necessary to operational thinking. What has also become evident, however, is that even when development is greatly delayed, the progression from stage to stage still occurs in the same order that Piaget outlined. Everywhere children become capable of concrete operations only after going through the preoperational stage, and if they do reach the formal operations stage it will invariably follow a period of concrete operational thinking. Cultural factors, that is, can affect *rate* of attainment; they do not alter developmental *sequence*.

In addition, it is also apparent that in every cultural group certain cognitive skills are valued more than others, and that as a result development of concepts within a stage will be differentially affected. A telling example comes from a study by Price-Williams, Gordon and Ramirez (1969) on 6- to 9-year-old Mexican children, some of whom had grown up in pottery-making families, while others came from families engaged in different skills. A series of conservation tasks was administered to the children, including a test of substance conservation which, as is customary, was assessed by means of transforming lumps of clay. All the potters' children were found to be greatly advanced in their understanding of substance conservation when compared with the other children. We can conclude that different cultures promote development in some areas of cognitive understanding more than in others, and that experiential factors are thus of rather more significance than was attributed to them by Piaget.

It is evident that a child's performance in an experimental task depends on a large number of factors over and above the specific task as such. The social setting, the child's interpretation of the adult's intentions, the procedures employed, the type of measure used – all may influence the results obtained, yet none of these was ever taken into account by Piaget. Even the familiarity of the language used in instructing the child needs to be considered. Piaget's question 'Are there more brown beads or more wooden beads?' when investigating children's understanding of whole/part relationships uses a form of wording that must sound peculiar to children; when rephrased by other investigators to make the question more meaningful, it was found once again that much younger children were capable of more advanced understanding than indicated by Piaget's results. Thus the total context in which the investigation takes place needs consideration in evaluating the findings – a conclusion particularly well illustrated when one considers the culture in which children live. As described in more detail in box 6.4, exporting Piaget's experiments to other cultures has provided some rather useful insights, especially by highlighting the role of experiential influences which Piaget on the whole neglected.

Let us turn to the second aspect of Piaget's theory which has aroused most controversy. *Does development take place in stages?* To distinguish a stage model from one that sees childhood in terms of a continuous process of change, three criteria have been proposed (Flavell, Miller & Miller, 1993):

1   *Qualitative changes.* At certain points of development children's behaviour and thought undergo change that is not just a matter of being able to do more of something or to do it faster or with more precision; it is rather a matter of doing something *differently*, such as by adopting another kind of mental strategy.

2 *Abruptness of change.* A stage-like model of development resembles a stair-case rather than an incline: whatever change there is occurs rapidly, not gradually.

3 *Across-the-board change.* Implied in the concept of stage is the belief that change occurs simultaneously in a wide range of functions: a new stage in reasoning, for example, affects all aspects of problem solving and not certain ones only.

Domain-specific, domain-general. Terms used to describe whether developmental processes apply only to certain mental functions or to all.

The attraction of a stage model such as Piaget's lies in its simplicity: it is easily grasped and easily summarized. But is it valid? Increasingly, psychologists in recent years have come to the conclusion that development assumes a more complex, uneven form, that change does not occur overnight, and that it is more accurately characterized as **domain-specific** than **domain-general**.

Take the example of egocentrism (described on pp. 174–5).

According to Piaget, children right up to the age of 7 are incapable of appreciating that another person may have a point of view different from their own, and instead assume that everyone else must perceive and feel as they do. It is only at the beginning of the concrete operations stage that children become capable of freeing themselves of their egocentric attitude and of coordinating other people's different perspectives with their own.

This account has been repeatedly challenged. Piaget relied for his evidence to a large extent on one specific test, the three-mountains task (see figure 6.1, p. 175). In a highly influential critique of Piaget's work, Margaret Donaldson (1978) has argued that this method of assessment is much too complex and meaningless to do justice to young children's abilities, and that situations which connect more with everyday life should be employed when young children are tested. As an example she quotes work by Martin Hughes, in which children are told to 'hide' a doll from two policemen in the set-up shown in figure 6.5, composed of two intersecting walls

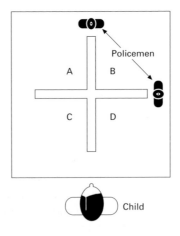

Figure 6.5   *Hughes's 'hiding' experiment to test egocentrism.*

high enough to obscure the doll. The task requires that children disregard what they themselves can see and consider only the point of view of the figures, i.e. that they act non-egocentrically. As Hughes found, children as young as $3\frac{1}{2}$ years are able to place the doll in the appropriate sector – a finding at variance with Piaget's conclusions but due, according to Donaldson, to the test making far more human sense to these children than the three-mountains task.

There have been many other demonstrations that children much younger than 7 can behave in a non-egocentric manner *under certain circumstances*. Much depends on the task and the demands it makes on the child; to propose that there is one particular age (whether it is 7 years or any other) when a perspective-taking ability clocks in is therefore not acceptable. What has also become apparent is that perspective-taking can usefully be differentiated according to the following three categories:

- *Perceptual* perspective-taking, i.e. the realization that another person sees and hears from a different viewpoint.
- *Affective* perspective-taking, the ability to assess another's emotional state.
- *Cognitive* perspective-taking, being able to comprehend what another person knows.

The developmental course of these three aspects is by no means identical. *Perceptual* perspective-taking is the earliest, as demonstrated by children's 'showing' behaviour (Lempers, Flavell & Flavell, 1977). Asked to show a toy to an adult sitting opposite, even 1-year-olds will hold the toy up. At $1\frac{1}{2}$ years children will not only hold it up but orient it so that it directly faces the other person. When given a hollow cube with a picture on the inside bottom surface and asked to show the adult that picture, 2-year-olds tilt the cube in such a way that the adult is able to see what is inside, even though this means the child deprives herself of the sight – surely as clear an indication of a non-egocentric attitude as one would wish. Thus already in the second year of life children are, in certain respects, aware that others see things differently; in addition, the development of this ability does not occur all at once but evolves in a gradual manner.

Affective perspective-taking develops somewhat later, yet still at a relatively very early age. This is seen, for example, in a study of preschool children who were told some short stories about a character and asked to select for each story whatever picture of a face showed the appropriate emotion (happy, angry, afraid or sad). Already at the age of 3 children had some limited success, and by age 4 they had become quite proficient in recognizing how someone else might feel in a given situation (Borke, 1971). As to *cognitive* perspective-taking, theory of mind studies (referred to in chapter 5 and described in more detail in chapter 8) have clearly shown how children in the later preschool years become capable of taking into account another person's beliefs, indicating that by age 5 or so they are quite sophisticated in making allowance for the fact that such beliefs may be quite different from their own. Thus being able to work out what other people perceive, what they feel and what is in their mind forms a gradual progression that continues through-out the preschool years.

The particular example we have taken, that of egocentrism, illustrates difficulties about Piaget's stage model which have also been found in other areas. Development rarely assumes the stepwise form that this model suggests: closer inspection reveals continuities which a theory based on periodically occurring qualitative shifts would not expect. It is also now generally accepted that Piaget's domain-general view needs to be replaced by a domain-specific view: that development frequently occurs at different tempos and in different ways across various functions which Piaget had originally put all under one umbrella.

Summary

Piaget's theory of cognitive development has a depth and a width that no other account of cognitive development can rival. His main contribution was to put forward a framework that not only linked together different cognitive functions by explaining them in terms of common processes (such as assimilation and accommodation, the formation of operations, egocentrism and so forth), but that also traced children's cognitive functioning from one age period to the next and so showed the basic continuity that exists from birth to maturity in children's efforts to know their world.

Intelligence, according to Piaget, should be seen as a means of adaptation to the environment, and his aim was to trace the way in which children become progressively more capable of achieving adaptation. He was not concerned with individual differences; it was rather the *nature* of development that interested him, namely, the manner whereby the limited psychological equipment of the newborn baby evolves into the sophisticated mind of the mature individual. To explain this progression, Piaget shied away from accounts based merely on the accumulation of knowledge, and instead stressed the active nature of even the youngest baby in attempting to find out about the world around her. Children are intensely curious about their environment; they want to explore and investigate; however, they do so not in a haphazard way but by selecting from their experiences whatever is in keeping with the psychological organization they already possess. Thus knowledge is *constructed*; it is derived from the child's active exploration of objects and ideas. The child, that is, acts like a 'little scientist': trying to make sense of new experience by experimenting, attempting to fit that experience into existing ways of understanding and, if this is not possible, extending these or creating new ones.

Piaget's observations convinced him that children's understanding of the world proceeds as a series of steps and not as a continuous line. There are, he believed, four major stages in the progression from birth to maturity, each of which represents a qualitatively different way of knowing:

1 The sensorimotor stage, from birth to the end of the second year, when children are not yet capable of mental representations and instead derive their knowledge of objects from directly acting on them.

2 The preoperational stage, extending from about 2 to 7 years, during which child-ren become able to engage in symbolic thought, language and pretend play.

3 Concrete operations, from about 7 to 11 years, when children acquire the ability to reason systematically and work out problems logically, though only if the prob-lems are applied to concrete objects and events.

4 Formal operations, from 11 years on, at which time children become able to reason about purely abstract and hypothetical ideas.

These stages form an invariant order; at each new stage mental strategies become available, and each represents an increasingly complex way of making sense of the environment.

While there is no doubt that Piaget's theory has greatly extended our knowledge of children's development, as well as making some useful contributions to educa-tional practice, it has also come under sustained criticism, with particular reference to two aspects. The first concerns Piaget's undue pessimism as to what young child-ren are capable of: by using different, more meaningful tasks, other investigators have found children to achieve success at tasks very much earlier than the ages Piaget had indicated. The second aspect that is questioned is the stepwise nature of develop-ment that Piaget proposed: as considerable evidence now indicates, change in cognitive functions occurs much less abruptly and not in such an across-the-board manner as Piaget's stage model indicates.

FURTHER READING

Boden, M. (1994). *Piaget* (2nd edn). London: Fontana. A paperback which not only describes the theory (under such chapter headings as 'The Intelligent Baby' and 'The Intuitive Child') but also relates it to other disciplines, namely, philosophy, biology and cybernetics.

Crain, W. (1999). *Theories of Development: Concepts and Applications* (4th edn). Englewood Cliffs, NJ: Prentice-Hall. Another short account, providing an outline of Piaget's biography and setting out his theory, followed by a useful evaluation of the contribution to our know-ledge of child development made by Piaget's writings.

Donaldson, M. (1978). *Children's Minds*. London: Fontana. A highly readable paperback that has become a classic critique of Piagetian methods and concepts.

Ginsburg, H., & Opper, S. (1983). *Piaget's Theory of Intellectual Development* (3rd edn). Englewood Cliffs, NJ: Prentice-Hall. A rather more detailed account, but aimed at the begin-ning student. The first chapter, which presents a brief biography and an account of Piaget's basic ideas, is especially helpful.

Miller, P. H. (2002). *Theories of Developmental Psychology* (4th edn). New York: W. H. Freeman. Contains a chapter outlining Piaget's theory. Short and clear, it is one of the best introductions there is.

Piaget, J. (1951). *Play, Dreams, and Imitation in Childhood*. London: Routledge & Kegan Paul. Piaget's own books are by and large difficult to read, for he writes in a dense style that is not easy to unravel and uses terminology that is very much his own. However, this par-ticular volume is probably the best for a first taste of the Piagetian approach, especially as it refers to some interesting topics and contains some fascinating observations.

CHAPTER SEVEN

The Child as Apprentice: Vygotsky's Theory of Socio-cognitive Development

Chapter Outline

The social context of cognitive development plays little part in Piaget's theory. Children, as he envisaged them, are solitary creatures; only rarely is the role of other human beings acknowledged as relevant to their development. The rattles, boxes and cups which figure so prominently in Piaget's observations of children's play and problem solving seem to appear from nowhere; the fact that their appearance is so often embedded in the interaction between child and adult is not regarded as pertinent. Whatever children achieve is considered to result from their solitary, unassisted efforts; children, according to the Piagetian view, are trying to understand the world on their own.

A very different conception emerges from the writings of the Russian psychologist Lev Vygotsky – a conception that has attracted increasing attention in recent times just because it does assign an essential role to the social context in shaping intelligence. Piaget and Vygotsky agree that development does not occur in a vacuum and that knowledge is constructed as a result of the child's active engagement with the environment. However, while Piaget conceived of that environment largely in asocial terms, Vygotsky was convinced that the particular culture in which children are embedded and the interactions with more knowledgeable people they experience form an integral part of cognitive development. Human nature cannot be described in the abstract; whatever course children's mental growth takes is to a large extent a function of the cultural tools that are handed down to them by other people. Thus the influence of the two writers was very different: whereas Piaget led us to think about children's internal mental processes and their transformation over age, Vygotsky drew our attention to the role of the social group and the interpersonal processes that can account for intellectual change.

Overview

The man

Lev Semeonovich Vygotsky (1896–1934) was born in Russia in the same year as Piaget. His educational background was primarily in history and literature, and after graduating from Moscow University in 1917 (the year of the Soviet Revolution) he taught literature at a secondary school. However, the range of his interests was wide, and he soon became fascinated by psychology, teaching the subject at a local teachers' training college and presenting a doctoral dissertation on the psychology of art. A paper he wrote on the nature of consciousness and presented at the 1924 Psycho-Neurological Congress in Leningrad attracted considerable interest, so much so that he was invited to join the staff of the Institute of Psychology in Moscow. This remained his professional base until, after a 10-year period of recurrent illness, he died from tuberculosis at the early age of 38.

Given such a brief lifetime it is astonishing that Vygotsky managed to write as many books and papers as he did. Clearly, his mind was a highly fertile and original one and one cannot help wondering what he would have achieved had he lived as long as Piaget did. Unlike the latter, however, he did not produce any fully fledged theory or coherent body of research; many of his ideas were not spelled out in detail; and it was not until many years after his death that his writings attracted international interest when his two major books, *Thought and Language* (1962) and *Mind in Society* (1978), were translated into English.

In addition, even in the Soviet Union Vygotsky's writings encountered difficulties – indeed, to such an extent that they were eventually suppressed by the Stalinist regime. This was paradoxical, for Vygotsky was a committed Marxian, who firmly believed that human behaviour is moulded by social organization and that the historical forces shaping our society need to be taken into account if we are to understand how children's development takes place. Having encountered Piaget's writings, he was convinced that a different conception of development had to be advanced – a conception that saw the child not as an individual but as part of the prevailing culture. The task of psychology is thus to investigate the tension between child and society and the way in which that tension is resolved in the course of development, and he believed that, by clarifying this process, psychology could be a means of creating a better socialist society. However, in the paranoid atmosphere that existed in the Soviet Union in the 1930s, Vygotsky's writings were greeted with suspicion: the politically acceptable theory of human nature at the time was based on Pavlovian conditioned reflexes, and the very fact that Vygotsky's ideas were considerably more sophisticated was sufficient for him to be treated as an outcast. He must have died a very bitter man.

The theory

Cognitive development is essentially a social process. This was the basic theme of Vygotsky's writings, and the task he set himself was to spell out the means whereby the higher intellectual functions – reasoning, understanding, planning, remembering and so forth – arise out of the child's social experiences.

He did so by considering human development in terms of three levels, namely, the cultural, the interpersonal and the individual, the integration of which determines the course that each individual child takes. We can summarize the levels as follows.

1 Cultural aspects

In accord with his Marxian beliefs, Vygotsky saw human nature as a socio-cultural product. Children do not need to start anew inventing the world, as Piaget seemed to believe. They can benefit from the accumulated wisdom of previous generations, and indeed cannot avoid doing so through their interactions with their caregivers. Thus each generation stands on the shoulders of the previous one, taking over the particular culture – including its intellectual, material, scientific and artistic

Cultural tools are the objects and skills which each society has perfected to carry on its traditions and which must therefore be handed down from one generation to the next.

achievements – in order to develop it further before handing it on to the following generation.

What is handed over? Vygotsky used the concept of **cultural tools** to describe the nature of children's heritage. By this he meant both technological and psychological tools: on the one hand, things such as books, clocks, bicycles, calculators, calendars, pens, maps and other physical devices, and, on the other hand, concepts and symbols such as language, literacy, mathematics and scientific theories, as well as values such as speed, efficiency and power. Acquiring tools such as these helps children to conduct their lives in particular ways regarded by our society as more effective and more acceptable; by their means they learn to understand how the world works. Take the example of time and the essential role that it plays in our society: from a very early age, children learn that their everyday experience is divided in terms of time units: language is full of words like morning, evening, soon, late, 1 hour, 3 hours, in a minute, Tuesday, next week and so forth, whereby the child's caregivers convey the need to place events in a temporal framework and to organize and think about their own activities in such terms. These psychological tools are reinforced with technological tools such as watches, clocks and calendars; to master these is not just a matter of acquiring some specific skill but is also intended to inculcate a particular way of thinking about the world which, in western culture, has come to assume a more essential role than is found in most other cultures.

Psychological and technological cultural tools usually exert their influence in tandem; certainly, in the individual child's development it is difficult to tell which comes first: the idea of time or an interest in watches and clocks; an awareness of literacy or a fascination with pictures and books. Yet there are occasions when technology appears to be in the driving seat and when its effects on development are initially unknown. A striking contemporary example concerns the role of computers: in a very short period these have come to assume a central part in all spheres of life, and in consequence children are being introduced to their use at ever earlier ages. Just how this latest cultural artefact will affect cognitive or, for that matter, social development remains a matter of conjecture; box 7.1 explores this intriguing issue further.

However, the most essential cultural tool that is passed on to children is language. Vygotsky saw language as much more important to the acquisition of children's intellectual skills than Piaget did. According to the latter, language in the early years exerts no formative effect on thinking; children's speech at that period is merely a self-directed by-product of the child's activities, with no communicative or regulatory function. Vygotsky, on the other hand, regarded language as playing a central role in several respects. For one thing, it is the pre-eminent means whereby society's experience is passed on: how others speak and what they speak about is the main channel of conveying culture from adult to child. In the second place, language enables children to regulate their own activities: the monologues which young children engage in and which Piaget saw as the main indication of an

BOX 7.1

Computers as cultural tools

There are few instances in history where a new technical invention has assumed such a dominant role in virtually all spheres of human activity as the computer. It has done so, moreover, most speedily, so that in the space of just a few decades computing expertise is regarded as an essential skill for even quite young children to acquire. With the gradual lowering of prices the use of computers is becoming ever more widespread, so that children may well encounter them at home or in preschool even before computers become part of their formal education.

Given such exposure, it is essential to investigate the psychological consequences of computer use, especially for children's development. A variety of questions have been raised, many to do with the effectiveness of computers as teaching devices and as providers of information, but others raising concerns about their addictive and socially isolating effects (Crook, 1994). However, many of the anxieties about the potentially destructive implications of computers for the social fabric of education have not been borne out: far from chaining individual children to individual machines, the computer in practice has often been found to function as a highly effective means of collaborative learning – something that was first brought about because economic necessity required groups of children to share computers in classrooms, but then because many teachers found such sharing to lead to more productive and motivated learning. A considerable body of research, much of it influenced by Vygotskian ideas about the social nature of learning, has confirmed that computer-based group work can have many advantages over and above individual computer usage, and that the individualization of learning is thus not a necessary consequence of modern technology (Light, 1997; Littleton & Light, 1998).

Very much less is known about the way in which computers affect children's cognitive activities. For example, is word-processing technology transforming the way children produce text when compared with traditional paper and pen methods, making them perhaps more productive or quicker or, because of easier editing facilities, more daring or more slapdash? Does the nature of computing promote particular ways of thinking or facilitate certain kinds of cognitive skills? This last possibility is suggested by research on video games, as carried out by Patricia Greenfield and her colleagues (Greenfield, 1994). For many children video games are their introduction to computer technology, and the particular symbolic systems and operating requirements they impose may well steer players towards certain kinds of competencies in the same way that, say, print literacy helps to develop particular cognitive skills. The studies reported by Greenfield focus mainly on one type of skill, namely, competence in processing spatial information. Most video games rely on rapidly moving icons, whose speed and distance the player is required to judge while attempting to guide them towards certain targets or while intercepting other objects. Manipulating icons quickly and accurately leads to success in many such games; these skills are thus valued and fostered by the medium. What Greenfield's findings indicate is that practice in video-game playing can generalize to a wide range of other situations also demanding spatial skill: interpreting visual images, manipulating them, mentally transforming them or relating them to one another – all abilities required in a great variety of educational and occupational tasks, especially in the fields of science, mathematics and engineering. Such transfer can occur even when children, having practised on the two-dimensional computer screen, are asked to navigate through three-dimensional real-life situations. The fact that females are by and large less competent at spatial tasks than males probably accounts for girls being less attracted to video games than boys; it is also noteworthy, however, that there are suggestions that practice with video games can serve as compensatory education for those who are relatively weak to start with at spatial performance.

Computers, like other cultural tools, can clearly constitute a potent source of cognitive socialization, in that they selectively foster some skills and neglect others. Such consequences are often unforeseen when technology first delivers these tools, making it all the more important to monitor their effects subsequently.

egocentric orientation are a sign that children have in fact become capable of using language as a tool for thought, originating from dialogues with others and thus essentially social in origin. Thirdly, language will in due course (around the end of the preschool period) become internalized and transformed into thought: an essentially social function thus becomes the principal tool for cognitive functioning.

2 Interpersonal aspects

It is here that Vygotsky made his main contribution, and the bulk of subsequent research inspired by him concerns the concepts he put forward to elucidate the nature of interactive processes relevant to cognitive development. We shall look at this research in greater detail below; here we will present a general outline of his ideas.

Children's cognitive development, according to Vygotsky, occurs essentially as a result of interacting with more knowledgeable and more competent others, who can pass on to the individual child the cultural tools required for intellectual activity – tools such as language which have been developed in the course of each society's history and which will enable children to function as members of that society. Children's lives are full of encounters with adults that have the potential to extend their knowledge of the world – in formal settings such as with teachers in school, or in informal ones with parents at home, and in each such encounter the child is given the opportunity not only to acquire certain specific problem-solving skills but also to become acquainted with the nature of the culture of which he or she is a member. Any advance the individual child makes intellectually is thus rooted in cultural and interpersonal contexts, and it is the interpersonal level that represents the meeting ground of the three sets of forces – cultural, interactive and individual.

Vygotsky believed that the child's ability to profit from help and instruction constitutes a fundamental characteristic of human nature – a characteristic nicely complemented by another, namely, the adult's ability to offer help and instruction. The contribution of a more advanced tutor is thus the key to cognitive progress: the ability to think and solve problems evolves through the guidance of people who can teach the child to use the appropriate cultural tools, and it is in the moment-to-moment interactions with such guides that children's intellectual development comes to be shaped. Being given the opportunity to participate in a wide range of social activities, children will therefore become acquainted with procedures that will in due course enable them to function independently.

Vygotsky thus proposed that intellectual competence emerges as a result of internalizing ways of solving problems that are first encountered in joint sessions with another person. As he put it in a much-quoted passage:

> Any function in the child's cultural development appears twice, or on two planes. First it appears on the social plane and then on the psychological plane. First it appears between people, as an interpsychological category, and then within the child, as an intrapsychological category. This is equally true with regard to voluntary attention, logical memory, the formation of concepts and the development of volition.
>
> (*Vygotsky, 1981a*)

Any intellectual skill therefore will first be performed jointly with a competent adult before the child takes it over and internalizes it. Cognitive development is thus a progression from the *intermental* to the *intramental*; from joint regulation to self-regulation. This conjures up a very different picture from that provided by Piaget: the child is not a solitary problem solver who has to profit from his or her own activity but is instead a partner in a joint endeavour – albeit a junior partner, namely, an *apprentice*.

The mutually adjustive nature of tutor–apprentice interaction is therefore the key to developmental progress, and some of Vygotsky's most interesting proposals concern the way such interactions take place. We shall consider these in more detail below; here let us note one basic and innovative point about Vygotsky's account, namely, his conviction that children's potential is best demonstrated by what they can achieve when working with a more competent person rather than when working on their own. Such an assertion goes, of course, directly counter to the generally accepted view, as seen in psychometric and other assessment procedures, that children's true capacities can only be revealed by tests administered to them in isolation. Vygotsky, while agreeing that children's solo performance is of interest, argued that a child's optimum level is achieved when working jointly with a more knowledgeable person, that more advanced ways of thinking are then revealed in comparison with solo conditions, and that children's ability to benefit from help can tell us more about their eventual capacities than their efforts at unsupported problem solving. Moreover, the gap between solo and joint performance is of great significance: this **zone of proximal development** ('proximal' in the sense of 'next'), as Vygotsky called it, came to assume a highly significant part in his theory, for it is here that the 'buds of development' are to be found rather than the 'fruits', and it is the former that Vygotsky considered to be of greater diagnostic value with respect to individual children's progress. As he put it:

Zone of proximal development.
According to Vygotsky, this is the gap between what children already know and what they are capable of learning under guidance.

> Imagine that we have examined two children and that we have determined that the mental age of both is seven years. This means that both children solve tasks accessible to seven-year-olds. However, when we attempt to push these children further in carrying out the tests, there turns out to be an essential difference between them. With the help of leading questions, examples and demonstrations one of them easily solves test items taken from two years above the child's level of development. The other solves test items that are only a half-year above his or her development.
>
> (*Vygotsky, 1956*)

Thus the two children differ sharply in their potential for further development, however similar they are in their actual development as conventionally assessed (see figure 7.1). Furthermore, it follows that adults need to pitch their tuitional efforts within the zone of proximal development if they are to have any effect on the child's development – a notion that draws attention to the need for sensitivity on the part of adults to children's abilities and potential and that raises the question of just how adults behave in their instructional role. As we shall see, much of the subsequent research stimulated by Vygotsky's writings is aimed at throwing light on these problems in order to understand the tutor–apprentice relationship in greater detail than Vygotsky himself provided.

3 Individual aspects

Vygotsky had very much less to say about this level than about the other two. Unlike Piaget, he made little effort to trace development over age: he did not aim to produce a stage-dependent theory like Piaget's, and what he did say about the

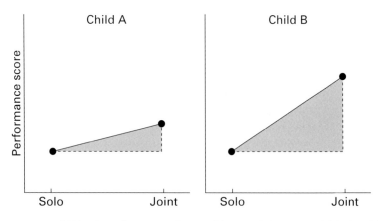

Figure 7.1   *Two children's performance when working on their own and jointly with a more knowledgeable person; the shaded area represents the zone of proximal development (after Siegler, 1998).*

child's role in joint problem-solving situations was equally applicable to preschool and to adolescent children. The only statement he made about age was to suggest that children up to 2 years are influenced primarily by biological forces and that the socio-cultural influences which form the focus of his writings do not come into play until after that age – an assertion clearly not supported by more recent work.

On the other hand, like Piaget, he saw the individual child as very much an active contributor to his or her own development. Children, that is, are not passive receivers of adult guidance: they seek, select and structure the assistance of those around them in learning how to solve problems, and to be effective the adult must therefore be aware of and follow the child's motivation to learn. Vygotsky paid little attention to the precise way in which children play their role and to the variations from child to child in what they bring to the interaction. He was content with the generalization that cognitive development must be thought of as a cooperative enterprise: on the one hand, children signal their requirements and provide adults with cues as to what they are able to achieve, and, on the other hand, adults need to be sensitive to these cues and to adapt the nature and timing of their interventions accordingly. Like Piaget, Vygotsky stressed the *constructive* nature of cognitive development: children play an active part in advancing their knowledge and becoming competent problem solvers. Unlike Piaget, however, he did not believe they can accomplish this task on their own: they can only do so in conjunction with other people in the context of joint enterprises. The position he advances has in consequence come to be known as **social constructivism**.

> **Social constructivism** is the position adopted by Vygotsky and others that children's learning is based on active striving to make sense of the world rather than on passive acquisition, and that they do so most effectively in conjunction with others.

From Other-assistance to Self-assistance

Vygotsky presented his ideas in broad-brush terms, with little empirical data to back up his theory. It has been left to others to fill in the details, and most of such subsequent work has focused on aspects of the interpersonal level, in particular on the way children profit from adult assistance in problem-solving situations. Vygotsky put forward the concept of the zone of proximal development (ZPD) as a unifying concept in attempts to understand children's progression from dependence on others to independence in their cognitive functioning, but left unanswered a number of questions which subsequent investigators have therefore had to examine. Let us review these.

What goes on in the zone of proximal development?

The ZPD is the gap between what can be achieved unassisted by a child and what can be achieved with the help of a more knowledgeable person. It is therefore the crucial area in which tuitional efforts ought to be pitched; the adult, that is, should be sensitive both to the child's achievements and to his or her potential, and sensitively gear intellectual challenges to just a step or so beyond what the child already understands. By building on existing knowledge, children can then be led to further achievements.

This progression through the ZPD has been described in detail in terms of three successive stages (Tharp & Gallimore, 1988):

- *Stage 1: Where performance is assisted by more capable others.* Before children can function independently, they must rely on the help of others. Initially, the child may have little understanding of the nature of the task or the goal to be achieved; the adult must therefore take a dominant part in demonstrating and directing, and the child will merely comply and imitate. For example, a very young child confronted by a jigsaw puzzle may have little idea of how to fit the various pieces together or, for that matter, what the end result should be; accordingly, the adult will need to act as a model, encourage the child to help and imitate, point out just what is 'right' and what is 'wrong', and draw attention to the way the picture is progressively built up and finally completed. On subsequent occasions, as the child becomes more competent, the adult will increasingly hand over responsibility to the child for certain specific aspects of the task, doing so at a rate and in a manner which, ideally, is closely geared to the child's progress, but remaining available for help and support whenever necessary. This outline applies to all tasks that children are expected to accomplish, whether we are talking of jigsaw puzzles or learning to read, whether the time taken is a matter of minutes or of years.

- *Stage 2: Where performance is assisted by the child.* The child increasingly takes over the major responsibility from the adult for accomplishing the task successfully, and can therefore often act independently and without requiring the adult's presence. Yet there is still a constraint: instead of relying on the adult's verbal directions, the child now relies on his or her own overt verbalizations – repeating instructions, requests and reminders, and so using self-directed speech for guidance through the task. Thus at this stage children's overt utterances, addressed to themselves, are a necessary means for regulating task actions, forming a transition from the regulating directives of others to the internal processes that will eventually take their place.
- *Stage 3: Where performance is automatized.* With repeated practice the child gradually relinquishes reliance on any form of overt self-guidance. Task performance now becomes smooth and is carried out automatically. Thus knowledge about task execution has become internalized, i.e. transferred from the social (or *intermental*) to the psychological (or *intramental*) level.

This progression may break down subsequently if interfered with – temporarily by tiredness or illness, or for longer periods by prolonged lack of practice or trauma. The individual will then no longer be capable of automatically carrying out the task and instead be thrown back to performance under conditions typical of the earlier stages, before once more progressing through the ZPD.

Let us note one crucial point: what goes on within the ZPD need not be confined to the explicit and didactic forms of instruction which Vygotsky mostly talked about. It also applies to a wide range of other kinds of interaction – ones which are quite casual and informal, involving mutual play or chat, but which nevertheless have similar potential to advance children's knowledge. It is for this reason that the term **guided participation**, introduced by Barbara Rogoff (1990) to characterize what goes on in the ZPD, is a most appropriate one, for on the one hand it draws attention to the mutuality of the instructional process and, on the other hand, it emphasizes the child's role in serving as an *apprentice* to more knowledgeable and competent individuals.

> **Guided participation** is the procedure whereby adults help children to acquire knowledge through collaboration in problem-solving situations.

How do adults assist children's task performance?

A child's first tutors are usually the parents, and tuition mostly goes on quite spontaneously and naturally in one-to-one situations. Take the following exchange between a mother and her 2½-year-old while putting together a jigsaw puzzle of a lorry (taken from Wertsch, 1979):

CHILD: 'Oh, now where does this one go?' (picks up a black cargo piece).
MOTHER: 'Where does it go on this other one? Look at the other truck and then you can tell.' . . .

CHILD: 'Well . . . (looks at copy, then at model) . . . I look at it . . . Um, this other puzzle has a . . . has a black one over there' (points at black cargo piece in model).
MOTHER: 'Um-hm . . . So where do you want to put the black one on this puzzle?'
CHILD (picks up black piece, looks at copy): '. . . Over there?' (inserts piece correctly in
copy).

Play or teaching? The distinction has little meaning, for whatever children of this
age learn is provided in a playful context, where children have fun and in which
they set the pace, willingly followed by the mother. The exchange between them
is far from didactic instruction; it takes the form of a dialogue, and the mother's
contributions are in question form that nevertheless serve to direct the child's attention and actions appropriately. It is the child, not the mother, who at the end of
this short exchange places the puzzle piece in the correct place, thus ensuring that
it is he who gets the satisfaction from having achieved the desired goal.

Adults employ a great diversity of behaviour patterns when assisting children
to solve problems, the precise nature of which depends on the task and on the
child's age and capability. Some general strategies do occur repeatedly, as listed
in table 7.1. However, these are not applied willy-nilly but are chosen
in full awareness of the child's ongoing efforts within the task situation, with the aim of involving the child to the maximum extent of his
or her abilities. The adult, that is, builds *scaffolds* to assist the child.

The concept of **scaffolding** was introduced by David Wood and his
colleagues (Wood, Bruner & Ross, 1976; also see Wood & Wood, 1996)
to describe the kind of guidance and support adults provide to
children in the ZPD, and thus to identify the sort of actions required
to promote learning. It arose originally from observations made by

Scaffolding is the
process whereby adults
offer help to a child in
problem solving, and
adjust both the kind
and the amount of
help to the child's level
of performance.

Table 7.1   Adults' strategies when helping children in one-to-one problem-solving
situations (e.g. completing a jigsaw puzzle)

Strategy	*Examples (from joint play with jigsaw)*
Attract attention to object	Point, tap, label
Structure task into sequences	'Start with the corners, and then the edges'
Break task into smaller components	'Let's just find the bits for the horse'
Highlight critical features	'Look, this is a corner piece'
Demonstrate	Hold piece over gap to be put in
Remind where got to	'We need to find the horse's tail now'
Act as memory bank	'Can you fit it in just like the square piece you put in before?'
Control frustration	'You're doing fine, it's nearly finished'
Evaluate success/failure	'Clever girl, you found that piece all by yourself'
Maintain goal orientation	'Just the rest of the house, then we're done'

Wood et al. (1976) of the teaching techniques which mothers used when their 3- to 4-year-old children were confronted by a task that they could not master on their own. The task involved a set of wooden blocks that had to be fitted together by means of pegs and holes to create a pyramid, the question being whether children could learn to do so with adult guidance. The results of the study show clearly that many of the children did learn to solve the problem independently after tuition; what was of most interest, however, was *how* tuition brought this about, and it is here that the term scaffolding arose as an appropriate way of describing the mothers' actions.

These took a variety of forms, such as helping the child to select a piece, showing how pegs fit into holes, removing pieces other than the one the child was working with, pointing out or naming some feature and so on. All these were designed to keep the child on task and to simplify the problem to an appropriate degree. However, crucial to success was the way in which the mothers adapted their interventions according to the child's progress. Wood identified two rules governing such adaptation: first, when a child is struggling the tutor should immediately offer more help; second, when the child is succeeding the tutor should give less help and fade into the background. By offering support that is always contingent on what the child is achieving, the child is given considerable autonomy and yet also has the opportunity at every step of relying on help. Thus the mother offers a level of control appropriate to what the child has learned – a level which gradually diminishes as the child takes over responsibility for completing the task (see table 7.2 for the levels used to assess the mothers' interventions in the block-assembly task).

The notion of scaffolding may evoke an image of a rigid and immobile structure, but this is not what is intended. The two contingency rules mean that the adult's behaviour is flexible and constantly modified in the light of what the child is doing. In this way one can ensure that all tuitional efforts are pitched within the child's ZPD; the nature and level of support are thus continually adjusted to the child's understanding of previous levels of instruction. As Wood acknowledges, sustaining contingency throughout a session is extremely hard to achieve; observations of both parents and professional teachers show that there are few who can remain contingent at all times. In so far as children nevertheless learn under such

Table 7.2 Levels of parental control applied during joint problem solving with child

Level		Examples
1	General verbal prompts	'Now you make something'
2	Specific verbal instructions	'Get four blocks'
3	Indicates materials	Points to blocks needed
4	Prepares for assembly	Orients pairs so holes face peg
5	Demonstrates	Assembles two pairs

conditions, it seems that something less than 100 per cent contingency is usually enough to ensure the child's success. However, the general principle stands: scaffolding is a contingent, collaborative and interactive effort that should lead in due course to the child taking over responsibility from the adult for completing the task.

There have been many other studies which have examined the joint problem solving of adults and children, employing the scaffolding concept in order to understand what goes on. The studies have involved children of different ages, interacting with a variety of partners such as fathers, teachers, unfamiliar adults and also more advanced peers, and tackling such diverse tasks as learning to count, retelling a story, looking at picture books, sorting objects, planning complex activities, acquiring handicraft skills and solving scientific problems (see box 7.2 for one example, namely, the way mothers help children to understand some of the first steps of numeracy). All of these involve a number of general features that typify effective tutoring (Rogoff, 1990):

1 Tutors serve to bridge the gap between a learner's existing knowledge and skills and the demands of the new task.
2 By providing instruction and help in the context of the learner's activity, tutors provide a scaffold to support the learner's problem solving.

BOX 7.2

Learning about numbers with mother

Children's developing understanding of number has attracted a great deal of research interest, and as a result we now know quite a lot about the kinds of numerical knowledge and skills which children acquire at various ages (see Gelman & Gallistel, 1978; Nunes & Bryant, 1996). However, we know less about *how* they acquire such competence for much of the research has involved testing *what* children know rather than asking about the origins of their knowledge. As a result, numeracy has mostly been treated as a purely intrapersonal process, and it is only fairly recently that its development under everyday social conditions has begun to attract interest.

What are the social contributors to number knowledge? As observational studies have shown (e.g. Durkin, Shire, Crowther & Rutter, 1986), children from infancy on become immersed in a great range of everyday activities involving the use of numbers. The conversation of adults that goes on around them is full of references to number, made quite spontaneously and with no particular intent to teach. Moreover, many of the routines that go on at home involve children in number-related activities: for example, helping to lay table ('we need to put two forks at each place'); going shopping ('let's get four of those cakes'); telling the time ('we are late for nursery school, it's already 9 o'clock'); cooking ('how about putting one more spoonful of flour in?'); choosing a particular TV channel, and so forth. In addition there are songs and rhymes ('one, two, buckle my shoe'), stories (about the three little pigs, or Goldilocks and the three bears), informal games (e.g. counting fingers or toes) and competitions (such as the number of times children can skip with a rope) – all of them activities that introduce children to the importance of number in a purely informal but meaningful way.

Of course, even at home there are more formal attempts to teach young children operations such as counting and adding. Putting such sessions under the microscope in order to see just how the teaching–learning process is conducted provides further evidence of scaffolding. Take a study by Saxe, Guberman and Gearhart (1987). Mothers of 2- and 4-year-old children were asked to work together on some simple numerical tasks such as counting the number of objects presented and matching objects in one array with those in another array. The sessions were videotaped, and analysis of the tapes showed just how the mothers quite spontaneously adjusted the level and kind of assistance they provided in order to further the child's own competence in these tasks. Thus, the mothers generally recognized the type of difficulty their children were experiencing and responded with instructions tailored to that difficulty. Following an error by the child they shifted to more specific instructions; following success they adjusted the complexity level of their guid-ance upwards. Mothers of younger and less able children simplified the task more by breaking it down into smaller and easier components; mothers also simplified their instructions when confronted with more difficult tasks. By such scaffolding moves they made it easier for children to progress to new levels of skill: the children were enabled to adjust their behaviour in the light of the mother's input, and could often accomplish a task with the mother's help that they had not been able to perform on their own. This change was, however, more common with the 4-year-olds than with the 2-year-olds; the former were clearly within the relevant ZPD for these particular tasks, whereas the younger children had apparently not quite reached it.

These observations provide evidence that is broadly consistent with Vygotsky's account of cognitive development. Children do not learn about number in isolation; they do so in conjunction with others who act, inform-ally and spontaneously in most cases, as helpers and instructors. Such help is usually provided sensitively, in full awareness of the child's general com-petence and moment-to-moment successes and failures. What is more, adults tend to make such sessions enjoyable, thus providing the motivation to repeat the experience and find out more.

3   Although the learner is involved in what is initially beyond reach, the tutor's actions ensure that the learner plays an active part in problem solving and contributes to the successful solution of problems.

4   Effective tutoring involves the transfer of responsibility from tutor to learner.

The main advantage of the term *scaffolding* is that it provides us with a vivid metaphor, reminding us that children's learning is a particular kind of joint effort in which adults need to make available supports of a special nature and at special times. By itself the concept does not actually explain how children internalize what their tutor provides; it does, however, draw attention to the conditions under which learning usually takes place and emphasizes the essentially social-interactive nature of these conditions.

What makes for effective assistance?

Not all adult efforts are equally successful in helping children to solve problems, so what accounts for the difference? Let us consider three sets of influences, stemming respectively from the adult, from the child and from the adult–child relationship.

- *Adults* vary greatly in their sensitivity to others, and the ability to tune in to children's requirements may well be grossly impaired in some. Yet such an ability is crucial if assistance is to be given in the contingent manner outlined above. Sensitivity involves understanding what components of a task the child can cope with on his or her own, what components the child can understand but only with help, and what components are beyond the child's current ability. An adult lacking sensitivity may overload the child with too much information, or give the information at an inappropriate level (too high or too low), or exert too much control and not allow the child space to try out his or her own solutions, or adopt the wrong strategy such as only giving verbal instructions when the child also requires non-verbal demonstration. Whatever form insensitivity takes, it deprives the child of the appropriate scaffold required for problem solution.

- *Children* vary in the extent to which they can profit from help. As we have previously emphasized, all adult–child interactions are bidirectional in nature; the effects children have on adults by virtue of their individual characteristics determine the nature of the interaction, and this applies to tuitional situations too. This becomes most obvious in cases of pathology such as Down's syndrome, for such children have considerable difficulty with employing attention in a flexible way, shifting focus in response to another person's attempts to redirect their behaviour and coordinating their actions with those of others – all activities required for profiting from joint problem-solving situations (Landry & Chapieski, 1989). The same applies to preterm children, at least in their early stages (Landry, Smith, Swank & Miller-Loncar, 2000), and for that matter any other child-based condition that interferes with adult–child synchrony.

- *Adult–child relationship* factors need to be taken into account because of indications that the kind of attachment that develops between parent and child can affect the child's ability to benefit from instruction – and not only from that parent but from others too (Moss, Gosselin, Parent, Rousseau & Dumont, 1997; van der Veer & van IJzendoorn, 1988). Securely attached children, it appears, have the confidence to tackle difficult cognitive problems even when working on their own or with an unfamiliar person; when working jointly with the mother, they know that their attempts at the task will be accepted and supported. Insecurely attached children, on the other hand, do not have that confidence; their past experience tells them that their actions are likely to be ignored or rejected, and as a result they are much less willing to use their own initiative. In general, insecure children interact with their mothers in a less supportive environment than secure children; mother and child are not so well attuned to one another in that the mother often fails to respond as meaningfully and contingently to the child's actions as found with secure pairs. As a result secure children's performance tends to improve after a joint problem-solving session with the mother, whereas this may not necessarily occur with insecure children.

Can peers act as tutors?

A distinction has been made between two sets of circumstances in which children help one another to solve problems:

- *Collaborative learning*, involving children at similar levels of competence working together in pairs or in groups – already referred to in chapter 4 as part of our discussion of peer relationships.
- *Peer tutoring*, where a more knowledgeable child sets out to provide instruction and guidance to another child in order to bring the latter up to a similar level of competence.

The latter is of relevance here, for according to Vygotskian theory the tutor–tutee model can incorporate any variant of pairs, such as parent–child, teacher–pupil and also peer expert–peer novice. In all there is an asymmetry of roles, in that in all of them knowledge is transferred from one partner to the other.

A considerable literature is now available on peer tutoring (see Foot & Howe, 1998; Foot, Morgan & Shute, 1990). Much of the interest generated stems from the practical implications that this work might have for educational practice: the idea that children are in a position to help each other has obvious attractions for hard-pressed teachers. Thus most of the peer-tutoring studies have examined school-age children and have frequently involved tasks of educational relevance such as reading, writing and spelling or science problems such as understanding the principles underlying floating objects or motion down an incline. Yet there is much of theoretical interest here too, for the greater the variety of type of partner one observes in joint problem-solving situations, the greater is the chance of learning about the way in which knowledge can be transferred.

Most of the studies on peer tutoring have reported positive results. Children do gain from being guided by a child tutor, even when the age gap between the pair is minimal; moreover, according to some studies teaching may benefit the *tutor* as well. Yet not all studies have found gains: under some circumstances children may even regress. Simply being with a more advanced partner is not sufficient; other conditions must be met too. Where, for example, the tutor has a greater but not a thorough understanding of the problem, the process of instruction may well fail; similarly, if the tutor dominates the interaction and does not give the tutee enough space, the latter is not likely to benefit. Clearly child tutors (like their adult counterparts) need to adopt certain strategies to be effective instructors: they too must show sensitivity to their partner's efforts, provide feedback at the right level and pace their instructions appropriate to the tutee's ability to absorb them (Tudge & Winterhoff, 1993). What is perhaps surprising is that children, at least from the middle years on, are often capable of adopting such strategies and can therefore act as instructors to less knowledgeable children.

What role do cultural factors play in adult–child tutoring?

When comparing the nature of children's instruction by others as found in different societies, it becomes apparent that there are marked differences in certain respects, yet also underlying similarities. Turning first to the differences, these can be seen in three aspects of instruction: *what, when* and *how. What* the subject is that children should be instructed in depends on the particular sets of skills and knowledge that each society values: hunting wild animals and skinning them in one; operating computers and making them work for you in another. *When* children should be instructed also varies according to cultural requirements: for example, in some African tribes heavily reliant on women's fieldwork, children aged 4 or 5 are instructed in the routines of child care, thereby letting the mother return to work as quickly as possible after the birth of another baby – all at an age when western parents would regard their children as still quite incapable of picking up the necessary skills.

How refers to the style of instruction – for example, the amount of support adults give to children's learning and the manner of giving it, the way in which the respective roles of tutor and tutee are perceived, and the extent to which the teaching–learning process is embedded in the everyday life of the community as opposed to being conducted behind closed doors in specialized education establishments. Cross-cultural comparisons illustrate the often quite considerable differences that exist in instructional style (see box 7.3 for one such example). Thus in some societies questions from children to adults are discouraged, as this is seen as impolite and insulting; in others, adults consider it ridiculous to ask a child a question when they themselves already know the answer. Variations exist in the emphasis placed

---

BOX 7.3

Mothers' and children's joint problem solving in Guatemala and the USA

In a highly ambitious cross-cultural investigation, Barbara Rogoff and her colleagues (1993) analysed in great detail how mothers and their young children from four communities, with very different cultural traditions, set about collaborating in solving problems. The four samples were drawn from Guatemala, the United States, India and Turkey, though here we shall concentrate on just the first two as they present the greatest contrast.

The Guatemalan group came from a Mayan Indian community called San Pedro, a small town in mountainous country that had been relatively isolated from outside influences and only recently acquired some of the products of modern technology such as electric light and radio. Most of the fathers were agricultural labourers or small farmers, struggling to make a living. The American families lived in Salt Lake City, the capital of Utah, a city of half a million people, and were mostly well-off middle or upper middle class. In each community 14 sets of mothers and children (aged 1 to 2 years) were intensively studied, with the focus of the investigation on the way in which the mothers helped their children to cope with two difficult tasks, i.e. to operate various novel objects such as a jumping-jack puppet and to put on clothes.

All the mothers worked jointly with their children on both tasks, providing help, support and encouragement. Yet the style of collaboration differed markedly in certain respects, highlighted by an analysis of the way in which the novel objects were tackled by each pair (see table 7.3). In San Pedro the mothers, unlike their American counterparts, did not see themselves as playmates of their children; to assume such a role was regarded as embarrassing, and they therefore preferred to call on one of their older children to play with the toddler and direct this child in helping the toddler to work the objects. These mothers saw themselves as basically supervisors and instructors, and while by no means uninvolved with the toddlers' activity they spent their time mostly on demonstrating what had to be done with the object and then turning it over to the child ('Now you do it!'). Thus, compared with the Salt Lake City

Table 7.3 Mothers' behaviour in joint problem-solving situations: a comparison of Guatemalan and US samples (percentage of episodes in which each behaviour occurred)

	Guatemala	USA
Mother acts as playmate	7	47
Mother converses with child as a peer	19	79
Mother uses baby talk	30	93
Mother praises	4	44
Mother shows mock excitement	13	74
Mother poised ready to help	81	23

Source: Adapted from Rogoff et al. (1993).

sample, a different atmosphere prevailed in the sessions: however helpful the Guatemalan mothers were, they provided assistance in a more formal manner, maintaining the difference in status between themselves and the child rather than treating the occasion as an opportunity for joint play as the American mothers did.

This difference was also seen in the patterns of communication adopted by the two groups. San Pedro mothers did not treat their children as conversational partners: whereas the Salt Lake City mothers would try to engage their children in dialogues, asking them questions and even trying to elicit their opinions, this was rarely seen in the San Pedro sample. The American mothers would often use baby talk in order to get down to the child's verbal level and establish a meaningful exchange; in order to motivate the child they spoke in tones of mock excitement; and in general they talked rather more whereas the San Pedro mothers relied more on non-verbal communication. The latter also rarely praised their children's efforts, and yet all along they closely monitored the child's activities and were poised ready to help whenever the child needed assistance.

Thus a detailed analysis of the way in which the two groups of mothers and children interacted when confronted with the same challenges highlighted marked differences in instructional styles. These reflect cultural variations in the role which each society assigned to parents and children. In Guatemala, for instance, children were seen as primarily responsible for their own learning, leaving the pace and direction of effort up to them; many of the toddlers' actions, for instance, occurred at their own instigation, with the mother merely holding a watchful brief. The American parents, on the other hand, considered themselves as having to motivate learning and structure the interaction session, but in the belief that they could do so most effectively by acting on the same level of play and talk as the child.

on watching and copying as the principal means of instruction as opposed to the child actively joining in with the adult; these differences in turn are related to whether responsibility for learning is assigned primarily to children or to adults. Variations can also be found in how much of instruction is explicit, carried out in specially set-up institutions such as schools, rather than implicit, going on informally as a by-product of everyday social life.

Yet despite this diversity, the theme of instruction as a collaborative enterprise, in which instructing adult and apprenticed child must establish shared understanding of means and goals, is a recurrent one, even in societies that otherwise adopt a very different tuitional style. Consider the following example of mothers from an Indian community in Central America (Rogoff, 1990):

> Mayan mothers . . . report that 1- to 2-year-olds observe their mothers making tortillas and attempt to follow suit. Mothers give children a small piece of dough to use and facilitate their efforts by rolling the dough into a ball and starting to flatten it. The toddler's 'tortilla', if it is not dropped in the dirt, is cooked by the mother with the other tortillas and eaten. . . . As the child gains skill in shaping tortillas, the mother adds pointers and demonstrates how to hold the dough in a position that facilitates smooth flattening, and the child can both witness the outcome of his or her own efforts and contribute to making meals. The child observes carefully and participates, and the mother, usually good-naturedly, supports the child's efforts by simplifying the task to make it commensurate with the child's level of skill by demonstrating and giving suggestions in the process of joint activity. Five- and 6-year-old children are able to make some tortillas for dinner, and girls of 9 and 10 can handle the process from grinding the corn to rolling and patting the tortilla to turning it on the hot griddle with their fingers, preparing the family's dinner when necessary.

We see here children participating in the activities of their elders, imitating them but also being encouraged by them with the use of a variety of scaffolding techniques – simplifying the task, breaking it down into components and giving the child responsibility for the easier ones, demonstrating, encouraging and in general adjusting instructions according to the learner's level of skill. Similar observations have come from other societies where different skills are being conveyed, such as tailoring in Liberia and weaving in Mexico – these too conform to the pattern of children gradually taking over responsibility for the task, adults relinquishing that responsibility, and the two working in concert to achieve this end.

Is joint problem solving superior to working alone?

We have now reached the crucial question, for it relates to the social origin of knowledge and so concerns one of Vygotsky's most basic propositions. A large number of studies are now available that have investigated this problem, the most convincing of which are those that have been specifically set up experimentally to test the proposition. Such a test usually takes the form outlined in table 7.4, whereby children's

Table 7.4   Research design for studies investigating the effects of joint problem solving

	Pre-test	Problem-solving practice	Post-test
Experimental group	Child's work on own is assessed	Child and tutor work together for a period	Child's work on own is assessed
Control group	Child's work on own is assessed	Child practises problem solving on own	Child's work on own is assessed

baseline of skill at some task is first established by assessing them on their own, succeeded by a period of working jointly with a tutor, and followed finally by assessing the child once more while working alone. The change from pre- to post-test can then give an indication of how much the child has benefited from the instructional period; this can be compared with any change that has taken place during the comparable period in a control group of children working on their own throughout.

Take as an example a study by Freund (1990). Children aged 3 and 5 years worked with their mothers on a task sorting toy furniture into the appropriate rooms in a dolls' house – sofa into the living room, cooker into the kitchen and so on. The mothers were encouraged to help their children in any way that they chose, though without any explicit teaching. Before the joint session the children's ability to sort on their own was assessed; immediately after the session with the mother they were assessed again on their own. When compared with a group of children of similar ages who practised by themselves instead of working with the mother, it was found that the 'joint' children made significantly greater gains than the 'solo' children (table 7.5). What is more, those mothers who provided the most helpful types of guidance to their children by, for example, discussing aspects of strategy (e.g. 'where do we keep the refrigerator at home?') and by maintaining goal direction (e.g. 'let's finish the bedroom and then do the kitchen') had children

Table 7.5   Pre- and post-test scores (percentage of correct responses on sorting task) by 3- and 5-year-old children experiencing joint or solo practice session

	Joint session		Solo session	
	Pre-test	Post-test	Pre-test	Post-test
3-year-olds	46	70	41	36
5-year-olds	52	94	51	64

Source: After Freund (1990).

making the greatest improvement in independent problem solving. Thus we can conclude, first, that the experience of active involvement with a more knowledgeable guide was directly responsible for a rise in the children's performance level, and secondly, that precisely what transpired in the joint session affected the degree of improvement: the more the children were exposed to certain kinds of guidance necessary for successful problem solving, the greater were their chances of coping with the task on their own.

A substantial body of evidence has now been accumulated indicating that children's ability to solve problems is raised by the experience of working with a supportive adult, and that this increase in ability carries over to future occasions of working independently. This applies as much to peer tutoring as to tutoring by adults; the effect has been found for mothers, for fathers and for unfamiliar individuals; and it has been demonstrated over a wide range of ages and tasks. Yet the findings are by no means unanimous. As we have already noted in the case of peer tutoring, and as has also been shown by some studies of adult tutoring (e.g. Kontos & Nicholas, 1986), the beneficial effects of joint work have not been confirmed by everyone: children have either failed to improve, or their improvement has been matched by a control group of children working on their own. It appears that the benefits are to be found under certain conditions only. For one thing, much depends on the tutor's technique: as Freund showed in the study just described, some kinds of guidance are more helpful than others. No blanket guarantee can be given for all forms of joint work, and under some circumstances the presence of a partner may even have a negative effect. For another, some tasks lend themselves more easily to the shared thinking that lies at the heart of successful tutor–tutee relationships than others. Where, for example, a task is most easily carried out by dividing it into simple parts, to be tackled by the child, and more difficult ones allocated to the adult, there will be no opportunity for a meeting of minds and the child's overall performance will not therefore improve.

Evaluation

Although Vygotsky's writings were 'discovered' only in the 1960s and 1970s, and although he did not live long enough to be anywhere near as productive as Piaget, his work has nevertheless become as influential as that of the latter. As though to make up for lost time, Vygotsky's theory has received an enormous amount of attention of late, and its contributions and shortcomings as a way of viewing children's cognitive development have thus gradually become clear.

Contributions

Above all, Vygotsky's legacy lies in his *contextualist* approach – the belief that it is meaningless to study individuals in isolation and that instead they must always be related to the social-historical-cultural context in which they are embedded. Vygotsky was by no means the first to advance such a view, but his analysis of what constitutes such a context and how it is related to intellectual development gave this approach a prominence which no other author had achieved.

Traditionally, the individual child has been seen as the point of departure for the study of development – either as the target for environmental stimulation, to be propelled in certain directions and moulded in particular ways, or as an independent agent busily constructing his or her own reality. In each case child and context were treated as antithetical: two separate units that somehow have to come to terms with one another in the course of development. To many, this seemed an almost commonsensical view; Vygotsky's writings, on the other hand, argued convincingly that *child-in-context* rather than *child-in-vacuum* should be regarded as the basic unit of analysis in our thinking about children. Take the following passage in which Vygotsky (1987) characterizes Piagetian theory and pours scorn on it:

> The child is not seen as a part of the social whole, as a subject of social relationships. He is not seen as a being who participates in the societal life of the social whole to which he belongs from the outset. The social is viewed as something standing outside the child.

Vygotsky's principal achievement was to have shown the gains to be made in our understanding when children are treated as part of the 'social whole' and not detached from their environmental context – when, that is, a more embracing approach is adopted than the traditional one.

What makes Vygotsky's theory particularly valuable is his attempt to spell out the nature of the context in which development occurs and the way in which this context impinges on children. Most unusually, the theory proposed that *context* is a multi-layered construct including far more than the immediate environment in which a child is functioning at any one time. Historical, political, economic, technical and literary influences – all these were introduced as an inherent part of the social milieu to which children belong. Take the concept of *cultural tools* which Vygotsky introduced – a novel way of appreciating how each society in the course of its history evolves particular means of thought whereby children are enabled to participate in that society's activities. Context, that is, is not some vague, global entity but a construct that can be specified and shown to have a definable role in children's development. Or take the concept of the *zone of proximal development* – a means of understanding the interface between child and society. This enabled Vygotsky not only to make the general point that culture needs to be handed down from one generation to another in the course of adult–child interaction, but also to indicate how this takes place and the mechanism whereby this can be accomplished most effectively.

Vygotsky did not undertake much empirical work himself, but the specific nature of many of his proposals has made it possible for others to follow up his ideas and a substantial body of research has thus been stimulated by the theory.

As we have seen, this applies in particular to the part that adults play in children's instruction, but other ideas too, such as the role of cultural tools in cognitive development, have given rise to a considerable number of investigations. In addition, two other areas of research owe much to Vygotsky's writings, namely, further attempts to specify just how we can most fruitfully define contextual influences (the ecological systems theory of Bronfenbrenner, 1989, being the best-known example), and cross-cultural comparisons such as those undertaken by Rogoff (1990) which derive their theoretical rationale from Vygotsky's stress on the symbiotic relationship between child development and socio-cultural milieu.

Shortcomings

There is much that is vague and unfinished about Vygotsky's writings, but let us focus on just two major omissions, namely, his neglect of the individual child's contribution and of emotional aspects.

As to the former, despite his aim of integrating the three main levels of culture, interaction and individual, Vygotsky paid scant attention to the last of these. Unlike his careful treatment of the other two, he failed to spell out in any detail the way in which children's individuality contributes to learning and development. He agreed with Piaget on the importance of seeing the child as active, yet the precise nature of what the child brings to the interaction with cultural partners is not sufficiently stressed or analysed. More attention is paid to the adult than to the child and to socio-cultural influences than to influences inherent in the child's nature. Admittedly, little was known about genetics at his time, yet other contemporary writers did acknowledge that there is no one typical child and accordingly did try to do justice to the nature of individuality in their accounts of development. The only concession Vygotsky made was his comment, when discussing collaboration with adults in the ZPD, that 'the child's performance is restricted to limits which are determined by the state of his development and his intellectual potential' (Vygotsky, 1987). Otherwise, he failed to give due weight to the role of individually based influences.

This is also seen in Vygotsky's neglect of age. His theory, unlike Piaget's, is not a truly developmental one; he conceived of a prototype child who functioned in the same way at age 2 as at age 12, never mind what maturational changes had taken place and what experiences had accumulated in the meantime. The ZPD shifts as the child gets older, but its nature and the roles which adult and child respectively play remain the same in Vygotsky's account, with no across-age comparisons made. New needs and abilities clock in as the child grows older, but Vygotsky gave no indication that, for instance, the child's definition of what constitutes her social context or the way she reacts to that context may change. Similarly, nothing is said about the way processes that underlie learning – such as sensory, attentional, memory and intellectual capacities – vary from one age to another and affect the tutorial interaction accordingly. For that matter, there is also no mention of the changes that normally occur in the identity of individuals the child accepts as tutors, as the range increases from parents to include other close adults, teachers and peers.

The other major shortcoming is the disregard of emotional aspects. While cognition was given a social appearance, Vygotsky's treatment of the child is as 'cold' as Piaget's. There is no indication of the struggles of learning, of the frustrations of failure and the joys of success. Nothing is said as to what motivates children to achieve particular goals, and the satisfactions and annoyances experienced in the course of attempts to reach these goals are passed over. This is a serious omission, though one shared with other major theorists. Vygotsky did write about the nature of emotions and emotional expression, but he made no attempt to link this up with his socio-cultural theory of cognitive development, which is thus not really the all-encompassing account he had set out to achieve.

Summary

Vygotsky's theory of cognitive development, like Piaget's, is a *constructivist* one: children, that is, actively interpret the world around them instead of passively relying on bits of knowledge being fed to them by others. Unlike Piaget's, however, his account can also be labelled a *contextualist* one: children are part of their socio-culture and their development is inextricably linked to the form of that culture.

Cognitive development is therefore essentially a social process and needs to be understood as the integration of three aspects: cultural, interpersonal and individual.

1 Culture plays a prominent role in Vygotsky's theory, in that he saw human nature as basically a socio-historical product, sustained by *cultural tools*. These refer to psychological devices like language and numeracy and to technological devices like books, clocks and computers. Such tools foster particular ways of thinking and enable children to understand the world in ways shared with other members of their society.

2 Interpersonal aspects describe the precise mechanisms whereby culture is passed on to children in the course of their encounters with more competent individuals. All knowledge, he proposed, is social in origin: cognitive development is a progression from the *intermental* to the *intramental*, in that any intellectual skill is first performed jointly with a more competent person before the child takes it over and internalizes it. When apprenticed to such a person, children are capable of functioning at a higher level than when working on their own, and their true potential is therefore best assessed in such joint performance rather than in isolation. The gap between solo and joint performance – the *zone of proximal development* – is, moreover, the area where the child is most likely to profit from instruction and where adults should therefore pitch their tuitional efforts.

3 The individual child's contribution to the learning process was acknowledged by Vygotsky but received little detailed attention. Other than seeing children as actively involved in their own development, he made little effort to spell out how factors such as age and individuality influence the course of cooperative learning.

Vygotsky's writings have stimulated a considerable body of research, much of it aimed at throwing further light on the way in which knowledge is transmitted from adults to children. Various descriptive accounts are available of the scaffolding strategies adults employ to help children acquire problem-solving skills, and a lot of evidence is now to hand confirming Vygotsky's basic hypothesis, that children's ability to solve problems is raised by joint work, even though the benefits are to be found under certain conditions only that are most effective in this respect.

The value of Vygotsky's theory lies, above all, in the importance attached to seeing children in the context of their socio-cultural background and not treating them as isolated units. Two major omissions are, however, evident; these are the neglect of children's age and individuality as influences on development and the failure to include emotional aspects in the treatment of cognitive and social factors.

FURTHER READING

Gauvain, M. (2001). *The Social Context of Cognitive Development.* New York: Guilford Press. Gauvain's book builds on Vygotsky's thesis, that not only what children learn but how they learn is inextricably linked to their socio-cultural background. By presenting recent work on such cognitive processes as problem solving, attention and memory, she demonstrates that the social setting in which children live provides both opportunities and constraints for their cognitive development.

Miller, P. H. (2002). *Theories of Developmental Psychology* (4th edn). New York: W. H. Freeman. A clear and concise account in a chapter entitled 'Vygotsky's Theory and the Contextualists'. Provides an overview of all the main features of the theory, evaluates it in the light of other theories, and traces its influence on subsequent research.

Rogoff, B. (1990). *Apprenticeship in Thinking: Cognitive Development in Social Context.* New York: Oxford University Press. Rogoff has been very much influenced by Vygotsky's theory but has put her own gloss on it and given particular emphasis to cultural influences. The book gives an account of both her theoretical position and her research activities.

van der Veer, R., & Valsiner, J. (1991). *Understanding Vygotsky: A Quest for Synthesis.* Oxford: Blackwell. A very detailed, comprehensive and sometimes rather technical account of Vygotsky's work. Presented in the context of his personal background and education, the book demonstrates the links between his views and Russian society and politics as they existed at the time.

CHAPTER EIGHT

Children as Information Processors

Chapter Outline

Modelling Mental Activity

In attempts to understand the workings of the mind, psychologists have found it useful to employ models of one kind or another, where the model represents particular human functions and thus helps us to gain insight into the way these functions operate. One such example is the telephone switchboard, used in the hope that we can thereby learn more about the way in which the brain receives incoming messages and establishes appropriate connections; another is the thermostat, which represents a further essential human function, namely, the ability to make use of feedback information in the attainment of goals. Models such as these serve as metaphors: the mind is seen as if it were such a device, on the assumption that this will further our understanding of the real thing.

Is the mind a computer?

The latest model so employed is that of the computer, derived from the *information-processing approach* to cognition (for detailed accounts, see Boden, 1988; Klahr & MacWhinney, 1998; P. Miller, 2002). This approach views mental activity primarily as a matter of handling information, starting usually with input through the senses and ending with some form of output such as goal-directed action. Understanding cognition is a matter of tracing the flow of information from one end to the other and of identifying the nature of the intervening processes. These include, for example, the encoding of information received in the form of symbols such as visual images or verbal labels; the storage of these symbols in the brain; their interpretation in the light of other stored material; the retrieval processes used to reflect upon and rework the acquired information; and the operations performed on such data in order to bring about particular forms of output. By experimentally manipulating the kind of input provided and analysing the way the individual deals with it under various output conditions, it becomes possible to infer what sort of processes intervene and to construct a flow diagram that illustrates the sequence of these processes (see figure 8.1 for an example).

Computers, like the human cognitive system, are also information-processing devices. They too accept certain kinds of input, and just as the human mind transforms that input into symbolic form to represent external stimuli, so computers need to convert their input into symbols in order then to register and store the data. And just as human beings then make use of stored symbols as the content of thought, so computers can perform a range of operations upon whatever material is to be found in their storage system. In certain respects at least, the mind is a computer; and though some advocates of the information-processing approach are content to consider this just as a metaphor, others have taken the comparison much further and, for instance, constructed computer programmes that aim to model the way we think, thereby putting to the test specific hypotheses about functions such as

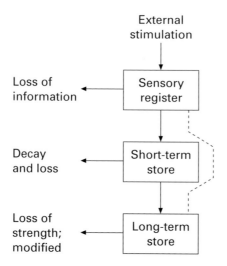

Figure 8.1 *Flow diagram: information received and stored (based on Atkinson & Shiffrin, 1968).*

attention, memory and problem solving. In this way, it is believed, we will be able to learn what individuals actually do when they are thinking.

Just as computers are described in terms of hardware (their physical components) and software (the operating programmes), so information-processing adherents consider it useful to differentiate between structures and processes when investigating human cognition.

- *Structures* refer to the building blocks of the cognitive system (hence the term 'cognitive architecture', which has also been used in this connection). These are the boxes that appear on flow diagrams as shown in figure 8.1, with labels such as sensory register, working memory and long-term memory. While purely hypothetical, they serve to draw attention to particular parts of the information-processing apparatus that carry out specific functions. There are relatively few such structures; moreover, they are enduring in that they do not change their functioning in the course of development or from one situation to another, and they are also universal in so far as they are part of the psychological equipment of all human beings. They are the hardware of the mind, and their characteristics provide the constraints on the kinds of programmes that can be run in individual cognitive systems.
- *Processes* are analogous to computer software – the programmes required to operate the system. Unlike structures, they are numerous, vary across age groups and from one person to another, and are highly adaptable to whatever circumstances confront the individual. From a developmental point of view in particular, it is useful to distinguish between *controlled* (or effortful) and

automatic (or effortless) processes – a distinction based on how much attention is required to carry out the process. Controlled processes demand all our attention: they are slow and laborious and take up a lot of 'cognitive space'. Automatic processes, on the other hand, occur speedily and easily, in that they involve familiar, well-practised routines and quickly assimilated stimuli. Much of cognitive development is concerned with proceeding from controlled to automatic processing. Compare a 5-year-old with a 10-year-old, asked to solve the problem 5 + 4 = ?: the former will spend a great deal of time comprehending what is required, working out ways of arriving at a solution and then checking the answer obtained; the latter, on the other hand, can produce an immediate answer on the basis of countless previous trials, and because of the minimal amount of attention required can thereby quickly free the mind to pass on to new mental challenges.

There have been many attempts to apply the information-processing approach to the study of children's cognition. These have, for example, involved the analysis of children's attempts to solve Piagetian tasks such as conservation and seriation; the approach has also been used with respect to educational problems in the areas of reading, writing and arithmetic; and much of the research on children's memory has profited from techniques and concepts developed by adherents to this way of analysing cognition. The general aim of such studies is to specify as precisely as possible the mental mechanisms children use in thinking: how they take in and represent information, how much capacity they have for storage purposes, what operations they use to retrieve and process stored information, and how young children differ from older individuals in the way they carry out these functions. The latter question is of particular interest, in that it attempts to shed light on the way cognitive development progresses. Piaget, as we saw, used the concept of stage for this purpose; most information-processing accounts, on the other hand, avoid all reference to stages and instead specify change over age in terms of such aspects as processing speed, storage capacity, and the number and flexibility of strategies available for storing, retrieving and making use of information (table 8.1 lists some examples of the developmental changes that have been proposed). Many of these developments are well documented: there is, for instance, no doubt that children's ability to repeat a string of digits, or of words, improves with age, reflecting improvements in their greater capacity to attend to information and store it in short-term memory (figure 8.2). What is not so clear is precisely what aspects of children's information-processing apparatus account for the improvement – whether, for example, children get better at recalling things as they get older because their basic storage capacity increases (i.e. a 'hardware' difference), or whether children become more efficient in employing various processing strategies (a 'software' difference). It is, of course, quite possible that both types of change take place, i.e. that brain growth occurs which in turn allows more functional development. At present, however, we know rather more about the *how* of change than the *why* – a common story in developmental psychology.

Table 8.1 Examples of developmental advance in the processing of information

Aspect of information processing	Nature of developmental advance
Processing capacity	Amount of information taken in through the sensory register increases with age
Processing speed	The speed with which the various parts of the cognitive apparatus function increases
Processing strategies	The strategies which individuals use for tasks such as remembering and problem solving become more numerous as children get older
Knowledge base	With increasing age the amount of relevant knowledge encountered by new experiences increases and facilitates (or sometimes hinders) the processing of new information
Parallel processing	Young children attend to one thing at a time; older children are able simultaneously to attend to several aspects of stimuli and combine them into one experience

What, then, are we to make of the information-processing approach? Does it help to think of the mind as a computer? A fierce debate has raged and is still raging around this issue, with some writers taking a strongly sceptical attitude. One of these is the philosopher John Searle (1984), who concluded:

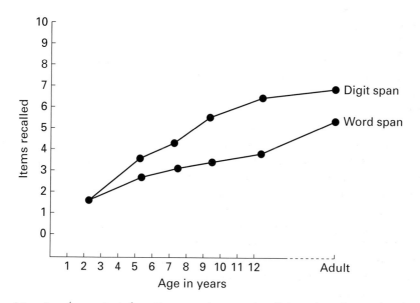

Figure 8.2 *Age changes in information-processing capacity: digit and word span (based on Dempster, 1981).*

The computer is probably no better and no worse as a metaphor for the brain than earlier mechanical metaphors. We learn as much about the brain by saying it is a computer as we do by saying it is a telephone switchboard, a telegraph system, a water pump or a steam engine.

Others have been rather more positive. Thus Margaret Boden (1988), after a very detailed examination of the various claims and criticisms made for using the computer as a model for minds, concluded that some distinct gains have been made for psychology by adopting this approach. In particular:

Computational psychologists are accustomed to seeking a degree of precision, in the description even of highly complex mental processes, which (at worst) highlights theoretical lacunae and (at best) helps us to fill them. This attention to precise theoretical detail is not a passing fancy, a trendy fad born of a technological society and doomed to obsolescence, but an enduring contribution to psychological science. It has provided a standard of rigour and clarity which must make us permanently dissatisfied with less.

Boden dismisses the fear that the comparison of mind with computers necessarily dehumanizes psychology, and does not regard as justified claims that a computer model is too mechanistic to cope with a mentalistic concept such as intentionality – one of the main criticisms put forward by Searle. Certainly, the computer as we know it nowadays is far from a passive mechanical device, and given the capacity for self-evaluation and self-modification there is no reason to believe that computers are incapable of simulating the more psychodynamic aspects of psychological functioning, such as motivation and even emotion. Admittedly, accounts of information processing have so far been almost entirely 'cold' in their treatment of human beings, describing them as purely cognitive systems and leaving out any reference to socio-emotional aspects. In principle, however, there is no reason why such aspects should not be included – see, for example, the efforts made to find links between attachment development and information-processing competence, based on the premise that children with secure attachments are more likely to have 'cognitive space' to attend to and cope with environmental challenges than insecure children. The evidence for this link (reviewed by Goldberg, 2000) is as yet sparse and by no means conclusive, but it does at least serve to remind us that there is a social dimension to all information processing that any complete account of children's cognitive functioning will need to include.

In the meantime, there is little doubt that, as Boden pointed out in the above quotation, one of the main advantages of the information-processing approach lies in its methodological and conceptual precision. The fine-grained analysis of the way we think, coupled with an equally detailed description of whatever task the individual is attempting to solve, is not only of theoretical but also of practical benefit. Error analysis, for example, applied to children's attempts to grapple with educational tasks, has the potential to go far beyond a global judgement of 'can't do', indicating instead with considerable precision the specific reasons for a child's failure and, in particular, pinpointing the exact location in the information-processing flow where the obstacle lies. Is it due to the child's limited ability to attend to and hold in mind a number of diverse items of information? Or to inadequate storage capacity? Or to poorly developed retrieval strategies? Or to lack of representational skills? Given such an approach, with its demand for explicit diagnosis of task and performance and their interrelationship in individual children, the chances of providing successful remedial action become appreciably greater in comparison with more globally based efforts (Siegler, 1998).

The Nature of Thought

Information processing in human beings is approximately equivalent to what is customarily referred to as thinking. While it is in fact not easy to define the boundaries of thought, there is general agreement that it covers such mental functions as reasoning, symbolizing, problem solving and planning – all expressions of the higher, more intellectual facets of the mind and all aspects to which information-processing approaches have given special attention.

The capacity for thought is surely *the* hallmark of the human species. There are indications that mental processes exist in other primates too; however, those in human beings are vastly more complex, flexible and far-reaching, particularly in the way they can go beyond the here-and-now and encompass abstractions and generalities. Yet, while we are all intimately acquainted with thinking from our own experience of it, trying to capture its nature is a challenging task. It appears to be something that happens inside our head, that goes on more or less continuously and over which we can exercise at least some degree of control. Its importance lies in the fact that it enables us to process information from the environment in an individual and creative manner, and the need to foster its growth in childhood is thus obvious. To pin down this elusive phenomenon in children and systematically investigate it may not be easy; nevertheless, it has been possible to find out a considerable amount about the characteristics of thought processes even in the early years of life.

The problem of access

Let us first consider how we can study something as private and unobservable as children's thinking. By what means can we reach a child's *inner* life? We cannot, of course, actually see or hear others' thoughts; however, by noting their behaviour in certain situations, we can *infer* that they are thinking and, moreover, surmise the nature and content of their mental processes. Below are some of the means that have been employed to this end in research on children's cognitive development.

- *Analysing conversations.* Children's participation in talk with others, whether adults or peers, provides one rich source of insights. Consider the following conversation of a 4-year-old with her mother (taken from Eisenberg, 1992):

    CHILD: Can we go to that park?
    MOTHER: Well, you didn't wear your shoes. You wore your ballet slippers.
    CHILD: Well, that's okay.
    MOTHER: No, because your ballet slippers aren't made to play outdoors in. They'll get torn up.
    CHILD: But can I wear my shoes?
    MOTHER: Well, we won't do that this weekend because it's beginning to get dark and in some places even parks are kind of dangerous after it gets dark.
    CHILD: Why?
    MOTHER: Well, because sometimes bad people come out at night and do things.

    We have a picture here of a child who is not content passively to have her mind filled by the dictates of others but who, on the contrary, is actively trying to think about social rules by enquiring, arguing and pushing the mother to elaborate on reasons for a particular course of action, and so become able to construct her own sets of such rules. Merely the use of the 'why' question (sometimes repeated with exasperating frequency by preschoolers) shows a child searching for reasons and order in the world around her, not prepared to accept events merely at their surface value. As Dunn (1988) has shown, children as young as 2 years do not just follow their parents' dos and don'ts and instead actively think about other people's expectations and attempt to understand why they are supposed to behave in certain ways rather than in others.

- *Recording monologues.* The way children talk to themselves can be as revealing as their talk with others. Indeed, in some respects it can be more revealing, as Katherine Nelson (1989) showed in a fascinating account of the monologues of one 2-year-old child (Emily) as she lay alone in her bed at night. Compared with her speech in conversations with her parents, Emily's monologues were in many ways richer, lengthier, more informative and linguistically more advanced, as she goes over her daytime experiences and narrates what has taken place and what she believes will take place. Here is an excerpt, concerned with an impending visit to the doctor:

    Maybe the doctor, took my jamas – I don't know. Maybe, maybe we take my jamas off. But, I leave my diaper, take my jamas off, and leave them off, at the doc – , my have get my check up, so we take my jamas off . . . The, and we maybe take my jamas off. I don't know what we do with my – maybe the doctor take my jamas, my jamas off cause my maybe get check up, have to to take my jamas.

Emily had been to the doctor before (though never in her pyjamas), and it appears that her outstanding memory is having to take her clothes off –

something that she attempts to integrate with what she is wearing at present, though without being able to make allowance for a change to day clothes. As Nelson points out, her repetitive 'maybe take my jamas off' suggests the emergence of an ability to make inferences based on prior experience; moreover, she appears to understand well the relationship between doctors and taking clothes off. This is just one example among many of Emily's attempts to think about and interpret what is happening to her in the course of her daily life, and thereby, as Nelson puts it, 'mentally construct an understandable world within which she can begin to take her place'. (See box 8.1 for further details of Emily's monologues).

- *Play techniques.* Psychotherapists have for long appreciated the value of play as a means of learning about the inner life of children. Children have a rich fantasy life which they may not normally verbalize; in play, however, they can reveal aspects of themselves that are too emotionally laden to be confronted directly. Thus doll play in particular has been used to tap children's representations of family relationships; similarly, by means of story-telling techniques, children are given the opportunity indirectly to disclose the way they think about others, about relationships and about themselves in the context of their real lives. Take the impact of maltreatment on children's mental life (Waldinger, Toth & Gerber, 2001): by a combination of story-telling and doll play one can explore how experiences of physical abuse, sexual abuse and neglect shape children's concepts both of themselves and of other people, and how their internal representations of relationships are differentially related to the particular kinds of parental treatment they have received. As the authors of one such study conclude: 'The same child who answered "fine" when queried about his relationship with his maltreating mother during a clinical interview session, elaborated on themes of maternal neglect, rejection, and punitiveness throughout the course of the narrative technique' (Buchsbaum, Toth, Clyman, Cicchetti & Emde, 1992).

- *Eliciting behaviour in experimental settings.* The above example refers to the *content* of thought, i.e. how children represent experience to themselves. Other techniques focus on the *form* of thought, i.e. the way in which children use their cognitive abilities. Take an experiment by DeLoache (1987), in which children aged $2\frac{1}{2}$ and 3 years watched while a miniature toy dog was hidden somewhere in a scale model of a room. The children were then asked to find a large stuffed dog in the same location in a full-size version of that room. To succeed the child had to use the model as a representation of the real room – a challenge which, as DeLoache found, most of the $2\frac{1}{2}$-year-old children could not meet whereas the 3-year-olds had no difficulty in solving the problem. Once again, an insight is provided into children's thought processes: at the younger age, children could not treat the model of the room both as an object in its own right and as a representation of something else; soon after, however, a shift occurred and the capacity for representational thinking began to emerge.

BOX 8.1

Emily's bedtime monologues

Emily is the first-born child of academic parents – a child clearly of high intelligence whose language development is well ahead of the average. Her bedtime routine included conversations with her parents and then, once they had left, a time when she would talk to herself before eventually falling asleep. For a 15-month period, between the ages of 21 and 36 months, Katherine Nelson, a psychologist interested in early language development, arranged with the parents to record both dialogues and monologues by means of a cassette recorder appropriately placed to pick up Emily's speech. The resulting tapes and transcripts were subsequently analysed by a number of scholars, each with somewhat different interests, and their reports were collected together in Nelson's book *Narratives from the Crib* (1989).

What most struck Nelson when first listening to the tapes was the contrast between Emily's speech when with her parents and when alone. It had always been assumed that it requires the support of a conversational partner to bring out a child's linguistic competence; formal analysis showed, however, that Emily's monologues were developmentally well in advance of what she contributed in dialogues. Particularly impressive was her ability to string together in a more or less coherent manner long sequences of comments on a single topic – far longer than the usual brief utterances in response to a question or comment by an adult. Thus one of the most frequent themes in Emily's discourse is to engage in narratives, when she recounts in story-like form what has been happening to her or what she imagines may happen. These narratives in particular provide excellent insight into Emily's thought processes and the kinds of meaning she attaches to her experiences.

Above all, the recordings indicate a child busily engaged in making sense of the world she lives in. She *thinks* about her experiences, in that she reflects on them, attempts to put them in some sort of temporal order, struggles with cause and effect, and through putting them in words can juggle with them in her mind – labelling, categorizing, generalizing and thus ultimately clarifying what may have been problematic or troublesome. It is as though her mind requires some sort of ordering of experience, and much of her discourse thus reflects her attempts to create a coherent mental world.

As Nelson points out, one important part of this is the discovery of herself as a thinking, feeling, acting person in interaction with other people who think, feel and act. Over the 15 months of recordings there is increasing use of personal references, as seen in the frequency of words like 'Emmy', 'I' and 'me' – as though she is becoming more conscious of herself and able to reflect upon herself as a distinct being. Developmentally, there are also other changes. For one thing, Emily becomes increasingly able to reflect not only on what has happened and what will happen but also on what should happen, indicating the appearance of standards to regulate her conduct and that of other people. Secondly, she becomes progressively able to insert fantasy elements into her narratives: instead of sticking to fact, she can pose invented scenarios and so engage in a much richer mental life in consequence. And thirdly, Emily shows increasing realization that experience occurs in time as more and more she uses words like 'tomorrow', 'later' and 'soon' – signposts that help her to order events in a temporal framework and think about them as arranged in particular sequences.

Emily may not be a typical 2-year-old – certainly not with respect to her advanced verbal development; also, the remarkable insights she shows into many of her experiences suggests an impressive sensitivity. On the other hand, her curiosity, her striving for understanding and her need to make sense of what is happening to her are characteristics found in virtually all young children, and by verbalizing these needs, especially in a situation of minimal constraints, they provide an insight into how children's thought processes can help them to cope with the challenges of their everyday experience.

Techniques such as these afford a glimpse of children's minds, even at quite young ages when they still have little ability to express themselves verbally. The conclusions we arrive at from applying them are, of course, based on inference: the children behave *as if* they are thinking. That, however, is the way in which we proceed in ordinary life: we have no doubt that we are surrounded by thinking beings because they behave in ways we ourselves would when thinking. In that sense, children indicate that they are already capable of thought at very early ages, though in the course of development this capacity soon becomes vastly more sophisticated.

Symbolic representation: Language, play, drawing

At the heart of thought lies the capacity to represent objects, people, events and experiences in symbolic form. Information-processing approaches regard representational skills as the hallmark of human cognition, and Piaget (as we saw in chapter 6) considered the passage from the sensorimotor stage to the preoperational stage as a momentous step because it is signalled by the emergence of *covert* rather than solely *overt* psychological functioning. Children, that is, no longer need to act on objects to produce results: they can represent them mentally and so manipulate them in symbolic form.

Symbolic representation can be defined as the ability to make one thing stand for another. Instead of the real thing a symbol is used – though often one and the same thing may be represented by a whole diversity of symbols. Consider how an apple can be represented: verbally, by the word 'apple', or 'pomme', or 'Apfel', or the equivalent in any other language; pictorially, by drawing or painting it in any of many different ways; gesturally, by means of some action that conveys the nature of an apple; or, as in play, by designating any object with some vague resemblance to an apple, such as a ball or a lump of clay, as the real thing. The relation between symbol and the thing it represents is in many respects an arbitrary one, in that there is no *necessary* connection between symbol and referent: the signs used in languages for the deaf, for example, need bear no resemblance to the things signified. However, symbols generally agreed upon and defined by social convention are usually the most convenient, so that (as in the case of language) they can be communicated to others.

Let us summarize the main uses of symbolic representation:

- Representations are private tools of thought: they can be changed and worked on as the individual wishes without the real thing being affected. Thus a child can have the most vicious fantasies about the newborn baby brother, yet do so in perfect safety without encountering the wrath of parents.
- By means of representations the past can be conjured up and the future anticipated. The individual is no longer confined to the here-and-now but can think about things in their absence, using previous experience in order to prepare for impending events.
- As seen especially with verbal labels, representations can be an economical way of referring to things by establishing abstract categories. The word 'toys', for instance, encompasses a wide range of specific objects, grouped together on the basis of a common feature, making it unnecessary for a child to mention every single one referred to.
- Representations are highly flexible: as we saw in the example of an apple, one and the same thing can be symbolized in many different ways. Equally, in fantasy any one object can serve many different purposes: for a child engaged in pretend play, a piece of wood can represent a boat one moment and a gun the next. Reality need not be a constraint.
- The symbols used in representation can be either shared with others or purely personal. Shared symbols are socially agreed and can therefore be used for communicative purposes: a gesture such as pointing is universally understood to signify an attempt to direct our attention; similarly, the Morse signal for SOS is used on the assumption that others will act upon it. Personal symbols are the individual's own: a child may invent a secret type of writing and so safely record his or her innermost thoughts in a diary, or a pair of twins may develop a language in which the two can communicate but that no one else is able to understand.

Symbolic representation takes many forms, but the most common in childhood are to be found in the three areas of language, play and drawing.

1 Language

By far the most common and efficient way of referring to things is verbally. A word, from one point of view, is simply a particular combination of sounds; from another, however, it is a most useful way of symbolizing things in the real world. Children begin to talk somewhere around their first birthday, using single words; by the second birthday they are able to combine words in phrases and sentences, and language then rapidly becomes a highly complex system of symbolic representation (see chapter 9 for a more detailed discussion of language development). The most intriguing step in this progression, however, is right at the beginning, when children make the momentous discovery that things have names.

The first 'words' children speak may not be conventional parts of our vocabulary and yet qualify as words because they are used meaningfully to designate particular things. For example Brenda, a little girl whose language development was studied in great detail by Scollon (1976) between the ages of 1 and 2, had a vocabulary entirely of her own at 14 months, in which sounds were consistently used in a meaningful manner, but one which others had to interpret from her behaviour and the context (see table 8.2). Sound and referent did not always have the precise one-to-one correspondence that adults expect: 'nene', for instance, was used to designate milk, juice and bottle, but was also occasionally applied to mother and to sleep. Such idiosyncrasies reflect the uncertainties of children as they first come to grips with the process of attaching names to things. Yet only 5 months later Brenda had a vocabulary of several dozen words, each of which was conventionally and consistently applied to certain specific things.

When children first use words, they do so only in the presence of the object named, i.e. in a purely associative manner, as though they do not realize as yet that the word stands for the object and can be used to refer to it in its absence. The transition from association to symbolization occurs somewhat later in the second year,

Table 8.2 One child's vocabulary at 14 months

Vocabulary	Meaning
aw u	I want; I don't want
nau	no
d di	daddy; baby
d yu	down; doll
nene	milk; juice; mother; sleep
e	yes
maeme	solid food
ada	another; other

Source: From Scollon (1976).

and has been regarded by some to account for the sudden spurt in vocabulary growth that occurs at that time in many children (McShane, 1991). Vocabulary size more than doubles between 18 and 21 months, and again between 21 and 24 months. Whether or not this is associated with the realization that things have names, there is no doubt that children suddenly become fascinated by naming. 'What's that?' becomes a regular feature of their talk with adults as they point to some new (or sometimes also to some quite familiar) object. They even invent their own labels when one is not readily forthcoming: 'fix-man' for mechanic, 'nose-beard' for moustache (Clark, 1982). Language acquisition is certainly no passive business!

Most early words are nouns that refer to certain objects of special interest to the child: 'bottle', 'ball', 'milk', 'kitty', or names of familiar people: 'daddy', 'mama' and the child's own name. This is hardly surprising; objects are easier to identify than actions or relational words, though some verbs like 'give' or 'pat', or terms such as 'more' or 'there', are also found quite early on. To some extent the emphasis on nouns may be determined by the nature of the language children are learning: Chinese children, for instance, begin with a preponderance of verbs and not of nouns because their language emphasizes the former rather than the latter (Tardiff, 1996). Even among English children there are differences in their preference for nouns: some (probably the majority) seem to focus all their efforts on the single strategy of learning names for things, and it is among these that the vocabulary spurt is so marked, while others acquire a more varied lexicon and do so in a more gradual manner (Goldfield & Reznick, 1990). In general, however, early references are to concrete things: toys, food, people, clothes, eating, playing, sleeping, crying. These are the aspects of children's lives that matter to them, and being able to refer to them verbally opens up all sorts of possibilities for both thought and communication. The need to refer to abstractions like 'happiness' or 'liberty' will come later as individuals become cognitively capable of thinking about such concepts.

2 Play

At the same time as language begins to blossom, the nature of play changes. Play can provide a most useful insight into children's cognitive capacities, and several developmental schemes have been proposed outlining the various levels through which play progresses as children grow older (table 8.3 gives an example). In this sequence the emergence of pretend play is a particularly noteworthy step: as Piaget pointed out, it signals the shift from sensorimotor to representational functioning, in that the child is no longer tied to objects as they are in reality but can use imagination to pretend that they are something quite different – a stick, waved about in the hand, is a sword but, clutched between the legs, becomes a horse; a piece of tubing one moment is a doctor's stethoscope but the next moment a snake; and children themselves can assume any number of fantasy roles: cowboy, prince or racing driver; pop star, queen or fashion model.

Table 8.3 Levels of play

Level	*Type of play*
Sensorimotor play (dominant in the first 18 months)	Exploring and manipulating objects by, for example, feeling, shaking, sucking, throwing, banging.
Constructive play (begins in the second year)	Objects are increasingly used to construct things, e.g. blocks are built into towers or are lined up side by side, puzzles are assembled, clay is made into shapes.
Pretend play (also begins in the second year)	Play becomes a vehicle for the child's imagination; it is no longer tied to reality and instead objects are used to represent anything that the child desires.
Socio-dramatic play (from about 4 years)	Children assume roles: cowboys and Indians, doctor and patient, teacher and pupil.
Rule-governed play (from the early school years)	Children now understand that play can be governed by rules to which they must conform, especially when taking the form of games played with others. These increasingly take the place of pretend play.

Source: Based on Belsky & Most (1981); Nicolich (1977); Rubin, Fein & Vandenberg (1983).

When pretending, children suspend belief in reality and interchange it for the imaginary. A banana makes a splendid telephone, and for a time it simply *is* a telephone. Yet children can just as easily dip back into reality; when the fantasy is exhausted they have no hesitation in eating the telephone. There are, admittedly, occasions when fantasies are so vivid and so prolonged that it may seem to worried parents that they are taking over the child. This is seen particularly in the case of imaginary companions: when one is continuously told not to sit on an empty chair because Casper is sitting there, it is easy to become exasperated and wonder whether the child may not be retreating too much into a fantasy world. Yet even when engrossed in the most vivid fantasies, children have little problem in maintaining the pretend–real boundary; the popular notion that young children live in a world where fantasy and reality are undifferentiated receives little support when empirically investigated (Woolley, 1997), and when fantasies do threaten to become too vivid children have devices for stepping back. Thus Garvey (1990) quotes the example of two boys starting with a quite realistic game involving a firetruck that had broken down, acting out the repair work needed to make it roadworthy again, but then drifting off into fantasies about having to fight off an 'Everything-Eating-Lamb' that had got into the truck and was devouring its engine. When they then began a new episode in which they were threatened by ghosts wanting to eat the tools used for repair, it all became a little too much for one boy who stopped and reminded his partner 'And by the way, we're only pretending'. A little while later the other boy too stepped back quickly to comment 'There's no such thing as ghosts' before resuming play by telephoning the Ghostbusters for help.

Clearly, pretend play – like all imaginary activities – has many uses: emotional, cognitive, social (P. Harris, 2000). As to emotional aspects, it gives the lonely child the chance to people the world with friends and so compensate for what reality cannot offer, and similarly the rejected child may construct an elaborate make-believe world in which she is found by her 'real' parents (usually royalty or at least very rich and famous but always kind and loving) and transported into a quite different environment. Fantasy can thus serve as a substitute for the real world, as seen also in children playing out forbidden acts in their imagination. Piaget (1951), for example, quotes a 5-year-old, angry with her father, who asks her imaginary companion Zoubab to cut off her Daddy's head: 'But she has some very strong glue and partly stuck it on again. However, it is not very firm now.' Even here, it seems, reality intrudes in the form of guilt – incomplete though it may be! Additionally, there are opportunities to prepare for unpleasant, frightening events such as an impending hospitalization; if the child takes on the role of doctor and assigns the patient's role to his teddy bear, he is at least in control of events and so has some opportunity of coming to terms with reality.

Among the cognitive consequences of pretend play, one must mention above all the development of imaginative powers. To quote Garvey (1990): 'The imaginative pretender has the experience of manipulating, recombining and extending associations between words and things, and between things, persons and actions. Thus it is reasonable to speculate that pretending is one of the experiences that facilitate the development of abstract thought.' Children who engage in a lot of pretend play have been found to have better powers of concentration, to produce more numerous and more varied ideas, to be more flexible in finding solutions to problems, and in the more mature stages of such play to show superior planning skills in organizing their make-believe activities.

The social dimension becomes particularly obvious when comparing the pretend play of different age groups. Just when children become capable of engaging in more complex, lengthier activities, their sociability also takes a step forward, and having previously engaged mainly in solitary play the most enjoyable activities are now often those carried out jointly with peers. However, integrating two or more sets of fantasies is a highly intricate business. This is shown beautifully in a very detailed account by Furth and Kane (1992) of the make-believe play of three girls aged between $4^{1}/_{2}$ and 6, who decided to enact 'The Royal Ball' – a drama played out over two days, involving queens and princesses and all the paraphernalia appropriate for a royal occasion. A considerable amount of planning and preparation went into this, much of it concerned with the assignment of roles (who is a queen and who is just a princess) and the possession of props like cloaks and telephones (!) – all requiring a lot of haggling and negotiation and so providing an opportunity to learn how to resolve conflict in a way acceptable to all. The frequent use of phrases such as 'how about . . . ?', 'OK?' and 'right?' shows that these children tried hard to seek agreement, though their bargaining sometimes took somewhat quaint forms:

CHILD A (pointing to a waistcoat on B's chair): Annie, since I found this first, can I use this?

CHILD B: If you want this, you can use it at the royal ball.

A: Just for the royal ball.

B: You can use it for the royal ball, the second royal ball. 'Cause at the first one I wear it, and the second one you wear it and the next one I wear it. We take turns. But this time I wear it.

Thus much of the children's efforts went first into the drawing up of certain formal rules applicable to a royal ball, such as the proper use of titles and of precedence, and only when these had been formulated and agreed could the play go ahead – which it did, with a clear beginning and end. In a joint activity such as this, therefore, make-believe is not merely a matter of spilling out various private fantasies, but an opportunity to learn how to fuse several sets of individual ideas and desires in such a way that the final product satisfies all the participants.

In pretend play children are offered scope to practise skills of various kinds: they can extend their imaginative powers and so learn the uses of symbolic representation; they can confront emotional problems and try to come to terms with them; and they can find ways of joining up with others for the sake of a common goal – and all this in an enjoyable context. In the course of the early school years pretend play gradually disappears from the overt behaviour repertoire of children as games with rules (football, marbles, hopscotch and so on) become predominant. Yet internal fantasizing remains a lifelong preoccupation – the little girl who played at being princess may become the woman who indulges in the rather more prosaic daydream of becoming boss of the corporation in which she is a low-level employee.

3 Drawing

A picture, just like a word or a toy, is a symbol that represents the real thing. It is distinctive in two respects. First, it is presented graphically and depicts three-dimensional reality on a two-dimensional surface. Secondly, a picture is not as arbitrary a representation as a word or a toy can be, but is generally expected to bear some degree of resemblance to the real thing.

Quite early on, from about the end of the second year, children realize that pictures are meaningful. They see a photo of themselves and happily announce 'me', or point to an apple in a picture book and then pick out the real thing in a fruit bowl while saying 'apple'. However, as with language, understanding precedes production: children take rather longer before they themselves can intentionally produce drawings that stand for real things. Their first efforts with paper and pencil take the form of scribbles, and though there have been various attempts to see form and meaning in scribbles the evidence is unconvincing: it is more likely that young children scribble for the sheer pleasure of it – an activity carried out for its own sake though also one that provides children with the opportunity to get to know the medium and to develop the fine perceptual-motor control that is required in drawing.

The ability to use drawing for representational purposes emerges gradually and usually in orderly fashion. To do justice to this progression we can turn to a developmental scheme proposed by Luquet (1927), an early student of children's drawings, which has been found useful by all subsequent investigators. It is based on the following four stages:

1 *Fortuitous realism.* Starting at about the age of 2 children may suddenly become aware that one of their scribbles resembles some real object – a ball, a bird, a table: anything that the child thinks is like that object even though others may see little resemblance. Although the child did not set out with the intention of drawing something real, such a post hoc interpretation is the first sign that the ability to consider pictures as representational symbols is now emerging. And when it does, it is helped on by adults' comments: 'Is that a house?' 'Are you drawing granny?'

2 *Failed realism.* Soon after, children do set out drawing with the deliberate aim of producing some particular picture. As yet, however, they cannot sustain the intention for any length of time, particularly not when their skill lets them down and the drawing fails even remotely to resemble the real thing. They may then switch intentions – 'granny' is declared to be a 'bush', or they revert to scribbling with no pretence at representation.

3 *Intellectual realism.* From about 4 years on both the intention and the skill to represent things graphically become much firmer. Children now want their pictures to be recognizable; however, what they draw is not so much a copy of the real thing as a symbol, albeit an acceptable one. Asked to draw the house they live in, they will not produce a picture of the real bungalow or semi-detached but a stereotyped house – something that includes the basic defining characteristic of houses and is thus more an expression of what they know about houses generally than what they see of some specific house.

4 *Visual realism.* Finally, at about age 7 or 8, children try to do justice to reality by drawing something intended to be a copy of the real thing. Houses are given distinctive characteristics; people are no longer portrayed in stereotypical form; more and more details are introduced; and some attempt is made to cope with such difficult technical problems as linear perspective and the size–distance relationship.

Among all the things children draw, the human figure is the most common. Here too an orderly progression is found in the way children tackle this task, and this has been described in great detail by Maureen Cox (1992, 1997) on the basis of many hundreds of such drawings by children of all ages. To start, once children are past the scribbling stage, they will nearly always begin by drawing 'tadpole figures' – composed simply of a circular shape set on two vertical lines (see figure 8.3). In

(1)   Tadpole stage (approx. 2½–4 years)

(2)   Transitional stage (approx. 4–5 years)

(3)   Canonical stage (approx. 5–7 years)

(4)   Realistic stage (approx. 8 years on)

Figure 8.3   *Developmental changes in children's drawings of the human figure.*

time some rudimentary facial features are added to the circle, and eventually arms are attached, though usually to the head. There is no torso: the head, or alternatively the space between the legs, serves for this purpose, as shown when children are asked to indicate the position of the belly button. Children aged 3 or more know, of course, all about tummies and chests, but the task of composing such a multi-part figure is still too much for them, and heads and legs take precedence in their order of things.

A tadpole figure may be a very primitive illustration of a human being by adult standards, yet even here the child is already using symbolic means of expression. Thus a straight line *stands for* a limb, two little circles for eyes, a vertical line for a mouth, and so on. There is as yet no attempt by the child to draw a photographic representation; the earliest drawings, on the contrary, are the most symbolic. However, as we see in figure 8.3, in time pictures become more realistic. Thus after their early tadpoles children generally pass on to what Cox refers to as a *transitional* stage, when the space between the legs is now systematically used as the torso and the arms accordingly moved down from head to legs. The child, we can conclude, is no longer thinking of single lines as standing for things such as limbs but as boundaries for spaces, which for their part can then be filled in. From about the age of 5 on the progression to realism becomes much more marked, as children adopt a *canonical* view when drawing – children, that is, attempt to draw people and objects in such a way that they become most easily recognizable. Asked to draw a cup, for example, a child will draw it with a handle even though the handle is not visible, for that is the defining feature of such an object. For the same reason, people are always drawn full-face, for that gives the most information about the person. Thus the drawing will always include both arms, both legs and both eyes; turning the person sideways would obscure some of these parts and so fail in the aim of providing all the information necessary to define the individual. Eventually, however, children come to recognize the limitations of such a point of view; from about 7 or 8 *visual realism* prevails and they now attempt to depict people as they really are, including finer details such as fingers and eyebrows, with the various body parts correctly placed in relation to each other and in their proper size proportions.

In all representations there are certain cultural conventions which children come to learn – conventions which, in the case of drawing, become very apparent when we compare the paintings of societies such as the Ancient Egyptian or the Chinese with our own. As adults, we often do not realize how pervasive such conventions are and how important it is that children have opportunities to learn them, for to us they seem merely 'natural' and require no effort to adhere to them. The practice of placing a figure vertically on the page to denote standing up but horizontally to show lying down is one example: children do not take much note of it at first, and if they are deprived of the necessary visual experience, as in the case of blind children, they may well fail to acquire this habit (see box 8.2).

BOX 8.2

Blind children drawing human figures

Below are a number of drawings of human beings, and they are remarkable because they are the product of congenitally blind children who had never actually seen a human being. The children form part of a group of 30 children, aged 6 to 10 years at the time, who were investigated by Susanna Millar (1975) and compared with a group of sighted children. All were asked to draw human figures, this being the first time that any of the blind children had undertaken such a task.

Figure 8.4 *Drawings of people by 10-year-old blind children.*

Not surprisingly, the sighted children produced much more accomplished drawings than the blind children. The latter were particularly deficient in the cohesion of body parts and in the number of details shown. What is surprising is that the blind children were able to draw anything at all that resembled the visual appearance of another person. Thus heads were drawn as circles, eyes as dots or small circles, limbs as lines. Admittedly, this was found primarily among the 10-year-olds (see figure 8.4); at younger ages, around 6 and 8, children were very much less successful in drawing anything recognizable as a human being. Thus there was a considerable developmental gap between blind and sighted in their ability to cope with the task. Yet even at the youngest age children made sensible attempts: as one 6-year-old blind boy put it when he started, 'I don't know how the head should go, but I think I will draw a circle'. How the blind children had acquired the rules for representing three-dimensional body parts in two-dimensional space – what part touch, for instance, plays in this respect – remains an intriguing question.

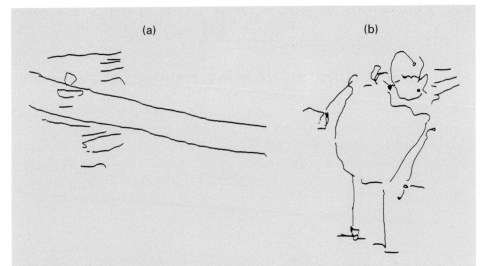

Figure 8.5   *Human figures drawn by (a) an 8-year-old blind boy; (b) a blind child aged 9 years.*

In one other respect blind children were also initially deficient: they had little conception of the need to place the figure vertically and in an upright position on a 'floor'. Nearly all the sighted children, even the youngest, followed this convention; many of the blind children, on the other hand, placed their figures in inverted, horizontal or near-horizontal positions (see figure 8.5). It appears that these children were simply not aware of any placement rule; thus, when asked to indicate the floor on their drawing, they either drew a circular scribble around the figure or indicated the whole of the page with their hand and said that the floor was 'all around'. Yet when informed, the children quickly acquired the conventional representation of 'floor' as a horizontal line at the bottom of the page. Thus one boy, having never drawn a human figure before, first produced a horizontally aligned, then an inverted figure; however, on being told that 'floor' is usually taken to be a line parallel to the bottom edge of the page, immediately drew a correctly aligned figure. The acquisition of such 'translation rules' can therefore be regarded as a necessary part of learning to represent things symbolically by making marks on a flat page.

Organizing the Mind

Whenever we encounter some new experience we immediately try to make sense of it by relating it to other experiences. We rarely perceive it as something entirely in its own right; were we to do so, we would be overwhelmed by the sheer diversity of all the unique things we encounter. Instead we try to comprehend each experience as the same as, or as similar to, or as different from, some other set of experiences, thereby giving the unknown meaning by relating it to the known. The mind, that is, automatically interprets our experiences by organizing and arranging them to fit into some more general framework, in this way simplifying and ordering our mental representations of the world. This is a tendency that is necessarily limited in very young children; nevertheless, its beginnings can be found at surprisingly early ages. We will examine it in relation to two such organizing activities, namely, concept formation and the construction of scripts.

Forming concepts

One way of making our world less complex is by grouping together things that share common characteristics. The end products of such grouping are **concepts** – mental categories which enable us to treat as one a diversity of things that can nevertheless be thought of as a unit for certain purposes. Thus 'animals' is a concept that makes it possible for us to classify together flies, dogs and elephants: creatures that are completely different except for certain characteristics that form a common core. Concepts such as these serve to cut up the world into manageable categories; they enable us to organize our experience into meaningful patterns, store them economically and draw inferences about new experiences without each time having to learn all about them afresh.

> **Concepts** are mental categories for the classification of diverse objects that share some particular characteristic.

Concepts are closely tied to language, for they are usually identified by some verbal label. Yet the ability to categorize can already be found at very early ages, even well before the acquisition of language. Give 18-month-old children a collection of objects to play with, some of which are used for eating and others for washing, and they will spontaneously sort them according to their use, even though the objects within a group may actually look quite different (Fivush, 1987). Categorization at an even earlier age can be demonstrated if another method, the *preference-for-novelty technique*, is employed. This involves repeatedly presenting children with a particular stimulus which, as it becomes familiar, will elicit less and less attention. When it is then paired with a different, unfamiliar stimulus, the child will prefer to attend to the latter. In this way, one can establish what even very young, nonverbal children regard as same and what as different. By employing this technique, Paul Quinn and his colleagues, in a series of experiments with babies (e.g. Quinn & Eimas, 1996; Quinn, Slater, Brown & Hayes, 2001), found that as early as 3 months of age children will consider as 'same' a wide range of perceptually quite different stimuli. For example, pictures of horses varying markedly in colour, orientation and stance were all treated as equivalent, and similarly with different pictures of cats – as though these babies had already formed a 'horse' category and a 'cat' category.

With age, children become ever more sophisticated categorizers. This is seen primarily in two developmental trends, namely, in the change from mainly perceptual to conceptual characteristics as a basis for forming categories and in children's increasing ability to arrange categories in hierarchies.

- *From perceptual to conceptual characteristics.* The earliest categories are mostly based on features that are visually obvious. Children asked to sort objects on the basis of 'whatever goes together' will put a cap with a ball because both are bright red rather than the cap with a scarf because they are both items of clothing. The latter involves an abstract criterion and therefore constitutes a mentally more complex task, to be mastered at a later age; still more abstract concepts such as time, space, liberty and life and death appear considerably later (see box 8.3 for the research carried out on the latter). Yet the reliance by young children on purely perceptual characteristics can easily be exaggerated. According to Piaget, abstractions of any kind are not possible until children leave the preoperational period at around school entry, but as with so much else in Piagetian theory, more recent evidence has shown that much younger children are already capable of classifying on the basis of non-obvious characteristics. Gopnik and Sobel (2000) demonstrated this by confronting children with what they termed a 'blicket detector' – a machine that lit up and played music whenever certain objects (labelled 'blickets') were placed on it; other objects (some the same, others different in appearance) could not produce this effect. Preschool children, some even as young as 3 years, quickly learned correctly to classify objects into 'blickets' and 'not blickets'; in other words, they showed that they could label and categorize objects according to their causal power, i.e. a functional characteristic, without any reliance on their perceptual characteristics.
- *Establishing hierarchical arrangements.* As demonstrated in figure 8.6, our conceptual world tends to be arranged in hierarchies. The higher the level, the more inclusive is the category and the more abstract in nature it is likely to be. According to Eleanor Rosch and her colleagues (1976), it is useful to distinguish between three levels: *basic, subordinate* and *superordinate.* Children find it easiest to establish categories at the basic level, for it is there that most similarity in terms of number of shared characteristics can be found. Thus 'dog' is a basic-level category; such a concept arises more naturally and will appear earlier than a superordinate concept such as 'animal' or a subordinate

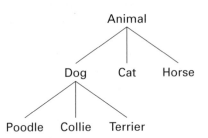

Figure 8.6 *A hierarchy of concepts arranged at superordinate, basic and subordinate levels.*

BOX 8.3

Children thinking about life and death

Amongst all the concepts that we form, those of life and death are surely the most basic. They are also amongst the most complex, at least from a child's point of view, and it is no wonder that a good many psychologists have tried to understand how children think about them. Piaget (1929) was one of these; thus, as part of his early work, he set out to determine whether young children can make a distinction between the animate and the inanimate, and did so by investigating what sort of phenomena they endow with life and consciousness. As we saw in chapter 6 (pp. 175–6), he concluded that initially the young child quite automatically attributes life to almost everything – the tendency to *animism*, as he referred to it. Being conscious themselves, children automatically attribute consciousness to almost any object: a stone rolling down a hill, a bicycle, the wind – all are seen in the child's image as knowing what they are doing. With age there is a gradual restriction in the range of things to which life is attributed, but not until mid-childhood will the child come to realize that only people and animals are conscious.

Later research has thrown doubt on this account. Piaget, it is believed, asked the wrong questions. He went on the assumption that life is a unitary concept and that children come to make a clear distinction between what is living and what is not living. More recent work suggests, however, that neither life nor death is a unitary concept and that instead each is made up of various components which do not necessarily develop concomitantly. Take the concept of life. According to some findings (e.g. Inagaki & Hatano, 1996; Rosengren, Gelman, Kalish & McCormick, 1991), it is essential to distinguish between a number of subconcepts that are inherent in the notion of life, such as growth, reproduction, self-initiated movement, inheritance and developmental change, and investigate these separately. When this is done, a rather different picture emerges from the one Piaget painted. For example, it appears that even 3-year-olds understand that animals get larger over time whereas objects do not, and so even the youngest children investigated apparently possess a primitive concept of growth as spontaneous change in size – a characteristic specific to humans and animals and not found in objects. Similarly with self-initiated movement: that too is in place very early on as a criterion for distinguishing the animate from the inanimate. During the preschool period children also begin to see that animals and plants have certain things in common and can therefore be classified together as live: at the age of 4, for instance, they understand that the two share certain functions such as a need for nutrition, whereas artefacts do not have such a requirement and are therefore a different class of phenomena. Even the notion of inheritance, at least in a restricted sense, is grasped by quite young children: they know that mummy dogs will have baby dogs and not baby cats, and that both animals and plants get their colouring from their parents whereas artefacts can get theirs only through human intervention. Tracing the development of children's concept of 'life' therefore requires attention to these specific components rather than lumping them together into one global characteristic.

Similar conclusions come from studies of the concept of death (e.g. Lazar & Torney-Purta, 1991). Four subconcepts have been distinguished here: irreversibility (the dead never come back to life), cessation (all biological and psychological functions end), causality (certain objective factors bring about death) and inevitability (death is universal and will apply to the child too). When each of these is studied separately, it is found that their onset and developmental course differ. Thus irreversibility and inevitability are the first to appear: certainly by age 6 children have a firm grasp of both these notions. The other two subconcepts, cessation and causality, are grasped somewhat later; understanding them appears to be conditional on at least one of the two earlier subconcepts being in the child's repertoire. Yet even then, when requested to give more detailed explanations, children often continue to give strange answers: asked about the causes of death, many of the 6- to 7-year-olds studied by Lazar and Torney-Purta mentioned cancer, heart attacks and AIDS, but some also included items such as 'from eating soap' and 'from the snow'. Curiously, relatively few gave old age as a cause.

We can conclude that children even in the preschool age range already differentiate living from non-living things in their thinking. However, their understanding then is still incomplete: initially it is evident with respect to just some aspects, whereas others appear at later stages. No doubt personal experience affects the developmental course: birth of a sibling or death of a grandparent will bring home to a child the realities of life and afford plenty of opportunities for obtaining objective information. Piaget was right in believing that gaining full insight is a protracted business: not until the age of 8 or 9 will children really grasp the proper meaning of life and death. However, by focusing on an undifferentiated notion of life, he missed some of the earlier indications of comprehension and so underestimated the extent to which even quite young children are already engaged on the task of concept formation.

one such as 'collie', where mental grouping is not so easy. Not everyone agrees that the developmental course of concept formation is quite so orderly; what is certain is that children gradually learn that they can arrange their mental representations in sequentially meaningful hierarchies and that these help them to think about the world in meaningful ways.

Constructing scripts

We think about the world not just in terms of static objects but also as series of ongoing events. Travelling to work or school in the morning, shopping at the local supermarket, family dinners, visiting relatives – these and many other routines occur as regular sequences in our ordinary lives, giving it a structure that is predictable and therefore reassuring. Our mental representations of these events are known as **scripts**.

> **Scripts** are mental representations of particular everyday events and the behaviour and emotions appropriate to them.

Scripts tell us 'how things are supposed to happen'. They are models of frequently repeated, stereotyped experiences and are therefore useful as guides to behaviour whenever the appropriate situation arises. Three characteristics of scripts are noteworthy (Nelson, 1978):

- A script contains certain obligatory activities in a particular sequence.
- It also has open slots for optional events.
- In addition, it designates certain roles that need to be filled by various actors.

A family dinner, for example, involves such basic activities as cooking, laying the table, eating and clearing up, which together define the event; however, what is cooked and eaten and who participates may vary to some extent from one occasion to another; nevertheless, who does the cooking and who lays the table or clears up needs to be determined. Thus the event as a whole has a coherent temporal structure that will always be repeated, even though some variability is possible with respect to certain of its features.

Children from at least the third year on are already capable of forming scripts for a considerable range of routine activities. They not only know how to behave in the relevant event, showing that they have understanding for 'what comes next', but they are also able to give a more or less accurate verbal account of the routine, which they appear to have stored in memory as an organized sequence of actions. Much of the original work on children's scripts was carried out by Katherine Nelson and her associates (1986; Nelson & Gruendel, 1981), who asked preschool children to recount various familiar events such as going shopping and eating at McDonald's. Here is one child's account of the latter:

> I walk in there and I, I, I ask my daddy and then the daddy ask the lady and the lady gets it. One small coke, one cheeseburger. . . . They want to eat here, so they don't need a tray. Then we go find a table. I eat it all up. All. And throw the . . . and the paper, throw the, the cheeseburgers in the garbage can. Goodbye. Goodbye. Jump in the car . . . Vroom! Vroom!

What is notable about these accounts is that even 3-year-old children tell their story in the appropriate temporal order. Young children are clearly sensitive to what follows what and store their representations of events accordingly. Violation of the 'correct' order can be very upsetting: a 2-year-old who was unusually given a bath before rather than after dinner became very upset because she thought she would not be fed that evening (Hudson, 1990). Temporal order is so important that children, told a story in which some of the component activities are presented in incorrect order, will subsequently retell the story with the incorrect sequence simply omitted. Experienced events have a time dimension, and even after just one experience children will arrange their account of that event in the appropriate order.

As children get older the nature of scripts changes in various ways. The most obvious change is that with age scripts become longer and more detailed. Older children are able to attend to and give an account of more of the component actions and thus produce a more elaborate narrative. In addition, older children make more allowance for variation from the usual; at age 3 children show that they have retained the basic structure of the event, whereas at age 5 they are also able to insert all sorts of optional extras ('you can order a hamburger or a cheeseburger'). One further developmental change: younger children's accounts focus almost exclusively on actions, whereas by 5 children also talk about the goals and feelings of the actors.

Scripts are important for both cognitive and social reasons. As to the former, Nelson has referred to them as the basic building blocks of cognition: all kinds of information about the world is organized around these mental structures, and in due course they serve as the foundation for more complex, more abstract cognitive skills such as the understanding of stories and the development of literary expertise. As to social implications, they provide a means of sharing knowledge about the world with others; in so far as they refer mostly to conventional routines, they offer children the opportunity to exchange experience with others, learn from their accounts and discuss what, in their various views, ought or ought not go on in these events.

Memorizing

An essential part of information processing involves access to knowledge gained from previous experience, as stored in our memory in the form of representations of the past. What is memory, and how does it develop in childhood?

The nature of memory

The popular picture of our memory is of a storage bin, into which we more or less automatically consign our experiences as they occur. From time to time we decide to retrieve a memory from the bin, though if it has been kept there for rather a long time it may well have deteriorated or even vanished altogether. Children's memorizing is thought to proceed in the same way, the only difference being that their storage bins are smaller than those of adults.

As a result of a very large body of research findings (see Tulving & Craik, 2000, for a review), we now know that this view is misleading in a number of ways. For one thing, the memory system is an extremely complex structure, containing not one but a number of 'bins', each with its own particular function. For another, there is nothing automatic about storing our experiences: on the contrary, it is a highly active, constructive process affected by various other processes such as the individual's goals, previous knowledge and social purposes. As far as children's memory is concerned, this may be more limited in capacity (though even that does not necessarily apply to all aspects), but it also functions qualitatively in ways that are not wholly identical to adults' memory.

As far as the structure of the memory system is concerned, the flow diagram shown in figure 8.1 (p. 223) gives some indication, though a greatly oversimplified one. It shows three principal structures:

- A *sensory register*, the function of which is very briefly to hold external stimulation when it is first received by the sense organs.
- A *short-term memory store*, which receives information from the sensory register but has limited capacity (somewhere around seven items). Its ability to hold information for any length of time is also limited; a telephone number, for example, will fade after some seconds or at the most a few minutes unless the individual employs some strategy such as rehearsal to keep it alive. Short-term memory is, however, not a unitary structure but is made up of three components: a *visuo-spatial* store, concerned with information received through the visual system; a *phonological* store, confined to auditory information; and a *central executive*, which performs various higher-level functions such as the coordination of information as it flows through the short-term system and the application of rehearsal and other strategies.
- *Long-term memory* receives information kept initially alive in the short-term store and can retain it there for months or years. Again, this is a structure containing a number of separate components; in particular, a distinction is usefully made between *episodic* and *semantic* memory. Episodic memory refers to our personal experiences – last night's party, the holiday in Turkey two years ago, the driving test we sat (and nearly passed) last month, or any other significant event in the past that can be retained in the form of scripts and stored in chronological order. Semantic memory, on the other hand, refers to our knowledge of facts about the world, arranged in various categories such as concepts but without any reference to the time when the knowledge was acquired – we know the capital of Sweden but have no recollection of when we learned this.

There is good reason to believe that all these various structures are separate, both in their location in the brain and in their developmental course. Neurological damage to certain areas of the brain may, for instance, result in impairment to the phonological but not to the visuo-spatial system (Gathercole, 1998), and similarly, the distinction between short-term and long-term memory is demonstrated by the way the former deteriorates much more rapidly in old age than the latter.

The development of memory

Given the complexity of the memory system, the developmental task confronting children is clearly not a simple matter of gradually 'getting better at remembering things'. There are four aspects to such development that can usefully be distinguished, referring respectively to changes in capacity, knowledge, strategies and metamemory.

1 Capacity

This would seem to be the most obvious candidate for any change with age in children's memorizing. Younger children's poorer performance could simply be due to less space being available in their information-processing apparatus, possibly due to neurological immaturity. Yet the evidence is far from straightforward, indicating that the capacity of neither the sensory register nor the long-term store varies with age. Only the short-term store shows such change, as illustrated in figure 8.2 (p. 225), for digit and word span. Yet even this may not be due to any increase in capacity as such but rather to the way capacity is used. For example, older children have greater knowledge of numbers and of words; such familiarity could well result in faster rates of identifying items and of remembering them more efficiently. In addition, older children are more skilled at employing various strategies for memorizing material; they are also more capable of thinking about memory as a mental activity and therefore working out ways of using it efficiently. Thus memory capacity is intricately related to knowledge, strategies and metamemory, and any developmental increase in ability may well reflect these other influences rather than a quantitative change in brain capacity.

2 Knowledge

What we know influences what we remember. The more familiar we are with a particular topic, the easier it is to retain additional information we obtain about that topic. Generally speaking, older children know more than younger ones and can therefore be expected to remember more.

But what if younger children happen to be more knowledgeable about some topic than older individuals? In a classic experiment Chi (1978) asked 8- to 10-year-old chess experts to reconstruct a chessboard arrangement that they had been shown for just 10 seconds, and compared their ability to perform this task with that of adults who had little knowledge of the game. The children were found to

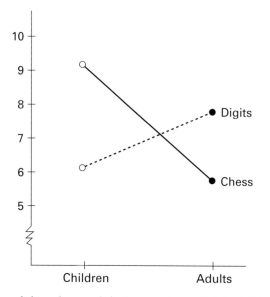

Figure 8.7 *Number of chess places and digits correctly recalled by child chess experts and adult chess novices (based on Chi, 1978).*

be far superior to the adults at remembering the position of the chess pieces; yet when given a standard digit-span test, the children performed at a poorer level (see figure 8.7). The children's greater ability to memorize was thus confined to the domain of chess; their expert knowledge overrode the effects of age.

3 Strategies

As children become older they get increasingly adept at using a number of strategies that will help them with all stages of memorizing – encoding the information, storing it and retrieving it. These are deliberately employed techniques, which for the most part are discovered by the children themselves as useful ways of enhancing their capacities (see table 8.4 for a list of the most common). Rehearsal is probably the most frequently used; when young children know that they will need to recall a string of words or of numbers, they can often be heard quietly repeating the items to themselves in the waiting period or be seen to move their lips while rehearsing them subvocally. However, this rarely occurs before the age of about 7; while younger children can be instructed to use a particular strategy in some specific situation, they cannot transfer the skill to any new tasks. From 7 on, however, both frequency and flexibility of strategy use increases, as a result of which the child becomes progressively more competent in making use of whatever memory capacity he or she has available.

Table 8.4 Memory strategies employed by children

Strategy	Operation	Example
Rehearsal	Repeating information over and over again	Subvocal repetition, as shown by lip movements
Organizing	Rearranging items into more familiar form	Random list of animal, food and furniture items ordered according to category
Elaboration	Constructing a link between otherwise unrelated items	Making up a sentence that includes the items, e.g. 'the *cat* drank a bottle of *wine* under the *sofa*'
Selective attention	Allocating attention selectively to items that need to be recalled subsequently	When told there will be questions about certain toys in an array, child will deliberately look at or name these during the waiting period
Retrieval strategies	Finding ways of making stored items more memorable if know they will need to be recalled	Breaking up a difficult name into components that are easier to retain

4 Metacognition

Metacognition
denotes the awareness
and knowledge
individuals have of
their cognitive
processes. It includes,
for instance,
metamemory and
metacommunication.

The term **metacognition** is used to refer to individuals' awareness of and knowledge about their cognitive processes. This includes *metamemory* – the understanding that one's own memory functions in certain ways, has various limitations, is better under some conditions than under others and can be enhanced in one way or another. Implied here is the ability to stand apart from oneself and take an objective look at the way mental processes are working. Again, it is only with increasing age that children acquire such capacity for conscious reflection, and the older they become, the more detailed and accurate their knowledge of memory will be. As a result of such self-knowledge children will also become more realistic in what they undertake to memorize; young children are often much too optimistic as to what they believe to be capable of, whereas older children are more objective in their self-assessments.

There are several conclusions that emerge from this overview of developmental aspects of memory. For one thing, it is apparent that memory is not some aspect of the mind functioning in isolation from all other aspects. As Kuhn (2000) put it: 'What we remember is an integration of what we currently experience, what we already know, and what we infer.' Our interests, purposes, skills and insights all play a part in any one act of remembering; the individual as a whole is involved and not just one bit of him or her. For another, remembering, whether we are talking about the storage or the retrieval part, is no mechanical, routine activity; it is a constructive endeavour for which we have perfected a variety of strategies to act as tools, helping us to reach whatever goals we have in wanting to remember. Finally, as far as these goals are concerned, people rarely remember as an end in itself; rather (to quote Kuhn again), 'they remember in the service of other goals inherent in the activities they pursue'. As box 8.4 shows, children are sometimes capable of quite unexpected memory feats if they have some good reason to remember; without such reason, memorizing carried out for its own sake can be a lot less effective.

BOX 8.4

Memory skills of Australian Aboriginal children

Numerous studies have investigated the cognitive abilities of Australia's Aboriginal people, using a diversity of assessment techniques such as IQ tests, educational achievement tests and Piagetian tasks. In virtually all instances Aboriginals were found to perform at an inferior level compared to white individuals, the difference often being quite substantial and evident in children as well as in adults. Does that mean that the cognitive capacities of Aboriginals are to be regarded as inevitably 'inferior' to those of whites?

There is, however, another possibility, namely, that the tests employed in these studies are not 'culture-fair', in that they do not tap abilities distinctive to individuals brought up in a very different environment from that associated with western life. Judith Kearins (1981, 1986) therefore decided to use a different approach, arguing that the kinds of behaviour that are most essential to survival in a society's natural environment are most likely to show an individual's abilities at their best. Traditionally, the Aboriginal people have lived in the large internal desert regions of Australia, in landscapes that are almost wholly featureless and lacking in distinctive characteristics that enable people to navigate their way from one location to another. Yet to survive in such an environment, Aborigines need to be able to locate water supplies at sites often visually unremarkable and to relocate their camp after a day of searching for food in barren areas. To do so successfully, they require an accurate memory for spatial relations. Kearins therefore devised tests that reflect the cognitive skills relevant to such a lifestyle and applied them to Aboriginal children and, for comparison, to white children.

The children, all in the age range of 7 to 16 years, were given a series of spatial relocation tasks, in each of which they were confronted with up to 20 objects arranged on a rectangular grid. They were asked to memorize the location of these objects during a 30-second period, whereupon the objects were mixed up and then had to be replaced in their original position. Some of the objects were rather more familiar to the Aboriginal children (e.g. seed-pod, feather, bone), others more to the white children (eraser, thimble, match-box, etc.). When scored for the number of objects placed correctly, it was found that on all tasks the Aboriginal children performed significantly better than the white children, even on tasks involving relatively unfamiliar objects. Thus the Aboriginals gave every indication that their spatial memory was superior to that of white children. In addition, Kearins noted that the two groups behaved differently while tackling the tasks. White children tended to move about, pick up objects and throughout mutter and comment on what they were doing. Aboriginal children, on the other hand, sat very still, paying close visual attention to the array but producing no overt or covert vocalizations. It appeared that the two groups were using different strategies for remembering: the Aboriginal children relied primarily on visual memory, whereas the white children used a verbal rehearsal strategy as an aid. This is borne out by the fact that for the white children familiar objects proved to be easier to remember than unfamiliar objects, presumably because they could attach verbal labels to them; the Aboriginal children, on the other hand, remembered both kinds equally well.

It is significant that rather similar results have been obtained from Eskimo children, whose spatial visual memory has also been found superior to that of Caucasian children (Kleinfeld, 1971). These children too are part of a society that lives in territory of a relatively featureless nature, where it is vital to foster those cognitive skills that people need for survival purposes. Assessing these skills indicates clearly that societies referred to as 'primitive' by whites may well outperform their white counterparts in these aspects.

Autobiographical memory

Even in the very earliest weeks of life children are capable of at least some rudimentary forms of memory. *Recognition* memory is the first to appear: immediately after birth babies can recognize the mother's voice, and soon after her face too. *Recall*, a more sophisticated form of memory, appears somewhat later: thus, by 8 or 9 months babies are capable of crying for the *absent* mother and can search for missing objects, and if a series of actions is demonstrated to them they can imitate these after an interval of time. These, and a range of other indications, are evidence that the ability to store information is present from the very beginning.

It is therefore curious that in later years we generally have no memory at all of anything that happened during the first 2 years or so, and that our memories even for the next 2 or 3 years tend to be fragile. This phenomenon, referred to as **infantile amnesia**, has attracted a great deal of speculation. According to Freud, it represents repression of sexually charged material, while others have variously invoked immaturity of brain mechanisms, the fragmentary nature of early memorizing skills, the absence in infancy of a self-concept, and the failure of young children to encode information in a form compatible with adults' understanding. However, while there is no shortage of proposals, there is a shortage of supporting evidence, and all such explanations consequently remain in the sphere of speculation.

> **Infantile amnesia** is the inability to remember events occurring in the first few years of life.

What is certain is that somewhere around the third year children become fascinated by the past and begin to talk about it in an increasingly coherent manner. An **autobiographical memory system** is being formed. Basically, autobiographical memory is about one's personal life history; it is a type of episodic memory composed of past events that are of significance to the individual and will therefore become an essential part of the child's emerging sense of self (Nelson, 1993). Children begin to talk about the past almost as soon as they are able to talk, but initially their references are merely to events that have just been completed. Between 2 and 3 years, however, a marked increase occurs in references to the more remote past, suggesting that children are now beginning to develop a definite sense of personal history.

> **Autobiographical memory system.** The store of memories referring to the individual's past history, the function of which is to provide a sense of personal continuity and which is therefore essential for children's acquisition of a self-concept.

This development first becomes apparent in the reminiscences children exchange with their parents. Take the following conversation of a mother with Rachel, her 21-month-old child (from Hudson, 1990):

> *MOTHER*: Did you see Aunt Gail and Uncle Tim last week?
> *RACHEL*: Yes, yes. Uncle Tim.
> *M*: What did we do with Aunt Gail and Uncle Tim?
> *R*: Said bye-bye.
> *M*: You said bye-bye to Aunt Gail and Uncle Tim?
> *R*: Yes, go in car, in car.
> *M*: In the car?
> *R*: Yes. Tim went in the car.
> *M*: Tim went in the car?
> *R*: Aunt Gail with Uncle Tim.

The excerpt shows that Rachel has a distinct memory for various aspects of that event, but also has some difficulty in giving a clear account of the experience. To a large extent this appears to be due to a lack of the necessary linguistic skills, reflected not so much in a restricted vocabulary as in difficulties in participating in a conversation and in providing a continuous narrative. What we also see, however, are the mother's efforts to 'scaffold' the child's contribution, by such means as initiating the exchange, offering appropriate prompts and repeating Rachel's utterances, and in general encouraging the child to talk about the experience and share the memory with the mother. It is this aspect of *sharing* that appears to be crucial in the development of early personal memories: from the interchange with the mother, the child can learn that the past is significant, that certain narrative techniques are required for sharing memories, and that memories can be useful when pursuing personal hopes and aspirations. As Reese (2002) has put it, 'Children are not just learning what to remember or how to remember, but why they should remember'. As a result of the help the parent provides, children become increasingly competent in organizing their memories and retrieving them in communicable form.

Parents, however, approach the task of reminiscing about the past with their children in different ways. Two styles have been distinguished, high-elaborative and low-elaborative (Hudson, 1990):

- *High-elaborative* parents speak often about the past and, when they do so, provide a large amount of detail about salient events. They encourage their children to offer similarly detailed narratives, asking many questions and greatly expanding on the child's answers.
- *Low-elaborative* parents show much less interest in the past, talking relatively little about events that they and their children had experienced and discouraging lengthy conversations dealing with such matters. In response to the child's memories, they offer little elaboration and tend to pose pointed questions requiring just a single correct answer.

Of particular significance is the finding that the children of these two sets of parents also develop different ways of talking about the past. Those with high-elaborative parents produce more detailed descriptions of remembered events, organize what they remember into a more coherent and meaningful story, and are more inclined to use the past as a guide to present action than children of low-elaborative parents. How parents jointly reminisce with their children, how they organize conversations about the past and how they support the child's own efforts to talk about experienced events appears to have a profound influence on the way in which children reminisce and think about personal memories. This is the *social interaction model* of the development of autobiographical memory – the belief that children's personal memories are dependent on parental socialization practices (Nelson, 1993). As Vygotsky proposed, cognitive skills such as memorizing have their origin in social interaction with more skilled partners: memory, that is, becomes first established through narratives that parent and child jointly construct and where the adult can scaffold the child's faltering efforts to recount past events. As a result of such support, the child will eventually become independently proficient at reminiscence – first as an overt activity in conversations with others, and subsequently as an internalized, covert function carried out in private. Parent-guided conversation about the past is thus the soil out of which the child's personal memorizing abilities grow.

Language clearly plays a crucial role in this progression from overt to covert memorizing. Parents provide linguistic tools for their children that enable them to describe and think about 'what happened'. Words are used to focus children's attention on significant aspects of their past experience, to attach meaning to these events and to facilitate representing them in memory. But it is not just talk about the past that affects the way children's ability to remember develops; talk at the time the event happens and the way that this talk is conducted plays a crucial part too. When Tessler and Nelson (1994) recorded what mothers and their 4-year-old children talked about during a visit to a museum, they found that those exhibits and activities that were *jointly* discussed by mother and child were subsequently much more likely to be remembered by the child than those that were referred to only by the mother or only by the child or, for that matter, not mentioned at all. This was confirmed in a subsequent study by Haden, Ornstein, Eckerman and Didow (2001), in which mothers' and children's behaviour was recorded during such special events as a bird-watching adventure and the opening of an ice-cream shop: again, those features of each experience that were *jointly* talked about at the time were the ones the children best remembered. What is more, verbal interactions (such as a mother naming something and the child then repeating and elaborating on that) appear to have a quite specific effect: when compared with non-verbal interaction (such as mother and child jointly handling an object), talk tends to be considerably more effective in committing something to memory and being able to retrieve it subsequently (Nelson, 2000). Language, we can conclude, is uniquely suited as a tool for representing experiences in memory: it organizes the experience in a meaningful way, it helps the child to store it in a coherent manner, and it makes it easier subsequently to recount it and share it with others. Perhaps it is not surprising that infantile amnesia is associated with the period when children have no or few skills to translate experience into verbal form.

Children as eyewitnesses

One practical consequence of the work on children's personal memory is that a great deal more is now known about the ability of children to act as eyewitnesses. In so far as children are increasingly called upon to provide testimony in court cases, the reliability of evidence obtained from children and the extent to which this changes with age have become important issues in memory research (for reviews, see Bruck & Ceci, 1999; Ceci & Bruck, 1995).

Most of the research on this topic takes the form of experimental studies, involving staged events which children are subsequently asked to recall after some specific interval, either freely or in response to interview questions. To summarize the main findings:

- The amount that children can remember in free recall varies according to age. Young children generally provide little material; from the age of about 5 this increases sharply.
- As to accuracy in what children can recall, there are surprisingly few age differences from about 6 years on, at least with respect to salient events that are personally meaningful. Schoolchildren's accuracy in free recall is as good as that of adults.
- Much depends, however, on the interval between witnessed event and recall. When the delay exceeds 1 month, age differences in accuracy become more pronounced: over such periods younger children forget more than older children.
- Younger children are more susceptible to suggestion when interviewed. When misleading questions are asked, they are more likely to be overawed by the person asking the questions and change their recall accordingly.
- However, suggestibility depends on a host of factors, including the way the interview is conducted, the type of questions asked and the perceived role of the interviewer.

Overall, the view that children in general are unreliable witnesses has not been borne out. What young children recall may be less detailed because they took in less information at the time the event occurred; they are also more susceptible to the social situation in which recall occurs and hence more suggestible. However, a lot more is now known about the conditions that facilitate recall in even quite young children, and, by applying interview techniques specifically developed for such children, it is now becoming increasingly possible to obtain usable testimony at all but the youngest age levels.

Thinking about People

Other human beings are the most fascinating as well as the most important part of any child's life, and it is no wonder that trying to make sense of others preoccupies children so much. They show this from quite an early age by the questions they ask: 'Why is Daddy so cross today?', 'Does John like me?', 'What will Mummy say about my torn trousers?' Just like adults, children need to understand other people, and for that purpose they assemble concepts for describing human beings and theories for explaining them. But are these concepts and theories the same as those employed by adults? Does the young child's social world correspond to that of older individuals? We shall look at this problem under two headings: the first concerned with the way children *describe* other people, i.e. in answer to the question 'What is he like?'; the second with children's attempts to *explain* people's behaviour, i.e. responding to the question 'Why does he behave as he does?'

Describing others

Listening to children's spontaneous descriptions of people they know makes it very apparent that there are considerable age differences in the kinds of qualities they attend to in others and in the kinds of labels they employ to characterize them. These differences are well illustrated in a study carried out by Livesley and Bromley (1973) on over 300 children aged 7 to 15, in which they were asked to write descriptions of various people known to them, concentrating on what sort of person the individual is rather than on their appearance. Here are two of the descriptions provided, the first by one of the youngest children in the sample and the second by one of the oldest:

> He is very tall. He has dark brown hair, he goes to our school. I don't think he has any brothers or sisters. He is in our class. Today he has a dark orange sweater and grey trousers and brown shoes. (7-year-old)

> Andy is very modest. He is even shyer than I am when near strangers and yet is very talkative with people he knows and likes. He always seems good-tempered and I have never seen him in a bad temper. He tends to degrade other people's achievements, and yet never praises his own. He does not seem to voice his opinions to anyone. He easily gets nervous. (15-year-old)

The two accounts are radically different, and indicate some of the changes that occur in the way children perceive people as they grow older. Let us summarize the dimensions along which these changes occur:

- *Outer to inner attributes.* Despite instructions to the contrary, the youngest children in Livesley and Bromley's study wrote mainly about their appearance, possessions and other external attributes; many did not mention a single psychological quality. Psychological qualities became more prominent at later ages, as though children gradually realize that the true identity of an individual is to be found in their mental rather than their physical characteristics.
- *General to specific.* Initially, children tend to use broad labels such as 'nice' or evaluative terms like 'good' and 'bad'. Subsequently they become increasingly precise, using words like 'modest' and 'nervous' that provide much more specific information about the person described.
- *Simple to complex.* At younger ages children tend to make sweeping statements about people. Thus they cannot comprehend that an individual can be both good and bad: if he is a good sportsman he cannot be a liar. As they get older, they come to realize the complexity of personality and allow for contradictions in any one person's make-up.
- *Global to differentiated.* Younger children tend to talk in terms of absolutes (e.g. 'he is horrid'); older ones (like the 15-year-old quoted above) make allowance for circumstances (e.g. shy but only with strangers) and introduce gradations (as seen in the phrase 'tends to'). Descriptions thus become more precise.

- *Egocentric to sociocentric.* The younger the child, the more likely it is that people are seen in terms of their impact on the child him- or herself (e.g. 'She is very nice because she gives me sweets'). Subsequently, descriptions become more objective; the child no longer figures centrally in the impression conveyed; moreover, children acknowledge that different people might have different ideas about one and the same individual.
- *Social comparison.* The older child quoted above includes the statement 'even shyer than I am' in his description. Such comparisons, either with oneself or with other people, become marked around the age of 10 to 11, whereas previously they are rarely found.
- *Organization.* In younger children's descriptions references to various characteristics are just thrown together; older children, on the other hand, make an attempt to create a coherent picture so that the uniqueness of the individual comes across more clearly.
- *Stability.* With age children increasingly appreciate that they can expect at least some degree of consistency in a person's behaviour, so that one can predict future actions on the basis of past actions. Younger children give little sign of thinking about such behavioural regularities and tend to confine their descriptions to past or to present.

The first developmental trend mentioned above, that referring to the change from outer to inner characteristics, has attracted most attention. It has been taken to indicate that young children are not aware of psychological characteristics and attend to nothing but people's external characteristics. More recent findings have shown, however, that this is a considerable exaggeration and largely a function of the methods used to investigate children's perceptions of others. Free-description procedures such as those employed by Livesley and Bromley ('tell me about . . .') are very demanding on children with limited verbal skills; when methods that are easier and more familiar are applied, even preschool children will show that they do have some ability to take into account psychological characteristics such as personality dispositions, motives and emotional states (Yuill, 1993). The proportion of inner to outer aspects may well be very much less than that found among older children and the young child's awareness of such features is by and large rudimentary. In that sense, the external-to-internal developmental trend is a real one. Yet, as we shall see below, from a very early age on children do take at least some account of other people's internal attributes and do not think of them entirely in terms of physical and behavioural characteristics.

Explaining others

Awareness that other people have minds may seem a highly sophisticated achievement, yet there is evidence that even toddlers already have some rudimentary knowledge of mental phenomena and the way they differ from physical phenomena. For example, 3-year-old children were told about two hungry boys, one of whom was thinking about a cookie while the other actually had a cookie. When asked questions such as 'Which boy can see the cookie?' and 'Which boy can't touch the cookie?', the majority of 3-year-olds had little difficulty in answering correctly (Wellman & Estes, 1986). Similarly, when 3-year-old children were confronted with a person wearing a blindfold and asked what that person could or could not do and think, most children correctly judged that she could think about an object but would not be able to see it (Flavell, Green & Flavell, 1995). Thus these children demonstrated that they already knew mental phenomena to have distinctive characteristics: in particular, that they related to a person's internal activity and that thoughts, unlike physical objects, cannot be seen or touched. By making comments such as that by one preschooler, 'People can't see my imagination', children of this age also show that they know mental phenomena to be private and not open to public scrutiny. Or take a remark, also by a preschool child, like 'Your mind is for moving things and looking at things when there's not a movie or a TV around': we have a clear indication here that these young children have some insight into the uses of mental activity and realize that the mind functions as a means of conjuring up things that may not exist in reality. Their conception of human beings is thus by no means confined to external actions: they have some understanding that other people are composed of psychological attributes too, and that these need to be taken into account if one is to explain their behaviour.

The same is revealed by children's descriptions of other people, when this is part of their spontaneous talk rather than elicited in question–answer sessions. According to one study (Miller & Aloise, 1989), labels such as 'nice', 'good' and 'bad' were used, respectively, by 70 per cent, 93 per cent and 87 per cent of 2-year-olds, and, as we saw in chapter 5 on emotional development, from about the age of $2^{1}/_{2}$ children increasingly refer to the feelings they assume other people are experiencing. Yet there are still considerable limitations in what young children know of other people. The labels they use are few in number, imprecise and highly subjective. They also refer mainly to temporary mental states rather than to stable personality traits. Also, children up to the age of 3 or 4 have not yet worked out the causal relationships between mental attributes and behaviour, e.g. that people will look happy if they get what they want and sad if they do not, or that a particular action results because the individual has the intention to bring it about. Young children may see people as more than a mere bundle of external attributes, but their conception is still lacking in coherence. Above all, they still need to develop a *theory of mind*.

As we saw in chapter 5, *theory of mind* is the term given to the realization that other people have an internal world which is distinctive to each individual. Having such a theory enables the child to explain observable events (people's actions) by postulating unobservable entities (desires, beliefs, etc.); it is thus a device for understanding why people behave as they do. In so far as the ability to impute mental states to others is a matter of inference which is then used to make predictions about their behaviour, employing the term *theory* draws attention to the fact that children engage in activities analogous to those of scientists when they use hypothetical entities to predict observable events: if X, then Y. Children's theories of mind are not, of course, explicit like the theories scientists construct; nevertheless, when fully developed, they too serve to explain observable phenomena on the basis of conjectural entities.

It is primarily in the age range 3 to 5 years that considerable changes in children's understanding of minds take place (Flavell, 2002). Increasingly, they become aware of the subjectivity of mental states: for example, that a picture they are look-ing at on a table will appear upside down to a person sitting opposite; that food they may dislike intensely may be another person's favourite; and that a much-loved dog could be an object of fear to another child. In general, children's understanding of the emotional aspects of mind precede their understanding of cognitive aspects: when Bartsch and Wellman (1995) analysed young children's spontaneous talk about people, they found that from the third year on children talked about others' desires, using words like *want, wish* and *like*; it was only in the fourth year, however, that these children began to use words like *think, know* and *wonder*, revealing an aware-ness of people's beliefs and thoughts, and it was not until the fifth year that the children began to use beliefs and thoughts as explanations of an individual's actions.

While children's mindreading abilities develop progressively throughout the early years, their understanding of *false belief* is generally taken as the litmus test for having acquired a reasonably sophisticated theory of mind. The concept of false-belief understanding refers to the child's realization that a person's belief about some particular real-world event is an internal, mental phenomenon that may differ from reality and from the child's own belief, and that beliefs may therefore be true or false and vary from one person to another. Consider the following story, acted out with dolls and toys, about two girls, Sally and Anne (see figure 8.8). Sally places a marble in a basket and then leaves the room, whereupon Anne moves the marble to another location. Sally returns and looks for the marble. The child being tested is then asked where Sally will look. Nearly all 3-year-olds will state that she will look in the new location where they themselves know the marble has been put – they cannot, that is, attribute a false belief to Sally and use that to predict her action. After 4 years, however, children give the correct answer: they know that others may have beliefs which do not accurately reflect reality and that their behaviour will reflect such false beliefs.

Thus younger children go on the assumption that there is only one world out there, namely, the one that accords with their own experience, and that other people will therefore act in the way the child would. They cannot as yet compre-hend that alternative models of a particular event may exist: one their own, the other an incompatible one describing another person's false belief about that event. After the age of 4, however, children acquire the ability to represent another person's view even though it conflicts with their own; they have come to realize, that is, that what is in our mind is only a *representation* of reality which is not necessarily accu-rate but which will still affect a person's behaviour. Thus the older child's theory of mind is a much more complex and useful device for understanding others than that of the younger child; their mindreading skill has become more sophisticated and their ability to predict others' actions is consequently more accurate. Theories of mind continue to develop after the age of 5 and show progressively greater refinement, but the conceptual change occurring in the 3 to 5 age range and high-

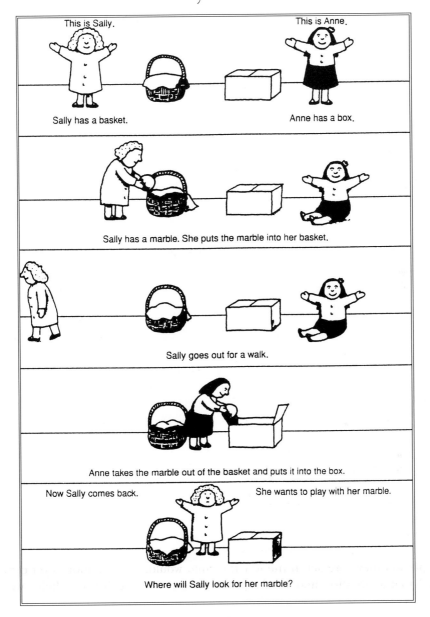

Figure 8.8   *The 'Sally–Anne' test of false-belief understanding (from Frith, 1989).*

lighted by the false-belief test heralds the most important step that children take
in their understanding of people's minds (Wellman, Cross & Watson, 2001).

Mindreading is clearly a crucial skill required for successfully interacting with
others – just how crucial can best be appreciated by considering individuals such
as those with autism who lack such an ability (Baron-Cohen, 1995). In view of its
importance, it may well be that its development is biologically determined, in that

it is part of the behaviour repertoire that is built into the human species. Yet, as Hughes and Leekam (in press) have shown, there are also indications that children's social experience influences various aspects of theory of mind development. Parenting style, attachment security, number of older siblings and amount of talk with others about inner states have all been found to contribute to the rate and extent to which children gain insight into the human mind. As with so many other facets of psychological development, biology may lay the foundations, but it requires nurture to foster what nature has provided.

Summary

One approach to understanding children's cognitive development is by means of an information-processing model. This views the mind as essentially a device for handling information, the flow of which needs to be traced between input through the senses and output in some form of action, linked by such intervening operations as assimilation, storage, transformation and retrieval. According to some writers, it helps to think of this process as analogous to the way computers function – like a computer, the mind depends on certain structures (hardware) and processes (software), and it is the joint operation of these that needs to be stipulated if we are to understand thinking and its development.

Thinking is dependent on the ability symbolically to represent things. In children this ability manifests itself mainly in three areas: language, play and drawing. Language enables a child to use a word to signify an object, and the discovery that things have names is thus a particularly important step forward in cognitive development. Similarly in play: when children become capable of pretending, they need no longer be tied to reality but can use their imagination to let one thing stand for another and so greatly expand the range of their inner life. In drawing, too, reality is transformed into a symbol, in this case a picture, and how children represent objects and people in their drawings provides further insight into their thought processes.

Thinking is facilitated if we can arrange our experiences in an orderly and economic fashion. One way of doing so is by forming concepts, i.e. by grouping together diverse things under a common heading. Another way is by constructing scripts – the name given to the way in which we mentally represent regularly occurring events in stereotypical form ('the way things are supposed to happen'). Scripts are formed from at least the third year on; they provide children with orderly structures for their daily routines and demonstrate how important temporal order is to young children.

How we think is intimately linked to how we remember. The human memory system is a highly complex organization; its developmental course is also not just a straightforward matter of 'getting better at it'. Four aspects need to be taken into account, referring to changes in the capacity of the various memory structures, the child's existing knowledge base, the strategies employed for memorizing, and children's metamemory, i.e. their awareness and understanding of their memory functions. Of particular significance is the development of an autobiographical memory – the means whereby a child builds up a sense of personal history. The intense interest children take in their past, seen from the third year on, first becomes evident in the reminiscences they share with parents; how parents 'scaffold' children's contributions to discussions about the past will influence the development of the ability to reminisce about the past and the way children think about personal memories.

Increasing knowledge of children's memorizing has also shed light on children's ability to act as eyewitnesses. Young children tend to recall less than older ones, especially after lengthy intervals; they are also more suggestible. Yet the view that children in general are unreliable witnesses has not been borne out; when appropriate interview techniques are employed, usable testimony can be obtained from all but the youngest.

The way children think about other people has been studied under two headings: how they describe others and how they explain their behaviour. The way children describe people changes with age in a number of ways; in particular, older children show greater awareness of others' psychological attributes and do not focus just on external characteristics such as their appearance and behaviour. Yet even quite young children do realize that other people have an 'inside' too, as shown, for example, by their references to various mental states attributed to others. Above all, however, it is necessary for children to develop a 'theory of mind', i.e. to realize that every individual has a distinctive mental representation of the real world and acts on the basis of that rather than reality itself. In particular, understanding that others can act on the basis of beliefs that are different from the child's own and may well be false is an important step forward in children's mindreading skills and enables them to predict others' actions much more accurately.

FURTHER READING

Bennett, M. (ed.) (1993). *The Child as Psychologist.* Hemel Hempstead: Harvester Wheatsheaf. Contains a number of useful chapters directly relevant to topics discussed here, including the development of script knowledge, children's descriptions of other people's personality and children's construction of a theory of mind.

Bjorklund, D. F. (2000). *Children's Thinking: Developmental Function and Individual Differences* (3rd edn). Belmont, CA: Wadsworth. A very comprehensive account that goes well beyond children's thinking and covers such other cognitive topics as perception and language development, as well as the study of intelligence.

Cowan, N., & Hulme, C. (eds) (1997). *The Development of Memory in Childhood.* Hove: Psychology Press. Includes a range of useful contributions that cover in an exhaustive manner what has been learned by recent research about children's memory development.

Mitchell, P. (1997). *Introduction to Theory of Mind.* London: Arnold. A concise yet comprehensive account of work on children's understanding of what other people think and feel, with special attention to the developmental course of this ability. Includes detailed account of work on autistic children and on the evolutionary origins of theory of mind skills ('Do apes have a theory of mind?').

Siegler, R. S. (1998). *Children's Thinking* (3rd edn). Upper Saddle River, NJ: Prentice-Hall. Written by one of the best-known present-day contributors to research on the development of thinking, this book presents an authoritative and clearly written account of the field.

Using Language

Chapter Outline

Repeatedly throughout the preceding chapters we have referred to children's use of language – in thought, in problem solving, in conversation, with adults or with peers or when alone, as an accompaniment of action or on its own. Language pervades a great range of human functions; without it we would be very different beings – less intellectually competent, less creative, less socially communicative. In this chapter, language and its acquisition during childhood will therefore be the prime focus, as we discuss its nature and developmental course.

What is Language?

Consider two deaf people holding a conversation. They are facing each other, their expressions are alert and animated as they are watching each other's hands, and these hands and fingers are sending a stream of messages which are clearly mutually intelligible. Throughout, of course, they are not vocalizing. Are they using language? This term is often equated with speech; yet, as we shall see below, this is not one of its defining characteristics. The vocal channel is one way of expressing language; however, it is not the only way: manual signs too serve the same purpose and in many respects function in the same way as words – hence the quite appropriate reference to sign *language* as used by the deaf.

The nature and functions of language

Language has been defined as an *arbitrary system of symbols* (R. Brown, 1965). As we saw in the last chapter, individual words 'stand for' things – objects, events, people – and it is children's task to learn the correspondence between symbol and whatever it refers to, and so accumulate a vocabulary with which to express themselves. The actual words (and the same applies to manual gestures and to the symbols we employ in written language) are for the most part quite arbitrary: there is, for example, no compelling reason why *dogs* should not be referred to as *cats*, why one particular combination of sounds has to be preferred to another – except, that is, for the very important consideration that symbols should also be recognized by other members of society. Language, after all, is an essential tool for communicating with other people; it enables us to share our knowledge and feelings with them, and there must therefore be agreement among members of each society as to what to call things. As far as the child learning to talk is concerned, it is necessary to realize that things have quite specific names which are the 'correct' ones to use. However, matters are not quite so straightforward: there are other lessons to be learned too. For one thing, the name used by the child may not be the appropriate one for other people to use. Father is 'Daddy' to the child, but 'John' to his wife, 'Mr Smith' to the postman, 'Smithy' to colleagues at work and (most confusingly) 'son' to the child's granny. A name is a symbol that depends not only on the person to whom it is applied but also on the person applying it. For another, what is 'correct' in

one society is not understood in another: children in Japan learn to sp
Japanese while those in Spain learn Spanish. Even the set of manual gestures lear...
by deaf children in America (American Sign Language) is in certain respects different from that learned by deaf children in Britain (British Sign Language). Thus
children have to find out that the ability to communicate via their particular code
has limitations, and that they need to acquire proficiency in other languages if they
wish to communicate with individuals outside their own society. Finally, there is
the all-important consideration that a language is more than just a collection of
words; it is also a coherent *system* in that there are rules for combining the words
in particular ways. The child, that is, must acquire not only a vocabulary but also
a grammar to become a proficient language user.

Language serves a number of functions. In particular, it is a device for communication, for thinking and for self-regulation.

1 Communication

The communicative usefulness of language is obvious. However, to talk to another
person requires a great deal more than being in possession of a language.
Acquiring a vocabulary and a grammar on their own is one thing; their use in everyday life is another. To talk to another person, it is necessary to show awareness of
the listener's ability to comprehend what is said; it is thus essential to adapt what,
when and how the message is delivered. Children may not be as egocentric as Piaget
believed; nevertheless, their ability to take account of another person's perspective
is not well developed. Young children tend to assume that others understand them,
seeing that they understand themselves; they are often not aware that their message
is inadequate and so get frustrated if what they say is meaningless to the listener.
They also need to learn that there are certain rules for using language in social
interaction – rules such as turn-taking, whereby child and partner alternate being
speaker and listener and so avoid simultaneous talk. Thus social skills go hand in
hand with linguistic skills; both are required for effective communication.

2 Thinking

As we saw in the last chapter, verbal symbols are powerful tools for thought processes; they enable us, *inter alia*, to conjure up the past and anticipate the present,
to combine things that are separate in real life, and to form concepts and other
abstractions. How language and thought are related to one another in development
has, however, been a matter of considerable controversy. On the one hand, we have
Piaget's view: thought is prior to language, in that the development of representational thinking makes possible the use of words. Language is merely a mode for
the expression of thought, and accordingly Piaget gave it relatively little weight in
his account of cognitive development. This contrasts markedly with the view put
forward by Vygotsky, who saw language as by far the most important psychological

tool the human species possesses, capable of transforming the way we think about the world and of altering (as he put it) 'the entire flow and structure of mental functions' (Vygotsky, 1981b). Language is thus prior to thought: developing the ability to use words makes representational thinking possible.

Piaget and Vygotsky also differed with regard to the nature of early speech. Both agreed that in the first few years speech tends to be egocentric, i.e. private in nature and usually directed at the self rather than at others, even though it is spoken aloud. According to Piaget, such speech has no particular function as far as thinking is concerned and simply fades away once representational thought develops. Vygotsky, on the other hand, saw private speech as externalized thought, which young children actively use in problem solving to guide thinking and plan action. However, by the age of 3 or so, children have learned to differentiate communicative speech from egocentric speech: both are still external, but the former is deliberately directed at others while the latter becomes a running commentary with which the child monitors actions. Towards the end of the preschool period, egocentric speech gradually disappears – not to fade away, as Piaget believed, but to go underground and become silent verbal thought. In the early school years, self-directed utterances can still be heard, especially when the child is confronted with a difficult task, but words are abbreviated and less audible and are clearly self-directed.

A considerable body of research on private speech has largely borne out Vygotsky's account and demonstrated how closely language and thinking become intertwined in the course of development. Private speech has been shown to be a frequent accompaniment of problem solving, even in young children; with age, however, it changes from being spoken aloud to becoming less and less audible and eventually silent. A study by Bivens and Berk (1990) plots this progression. Children aged 6 to 7 were closely observed in their classroom while working individually on mathematical problems, and note was taken of incidents of private speech and its manner of expression, i.e. whether it consisted of overt remarks irrelevant to the task in hand, or overt remarks but task-relevant, or such task-relevant manifestations of inner speech as inaudible muttering or lip movements. The same procedure was repeated 1 year and 2 years later. The overall incidence of private speech while the children were working was found to be extremely high; what is more, it remained at a similar level over the 3 years of observation. However, the nature of such speech changed markedly over this period. As shown in table 9.1,

Table 9.1   Changes over age in incidence of private speech

Private speech type	6–7 years	7–8 years	8–9 years
Overt, task-irrelevant	4.6	1.4	1.2
Overt, task-relevant	23.8	10.3	6.9
Inner, task-relevant	31.9	48.7	50.8

Source: Adapted from Bivens & Berk (1990).

both task-relevant speech and task-irrelevant overt speech declined; task-relev
inner speech, on the other hand, increased greatly. Thus, as children gradu......,
relinquish the more audible, less mature forms of externalized private speech, they
make increasing use of internalized private speech, strongly suggesting that overt
speech is becoming replaced by covert thought and so confirming Vygotsky's views
about the developmental role of private speech.

3 Self-regulation

Language affects not just thinking but also action. When Furrow (1984) observed
2-year-olds at play in their own homes, he noted how time and again they gave
themselves instructions: 'No, not there'; 'I put that there'; 'Put it', and so forth. It
is also notable that in the above-mentioned study by Bivens and Berk, the development of internalized speech was paralleled by children's greater ability to inhibit
extraneous movements and restlessness and to pay closer attention to the task –
consistent with Vygotsky's belief that private speech comes increasingly to promote
self-control. According to Luria (1961), one of Vygotsky's colleagues and follow-
ers, there are three developmental stages in children's ability to use language to
direct their behaviour. In the first, up to about 3 years, another person's verbal
instructions can activate an action but not inhibit it. Given a rubber bulb to squeeze,
children will correctly respond to the command 'Squeeze'; when told 'Stop' they
will squeeze again. In the second stage, up to about 4 or 5 years, they respond to
instructions in an impulsive manner: told to press the bulb when a light comes on,
they will press repeatedly, responding not so much to the contents of speech but
to its energizing quality – thus the louder the instructions, the more often they will
press. Finally, after about 5, they will respond to the contents of speech and become
capable of using that to inhibit as well as activate their actions. Verbal regulation
of behaviour, whether by children themselves or by another person, thus comes
to play a major role, though one that needs to develop progressively in the course
of early childhood.

A uniquely human ability?

The use of language is widely regarded as an ability confined to the human
species. Of course, other species do have various ways of communicating with their
companions, and these sometimes take quite elaborate forms, as seen in the dance
performed by bees on return to the hive whereby they inform other bees about
the precise location of a source of pollen-rich flowers. However, such messages do
not add up to a language; the actions performed may be representational but are
not based on an underlying system of rules which enables the individual constituents
to be combined in a variety of different ways. Animals, that is, may have a (mostly
very limited) vocabulary but they lack a grammar.

There have been a number of attempts to find out whether apes are capable of acquiring language (see Savage-Rumbaugh, Murphy, Sevcik, Brakke, Williams & Rumbaugh, 1993, for a brief historical account). Most of these studies have involved rearing young chimpanzees in the investigators' homes, sometimes together with their own children, in order to teach them a range of human-like skills: eating with a spoon, unlocking doors, recognizing and sorting pictures, and so on. Together, these studies indicate that chimpanzees can become very much more proficient at acquiring such feats than had been thought possible; attempts to teach language, however, have produced rather more mixed results. Training chimpanzees to produce vocal speech has been largely unsuccessful – unsurprisingly, in view of apes' very different vocal apparatus compared to that of humans. On the other hand, making use of chimpanzees' manual dexterity and teaching them a sign language such as that used by the deaf has resulted in somewhat more positive findings. One of the best-known attempts was that by Gardner and Gardner (1971), who adopted a chimpanzee named Washoe and taught her American Sign Language (ASL). From infancy on, ASL was the sole means of communicating with Washoe: nobody was allowed to use spoken language in her hearing, and all signing was integrated into the animal's everyday routines. Washoe was unable to acquire signs by imitation, as do human children; on the other hand, when the Gardners moulded her hands to produce the appropriate signs, she soon began to accumulate a vocabulary, reaching 85 different signs by age 3 years. Her ability to combine signs, however, was limited: producing 'sentences' based on subject–verb combination ('Washoe eat') or verb–object combination ('drink juice') appeared to be beyond her capacity. Subsequent efforts by other investigators, working with various kinds of apes, using lexical keyboards instead of manual gestures and focusing not just on the production but also on the comprehension of signs, have mostly indicated a rather greater range of linguistic skills than the older studies, including the ability to combine signs into meaningful sentences and use these for communicative purposes (Savage-Rumbaugh et al., 1993). Nevertheless, the work remains controversial: various alternative interpretations have been advanced for the animals' success, denying them true linguistic understanding; moreover, whatever animals achieve is of a far more limited nature and is obtained much more slowly and laboriously than is the case with children's language acquisition. And no wonder: using language in whatever form is not a natural skill employed by animals in their natural habitat, and whether they can be taught some rudiments of this skill is therefore not a very significant issue.

There are a number of additional considerations that point to language being a human prerogative. Discussed in detail by Lenneberg (1967), they include the following (see Bjorklund, 2000, for a summary):

- *Language is species uniform.* All normal human beings, reared under normal conditions, develop language. Even the most 'primitive' societies have languages every bit as complex as those found in more advanced societies.
- *Language is difficult to retard.* It takes quite exceptional circumstances, such as severe isolation or deprivation, to prevent children acquiring speech. Even

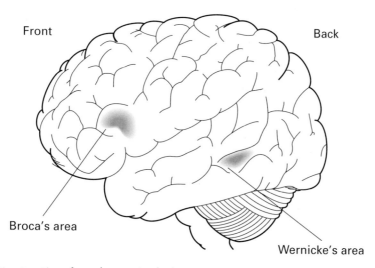

Front   Back

Broca's area

Wernicke's area

Figure 9.1 *Location of speech areas in the brain.*

deafness or other forms of disability cannot interfere with the urge to communicate; other channels such as sign language are then resorted to.

- *Language unfolds lawfully and in regular sequences.* The order and timing of
  various linguistic milestones is similar in all typically developing children, and
  even in retarded children the order is the same though timing is slowed down.
  This suggests maturational influences, i.e. that language development is
  determined by a biological plan inherent in humans in the same way that
  motor development is determined.
- *Language is based on various specifically evolved anatomical structures.* These include
  the vocal apparatus in the mouth and throat, which has specifically developed
  in humans to serve speech and is not found in other primates. They also
  include central structures in the brain, where the left hemisphere is the
  primary locus for language functions. Two areas in particular are implicated, namely, Broca's and Wernicke's (see figure 9.1); patients with lesions
  confined to these locations will develop language disabilities but show no
  other symptoms.
- *Language emerges from preadapted abilities present from early infancy on.* This is an
  additional consideration, based on two lines of research carried out subsequent to Lenneberg's book but giving further support to his belief in the
  importance of biological factors in the development of human speech. First
  are the findings mentioned in chapter 3, showing that young babies pay attention to the human voice above all other sounds; they are, that is, genetically
  ready to be especially responsive to the speech of others. Secondly, it has
  been established that babies can segment the complex sound signals that make
  up speech in the same way as adults, showing a sensitivity to acoustic distinctions
  found in speech long before they can understand speech (Eimas, Siqueland,

Jusczyk & Vigorito, 1971). It appears that from birth there is unique correspondence between children's auditory sensitivity and the speech that they hear from people around them.

We can conclude that human beings have a potential for language that is part and parcel of the heritage of our species (see Pinker, 1994, for a detailed account). Children are 'language ready' from birth on and will develop the ability both to comprehend and to produce speech under a wide range of conditions. This does not, of course, minimize the role of these conditions; as we have seen repeatedly, nature does not exclude nurture. The raw material for language development needs to be supplied by the environment: how and how much adults provide that material in the form of verbal stimulation will also play a highly significant part in the acquisition of language.

The Developmental Course of Language

When do children start acquiring language skills? There is no simple answer to this question, for it all depends on what criteria we use for language acquisition. If children are in certain respects biologically preadapted to attend to and process speech, the course of development is already on the way at birth. If comprehension of specific words is the criterion, evidence can be found in most children around 9 months or so. If, on the other hand, we use the most popular criterion, the ability to produce a comprehensible word, the age of 12 months or so would be the choice.

However, just to make matters more complicated, there are four distinct aspects of language, each with its own timetable:

Phonology is the study of the sound systems that make up languages.

- **Phonology**, which is concerned with the way speech sounds are produced. Phonological development is a protracted business. In the early months of life babies' vocalizations are limited to cooing and crying, and it is only when they begin to babble around 5 to 6 months that an increasingly varied, much more speech-like pattern emerges. Once 'real' words appear the range of sounds a child can make becomes ever larger. Full phonological competence, however, is often not achieved till school age: even preschoolers find some sounds more difficult to produce than others, so that, despite being able to use proper words, their speech may still at times be hard to understand.

Semantics is the branch of linguistics concerned with the meaning of words and how we acquire them.

- **Semantics** refers to the meaning of words. Whereas in the babbling stage sounds are produced just for the sheer pleasure of it, so that a baby can lie for lengthy periods happily repeating *bababa*, at the beginning of the second year the child learns that a particular sound like *mama* actually means something. Here too development is protracted, not only because the child has to learn a very large number of words, but also because meaning becomes ever more complex, abstract and interwoven with the meanings attached to other referents.

- **Syntax** involves the knowledge we possess of how to combine words into sentences. Children need to learn not only the individual words that make up the elements of sentences, but also the grammatical rules whereby we convey different meanings by producing different combinations of words: 'Daddy kiss' means something very different from 'kiss Daddy'. Yet word order is only one aspect of syntax; there are many other grammatical rules to learn, such as those applied to the asking of questions, the expression of negatives and the use of passive sentences. In this respect, too, acquiring the relevant knowledge takes us well into the school years and in many people may never be complete, even though such knowledge is usually implicit rather than explicit.

  > **Syntax** refers to the grammar of language, i.e. the rules whereby words are combined to make up meaningful sentences.

- **Pragmatics** concerns the use of language in a social context. Language is a tool essential for communicating with others and needs to be adapted to the particular people we are talking to, the situation in which we find ourselves and the reason why we are saying something. Thus children need to learn a considerable range of conversational principles if they are to be effective communicators. They must find out, for example, that information conveyed to another person has to be adapted to that individual's existing knowledge; that it is necessary to talk louder to a person at a distance than to someone near; and that tone of voice can convey meanings such as mystery or hostility over and above the content of what is said. Children, that is, need to learn not only how to talk, but how to make use of talk.

  > **Pragmatics** is the study of the rules that determine how we use language for practical purposes.

Acquiring language involves competence with respect to all of these four aspects, and each covers a considerable range of different skills. What is so surprising, given the complexity of the task, is that children become competent so quickly: by the age of 5, nearly all the essentials of linguistic competence are in place, even though development continues for quite some time yet. Below we shall look at some of the main features of this developmental progress in rather more detail.

First words

When children begin to speak, mostly somewhere around their first birthday, the first 'real' words they produce are similar to the babbling sounds they had been making for some time. They choose words that phonologically are the easiest; as Siegler (1998) has pointed out, this explains why the words chosen for mother and father are so similar across a great range of different languages (see table 9.2).

Table 9.2 Young children's words for mother and father in diverse languages

Language	Mother	Father
English	mama	dada
Hebrew	eema	aba
Navajo	ama	ataa
Northern Chinese	mama	baba
Russian	mama	papa
Spanish	mama	papa
Taiwanese	amma	aba

Source: From Siegler (1998).

Considering that babies' babbling is virtually identical the world over, irrespective of the language they hear around them, this is hardly surprising.

Also the kinds of things children's first words refer to are similar the world over. They are the parts of their experience that matter to a 1-year-old: parents, siblings, pets, toys, clothes and food. Things that move are more likely to be named than immobile things: *car* rather than *lamp*, *bus* rather than *street*. One cannot, however, take it for granted that the child's use of a word is necessarily identical to the way an adult would use it, for initially children are inclined both to overextend and underextend words. *Overextension* is a matter of generalizing a word to a wider range of things than the conventional use of the word demands: having learned *doggie*, the child may call cats, rabbits, lambs and various other small animals by that name too. *Underextension* involves a narrowing of conventional usage, as when the child thinks that *doggie* is the name given to the family pet and is therefore inappropriate for any other dog, or when a word is applied to an object in just one specific context and in no other. For example, Martyn Barrett (1986) quotes his 1-year-old son as using the word *duck* only when hitting his toy duck against the edge of the bathtub, but never while playing with it in other situations and never when seeing real ducks. Both over- and underextension show that it takes time and social experience for children to learn to align their usage of words to that of others. Early idiosyncrasies of children's speech may have a certain charm, but they can also give rise to confusion and parents are unlikely to accept them passively for long.

What is still not clear is precisely how children learn the meaning of specific words in the first place. Even when an adult makes things easy by giving 'vocabulary lessons', for example by pointing to a dog and saying *doggie* at the same time, it is not obvious whether the word refers to the whole animal, or to some specific part, or to its colour, or to the particular activity it is engaged in. It has been proposed that in such a situation a *whole-object constraint* is operative, i.e. that in the absence of any other information the language-learning child automatically assumes that the reference is to the object as a whole (Markman, 1989). This explanation might well explain why children's acquisition of nouns takes place so quickly, and indicates one of a number of strategies that children bring to the task of word learning (see Messer, 1994, for a fuller account).

However, more often than not children do not hear words in the context of easy vocabulary lessons but as part of a rapidly spoken, continuous flow of language. How can they segment such a flow where pauses between words are rare, and acquire meaningful words when they are still in the single-word stage themselves? One answer is that adults, often quite automatically and unknowingly, adapt their language to the child's ability to process speech input and so provide extra help and support to the learner. For instance, they will leave pauses between words, slow down their speech, give extra emphasis to certain parts of sentences, ensure that the child's attention is appropriately focused, and embed the words they utter in a context of gestures and other non-verbal cues that will provide the child with additional information and so make the task of understanding and imitating words a lot easier. We shall look at the sort of help adults provide in more detail below; here let us note that there is little doubt that the acquisition of language is very much a social interactive process and that any attempt to understand it in terms of the activities of the learner alone is doomed to failure. Nevertheless, as seen in the following example, the ability to segment sentences is far from perfect at first (Ratner, 1996):

> *FATHER*: Who wants some mango for dessert?
> *CHILD*: What's a semmango?

What is noteworthy is not that children occasionally make mistakes such as this but that in most cases they get it right.

The growth of children's vocabulary gets off to a somewhat slow start. In the first half of the second year they acquire something like eight new words per month; thereafter, however, a positive explosion of vocabulary suddenly takes place, children being transformed into what Pinker (1994) referred to as 'vacuum cleaners' for words, acquiring up to nine new words per day (see figure 9.2). For much of early childhood the acquisition of new words proceeds at a quite astonishing rate (see table 9.3). As Susan Carey (1978) put it:

> By age six the average child has learned about 14,000 words. On the assumption that vocabulary growth does not begin in earnest until the age of eighteen months or so, this works out at an average of about nine new words a day, or almost one per waking hour.

If learning a new word were a slow and difficult process, requiring many trials and repeated practice as it does subsequently when children start to learn a second language, this rate would be impossible. However, for the most part it takes only a relatively few exposures, and sometimes only a single one, before children in the first 5 years or so can learn the meaning of a word they have heard someone else use and become able to use it themselves. The meaning is often only partial and needs to be followed up in subsequent months or years by gradually modifying and

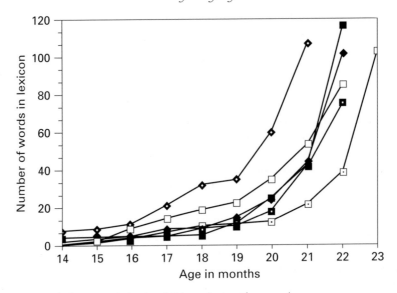

Figure 9.2   Vocabulary growth in six children during the second year.

refining the ways in which the word can be used. Nevertheless, the initial step indicates the child's impressive capacity for learning language. Such rapid acquisition
is known as *fast mapping*, and while it occurs in children as young as 2, it eventually slows down and becomes much rarer in later childhood.

Table 9.3   Vocabulary growth in the first 6 years

Age (years–months)	Size of vocabulary
1–0	3
1–6	22
2–0	272
2–6	446
3–0	896
4–0	1,540
5–0	2,072
6–0	14,000

Source: From various publications.

Forming sentences

From about 18 months on children begin to string words together to form 'sentences'. Initially, these are very different from those used by adults – hence the
quotation marks. They are brief, simple and often grammatically incorrect, yet for

the most part their meaning is surprisingly clear. 'More milk'; 'Sit chair'; 'Cow moo'; 'See baby'; 'Bye bye car' – in each case the child is attempting to convey something and, despite the *telegraphic speech* quality (R. Brown, 1973) of the utterances, usually succeeds in doing so. It is true that reference to the context is sometimes required to know which of several possible meanings the child has in mind. To take a much-quoted example: Lois Bloom (1973) observed a child use the phrase *Mommy sock* on two different occasions. The first time she said it as she picked up one of her mother's socks; the second while her mother was putting a sock on the child. In the former case her meaning was 'This is mommy's sock', while in the latter the full sentence would have been 'Mommy is putting a sock on me'. In both cases, however, the fact that the child can produce combinations of words means that much more complex meanings can be expressed than was possible with single words; instead of merely referring to or naming something, the child is now cognitively able to express relationships between, for example, mother and sock.

From the third year on there is a rapid increase in the length, complexity and grammatical correctness of sentences. Considering how very complex the rules for forming sentences are, children (unlike apes) become able to master them from quite an early age on. Thus they soon realize that a sentence is more than just a string of words, and that the way the words are ordered is all-important to conveying meaning. 'Daddy kiss' is very different from 'kiss Daddy', yet this is not a lesson that has to be taught to children but one they pick up spontaneously and work out for themselves. Indeed, the creative nature of children's language acquisition is nowhere as striking as at the phase when they are busily getting to grips with the rules underlying the formation of meaningful sentences. Take the rule that '-ed' is generally added to English verbs in order to indicate the past tense. Initially, children disregard this rule; when they describe past events they will say such things as 'Granny play piano this morning', or 'I sleep last night in big bed'. Sometime in the third year they learn the '-ed' rule but apply it to *all* references to the past: 'play' becomes 'played' but 'sleep' becomes 'sleeped'. The very fact that they have picked up the rule at all is significant: nobody has taught them about it, and as many observational studies have shown, parents very rarely correct their children's grammar. It is as though the child is actively and quite spontaneously involved in rule learning, which thus comes to occupy a major role in language acquisition. *Overregularization*, i.e. the tendency to apply a rule indiscriminately to all instances of language use, means that for a time words like *goed, wented* and *comed* will be used – words that the child will obviously not have heard adults speak and are therefore not explicable by imitation, but that result from the child's creative efforts in the course of making sense of the whole business of how to talk. In time they will learn that there are exceptions to the '-ed' rule; however, according to a study by Kuczaj (1978), even 6-year-olds are sometimes still uncertain about specific instances: asked to indicate whether a particular word is OK or silly, most considered *eated* as silly but judged both *ate* and *ated* as acceptable.

There are other linguistic conventions which children must also acquire, such as how to form a sentence into a negation or how to ask a question. At first children deal with these matters quite simply: in the one case by putting *no* or *not* in front of the usual utterance ('not I have medicine', or 'no I go'); in the other case by merely adding a rising inflection to the end of the sentence. In time they learn that more complex structures are required and will begin to produce grammatically correct sentences. The rule that the letter *s* needs to be put at the end of nouns to indicate the plural provides us with another example of overregularization: having first become aware that there is such a rule, children apply it indiscriminately, as seen in their talking about *foots*, subsequently modified to *feets*, before the correct usage is finally adopted.

In subsequent years children learn to form various other kinds of complex sentences – sentences which contain coordinating conjunctions, such as 'Baby cried but I kissed her and she stopped'; passive sentences: 'The window got broken'; sentences with embedded clauses: 'Can I go out to play when it stops raining?'; sentences with tag questions added: 'I did the best drawing, didn't I?', and so forth. In each case there is an orderly progression in the way the child arrives at the correct form. Take the development of asking questions. Having first marked questions by merely adding rising intonation at the end ('I ride bike?'), from about the third year on children become able to produce 'wh' questions, though in greatly simplified form ('Where teddy?'). Subsequently children learn that auxiliary verbs such as *does* need to be added, though they are still unsure how to fit these into a grammatically correct sentence and will say, for example, 'Why does Annie cries?' Eventually questions become properly formed as long as they involve brief sentences; more complicated questions, on the other hand, continue to present difficulties right into the early school years. The progression, we may note, is quite spontaneous: children are rarely specifically taught how to ask questions; if such an attempt is made, it is usually in vain. A certain degree of cognitive agility is required to formulate some kinds of sentences; once children have acquired this, their speech will be adapted accordingly. Given this link to cognitive development, it is not surprising that both the order in which different forms of grammatical constructions appear in children's speech and the timing of the various milestones are similar among children generally – indeed, so much so that even deaf children using sign language show the same regularities of development as children acquiring spoken language (see box 9.1).

Are there critical periods in language acquisition?

As we have seen, the development of language generally takes place in an orderly fashion at predictable times. Most of the basic language skills appear in the age range $1\frac{1}{2}$ to 5 years, and unfold in a regular manner rather like the development of children's motor skills. As with motor development, the age-dependent nature of language learning suggests that maturational processes are operating, i.e. that children, when brought up under typical circumstances, acquire language according to a programme built into their nervous system as part of their genetic endowment.

BOX 9.1

Acquiring sign language

Children born with severe or profound hearing impairment have great difficulty in learning to speak, and are therefore more likely to acquire some manual means of communication such as American Sign Language (ASL) or British Sign Language (BSL). As a considerable number of studies, especially of ASL, have shown, these are 'real' language systems, differing from spoken language only in their modality, in that they are expressed manually rather than by vocal means. Each sign language has a clearly defined structure of its own, with characteristics that in certain respects are not identical to or derived from those of spoken language. Sign language is thus not a straightforward translation of speech; for example, the question in English 'What is your name?' becomes 'Name you what?' in BSL. However, as is the case with spoken language systems, all sign languages are both symbol-based and rule-governed (for further details see Bishop & Mogford, 1993, and Klima & Bellugi, 1979).

As with words, individual signs are for the most part arbitrary in nature, consisting of a particular combination of the way in which the hand is held, where it is held in relation to the body and how it is moved (see figure 9.3).

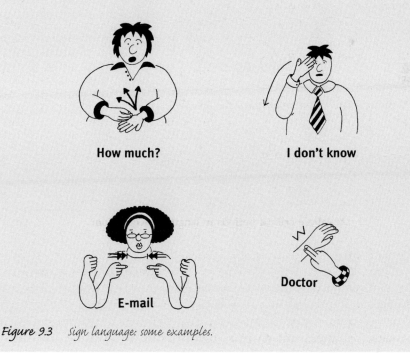

How much?   **I don't know**

E-mail   **Doctor**

Figure 9.3   *Sign language: some examples.*

Facial expression and bodily movement may also play some minor part. In a few instances the sign is iconic – that is, the manner of expression is indicative of its meaning. For example, in ASL crying is shown by a finger drawn down each cheek as though tears were flowing, while the sign for tree looks rather like a tree waving in the wind. But whatever the nature of the sign, it is a conventional one, agreed by all members of that particular linguistic community and used as a means of communicating with others.

When the parents are also deaf (though this occurs only in about 1 in 10 cases) and are competent in signing, children acquire sign language as readily as hearing children acquire speech. In such children the first signs generally appear towards the end of the first year, at about the same time as words are first heard in hearing children. During the second year two-sign combinations appear, again at a comparable age to the start of two-word utterances, to be succeeded in the following months by longer and increasingly complex combinations. But it is not only the age of onset but also the nature of the combinations that is comparable: for instance, the individual signs are frequently arranged in subject–verb–object order (such as 'I hug baby'), showing that the child has become able to apply syntactical rules in a meaningful and consistent manner and has thus acquired the basics of grammar at the usual age. Even syntactical errors are made in signing at the same time as they are found in speaking children; deaf children, for example, have just the same tendency to overregularization and will produce signed versions of verbs like *goed* and *sleeped* as their first efforts to indicate the past tense.

Of particular scientific interest are deaf children whose parents are unable to sign and who consequently have no access to any language, oral or signed, in early childhood. As Susan Goldin-Meadow and her colleagues have shown (e.g. Goldin-Meadow & Morford, 1985), the urge to communicate is so strong that these children will construct their own sign language, based in the first place on natural gestures such as pointing and pantomimed actions (e.g. a fist held to the mouth in order to signify eating). Thus quite spontaneously, without tuition or example, the children build up a vocabulary to indicate people, objects and actions, which in due course are combined into 'sentences' containing signs consistently ordered according to the rules of grammar. Being cut off from any source of linguistic input, the children's further language development will not progress very far; what we can see again, however, is how closely the course of such development in children deprived of the usual opportunities to express themselves parallels that of spoken language.

But what happens when, for one reason or another, this process is interfered with and the child does not have the necessary opportunities to acquire spoken language within the customary age range? Is it too late to learn language subsequently? Are there critical periods for such learning? The concept of **critical period** has been put forward to indicate that psychological functions will develop only if children are provided with certain essential experiences at certain specific times; without these, development will not occur. The support for this proposal is somewhat mixed. On the one hand, in the case of binocular vision, there is sound evidence that children need to have the proper use of both eyes in the first 2 or 3 years; it is, for example, essential to correct squints at this time so that children learn to coordinate the two eyes at this early age (Banks, Aslin & Letson, 1975). With regard to attachment formation, on the other hand, there is now good reason to believe that children deprived of the opportunity at the usual age can still make up at later ages – within certain limits at least (Schaffer, 1998).

> **Critical periods** are those times in the course of development when an individual must be exposed to certain experiences in order to acquire a particular skill.

Support for a critical period in language learning has come mainly from Eric Lenneberg (1967), as part of his case for the biological foundations on which language is built. Such a period is said to extend between $1^{1}/_{2}$ years and puberty, during which time the brain is thought to be particularly adept at acquiring linguistic abilities; language acquisition is therefore easier early on in childhood and may indeed be difficult, if not impossible, for adolescents and adults. According to Locke (1993), evidence to evaluate this claim can be drawn from four sources:

- *Second-language learning.* When Johnson and Newport (1989) tested Chinese and Korean immigrants to the United States for competence in English, they found that their knowledge of grammar was closely related to the age at which they had started to learn English. Those who had arrived in the USA before age 7 were just as proficient as native speakers; those who came after 15, however, showed considerable ineptitude, even when they had lived as long in their new country as the younger people. The age-dependent nature of language learning is thus supported, at least for second languages, though there is no indication that there is a definite end to acquiring such an ability.
- *Late exposure to language in deaf children.* Some deaf children are not provided with any opportunity to acquire a formal language, oral or manual, until comparatively late on in childhood. Studies of such children (e.g. Newport, 1990) produce results similar to those obtained from second-language learning: the later that first exposure to language takes place, the more difficult it is for the individual to become proficient in it. Again, however, no specific cut-off point has been found.
- *Effects of brain damage at different ages.* It has repeatedly been demonstrated that the consequences of specific damage to the language areas located in the left hemisphere of the brain are largely dependent on the individual's age

at the time the injury was sustained. The younger the child, the more likely it is that other areas will take over and enable the child to recover the lost functions. With growing age such plasticity diminishes, making it more difficult for the individual to attain linguistic competence.

- *Children reared in isolation.* A considerable number of cases have been reported over the centuries of children who have had no or very minimal contact with human beings and therefore with language (Newton, 2002). Among the most famous of these is the Wild Boy of Aveyron (as he came to be known), who in the winter of 1800 emerged from the woods near Aveyron in France, having apparently been abandoned as a toddler and having lived there without any human contact ever since. When found at an estimated age of 12 years he was naked, sometimes took to running on all fours, was used to a diet of acorns and roots and, of course, could not talk. He was taken to Paris and placed in the care of Dr Itard, a young physician at the Institute for Deaf-Mutes, who for the next few years devoted the major part of his daily life to making the boy 'human', i.e. teaching him social skills and above all to acquire language. Yet after several years of concerted effort, Itard had to concede failure: the Wild Boy never learned more than a few words, and though he lived into his forties, speech remained beyond his capabilities. There have been other children similarly deprived of acquiring language at the usual age, though under different circumstances. Of most interest is 'Genie', who came to notice in the 1970s, having been kept in a locked room from the age of 18 months and hardly ever exposed to speech. When eventually discovered at age 13, she was totally unable to talk; given intensive language training over a period of years she made some limited progress, but she too never acquired normal language (see box 9.2 for more details). Like the Wild Boy of Aveyron, it seemed too late for her to make up for lost time.

Is there a critical period for language acquisition? One cannot give an unequivocal answer, for inevitably the evidence has to be drawn from 'experiments of nature', and conditions other than linguistic deprivation, such as social isolation, malnutrition and cruelty, may play their part in bringing about the end result. The critical period concept originated in work with animals, where it is possible experimentally to manipulate such aspects as the conditions of isolation, the length of such treatment and the age when it is applied. Even there findings have not turned out to be as clear-cut as had been expected; in particular, it has become apparent that the age range of susceptibility is flexible and under certain conditions can be drawn out considerably. The term **sensitive periods** is now used instead, indicating that at certain ages new developments are *more likely* to occur than at other ages. This is also the one safe (and not very startling) conclusion from the above evidence about linguistic development in humans: childhood is the optimal period for language learning. There is, however, some flexibility in the precise age when children need to start on this task, and there is also

Sensitive periods are the times during development when an individual is more likely to acquire some particular skill than at other times.

BOX 9.2

Genie's story

It would be difficult to imagine a more tragic story of cruelty and neglect than that of Genie (see Rymer, 1994, for a detailed account). From the age of 18 months on her father, a mentally sick man with a hatred of children, imprisoned Genie in a small room, where she spent her time tied to a child's potty chair, hardly able to move. She was given no toys to play with and throughout this period had hardly anything to look at or to touch in her barren surroundings. There was also no auditory stimulation – no radio or TV, no talk from her father or her cowed and semi-blind mother, and if she herself vocalized her father beat her. At night she was caged in a cot, where again she was rigidly constrained. When at last, in 1970, her mother summoned the courage to leave home, taking the child with her, Genie, then aged $13^{1}/_{2}$, was unable to stand erect, was doubly incontinent and so severely malnourished that she had to be hospitalized. She was also emotionally extremely disturbed, quite inept socially and almost mute.

Various attempts (unfortunately often uncoordinated and made ineffectual by personal rivalries among the professionals involved) were made to help Genie with her multiple psychological and physical problems. Above all, her lack of speech was seen as a challenge by psychologists to find out whether a child could still acquire language beyond the age of puberty, and a concerted and carefully planned effort was accordingly made by Susan Curtiss (1977), a graduate student specializing in psycholinguistics, to teach Genie language skills. Over the next few years Curtiss devoted a great amount of time to this effort, attempting to stimulate Genie's interest in learning to communicate with others by means of speech, while testing and recording in detail whatever progress the child made. Gradually Genie began both to understand and to produce words and so build up a vocabulary, and having gone through the one-word stage she eventually began to combine words and produce more complex utterances in the same way as seen in other children. However, her progress was slow: for example, after 4 years of intensive tuition, she scored only in the range of a typical 5-year-old on standardized vocabulary tests, and her store of two-word phrases reached no more than 2,500 utterances. Not only was her progress slow, it was also severely limited, and especially so in learning the rules of grammar. She never mastered negative sentences, or how to ask questions, or how to form relative clauses or passive sentences. Thus her speech remained atypical, full of sentences like 'I want Curtiss play piano', 'Like go ride yellow school bus' and 'At school scratch face'. Whereas most children develop the ability to form the main sentence structures of English in the space of about $2^1/_2$ years, Genie's speech even after 4 years of starting to combine words was still severely deficient in this respect.

One finding from the many tests which Genie underwent is perhaps especially relevant to her linguistic limitations. Whereas normally language involves the left hemisphere of the brain, in Genie the right hemisphere was the main site of electrical activity during speech. It is indeed interesting to note that the nature of her grammatical deficiencies is similar to that of individuals recovering after surgical removal of the left hemisphere and therefore having to shift control to an 'unnatural' part of the brain. Why this shift took place in Genie's case, however, we do not know, though it is possible that one of the consequences of her ill treatment in childhood was damage to her brain, localized in certain areas.

Genie is still alive at the time of writing – a deeply unhappy, emotionally disturbed middle-aged woman who remains isolated from others because of her highly restricted abilities to communicate. Whether her failure to acquire proper language was indeed a matter of 'too late' remains conjectural; there were just too many other adverse things that happened to Genie in her early years to conclude with any degree of certainty that missing language acquisition at the usual time was the decisive factor.

no definite indication supporting Lenneberg's contention that puberty is the point beyond which any further learning becomes impossible.

Communicative competence

Linguistic competence must go hand in hand with communicative competence. Perfect speech is not sufficient on its own; it is essential for individuals to adapt what they say to the particular social context in which they are operating. A message addressed to an adult may not be appropriate when addressed to a young child; talk to a stranger tends to take a different form compared with talk to a familiar person; somebody who is quite ignorant about the topic will need to be given different information than somebody familiar with it. Just as there are rules for grammar, there are rules for the communicative use of language, and children need to learn about the latter as well as the former.

According to Grice (1975), there are a number of *conversational principles* that embody the kinds of rules governing linguistic exchanges. These include:

- *Quantity*. It is necessary to give as much information to the other person as is required for understanding the message – no more and no less. Children need therefore to learn how to take into account the other person's existing knowledge and adapt their message accordingly.

- *Quality.* We generally go on the assumption that what is said is truthful. Children need to learn that they are expected to tell the truth, though they must also find out that there are certain permissible exceptions to this, such as jokes, teasing and sarcasm.
- *Relevance.* In any exchange between two individuals it is essential that both address the same topic and follow up the other person's contribution when it is their turn to talk. This is sometimes strikingly absent from young children's conversations, which can be more like two monologues than a dialogue.
- *Manner.* For a proper exchange it is necessary that individuals take turns in speaking and listening. Interrupting someone is not polite, but it is also not helpful in conveying a message from one person to another.

Young children are at first not very competent in their ability to follow these principles. Warren and Tate (1992) recorded 2- to 6-year-old children's telephone conversations with an adult, of which the following exchange between 3-year-old Alice and her grandmother is an example:

> *ALICE*: 'I got a green one' (opening topic).
> *GRANDMOTHER*: 'You got a what?'
> *ALICE*: 'A green one.'
> *GRANDMOTHER*: 'A green one . . .'
> *ALICE*: 'There's a baby out there' (points to window).
> *GRANDMOTHER*: 'There is . . .'
> *ALICE*: 'Is a baby out there.'
> *GRANDMOTHER*: 'My goodness.'

Alice is clearly violating several conversational principles but most of all the first one, in that she provides insufficient information to her grandmother at the other end of the telephone line by not specifying what the 'green one' refers to or just where the baby is that she is pointing to. As Warren and Tate found, such failures are common in the preschool years, and especially so during telephone rather than face-to-face conversations. Thus the children they recorded frequently shook their heads without saying 'no' or nodded without saying 'yes', pointed without also giving verbal information and made remarks such as 'Look at this' as though the listener were physically present. By age 6 there were far fewer such incidents; by then children found it easier to take the other person's perspective and were no longer caught up in their own egocentric view.

While egocentrism undoubtedly plays a part in limiting young children's communicative competence, there are also plenty of observations showing that Piaget's assertions about preschool children being wholly incapable of conducting a dialogue with another person are greatly exaggerated. Eleanor Keenan (1974) recorded talk by her twins, aged 2 years 9 months at the time, while still in bed in the early morning hours. The following is an example:

TOBY: (alarm clock rings) 'Oh oh oh, bell.'
DAVID: 'Bell.'
TOBY: 'Bell. It's mommy's.'
DAVID: (mumbles indistinctly)
TOBY: 'Was mommy's alarm clock. Was mommy's alarm clock.'
DAVID: 'Alarm clock.'
TOBY: 'Yea. Goes ding dong, ding dong.'

There is a definite coherence to this exchange, no doubt made easier by the twins' familiarity with each other but still impressive in children of this age. For one thing, the children alternate their remarks in orderly fashion, each waiting for the other to finish before starting his own contribution. For another, the children clearly listen to the content of each other's remarks, imitating or expanding what they have just heard and so preserving continuity by repeatedly addressing the same topic. These are essential skills to develop if children want to communicate with another person. Another example is the ability to adapt one's speech to the level of understanding of the listener, and as demonstrated in a study by Shatz and Gelman (1973), this too becomes apparent before the end of the preschool period. Four-year-olds were paired in turn with another 4-year-old and a 2-year-old and asked to explain to their partner how a toy works. Analyses of their speech showed that the children systematically modified the way they talked: when addressing the younger child they used shorter utterances, simpler sentences and more attention-getting devices than they did with a peer. Impressive sensitivity to the needs of the conversational partner is clearly apparent here.

As with linguistic competence, so the development of communicative competence is a complex, long-drawn-out affair that extends throughout much of childhood. In its course children learn to express a considerable variety of *speech acts,* i.e. to use language to accomplish particular objectives such as to seek information, make requests, assert oneself, change another's behaviour, express feelings, strengthen or sever a relationship, and so on. Children, that is, come to learn that one can get things done by using words; what one says may bring about practical consequences. There are, however, conventions in the way speech acts are expressed for optimal effectiveness. If, for example, a child wants a drink, the simple one-word utterance *drink,* which was sufficient in an 18-month-old to be accepted by others, is unlikely to be tolerated in a 6-year-old. Such a child would be expected to have learned certain politeness conventions and know that *please may I have a drink* is the 'proper' way of requesting, even though the utterance is in the form of a question and the child's aim is to obtain action such as the mother pouring out a drink and not the answer 'yes'. It is interesting that most parents, while rarely correcting a child's grammar or pronunciation, will spend a lot of effort on the teaching of politeness rules – presumably because they realize that with the former two they are unlikely to be successful, whereas with the latter instruction does bring about the desired change.

The learning of speech acts is part of a more general development, namely, the acquisition of *metacommunication.* From at least the early school years on children begin to think about words in their own right: thus, they treat words as objects, plan how to use them for particular purposes and increasingly monitor their own speech. This is seen in their realization that a message they are sending may not be adequate and needs correction or some additional information. Thus, when a 7-year-old says 'We went to – erh, me and Jane went to the shop, you know the one round the corner that sells sweets and stuff', she appears to realize that her companion does not know who 'we' refers to and needs to be told just which shop they visited. It is as though she is listening to herself, thinks about the effectiveness of her communication and is able to take appropriate action by carrying out the necessary verbal repairs. Metacommunication skills develop throughout the school years; they enable children, among other things, to play with words by creating puns or nonsense words; they help in the understanding of metaphors and sarcasm; and they bring about the ability deliberately to create confusion in the other person. It is as though children learn how to put distance between themselves and their speech, come to view the latter objectively, and as a result become more effective in using language for communicative purposes.

A note on literacy

Language takes not only a spoken but also a written form. Writing, just like speech, is used to construct and convey meaning; unlike oral language, however, literacy is not an integral part of being a human being but appeared comparatively late in the history of our species. It is thus a cultural achievement, though one that we now regard as essential to our social and intellectual life – hence the emphasis placed on teaching children the skills of reading and writing.

The relation between spoken and written language is by no means a simple and straightforward one, in that the one is not merely a version of the other in a different medium (Wood, 1998). There is no one-to-one correspondence: we do not write as we speak, and this is one reason why children find it so very much more difficult to acquire literacy than speech. Spoken language is acquired quite naturally in the flow of social interaction: children comprehend what other people's utterances mean with the help of a great variety of gestural and environmental clues in which speech is embedded; their own utterances get immediate feedback from others as to whether they are comprehensible or not; and there is no need to form syntactically perfect sentences, for incomplete utterances are often sufficient for the other person to guess what the child is trying to convey. Writing, on the other hand, is a much more deliberate, more carefully planned affair: children need consciously to reflect upon the structure of language in order to form their sentences; they must be aware of the conventions of writing (proceeding from left to right, leaving spaces between words, use of capitals and punctuation, and so forth); and all this is carried out in a solitary context where no immediate feedback is available from a partner. Learning to write therefore makes far greater demands on children than learning to talk; no wonder it occurs several years later in the course of development and requires the skilled help of adults.

Emergent literacy
refers to the very first
stage of becoming
literate, namely, the
realization that written
language is meaningful
and interesting.

Becoming literate is not just a matter of acquiring a set of technical skills concerned with such aspects as letter recognition, handwriting and spelling. Learning how to read and write has been covered in detail in many sources (e.g. Adams, 1990; Harris & Hatano, 1999; Oakhill, 1995); here we shall focus instead on the very beginnings of becoming a literate being, namely, on what has come to be called **emergent literacy** – the term used to denote children's earliest awareness of and attitudes towards written language (Whitehurst & Lonigan, 1998).

The concept of emergent literacy draws attention to the all-important idea that becoming literate involves not only *knowledge* of how to read and write but also having an *interest* in reading and writing – something that begins long before formal schooling (McLane & McNamee, 1990). In modern society children are born into a world in which they are surrounded by print: on the posters pinned to their bedroom walls, on the slogan-bearing T-shirts they are dressed in, on the Coca-Cola bottles from which they drink, on the newspapers and magazines they see lying around at home, and on the shop signs and advertisements they encounter outside. As they soon discover, these print symbols are more than just visual images – other people pay attention to them and appear to derive some sort of meaning from them. However, the main motivation for an interest in literate activities comes through direct involvement in them, and that is usually initiated by the parents. Joint picture-book reading provides the clearest early example – an activity that has been closely investigated by a large number of studies (see Snow & Ninio, 1986). When parents and young children look at books together, they generally participate in a highly interactive, collaborative process: the parent is not just the reader and the child the listener, but the two frequently engage in conversations about what is happening and in question-and-answer sessions to clarify the narrative. Thus the parent will point to a picture and ask 'What's that?', or make some comment such as 'Do you remember when we went on a train like this one?' Children are thus challenged to respond and so become active participants in a shared enterprise; their interest is aroused, and at the same time they learn about what books are for and how to use them – that books are for reading and not for playing with, that pages need to be turned one at a time, that pictures and text usually go together, and above all that printed material conveys meaning and can be the source of great pleasure.

The more parents provide the motivation for an early interest in literacy activities, the greater children's progress will subsequently be at school in the more formal process of learning to read and write (Senechal & LeFevre, 2002). Parents' own interest in literacy plays a part: such indices as number of books in the home, time spent by them on reading and frequency of visits to public libraries are all predictors of children's educational competence. Children profit from example; they also profit from parents making available materials for literacy-related activities, such as paper and crayons for scribbling and picture books for looking at. By at least the age of 3, children come to incorporate these materials in their pretend play: they assume roles such as that of TV announcer reading the news (though

(a)   2½-year-old

(b)   3-year-old

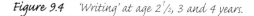

(c)   4-year-old

Figure 9.4 *'Writing' at age 2½, 3 and 4 years.*

from a blank piece of paper), or of a traffic warden issuing a ticket that has to be filled in, or of a waiter taking down an order from a diner. The scribbles they produce on such occasions can be highly revealing of their understanding of text: as figure 9.4 shows, 2½-year-olds still have little grasp of the form that writing takes; at 3 they are likely to produce a linear squiggle; by age 4, however, they know both that writing proceeds sequentially from left to right and that spaces need to be left between words, even though they may still be incapable of producing the words themselves in recognizable letter form.

Thus children learn a great deal *about* reading and writing before they learn *how* to read and write. These skills have their origins in children's social interactions at home, and in particular in the extent to which they are shown that literacy is a valued, useful and above all a pleasurable activity. By means of such precursors the child can then progress to 'proper' educational competence.

Explaining Language Acquisition

We now turn from description to explanation, from *when* and *what* to *how* and *why*. There is far more uncertainty about the mechanisms that enable children to develop linguistic skills, and the various theories that have been put forward to help us understand this development differ sharply in many respects in the approach they take. There are three major types of theories: behavioural, nativist and social interactional.

Behavioural approaches

Around the middle of the twentieth century the tradition of behaviourism was dominant in psychology, especially in the United States. Much of this was due to the work of B. F. Skinner, who in his 1957 book *Verbal Behavior* set about applying behaviourist principles to the acquisition of language. According to this proposal, children learn language just as they learn all other forms of behaviour, namely, through **operant conditioning**, i.e. by being reinforced for acts which are deemed to be the 'correct' acts by adults. Reinforcement of verbal behaviour is brought about through rewards such as parental praise or by showing in some way that the child's utterance has been understood, as a result of which the child is more likely to repeat that behaviour on future occasions. Thus when an infant utters 'ma', the mother may respond with great delight 'Mama, yes, I'm mama', thereby both accepting the utterance and attempting to shape it into a proper word for the child subsequently to repeat. Children may also spontaneously imitate adults' speech, and if this is followed by some form of reinforcement learning will also occur.

Operant conditioning refers to the procedure whereby an individual acquires a particular behaviour pattern as a result of being rewarded for performing it or punished for not performing it.

This account is no longer held to be credible. The main reasons why it is regarded as unsatisfactory are the following:

- There is no evidence that parents act as the language teachers that Skinner envisaged. On the contrary, parents are very tolerant of their children's verbalizations during the early years, whatever the form; thus, if the child says 'Me bigger than Joe', they are more likely to respond by challenging the truth of the statement than by attempting to correct its grammar. Mistakes such as overregulation (e.g. *goed* instead of *went*) are nearly always accepted and thus reinforced, yet children do not retain such utterances but soon learn to correct them on their own initiative.
- When parents do attempt to act as teachers, their children's language development is slowed down rather than speeded up. The more a parent attempts to interfere with and direct the child's natural ways of expression, the more likely it is that she is defeating her own ends by impeding her child's further progress.
- Imitation plays a role in the acquisition of single words, but it cannot explain the acquisition of grammatical structures. There is no evidence that children try to imitate adults' sentences; as we have seen, they create their own, and do so in whatever way is natural to their particular stage of development.
- Most basically, Skinner put all the onus on adults and their role as reinforcers and teachers, while seeing children merely as passive recipients of these efforts. Yet descriptions of the course of language acquisition show vividly how active children are in attempting to master ways of communicating and how hard they try to work out the rules which govern language. This creative aspect

of development is completely neglected in the mechanistic approach which the behaviourists adopted and, more than any other criticism raised, doomed the theory to failure.

Nativist approaches

The main contention of the nativist position is that the explanation for language development is found primarily in the child's inborn equipment, and not in any environmental influences such as teaching or modelling. The most significant proponent of this view was undoubtedly Noam Chomsky (1986). It was he who was mainly responsible for the demise of the behaviourist position, accomplished by his 1959 critique of Skinner's *Verbal Behavior* – surely one of the most devastating book reviews ever written. As he put it, 'I can find no support whatsoever for the doctrine . . . that slow and careful shaping of verbal behavior through differential reinforcement is an absolute necessity'. In particular, he criticized Skinner for being unable to account for *linguistic productivity* – the ability to make use of whatever words the child has learned by combining them in many varied ways and so being able to create sentences never heard before by the individual. This, according to Chomsky, is the essence of language, and no account based on operant conditioning can possibly explain how children acquire the rules which govern sentence construction.

Thus for Chomsky it is the acquisition of grammar that must be the focus of any attempt to explain language development. There are, he believed, two aspects of language that need to be distinguished:

- The *surface structure*, namely, the speech which children actually hear their parents and other adults use. This on its own, however, is of little help to the language-learning child, for adult speech is mostly too ambiguous and too complicated to enable a young child to deduce the rules on which it is based.
- The *deep structure*, namely, the underlying system that governs how we arrange our words to produce meaningful utterances. It is knowledge at this level which children need to acquire as their main task in language acquisition; yet given on the one hand the great complexity of language, and on the other hand the speed with which children nevertheless learn to speak, one must conclude that from birth on some inborn mechanism is at work that drives the language acquisition process.

Language acquisition device (LAD). According to Noam Chomsky, this is an inborn mental structure that enables children to acquire knowledge of the complexities of grammar with remarkable speed.

Thus, according to Chomsky, human beings arrive in the world equipped with a **language acquisition device** – LAD for short – which enables us to develop linguistic skills with comparative ease. He envisaged this hypothetical entity as some kind of brain structure found

Universal grammar
denotes those rules of
language formation
that are found in all
possible human
languages.

in all human beings (and only human beings) that embodies the inborn knowledge we have of **universal grammar**, namely, those aspects of language common to all the world's languages (e.g. the distinction between nouns and verbs). The particular language a child hears others use is filtered through this device, which then extracts whatever regularities occur in it (e.g. 'always add the letter *s* to nouns to indicate the plural') and so provides the child with the set of rules required for comprehending and producing acceptable speech. LAD is thus a programme, built into the human species, which ensures that children learn the intricacies of grammatical language quite readily – certainly much more so than if they depended on adults' teaching and modelling.

As we have already seen, there is no doubt that various aspects of language development depend on our biological make-up. Moreover, the impressive consistency with which all children (including deaf children using signing) go through the same developmental stages in acquiring language is a strong indication that maturational processes are at work in guiding sequence and timing. However, whether to add Chomsky's LAD to this list is more controversial. Doubt has been expressed, for example, regarding the idea of a universal grammar: as Slobin (1986) has shown, there is far greater diversity among the world's languages in the grammatical rules they employ than Chomsky's proposal would allow. In addition, Chomsky can be criticized for going too far in the opposite direction to Skinner along the nature–nurture continuum: while the latter neglected biological contributions, the former had virtually nothing to say about the role of environmental contributions, making little effort to integrate these into the theoretical framework he proposed.

Social interaction approaches

The proponents of the third perspective on language development agree that human beings are biologically set to acquire linguistic skills, but consider that far more attention needs to be paid to social factors, with particular reference to the communicative interactions which children have with adults in their early years. A considerable amount of research has been conducted to substantiate this claim; we shall accordingly devote rather more time to this approach than to the other two.

Most influential has been the work of Jerome Bruner (e.g. 1983). As he put it, 'We shall make little progress if we adhere either to the impossible account of extreme empiricism or to the miraculous one of pure nativism'. A middle way needs to be found that does justice to the intricate interweaving of children's inborn linguistic dispositions with their social experiences of language use. These experiences begin in the preverbal period, where children are given plenty of opportunities to learn about the use of language in the context of exchanges with familiar, responsive adults. Take the following 'conversation' of a mother and her young baby (from Snow, 1977):

BABY: (Smiles)
MOTHER: Oh, what a nice little smile!
   Yes, isn't that nice?
   There.
   There's a nice little smile.
BABY: (Burps)
MOTHER: What a nice wind as well.
   Yes, that's better, isn't it?
   Yes.
   Yes.

The mother here is taking both parts, the child's as well as her own, but by leaving pauses between her utterances as though she is expecting the child to respond, and by even asking questions, she is treating the child as though he were an equal partner and thus acquainting him with the art of conversation. Learning *about* language thus gets started well before the first words appear; it takes place in the context of familiar, everyday routines, and is made easy by the way in which mothers and other adults carefully present language to the young child. Chomsky's notion, that children are surrounded by a bewildering array of other people's utterances, from which their LAD somehow manages to abstract the rules underlying language use, is rejected by Bruner. Children acquire language by virtue of LASS – a **language acquisition support system**, as Bruner labelled the various forms of help and support which adults provide, and it is these and not only the child's inborn acquisition mechanisms that bring about language learning. LASS, that is, works hand in hand with LAD.

> **Language acquisition support system** (LASS). Jerome Bruner proposed this term as a counter to Chomsky's reliance on inborn knowledge, to draw attention to the collection of strategies adults employ to help and support children's acquisition of language.

Adults' support of language learning takes various forms. We shall single out two that are thought by many to play a particularly significant role and have thus been most closely scrutinized by research workers. Respectively, they are concerned with the *style* of adults' speech and its *timing* in relation to the child's ongoing behaviour.

1 The style of adult speech

Adult talk to a young child is very different from adult-to-adult talk. This is not just a matter of *what* is said but also *how* it is said. Quite unconsciously, a different style is adopted, whereby the manner of speech is adjusted to the child's ability to comprehend (Snow & Ferguson, 1977). Initially, this style was referred to as 'motherese', as mothers were the only people investigated; since then it has become clear that virtually anyone – fathers, men and women with little experience of child care, even older children – will adopt the same style when confronted by a young child. A-C (adult-to-child) speech, as it is now referred to, is characterized by a great many features, some of which are listed in table 9.4; in sum, these make speech to children simpler, briefer, more complete, more repetitive and more

Table 9.4   Some features of adult-to-child speech

Phonological characteristics	Semantic characteristics
Clear enunciation	Limited range of vocabulary
Higher pitch	'Baby talk' words
Exaggerated intonation	Reference to here-and-now
Slower speech	
Longer pauses	
Syntactic characteristics	**Pragmatic characteristics**
Shorter utterance length	More directives
Sentences well formed	More questions
Fewer subordinate clauses	More attention devices
	Repetition of child's utterances

attention-worthy than speech to adults. Thus sentences tend to be short, simple and grammatically correct; pauses between utterances are long; intonation is exaggerated; pitch is high and variable, and reference is mostly to the here-and-now. These features have been reported for a wide range of languages; they have even been identified in parents' signing to deaf children (Masataka, 1993). The younger the children are, the more marked the characteristics of A-C tend to be; adults, that is, 'fine-tune' their speech in relation to the child's perceived linguistic competence (Snow, 1989).

In theory at least, such a style should be an excellent teaching device for language-learning children. But is it? Research has produced some very mixed results: some studies support an association between A-C speech and language development; others find no such relationship; still others find connections at only some ages or with respect to only certain aspects of language; and it has even been suggested that simplification of verbal input may hinder children's development (see Messer, 1994, for a summary). Such uncertainty is surprising; it seems, after all, common sense that learning should be easier if the task is made easier. The problem is partly methodological, in that the majority of studies depend on correlational results and these do not allow any assumptions to be made about the direction of causation. Thus it is possible that the direction is not from adult to child but from child to adult: instead of adults being responsible for children's advances in language development, it may be that the more competent a child is the more adults will no longer present simplified speech. As with so many other aspects of socialization, it is likely that the direction of influence goes both ways: adults and children influence each other in a continuing reciprocal process difficult to disentangle.

There is one further consideration: however widespread A-C speech is, it is not universal. In certain societies it is completely absent from the interaction of parents with young children – in some because the parents talk to the child as they would to an adult, in others because it is just not done to talk to an infant at all. Box 9.3 gives some further details; in all instances, however, there are no

BOX 9.3

Parental speech in its cultural context

The particular modifications which parents make in talking to children are so widespread in western society that they have been assumed to be universal – part of the package of being a sensitive, helpful parent. It has therefore come as a surprise to find from observations carried out in other societies that this is not so and that other styles of parental speech linked to different cultural practices are prevalent elsewhere. Such variation not only refutes the notion of universality but also provides an 'experiment of nature', in allowing us to test whether the A-C style is a necessary precondition for children's normal language development.

Consider the case of Samoan parents and their children, studied intensively by Elinor Ochs (1982; Ochs & Schieffelin, 1984). Samoan society is highly stratified: everyone is assigned a particular status, and social life revolves around the relative ranking of participants. Thus having a title or not, or being of an older or younger generation, matter a great deal to the way people behave to each other and the roles they play in all aspects of everyday life – even in child care. Children are generally looked after by a range of caretakers, including the mother, unmarried aunts and the child's older siblings, and from the beginning babies are expected to learn that their behaviour towards these individuals must depend on their ranking and that, moreover, they themselves are at the bottom of the ladder.

This is reflected even in the way in which children are referred to. For the first 6 months they are known as *pepemeamea* – literally, 'baby thing thing', as though they are not quite real human beings. During this period they receive a great deal of physical contact and are almost constantly with the mother, assisted by other carers. However, direct verbal interaction is virtually absent: the baby is frequently talked *about* by others but not talked *to*, for children at this age are not treated as conversational partners. Language addressed to the child is confined to songs or rhythmic vocalizations; no attempts are made specifically to direct any other speech to children.

This changes somewhat once babies start crawling and become mobile. From then on they are referred to as *pepe*, 'baby', as though they have now assumed a slightly higher rank. Somewhat more speech is addressed to them by the mother and others, uttered in a loud and sharp voice, but usually as a command and not as an attempt to get the child to respond in some way. What is more, such speech is not simplified in any way: the usual features of A-C speech as known in the West are totally absent, in that adults talk to children as they would to other adults. The onus is on the child, being of lower rank, to learn to understand others. Similarly, when children produce unintelligible utterances, adults make no effort to interpret their meanings: they do not, as would western mothers, help the child to clarify the utterance by expanding or repeating it: once again, the onus is on the child to learn to produce intelligible speech. Children, that is, are expected to adapt to others rather than others adapting to them. From birth on children are thus taught not to expect adults to assist them in their communicative attempts and instead to rely on their own skills. And yet Samoan children are said to become fluent speakers at the usual time.

Similar findings have been obtained from other societies. One such example comes from the Kaluli in Papua New Guinea (Ochs & Schieffelin, 1984; Schieffelin & Ochs, 1983) – a society we have already come across in chapter 2 (pp. 26–7). Here, too, little attempt is made to involve young children in any form of direct talk. Apart from being greeted by name, children rarely have any other utterance addressed to them until their second year, and then adults' talk consists mainly of 'one-liners' that do not call for any response from the child. Another example comes from Pye's (1986) study of children learning the Mayan language Quiche in South America: here also, no evidence was found that adults in any way adjust their speech when talking to children; in any case, the mothers, though solicitous and caring, rarely take time off from serious occupations like weaving in order to involve their children in playful interactions such as story telling, lullabies or games. Again, both Kaluli and Mayan children are reported as developing language normally.

These observations show, first, that the A-C style is not universal and therefore biologically given; secondly, that the process of language acquisition must be seen as linked to more general cultural beliefs and practices; and thirdly, that children's acquisition of language can proceed normally even without specific parental help. Just one caveat about the latter conclusion: the cross-cultural studies cited did not formally follow up and assess children's language development with standardized tests but relied on general impressions. The possibility of some delay compared with western norms cannot therefore be ruled out, though it is unlikely that this is anything but mild.

indications that children's language development is in any way held back in relation to western norms. For that matter, the speech of depressed mothers lacks some of the features of A-C speech, and these children too do not appear to be handicapped thereby (Bettes, 1988). It may be that the modifications found in A-C speech facilitate language learning but are not necessary for it. Further research is required to provide more decisive conclusions; in the meantime, it is difficult to believe that a naturally occurring, quite unconsciously adopted and very widespread pattern of communicating with young children does not have beneficial effects.

2 The timing of adult speech

As a large number of observational studies have shown, parental talk to young children is generally timed to coincide with whatever the child is currently attending to. Take the following common scenario of a mother and her 2-year-old child playing with a set of toys: the child inspects the toys, selects one of them, picks it up and begins to play with it; the mother thereupon starts talking about that toy: she may name it, point out its uses and features, comment on the child's previous encounters with it or similar toys, and in this way verbally enlarges on the specific topic that the child is attending to at that moment. Talking about some other toy that the child is not interested in just then would be inappropriate and insensitive, depriving the child of valuable opportunities for language learning in a meaningful situation. The establishment of **joint attention episodes** such as this provides the context for developmental progress in a range of cognitive functions (for more detail see Moore & Dunham, 1995); it ensures that child and adult share a particular topic of interest and, as Vygotsky originally pointed out, provides the adult with the opportunity to start where the child is and so introduce new information at a time when the child is most likely to retain it.

> **Joint attention episodes** are those situations in which an adult and a child simultaneously focus upon some object and together carry out actions upon it.

Joint attention episodes can play a particularly effective role in getting language off the ground. Consider the following findings, taken from some of the large number of reports that have investigated the association between such episodes and language acquisition:

- Quite a number of studies (summarized by Schaffer, 1984) have shown that parents at play with their young children tend quite naturally and automatically to monitor the child's focus of attention and home in on whatever the child is interested in at the time. They do so by using a variety of cues offered by the child, such as direction of gaze, pointing or touch, and having thus established a shared topic they will then talk about it, naming it or commenting on its characteristics. Take a study by Murphy (1978) of mothers looking at picture books with their 1- to 2-year-old children. The children frequently used pointing as an expression of interest in a picture; whenever they did so the mother would generally follow with some comment, thus using their shared attention as an opportunity to provide verbal information timed to coincide with the child's spontaneous interest and ensuring that the language input was made a meaningful experience. The nature of that input was adapted to the child's stage of language learning: with 1-year-olds the mothers mostly named the object being examined; older children, on the other hand, were often asked 'wh-' questions such as 'What's that?', thereby challenging the children to demonstrate what they had learned by then and, by praising the answer, reinforcing that knowledge.

- The more time children spend in joint attention episodes, the more progress they make in language acquisition. For example, Tomasello and Todd (1983) videotaped mother–child pairs periodically at home in a play situation, beginning at the child's first birthday and continuing for 6 months. At the end of this period children who had experienced the longest time in joint attention situations with their mothers were found to have developed larger vocabularies. Similarly Wells (1985), by sampling preschool children's natural speech at home by means of radio microphones, was able to demonstrate a relationship at age $2^1/2$ between rate of language development and the amount of speech addressed by the mother to the child in such contexts of shared activity as joint book reading, conversations, play and doing the housework together.

- It has long been known that the language development of twins lags well behind that of other children. While there are various explanations for this lag, one possibility is that twins tend to be rather less involved in individual joint sessions with their parents. Tomasello, Manule and Kruger (1986) observed both twins and singletons, all in their second year, at home and found considerable differences between the two groups in the amount of speech directed at them individually and in the time spent by each child in joint attention episodes – a situation little changed even when taking into account the attention given to both twins simultaneously (see table 9.5). A link between attention deprivation and language retardation is thereby indicated.

- Considerable differences exist among mothers in their responsiveness to their children, that is, the extent to which they are 'tuned in' to cues such as gaze direction, pointing or other indications of the child's attention. These differences have repeatedly been found to predict children's rate of language development: the more responsive the mother, the more likely it is that her child will make rapid progress in acquiring language. For example, Tamis-LeMonda, Bornstein and Baumwell (2001) videotaped the interactions of mothers and children in free play when the latter were around 1 year of age and obtained

Table 9.5 Mothers' speech to singletons and to twins

	To singleton	To individual twin	To individual twin plus to both twins
No. of maternal utterances	198.5	94.9	141.0
Time spent in joint attention (sec)	594.0	57.0	208.0

Source. Adapted from Tomasello et al. (1986).

various indices of maternal responsiveness to the child's activities. The children's progress in acquiring language was assessed throughout the major part of the second year, and was found to be closely associated with the degree of mothers' responsiveness: the greater the latter, the quicker the former.

- One further feature of adult behaviour is noteworthy as having a direct bearing on children's language progress. As Carpenter, Nagell and Tomasello (1998) found in a follow-up study of children aged 9 to 15 months, mothers' use in joint play of 'attention-following' strategies facilitated the children's linguistic development to a far greater extent than 'attention-shifting' strategies. In other words, when a mother allowed the child to choose the focus of interest and followed into it with her subsequent talk, she made it easier for the child to acquire the name and other relevant linguistic information about the object than when she herself determined the focus and then set about shifting the child's attention to that. There are consistent differences between mothers in this respect, creating contrasting language-learning environments for their children.

There can be little doubt that joint attention episodes provide optimum occasions for language acquisition by young children, and especially so when adults take care that their speech input is relevant to the child's interest at the time. By sharing that interest, they ensure that the language the child hears is meaningful, and what is meaningful is more easily incorporated in the child's repertoire. Joint attention is especially important in the early stages of language development when children learn how to label things verbally and so build up a vocabulary; there is evidence, however, that it also plays a significant part subsequently in the acquisition of syntax (Rollins & Snow, 1999). Furthermore, if joint attention leads to shared experiences, it also allows the partners to cement their interpersonal bonds and so has a more general social function than only language learning.

One concluding note: whatever help children get from their social partners, and however important their biological endowment is in laying down a basis, it is unlikely that these tell the whole story of language acquisition. Accounts based on these two sets of influences alone are in danger of seeing the child as passive – driven along by a combination of environmental and inborn influences. As with other aspects of development, children's active role in their own progress must also be acknowledged. Children are creative, sense-making beings, and in no other human function is this seen so clearly as in language learning. New theoretical approaches have given this consideration increasing recognition; thus Lois Bloom and her colleagues (e.g. Bloom & Tinker, 2001), in putting forward their *intentionality model* of language acquisition, have stressed that the child's role is primary in all aspects of learning to talk – in particular, in that children's intention to communicate with others and to establish themselves in a social world motivates them to express overtly by means of more and more sophisticated linguistic means the increasingly complex intentional states they experience. It is thus the child's internal resources, and not so much external guidance, that provide the driving force for language acquisition.

Whatever the merits of the precise formulation of this model may be, it does draw attention to the constructive nature of children's minds – the fact that development is the end result of children's interpretations and evaluations as well as of genetic and environmental influences.

Summary

Language is an arbitrary set of symbols, used for communicating, for thinking and for self-regulation. Its expression is not confined to spoken forms; manually signed language, as used by the deaf, is an example of another form it can take. Language is more than a collection of words; it is a coherent system with rules for combining the words in particular ways. Children must therefore acquire not only a vocabulary but also a grammar to become proficient language users.

Language is a uniquely human function, as seen by the largely unsuccessful efforts to teach it, even in signed form, to apes. The fact that language is based on certain specific structures in the human brain, and the selective responsiveness to human speech found from birth on, support the conclusion that language is a biologically influenced species-specific ability.

The developmental course of language acquisition also indicates that much of it is dependent on a biological plan inherent in the human species generally. For example, nearly all children begin to string words together towards the end of the second year; considering the complexity of the rules for forming sentences, they master the necessary conventions in a surprisingly short period – despite the fact that they are rarely, if ever, given direct tuition. However, the support for critical periods in language learning, i.e. the notion that this must take place within a particular age range beyond which it is no longer possible, is somewhat mixed. The evidence comes mainly from 'experiments of nature' such as from children reared in isolation, where too many other conditions play a part in the subsequent linguistic retardation found to arrive at conclusions.

Four aspects of language need to be distinguished: phonology, semantics, syntax and pragmatics, each with its own developmental timetable and each covering a range of specific skills. Especially noteworthy is the fact that children need to acquire not only linguistic competence but also communicative competence. The latter concept concerns individuals' ability to adapt what they say to their partner's ability to understand. Its development is a complex, long-drawn-out affair, requiring a capacity for taking the perspective of others – something present in rudimentary form quite early on but not fully evident till the middle years of childhood. Communicative competence is also dependent on the acquisition of metacommunication, i.e. the ability to think about words in their own right and reflect upon the structure of sentences – an ability, moreover, essential to the development of literacy. Literacy involves a lot more than learning to read and write; as work on emergent literacy has shown, it also entails children's interest in and attitudes towards reading and writing. Such attitudes are first formed in the preschool years, and depend greatly on the motivation that parents provide in literacy-related activities. They do this partly by their own example, partly by ensuring that children have access to necessary materials, but mostly by including children in shared activities such as joint picture-book reading.

There have been a number of attempts to explain how children acquire language. Behavioural approaches, such as Skinner's, saw language as something to be learned piecemeal, mainly through operant conditioning and imitation. Nativist approaches, associated primarily with Chomsky's work, place the emphasis on inborn mechanisms, such as a language acquisition device for the learning of grammar. Social interaction approaches have paid most attention to the help and guidance adults provide, such as by adapting the style of their talk to the child's ability to comprehend and by involving the child in joint attention episodes. No one of these approaches is sufficient on its own; moreover, it is necessary to do justice to children's own role in actively wanting to acquire the linguistic means whereby they can express their mental states and can communicate these to other people.

FURTHER READING

Cattell, R. (2000). *Children's Language: Consensus and Controversy*. London: Cassell. Written for anyone interested in the development of children's language, whatever their previous knowledge. Covers most of the main topics in the area, and presented with a light touch.

Gleason, J. B. (ed.) (1997). *The Development of Language* (4th edn). Boston: Allyn & Bacon. A 'big' and comprehensive edited collection where different experts contribute chapters on their particular topic.

Hoff-Ginsberg, E. (1997). *Language Development*. Pacific Grove, CA: Brooks/Cole. Another 'big' book – comprehensive, detailed, authoritative. Covers not only the most commonly discussed topics but also gives accounts of language development in such special populations as mentally retarded, blind and autistic children, as well as describing language change in adulthood and old age.

McLane, J. B., & McNamee, G. D. (1990). *Early Literacy*. London: Fontana; Cambridge, MA: Harvard University Press. A short, delightfully written account of the way in which preschool children learn about the nature and functions of reading and writing by means of play with picture books, crayons and other literacy-related materials and activities.

Messer, D. J. (1994). *The Development of Communication: From Social Interaction to Language*. Chichester: Wiley. The focus of this book is on the development of communication in general, but by tracing the origins of language in the child's interactions with others it also gives a detailed account of the onset of language in the first 3 years of life.

CHAPTER TEN

Towards Adulthood

Chapter Outline

Socialization is the umbrella term for all those processes whereby children are helped to acquire the behaviour patterns and values required to live in their particular society.

Individuation is the umbrella term for all the processes employed in children's acquisition of a personal identity (see **social identity**).

As William Damon (1983) once suggested, when thinking about children's development it is useful to distinguish between two distinct developmental trends. On the one hand there is **socialization** – the process whereby children become integrated into their community by learning about and adopting as their own the values and customs prevailing therein, and, on the other, there is **individuation** – the process that enables children to form a personal identity which expresses their own unique pattern of psychological characteristics. The two aspects are the converse of one another and yet are closely interconnected. Thus socialization ensures that children become *like* other people, while individuation results in their being *different* from others; yet, paradoxically, the two arise from the same matrix of psychological growth and experience and their interplay constitutes a basic theme as children progress towards maturity.

Much of what we have discussed so far concerns socialization. However, in this chapter we shall focus primarily on individuation. What accounts for psychological uniqueness? How does the course of childhood development give rise to the mature personality of the adult? These are important questions; we shall consider them by enquiring, first, how children set about the vital task of establishing themselves as persons, and then by asking about the means whereby childhood and maturity become interconnected and the extent to which early characteristics foretell what kind of person will eventually emerge as adult.

Becoming a Person

Until fairly recently, surprisingly little attention was paid by developmental psychologists to differences among individuals. The focus was mainly on group averages and norms – useful data to establish, of course, but what a peculiar being an average child would be! What is interesting about people of any age is their individuality, but how is this established?

Biological underpinnings of individuality

Temperament refers to the set of inborn characteristics that distinguish one person from another in the behavioural style they manifest.

Children are individuals from birth on, and indications of their individuality are to be found in virtually every aspect of behaviour in even the youngest babies. Initially, these differences reflect children's inherent **temperament** – the term used to designate those aspects of behaviour that describe a person's general style of response to the environment, especially the emotional vigour, tempo and regularity with which activities are customarily carried out. As a considerable body of research (summarized by Molfese & Molfese, 2000; Rothbart

& Bates, 1998) has demonstrated, these qualities are part of each person's inborn make-up and are almost certainly genetically determined. They can be discerned from the early weeks of life on and, to some extent at least, remain influential thereafter.

It has not been easy to identify the precise qualities that constitute temperament. Table 10.1 gives details of three proposals putting forward somewhat different classifications. In due course the divergences will no doubt be resolved and a common scheme emerge; in the meantime, it is generally agreed that temperament, however described, can be considered to represent the biological foundation of individuality. Whether it is correct to think of temperamental characteristics as 'early emerging personality traits' (Buss & Plomin, 1984) is still in doubt, for the extent to which they are in fact continuous with individual differences in adolescence and adulthood is, as we shall see later, not yet firmly established. But whatever the inborn origins of individuality may be, the nature of personality will undergo various kinds of change as an inevitable accompaniment of development – changes such as the following:

Table 10.1   Three schemes for classifying temperament

Thomas & Chess (1977)	
'Easy'	Highly adaptable, positive and moderate in mood; accept frustration with little fuss
'Difficult'	Lacking adaptability, moods intense and often negative
'Slow to warm up'	Wary and shy in new situations; becoming increasingly positive and adaptable
Buss & Plomin (1984)	
Emotionality	Refers to the amount of arousal in response to stimulation, whether manifested in distress, fear or anger
Activity	Relates to motor tempo and vigour; even young babies already show consistent differences in this respect
Sociability	The extent to which the individual prefers others' company as opposed to being alone. Here too young babies differ, e.g. in seeking attention and initiating contact
Rothbart, Ahadi, Hershey & Fisher (2001)	
Negative affectivity	Covers sadness, fearfulness, lack of soothability and frustration – similar to neuroticism
Control	The extent to which individuals exert constraint, inhibition and conscientiousness
Extraversion	Includes lack of shyness, impulsiveness, intense pleasure – similar to sociability

The first scheme above refers to categories of individuals, the other two to behavioural dimensions.

- With age, children's personality structure becomes an increasingly complex organization. Initially, relatively few terms are required adequately to describe an individual; when referring to a baby, words like 'honest' or 'altruistic' are not likely to be chosen. Subsequently, children's personality undergoes more and more elaboration and attributes need to be acknowledged that did not exist at earlier stages.
- With age, personality becomes more coherent. The term 'personality' in itself implies more than a bundle of separate traits; it is a constellation which increasingly functions as a unit in which it is the *interaction* of various characteristics that is of significance. To illustrate: in order to predict adult criminality, Magnusson and Bergman (1990) had to take into account a combination of 13-year-old children's aggression, hyperactivity, inattention and poor peer relationships; individually, these characteristics had no predictive power.
- With age, the way in which personality traits are expressed undergoes change. At younger ages, for example, aggression is usually manifested in some physical form; later on, in response to social pressures, it is more likely to take a less overt, more indirect form.
- With age, children become increasingly aware of their own personality characteristics. Self-evaluation takes place, and by monitoring their activities and comparing themselves with others children become capable of acquiring sufficient insight into their motives and propensities deliberately to bring about some degree of behavioural change in an effort to modify their existing personality characteristics.

Constructing a self

The last of the points just listed is of particular significance, for it brings us to the pivotal role which an individual's self-concept plays in personality development. 'Who am I?' is a question that challenges children right through into adolescence, and a considerable part of childhood is devoted, in one way or another, to finding an answer. But what is the self? It is clearly a hypothetical entity and not a substantive one experienced through the senses. Perhaps the best way of thinking about it is as a 'theory' that each one of us develops about who we are and how we fit into society. It is a theory that is repeatedly revised during childhood in the light of both cognitive development and social experience: on the one hand, as children get older they become more competent at self-awareness and more realistic, and, on the other hand, other people's perceptions and responses will come to play a more central role in shaping the nature of that awareness. Thus the theory is built up gradually during childhood, taking somewhat different forms at different developmental stages. Its formation is, moreover, never complete, for at no time does the self function as a wholly closed system – on the contrary, it will always be affected by experience and, in particular, by other people's evaluations. Having such a theory is clearly useful: for one thing, it provides us with a sense of permanence and, for another, it supplies a source of reference in our attempts to organize behaviour towards others and to make choices among alternative courses of action, seeking out those experiences that fit in with our self-image.

The self may feel like a unitary entity, but it is useful to distinguish various constituents, each with its own characteristics and developmental course. In particular, the following require mentioning:

- **Self-awareness**: the realization by children that they are each a distinct being – an entity separate from all others and possessing an identity of their own.
- **Self-concept**: the kind of picture which children form of themselves ('I am a girl'; 'I am generous'; 'I am left-handed').
- **Self-esteem**: the evaluative aspect of the self, answering the question 'How good am I?' and thus referring to the worthiness and competence an individual experiences in relation to him- or herself.

Self-awareness is the very first step in the formation of a self and refers to the realization by children that they are distinct beings with an existence of their own.

Self-concept refers to the image that children build up of themselves, providing an answer to the question 'Who am I?'.

Self-esteem concerns the value that children attach to their personal qualities, answering the question 'How good am I?' and ranging from very positive to very negative.

Self-awareness is, of course, the very first constituent that emerges. In early infancy children do not yet have a sense of self: initially, they are unable to conceive of themselves as separate beings with an existence and characteristics of their own. One simple technique for testing whether consciousness of self has appeared in a child's behaviour repertoire is the *visual recognition test*, developed first with chimpanzees and then applied by Lewis and Brooks-Gunn (1979) to young children. These investigators asked mothers unobtrusively to apply a spot of rouge to their children's nose, and then to place the children in front of a mirror to see how they responded to their image. Their assumption was that if children are able to recognize that the mirror-image is of themselves, they will reach for the spot on their *own* nose, not the nose in the mirror; they can then be regarded as having a sense of self-awareness. Such behaviour, however, was rarely found before 15 months of age: at 1 year children were often amused by what they seemed to think of as another child but showed no particular interest in the spot of paint, and only by the middle of the second year did they give definite indications that the spot was of interest *and* that they realized it was theirs. Visual recognition is, of course, only one indication of self-awareness; others such as children's ability to name themselves when presented with their photo (Bullock & Lutkenhaus, 1990) and the use of self-related terms like 'I' and 'me' (Bates, 1990) can also be taken as evidence and also generally appear in the second year. What is certain is that by the end of the second year, the child has taken the first and most essential step in the development of the self-concept, namely, the establishment of a separate, distinctive identity.

Table 10.2 summarizes the series of developmental changes that occur right up to adolescence in the way children think of themselves. In many respects these

Table 10.2 Developmental changes in self-concept

From	To	Nature of change
Simple	Differentiated	Younger children form global concepts; older children make finer distinctions and allow for circumstances
Inconsistent	Consistent	Younger children are more likely to change their self-evaluation; older children know about the stability of the self
Concrete	Abstract	Younger children focus on visible, external aspects; older children focus on invisible, psychological aspects
Absolute	Comparative	Younger children focus on self without reference to others; older children describe themselves in comparison with others
Optimistic	Realistic	Younger children give a rosy account of themselves; older children are more balanced in mentioning weaknesses as well as strengths
Self-as-public	Self-as-private	Younger children do not distinguish between private and public behaviour; older children consider private self as 'true' self

changes are similar to those found in children's descriptions of other people (see chapter 8, pp. 259–60). Thus, the accounts become increasingly specific, able to take note of ever-finer nuances; they grow more consistent from one occasion to another as though children gradually come to appreciate the stability of the self; they become increasingly socio-centric in that they include more comparative references to other people; and, above all, the trend from a focus on physical characteristics to inclusion of psychological characteristics is evident. Thus young children will see themselves mainly in terms of their appearance and possessions ('I have got blue eyes'; 'I have got a bike'), and will subsequently progress to what they do ('I can skate'; 'I help with the shopping'). At the beginning of the school years they will start to mention psychological traits ('I am brave in the dark'; 'I am good at reading'), and these gradually become more and more sophisticated and comparative ('I don't get as upset as the other girls in my class'; 'Others will often come to me with their problems, because they see me as someone willing to help and give good advice'). At the same time, children become more realistic about themselves: whereas preschoolers' self-descriptions generally suggest a very optimistic picture that refers only to positive features, older children will provide a more balanced account which mentions weak spots as well as strengths.

One further developmental trend deserves special mention, namely, the appreciation by older children of what many regard as the essence of the self, i.e. its private nature. This is by and large a relatively late development; according to Robert Selman (1980), children younger than 6 cannot distinguish between private feelings and public behaviour, regarding the distinction as meaningless, and only from about 8 years on will children acknowledge the inner nature of the self and come to think of it as the 'true' self. Admittedly, some specific aspects of the self are considered to be private at much earlier ages; for example, children as young as 3 appear to realize that their thoughts are invisible to anyone staring into their eyes – though their explanations tend to take the form of 'Thinking can't be seen because the skin is over it'. The idea of the self as private continues to be developed right into adolescence; it is only then, according to Selman, that young people become 'aware of their self-awareness' and know that they can consciously monitor their own experience. Even then adolescents initially tend to have a rather naive faith in the ability of private thought to control public behaviour; it is not until the later years of adolescence that they also come to appreciate the role of unconscious influences and hence the limits to the effectiveness of self-control.

Self-esteem: Its nature and development

In talking of the self, we refer not only to the way we perceive ourselves but also to the way we evaluate ourselves. A useful definition of self-esteem comes from writings by Coopersmith (1967), one of the earliest noteworthy contributors to research on this topic:

> By self-esteem we refer to the evaluation which the individual makes and customarily maintains with regard to himself; it expresses an attitude of approval or disapproval, and indicates the extent to which the individual believes himself to be capable, significant, successful and worthy.

Self-esteem is a function of the discrepancy between the *ideal* self and the *real* self as perceived by the individual. Where there is little discrepancy, the individual experiences feelings of worthiness and satisfaction; where the discrepancy is great, feelings of failure and unworthiness result. Indeed, much of the motivation for investigating this phenomenon comes from the belief that self-esteem is closely linked to future mental health. Thus medium to high self-esteem is considered to give rise to happiness and satisfaction, whereas low self-esteem has been associated with depression, anxiety and maladjustment. Efforts to increase unduly low esteem are therefore regarded as well worthwhile in preventing later psychological problems (Harter, 1999).

However, it has also become clear that self-esteem ought not to be thought of as a unitary entity, something that one can represent by a single score on a low–high continuum. Rather, individuals evaluate themselves separately in relation to various specific domains, and their assessment of one need not have any implications for their assessment of any other. Susan Harter (1987, 1999), in a highly ambitious programme of research on self-esteem, has found it useful to distinguish five separate areas in which to assess children's beliefs about themselves:

- *Scholastic competence*: how able the child considers him- or herself at schoolwork.
- *Athletic competence*: the child's feelings of competence in sport activities.
- *Social acceptance*: whether the child feels popular with peers.
- *Physical appearance*: how good-looking the child believes him- or herself to be.
- *Behavioural conduct*: to what extent the child considers his or her general behaviour to be acceptable to others.

Harter has combined these five domains to make up one assessment tool, the Self-perception Profile for Children, to which one further aspect is added, namely, a global self-worth scale that asks how much children like themselves as people. A number of questions are asked under each heading (see figure 10.1 for a sample item), and from children's answers to these a profile is constructed that indicates a child's self-esteem in each domain. The hypothetical examples shown in figure 10.2 illustrate that profiles can take many forms: consistently high, consistently low or varying from one domain to another in all sorts of ways. Separate estimates for each area are clearly useful in arriving at a picture of children's feelings about themselves. However, as individuals get older, more domains require to be added: for example, for adolescents close friendship, romantic appeal and job competence must also be taken into account, and to assess adults' self-esteem still further domains have to be considered.

Figure 10.1   *Sample item from Harter's Self-perception Profile for Children.*

In the course of childhood considerable changes take place in the way children evaluate themselves. Take the following account of himself by a preschooler:

> I'm four years old and I know all my A, B, Cs. Listen to me say them: A, B, C, D, E, F, G, H, J, L, K, O, M, P, R, Q, X, Z. I can run faster than anyone. I like pizza and I have a nice teacher. I can count up to 100, want to hear me? I love my dog, Skipper. I can climb to the top of the jungle gym. I have brown hair and I go to preschool. I'm really strong. I can lift this chair, watch me!   (***From Harter, 1987***)

There is certainly nothing negative about this little boy's picture of himself! His account is also very disjointed, consisting of a list of features strung together in a higgledy-piggledy manner and thus reflecting the lack of organization that typifies the preschooler's self. Children at this stage are still focused on their separate activities; making a global judgement about themselves remains beyond their capacity.

At the beginning of the school period considerable changes occur in the nature and organization of self-esteem. A study by Marsh, Craven and Debus (1998) illustrates these well. A sample of nearly 400 Australian children were administered

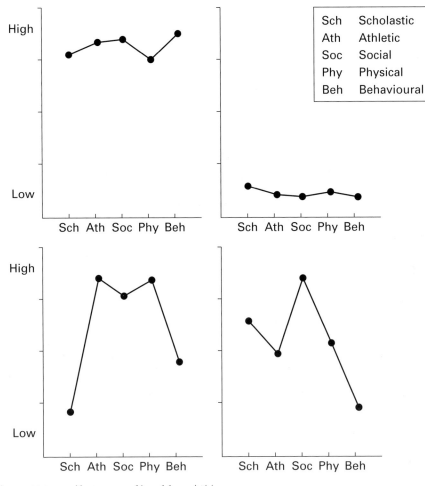

Figure 10.2 *Self-esteem profiles of four children.*

self-esteem tests when aged between 5 and 7, and then reassessed a year later. The findings indicate, in the first place, that even within this relatively brief age span older children show greater stability from one testing to another than younger children: over age, self-esteem judgements were becoming more consistent. In the second place, the older children were more discriminative in their appraisal and no longer provided consistently high estimates. Thirdly, presumably because of the last trend, the children's self-assessments became more closely aligned with such external indicators as teacher ratings and school performance. In general, from about the age of 7 on children become much more realistic and also much more coherent in the way they evaluate themselves. As a result, an overall dip occurs in level of esteem, for now children are prepared to acknowledge failings as well as accomplishments, negative as well as positive features. These trends continue through the school years; at the same time, particular domains of behaviour become more important to children than other domains: in mid-childhood, for example, peer acceptance and sporting competence become more prominent in most children's evaluations, and from puberty on physical appearance assumes a salient role for nearly all youngsters.

The self in adolescence

Adolescence is a period of considerable psychological as well as physical change, and it is no wonder that it has been designated a time of turmoil. The physical changes are such that children's appearance alters markedly in many respects: inspecting themselves in the mirror (and what adolescent does not do so at frequent intervals?), they find that they really *are* different and that some drastic adjustments need to be made to their self-image. For one thing, with the onset of puberty a quite spectacular increase in height takes place – as much as 9 inches in boys and 7 inches in girls during the following 3 years. However, this spurt does not take place evenly throughout the body; thus hands and feet generally outgrow all else, causing the clumsiness that is such a frequent accompaniment of early adolescence. In addition, in boys a marked increase in shoulder breadth occurs and also a considerable general increase in muscle; in girls the increase is mainly of fat and is found especially around the hips. And, of course, the secondary sexual characteristics appear, such as girls' breast development, boys' deepening of voice, and bodily hair in both sexes. There are certainly plenty of reasons why a sharp increase in self-consciousness should set in when children so suddenly find themselves with such a markedly different body. This feeling is heightened by the great variations in the age when all this takes place: in girls puberty generally occurs sometime between 8 and 14 years, in boys between 10 and 16. As a result, variations in height alone among children of the same age is greater at this time than at any other, making both the very early and the late developers feel 'different'.

An increase in introspectiveness is perhaps inevitable under these circumstances. The question 'Who am I?' assumes a new urgency. But there is also another question that requires an answer, namely, 'Do I like myself?' Most adolescents have an *ideal self,* formed in part by the standards set by the peer group and in part by particular idols from the world of sport, pop, public life or other valued spheres, and are acutely aware of the discrepancy with the *real* self, at least as perceived by the individual. Dissatisfaction with the real self is common at this period, and this is reflected in the sometimes quite drastic drop in self-esteem that takes place in the earlier stages of adolescence. The drop is most marked among girls, and applies especially to feelings about attractiveness. As being thin is regarded by young girls as something desirable in present-day society, the increase in fat that normally occurs following puberty gives rise to dissatisfaction among many and, in some, to drastic dieting and even to anorexia. A great deal of publicity has been given to anorexia;

it is, however, a relatively rare condition and, when it persists, is generally associated with disturbed family relationships and pre-existing emotional problems (Attie & Brooks-Gunn, 1989). Overall, the drop in self-esteem is only a temporary phenomenon: in later adolescence the majority of individuals manage to adjust to the changes that have taken place in themselves and to accept their new body image, and in consequence self-esteem rises once more to previous levels.

It is largely due to the writings of Erik Erikson (e.g. 1965, 1968) that adolescence has come to be thought of as a time of **identity crisis**. Identity, according to Erikson, is 'a subjective sense of an invigorating sameness and continuity', and the crisis needs to be regarded as a normative event that adolescents have to experience in order to proceed to adulthood. Erikson incorporated his views of adolescence in a more general account of psychological development from birth to death, depicted by him as a series of stages each characterized by a **developmental task** that has to be mastered if the individual is to continue to further stages (see table 10.3 for an outline). Thus in the first stage the task confronting the young child is to establish 'basic trust' – to find out, that is, that the world is a good place where one can feel secure and be assured of love and understanding. If the child does not have the chance to acquire such knowledge, a general feeling of mistrust will result, with implications for all subsequent attempts to get to grips with the world and in particular with other people.

The quest for identity is, according to Erikson, the main theme of life, and is evident in different forms at all stages. However, it is in adolescence, when children become aware of themselves as developing persons with the potential to take control of their lives, that the need to establish a coherent identity becomes the major challenge to tackle. All adolescents must go through the identity crisis – referred to as a 'crisis' because it is a source of conflict within the individual experiencing it. By resolving the conflict, the young person is able to proceed to early adulthood and face the next task; failure, on the other hand, results in identity confusion, characterized by continuing bewilderment as to the individual's role in life. Such a failure may be due to problems at the time, like lack of parental support or excessive educational demands; it may, however, also be due to failures at earlier stages in resolving tasks confronting the individual then.

Although subsequent research has not confirmed all the specific details of Erikson's stage model, and although there is some question whether the identity crisis is as common or as severe as he believed, Erikson's writings have considerable intuitive appeal. They offer many an insight into the uncertainties and struggles of adolescence and the attempts made by young people to define anew their role in life and the goals they are aiming for. This is the period when, in our society, individuals are expected to make educational and occupational choices that may well have long-term implications. Young people know that these choices are crucial,

Identity crisis. Associated primarily with the writings of Erik Erikson, this term denotes the period of confusion and low self-esteem that is (controversially) said to be typical of adolescence.

Developmental task. According to some writers such as Erik Erikson, childhood can be divided into a series of stages, each one of which presents the individual with some major challenge that must be met in order successfully to continue to the next stage.

Table 10.3 Erikson's stages in the life cycle

Approximate age	Developmental task
0–1½ years	*Trust vs. mistrust:* Developing confidence in others' dependability
1½–3 years	*Autonomy vs. shame:* Developing self-assertiveness and self-control
3–6 years	*Initiative vs. guilt:* Developing a sense of purpose in independent action
6–11 years	*Industry vs. inferiority:* Developing motivation to learn and acquire skills
Adolescence	*Identity vs. role confusion:* Developing a sense of self as a unique individual
Young adulthood	*Intimacy vs. isolation:* Developing emotional commitments to other people
Middle age	*Generativity vs. stagnation:* Developing a sense of commitment to work
Old age	*Integrity vs. despair:* Acceptance of life and death

yet they are often fearful of the consequences of whatever course they adopt. As Erikson put it, they are led to conclude that 'I ain't what I ought to be, I ain't what I'm gonna be, but I ain't what I was'.

Given these stresses, one can understand that adolescence is often referred to as a crisis period. While an increase in the incidence of various forms of psycho-pathology does take place during the teenage years, it is nevertheless easy to exaggerate the extent of upset. As spelled out by Rutter and Rutter (1993), it is not that the overall rate of psychiatric problems changes greatly, but rather that the particular mix of conditions alters. Behaviour disorders associated with childhood, such as bedwetting and sleep disturbance, become less prominent; on the other hand, conditions such as depression, especially in girls, and problems related to substance abuse increase markedly, as do various psychotic illnesses. But emotional upset, as a kind of mental echo of the physical upheaval that takes place in the wake of puberty, is not an *inevitable* part of adolescence. In some societies, such as the Pygmies of the Kalahari Desert, adolescence is not recognized as a separate stage, in that children, once they reach puberty, are regarded as adults and ready not only to contribute economically to the general welfare but also to marry and become parents (Shostak, 1981, quoted by Cole & Cole, 2001). The 'storm and stress' traditionally associated with adolescence in the West do not occur under such circumstances. By contrast, in our society adolescents find themselves in a kind of no-man's land – neither child nor adult but a separate, ill-defined species, ready to procreate but not allowed to do so, expected to continue formal education whether they wish to or not, dependent on parents even though increasingly their preferred company is with age-mates. Adolescence, it appears, is a culture-specific phenomenon, and puberty, though widely acknowledged as an important milestone, has both social and emotional repercussions that vary from one society to the next.

Influences on self-development

The self is the mechanism whereby children develop ideas about their distinctiveness. As we have seen, the way these ideas are expressed differs from one developmental level to another: as children become cognitively more sophisticated, the self becomes more coherent, more stable and more realistic. But what accounts for the great variation in content of ideas at any one level – why, for example, are there individual differences in the extent and expression of self-esteem? Why are some children more self-confident? Why do some think of themselves as helpful or as clever or as unwanted or as generous?

One answer points to the child's social context – to the attitudes, expectations and perceptions of other people, particularly those who are important to the child. At its most extreme, this view gives rise to the *looking-glass self*, as Cooley (1902) referred to it, the notion that the self is a reflection of the way others see us. It is highly unlikely that things are that straightforward and that children develop a self solely in response to what others think; what cannot be doubted is that interpersonal influences do play some part, and probably a weighty one. Take Coopersmith's (1967) study of self-esteem in 10- to 11-year-old boys: parents of high-esteem boys were found in many respects to differ considerably from parents with low-esteem boys. The former were more accepting and, while setting clear limits, allowed their children considerable freedom within these limits, thereby boosting their self-confidence; the latter, on the other hand, related to their children in a rejecting, distant manner and were either autocratic or overpermissive in their attitudes, as a result of which the boys presumably felt unappreciated and developed poor opinions of themselves.

Such findings bear out the expectations of attachment theory: as we saw in chapter 4, it is an integral part of this theory that children's sense of self is closely related to the quality of their interpersonal relationships and that the internal working models which they develop of self and others are a function of the kind of attachment patterns that grow out of their early experiences. Thus the accepted child will develop a model of self in predominantly positive tones; the rejected child, on the other hand, will come to regard him- or herself as unworthy and unlovable, and consequently become insecure and lacking in confidence. At present the evidence linking the various types of attachment patterns to self-images is somewhat sparse and inconsistent (Goldberg, 2000); however, studies of maltreated children do indicate that a markedly deviant relationship can have profound implications for the child's development of self. When Bolger, Patterson and Kupersmidt (1998) compared children who had experienced different kinds of parental maltreatment with non-maltreated children, they found various kinds and degrees of impairment in self-esteem among the former, but especially among those who had experienced sexual abuse even where this involved isolated incidents. Among physically abused children the effects depended to some extent on frequency of maltreatment: where this had been persistent, children developed ideas of themselves as deserving of punishment and as incompetent. Emotionally abused and neglected children, on the other hand, did not show impairments in self-esteem; the consequences of their treatment manifested themselves in other areas instead.

The family is no doubt the cradle of children's sense of self, but as they get older the range of significant others able to influence the way children perceive and evaluate themselves increases. Approval of peers becomes particularly important in the course of the school years: to be popular and liked, or on the contrary to be rejected, has repercussions for all sorts of developing psychological attributes but especially so for children's feelings about themselves. Thus rejection from and isolation by the peer group have repeatedly, at all ages from middle childhood on, been found to be linked to lowered self-esteem (Harter, 1998); in that respect at least, the concept of the *looking-glass self* can be justified. This is also one of the reasons why bullying needs to be taken so seriously; as a considerable body of research has demonstrated, bullied children are especially liable to suffer from low self-esteem (see box 10.1 for further details). And yet, children who encounter rejection and victimization do not necessarily respond in a passive manner by absorbing whatever their peer group inflicts upon them; rejected by their usual company because, for instance, their behaviour is too disruptive, they may then seek to join a delinquent gang where such behaviour is the norm – a socially undesirable step no doubt, but one that is constructive from the individual's point of view as a way of maintaining and enhancing self-reputation.

BOX 10.1

Victims of bullying and their selves

Bullying of children by children is a worldwide phenomenon that can have serious and sometimes long-term consequences for the victims. Estimates of the incidence of bullying vary: more occurs in primary than in secondary schools, more among boys than girls, and more in some social communities than in others. Much depends on how one defines bullying: for instance, should teasing be included? Much also depends on how it is assessed: as it is difficult to observe one normally relies on reports, but self-reported and peer-reported bullying do not necessarily produce the same results. Roughly speaking, up to 20 per cent of children are reported as being bullied and up to 10 per cent as being bullies – certainly sufficient to take preventive action.

Not surprisingly, it has repeatedly been shown that bullying affects the victims' self-esteem. When children are singled out as targets for others' sustained aggression, they may well interpret such acts as reflecting upon themselves, indicating that they are in some way inferior in status within their peer group and so affecting the way they perceive themselves. For example, Boulton and Smith (1994) investigated bullying among a large group of 8- to 9-year-olds, and found 13 per cent among them could be classified as bullies and 17 per cent as victims (with a further 4 per cent as both bullies and victims). When given the Harter Self-perception Profile for Children, victims scored significantly lower than other children on some of the dimensions of the test, namely, the athletic competence, social acceptance and global self-worth scales; their view of themselves as given by such other scales as scholastic competence appeared not to be affected, underlining the importance of not treating self-esteem as a unitary entity. In a review of all relevant studies on the psychological consequences of bullying published during a 20-year period, Hawker and Boulton (2000) confirmed the link with lowered self-esteem: a general trend emerged from all these findings for bullied children to score low on global self-worth and, among the specific scales, lowest on social acceptance. It is thus in the interpersonal domain that such children are most likely to develop a negative view of themselves. The review also found, however, that certain other aspects of personal adjustment were even more seriously affected, with depression in particular being a prominent symptom in these children.

Just how do bullied children interpret what is happening to them? Do they ask 'Why me?' To what do they attribute being singled out? According to a study by Graham and Juvonen (1998), self-blame is a common response: a considerable number of bullied children, rather than putting the onus on the bullies, saw themselves at fault in eliciting aggression from others. This applied primarily to children who put the blame on something about their character in general ('It's something about the way I am') rather than on specific, usually just temporary behavioural attributes ('It's something about what I did in this situation'). In the former case, because self-blaming implicates the child's personality as such and so reflects on the self, children were found to suffer from a range of adjustment difficulties including low self-esteem, whereas in the latter case the bullying episode was interpreted as being due to something that the child could easily rectify and so did not lead on to further psychological problems.

It is perhaps easy to assume that the relationship between being bullied and having low self-esteem is one of cause and effect. Most studies, however, have been correlational in nature, that is, they could only determine that the two tended to coincide. Might it not be that the cause–effect sequence is in the other direction, namely, that children with low self-esteem have characteristics that elicit bullying by others? Victimized children have been described as lacking humour and self-confidence, crying easily, being lonely and disliked by other children and lacking skills in social situations; others are said to be disruptive, aggressive and argumentative (Perry, Perry & Kennedy, 1992). In a longitudinal study entitled 'Does low self-regard invite victimization?' Egan and Perry (1998) assessed 10- to 11-year-old children at two different points of time and, by being able to trace the developmental course of self-esteem and being bullied, found that the cause–effect sequence often goes in both directions. On the one hand, a child's sense of personal inadequacy can lead to being singled out as a victim, and on the other hand, being maltreated by peers tends to bring about further impairment of self-regard. Low self-esteem is thus both cause and effect of being bullied – an indication of how complex a phenomenon bullying turns out to be.

Let us emphasize that, as with other aspects of development, the building-up of a self is not just a matter of being pushed along by forces in the environment; it is also governed by children's own increasingly intentional role. Children are active, self-determining beings who monitor, appraise, construe and interpret their own behaviour and the effects it produces, and in that light gradually come to build up an image of the sort of individual they believe they are. By thus reflecting on themselves, by comparing themselves with others and by accepting or rejecting the views of others about their character, they form a series of hypotheses in an attempt to gain an understanding of themselves – hypotheses that in due course come to coalesce into a more or less coherent theory, designed to answer the 'Who am I?' question.

Acquiring a sense of gender

Personal identity refers to those aspects of an individual's personality that distinguish him or her from other individuals.

A distinction is customarily made between **personal identity** and **social identity**. The former refers to all those specifically individual attributes that distinguish one person from another; the latter designates membership of broad social groupings like gender, ethnicity, socio-economic status and occupation that we share with many other individuals but that also distinguish us from other groups of individuals. A sense of membership of particular groupings also comes to be incorporated into the child's self-image.

Social identity refers to an individual's sense of belonging to particular social categories like gender and ethnicity.

The most basic of all such categories is gender (denoting thereby psychological differences between males and females, whereas sex refers to physical differences). A child is born male or female; how he or she is treated thereafter depends very much on which sex he or she belongs to. As a result, children soon acquire a sense of gender identity ('I am a boy'; 'I am a girl'); they also quickly realize that others can be so classified. Yet a full understanding of what is involved in the concept of gender is not achieved till mid-childhood; it is a gradual process which, according to Lawrence Kohlberg (1966), involves three different aspects, each emerging at a different time:

- *Gender identity* (appearing at about $1^1/_2$ to 2 years). The child becomes aware that everybody, themselves included, belongs to one of two groups – boys or girls, men or women. When asked 'Are you a boy or a girl?', children can answer correctly from at least the end of the second year on; shown another child, they can correctly identify the child's sex from the beginning of the third year on, basing their judgement on certain obvious characteristics such as hair and clothes. At first, however, these are mere labels that can be attached to people rather like a name, with no further significance.
- *Gender stability* (from about 3 or 4 years). The child now realizes that an individual's sex remains a constant feature throughout life. Asked 'When you were a baby, were you a little boy or a little girl?', or 'Will you be a mummy or a daddy when you grow up?', children from the fourth year on (but not before) can answer correctly. However, the child's understanding is still severely constrained: asked 'If a boy puts on a dress, will he be a girl?', most preschool children will answer in the affirmative, believing that sex is defined by superficial characteristics and can thus be changed.
- *Gender consistency* (appearing around 5 or 6 years). From now on children realize that masculinity and femininity are attributes that remain consistent over context as well as time, and are not defined by the individual's appearance or actions. A girl, that is, is still a girl even when she cuts her hair short and wears boys' clothes. Gender understanding is thereby completed.

From a very early age on children also come to know that certain kinds of behaviour are regarded as appropriate for boys and others for girls. Such **gender role knowledge** is revealed from about $2^1/2$ years on when children are asked about the kinds of activities boys and girls usually engage in. The following are examples of the sort of answers they give:

> **Gender role knowledge** is the awareness by children that certain kinds of behaviour are considered as 'right' for boys while others are 'right' for girls.

'Boys hit people.'
'Girls talk a lot.'
'Girls often need help.'
'Boys play with cars.'
'Girls give kisses.'

Stereotypes about what is appropriate for males and females are apparently early in place, and despite considerable changes in the last half-century or so about gender roles they are still evident, both in the way children actually behave and in the actions and expectations of those responsible for their socialization.

The search for gender differences in children's behaviour has taken place in three main areas: in the development of personality characteristics, in preferences for particular toys and play activities and in the choice of playmates. Below is a summary of findings for each area:

- *Personality characteristics.* Cultural stereotypes still persist as to what is 'correct' behaviour for males (active, dominant, aggressive, confident) and for females (nurturant, caring, passive, compliant). However, comparison of boys' and girls' behaviour yields only limited supportive evidence for such a dichotomy. There are some indications (to quote one example) that male babies tend to be more active than female babies (Eaton & Yu, 1989) – a difference that might account for the greater incidence of rough-and-tumble play among boys that is commonly found in later years. Yet when Maccoby and Jacklin in 1974 reviewed the 1,600 articles that had been published by then on gender differences, they found that hardly any of the many psychological attributes they examined clearly differentiated the sexes – a conclusion that subsequent work has by and large confirmed (Ruble & Martin, 1998). There is some evidence that boys exceed girls in aggressiveness, yet when non-physical as well as physical aggression is taken into account the difference becomes minimal. There are also indications that girls outperform boys on verbal tasks while boys outperform girls on spatial tasks. In general, however, personality and cognitive differences are far fewer in number than is commonly believed and, where they do exist, are moderate in extent and are quite probably becoming less evident as society redefines the roles of the sexes.
- *Toy preferences.* Rather more evidence of gender differences is found in children's choice of toys and play activities. In general, boys tend to play with trucks, blocks and guns; girls with dolls, soft toys and domestic articles (Golombok & Fivush, 1994), and they do so well before becoming consciously aware that some toys are considered to be more appropriate for one sex than the other. Boys engage in more active, rougher play activities like cops and robbers or cowboys and Indians; girls prefer playing house and skipping or ball games. It could be that such differences are due to characteristics inherent in children: boys are more active and aggressive; girls more passive and nurturant, and each sex chooses those toys and games that are most appropriate to these types of behaviour. However, it could also be due to socializing pressures: parents, peers, schools and the media send out a great many messages to children of all ages about what is regarded as sex-appropriate in our society. Table 10.4 summarizes some of the relevant findings; there is now a considerable body of evidence available indicating that adults have certain expectations about children's behaviour that are sex-typed and constitute definite pressures on children to conform to the accepted norm. These pressures are targeted mainly on specific sex-typed activities and interests,

Table 10.4 Some examples of adults' sex-typed behaviour towards children

Socialization area	Findings	Reference
Choice of toy	Adults encourage children, especially boys, to play with sex-typed toys (e.g. trucks vs. dolls)	Fagot & Hagan (1991)
Style of play	Boys encouraged in and girls discouraged from vigorous, active play	Fagot (1978)
Task assignment	Boys are given 'male', girls 'female', household tasks	White & Brinkerhoff (1981)
Aggression	More attention paid to aggressive, assertive behaviour in boys than in girls	Fagot & Hagan (1991)
Control	More verbal and physical prohibitions shown to boys than to girls	Snow, Jacklin & Maccoby (1983)
Autonomy	Parental talk to boys contains more encouragement to autonomy than talk to girls	Leaper (1994)
Emotional awareness	Parents discuss feelings more with girls than with boys	Kuebli, Butler & Fivush (1995)
Emotional control	Boys encouraged more than girls to control expression of emotion	Fagot & Leinbach (1987)

and appear to be at their most intense in children's second year of life, i.e. at the time that gender development gets under way (Fagot & Hagan, 1991). However, whether these socializing influences do have the intended effects, or whether parents are merely reacting to pre-existing differences in their sons and daughters, remains a controversial and as yet unresolved issue (see box 10.2 for some attempts to answer this question).

- *Playmate choice.* By far the clearest indication of gender differences is to be found in children's choice of companions. Boys play with boys, girls with girls, and moreover they show this preference as early as the third year (see figure 10.3). As Eleanor Maccoby (1990, 1998) has pointed out, gender segregation is a highly significant phenomenon. It is universal, found in all cultural settings for which we have data. It is seen even in the play of other primates at similar developmental levels. It occurs spontaneously, without pressure from adults, and is highly resistant to enforced change. It increases in strength, becoming especially notable in the school years, and remains at a high level right into adolescence, when despite the demands of sexuality gender segregation by no means disappears. And it is of considerable psychological significance because, according to Maccoby, peers make a major contribution to children's socialization, and the very distinctive interaction styles

BOX 10.2

The Baby X experiments

From the very beginning the way adults respond to a child is influenced by the child's sex. For example, in a study of parents' initial reactions to their newborn babies (Rubin, Provenza & Luria, 1974), both mothers and fathers referred to their sons as stronger, bigger, better coordinated and more alert; daughters were considered to be smaller, softer, more finely featured and less attentive. Clearly, adults bring sexual stereotypes to their interactions with children, but are these expectations responsible for creating behavioural differences in the children or do adults react to differences that are already present? What is the direction of influence?

A series of studies, starting in the 1970s and collectively known as the Baby X experiments, set out to answer this question. Let us take one (by Condry & Condry, 1976) as an example. A sample of over 200 adults, both men and women, were shown a videotape of a 9-month-old baby who was introduced to some as a boy ('David') and to others as a girl ('Dana'). Both in appearance and in dress the baby was neither markedly masculine nor feminine. The baby was shown responding to various toys such as a teddy and a doll and to such stimuli as a jack-in-the-box and a sudden loud buzzer, and for each of these the adults were asked to describe the emotion displayed. The results clearly show the influence of the child's presumed sex. For instance, when 'David' reacted to the jack-in-the-box by crying, most of the adults perceived this as anger; when 'Dana' showed exactly the same behaviour, it was perceived as fear. The same baby reacting in the same way was judged to respond differently, depending on the gender label supplied. As the authors conclude, differences between male and female infants appear to be in the eye of the beholder.

There have been many other studies investigating reactions to Baby X (see Golombok & Fivush, 1994, and Stern & Karraker, 1989, for reviews). While using the same basic approach, there are variations among these studies in procedural details and in samples – for example, whether the baby is presented live or on videotape, whether the adults are asked to interact with the baby or not, the amount of experience that the adults have of children, the kind of judgements they are expected to make, and so forth. Some of these studies have found the same clear-cut results as reported by Condry and Condry in the study quoted above, indicating that knowledge of a baby's gender is a definite influence on adults' behaviour. Provided with a collection of toys, for example, some sex-typed as masculine such as a car or a rubber hammer and others as feminine such as a doll or a tea set, adults were more likely to offer the masculine toys to the baby when labelled as a boy but the feminine toys when the same baby was labelled as a girl. Similarly, they were more likely to encourage the 'boy' to play vigorously and to explore the toys actively, whereas the 'girl' was treated more gently and as more dependent on adult help. However, other studies have obtained rather less clear-cut results, finding, for instance, a sharp difference according to type of measure employed. Thus, when adults were asked to rate the baby's personality characteristics (how friendly, how cooperative, etc.), few differences according to gender labelling emerged: the baby's real characteristics played a more important part in the way the child was perceived. On the other hand, the way the adults actually behaved towards the baby was more likely to be affected by the label provided: their style of interaction, the kind of stimulation provided and the kinds of toys chosen did reflect the knowledge they had been given regarding the child's sex. And one other curious finding: when children are asked to interact with a Baby X, they are more strongly influenced by knowledge of the baby's alleged sex than adults – possibly because they are still forming their own gender identity and therefore adopt rather more extreme and inflexible attitudes in perceiving and responding to males and females (Stern & Karraker, 1989).

It appears therefore that the gender-labelling effect is not as strong as originally thought. Whether a child is considered to be male or female is only one of several influences on the way others react. It is strongest when little other information is available about the child such as his or her real characteristics or when that information is ambiguous. However, when gender-label effects are found, they are almost invariably in keeping with cultural stereotypes of the sexes and may well therefore play a part in children's gender development.

that boys and girls respectively manifest and develop in their gender groups have implications for social behaviour well beyond adolescence into adulthood. In the case of males, this style may best be labelled as *constricting*: boys use more commands, threats, interruptions and boasts than girls; there is a lot of concern with issues of dominance; there is much rough play and risk-taking; and speech serves largely an egoistic function, in that each individual is engaged in some form of self-display and in attempts to establish and protect his turf. Girls, on the other hand, adopt an *enabling* style: their agenda is to sustain relationships rather than to assert themselves; in their gender group they are therefore more likely than boys to express agreement, give someone else a chance to speak, acknowledge points made by others and use speech for socially binding purposes. Naturally, some overlap in group style occurs: girls too can be assertive, just as boys will also work for the

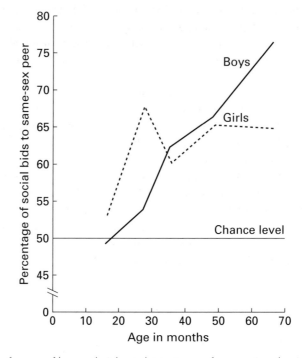

Figure 10.3 *Preferences of boys and girls aged 1 to 6 years for same-sex playmates (based on La Freniere, Strayer & Gaulthier, 1984).*

common good. Nevertheless, male and female groups tend to operate differ-ently, and the interactive styles promoted therein remain a lifelong acquisi-tion that forms an essential part of each individual's gender identity.

Continuity and Change

Most of us are convinced that we are basically the same individuals we were when younger. We may know more, we have developed a range of social and cognitive competencies, we have extended our horizons in society and become part of diverse interpersonal networks, but essentially we remain the same person we can remember from our earliest times. Such a sense of self extending in time, where we connect the way we are now with the way we were in the past, is psychologically advanta-geous from a great many points of view (Moore & Lemmon, 2001), but to what extent are we really the same? Following up children as they develop, that is, look-ing forward over the years rather than looking back, provides a rather more complex picture, one where there is both continuity and change and where the idea of devel-opment as merely a process of cumulative accretion needs to be replaced by one which also makes allowance for periodic qualitative changes. Such changes may be brought about by internal reorganization of the kind Piaget envisaged in describing his progression of cognitive stages; they may also be brought about by the impact of drastic experiences such as the death of a parent, prolonged hospitalization or an episode of abuse. Whatever their nature, the child is not quite the same individual after as before.

Questions of continuity and discontinuity not only challenge our theoretical conceptions of development, they also have implications for the potentially useful issue of predictability. Being able to predict that certain individuals will become antisocial long before they actually do so brings with it the hope of prevention; if particular kinds of psychological profiles in childhood can lead one to expect delinquency and criminality in adolescence and adulthood, there is at least the possibility of helpful action being taken early on. Consistency in the developmental course would guarantee successful prediction; if, on the other hand, children's early characteristics bear little relationship to adult personality, prediction would not be possible. It is certainly no wonder that a lot of effort has gone into investigating the connection between early and later status.

Investigating continuity

Assessing the extent to which individuals remain the same or change in the course of development is by no means a straightforward matter. A major problem is that *continuity* has a number of quite different meanings, each requiring a different kind of assessment (see Caspi, 1998, for an extended discussion). Two in particular need to be distinguished:

- *Relative continuity.* This refers to individuals retaining their rank order within a group. If a class of children is assessed by their teacher for anxiety level at the age of 6 and then reassessed at the age of 10, we can correlate the two scores and so determine whether changes have taken place from one age to the next. The correlation coefficient, however, expresses only the extent to which children have retained the same status in comparison with other children in the group, whether, for instance, those who scored highest on the first occasion remain among the highest on the second. It does not tell us about the actual level of anxiety on the two occasions; thus the correlation coefficient may obscure the fact that the group as a whole has become very much less anxious in the period between the assessments.
- *Absolute continuity.* This refers to the extent to which some particular attribute remains constant in individuals over periods of time. Is the highly aggressive 5-year-old still highly aggressive at age 15? The same question can also be asked about groups of individuals: is the sample of inner-city, deprived children assessed for aggressiveness at school entry still showing the same level of aggressiveness 10 years later? Comparison of means is employed to answer questions of this type rather than correlation coefficients.

Ideally, when investigating continuity from one age to another the same measurement tools should be employed right through, yet in practice this is often difficult. What is appropriate for assessment purposes at one age may not be so at another, for the way a particular attribute manifests itself in overt behaviour can change with age even though the attribute itself remains constant. Young children, for example, express their aggressiveness directly in physical form; questionnaires or observation schedules used to investigate it would therefore ask about symptoms like punching, kicking, biting and pushing. With age, such direct manifestations become increasingly infrequent yet may well be replaced by more indirect, verbal means such as hurtful comments and social exclusion. Different items therefore need to be included in questionnaires and schedules to make them age-appropriate: yet, by the same token, comparison with earlier ages then becomes difficult. The same problem arises with respect to most psychological functions: as detailed in box 10.3, our ability to predict intelligence from tests at very early ages

BOX 10.3

Can later intelligence be predicted from behaviour in infancy?

Parents, educationalists and child-care workers would all find it useful to know as early as possible how intelligent a child is going to be and so plan accordingly. But how early can one tell? The notion that intelligence is fixed once and for all by an individual's genetic endowment was abandoned long ago as untenable, but given a reasonably steady environment intelligence too should remain fairly steady. So is it feasible to predict from the early years or even months to later on in childhood?

A number of developmental tests are available for the first 2 or 3 years of life, yielding a DQ (developmental quotient) analogous to the IQ and making it possible to compare any given child's progress with that of others of the same age. However, these are essentially perceptual-motor tests, in that they assess skills such as visually following a moving target, fixating and grasping an object and placing one block on top of another. These are of a very different nature from items included in most intelligence tests, which rely heavily on verbal ability and abstract reasoning. When DQ scores obtained in infancy are compared with later IQ scores, the correlations are generally near zero, suggesting that infancy tests may be of use in assessing current status but not in predicting future progress. Whatever the early tests measure, it appears not to be intelligence.

Rather than leave it at that, a search has been mounted for other ways of getting at intelligence in infancy (see McCall & Carriger, 1993, and Slater, Carrick, Bell & Roberts, 1999, for detailed accounts). These have mostly focused on various aspects of information-processing ability that are already evident in the early months, on the basis that the speed and efficiency of such a function are essential ingredients of most kinds of intellectual performance. In particular, measures of habituation to visual stimuli have been employed. This refers to the decline in looking time that occurs when the same stimulus is repeatedly presented, on the assumption that the speed with which a child habituates is an index of how quickly that child is able to process the stimulus, memorize it and on subsequent appearances recognize it as already known and therefore cease looking at it.

A considerable number of experiments employing this procedure have been employed with babies and young children of various ages, who were then followed up into later childhood and tested with conventional IQ tests. The results have been mildly encouraging, in so far as performance even in the early months has been found to be more closely related to later IQ than is usually the case with DQ scores. Various points have emerged:

- Prediction is never more than modest: expressed statistically, correlations between infancy habituation and later IQ tend to be in the range 0.3 to 0.5 rather than near to perfection at 1.0.
- Not surprisingly, the shorter the age interval between the two assessments, the easier it is to predict from the earlier to the later.
- For some as yet unknown reason, prediction from habituation performance is more certain when made between 2 and 8 months than earlier or later in infancy.
- Prediction is easier for 'at-risk' children (e.g. very premature and handicapped children) than it is for others.
- Fast information processors are generally also more efficient processors.
- As with intelligence generally, drastic changes in lifestyle such as gross deprivation may upset the ability to predict later status.

We must conclude that even with the new approach to early testing, prediction of childhood intelligence is still an uncertain business. Various measures other than habituation speed have been explored, such as recognition memory, visual anticipation and visual reaction time – all with the advantage that they lie within the behaviour repertoire of even very young children and can thus be easily obtained. All, moreover, are concerned with information processing and thus are conceptually more closely associated with intelligence than perceptual-motor behaviour and accordingly more promising. However, a lot more work is required before firm conclusions about the early predictability of intelligence can be reached.

is as yet restricted because the mainly verbal items included in conventional IQ tests for older children are of no use in infancy. As an alternative approach, rather than look for tests identical in form across the whole age spectrum, investigators are now searching for measures that are *conceptually* related to intelligence but can be applied even to babies. If it is possible to establish that the same underlying predisposition manifests itself in different ways at different ages, it becomes easier to provide an answer to the question of developmental continuity.

Predicting from early behaviour

Considerable effort has gone into attempts to trace the developmental progression of particular personality attributes from early childhood to adulthood. Quite a lot of knowledge has accumulated as a result; however, the story that such knowledge tells us has turned out to be a rather complicated and convoluted one. Human beings do not simply progress in a straight line: there is continuity but there is also change, and though in some respects we bear the same attributes throughout, in others we become rather different individuals from the way we started. Let us illustrate with reference to the developmental story of two very different personality attributes, shyness and aggressiveness.

1 *Shyness*

Shyness encompasses a considerable range of behaviour patterns: quietness in social situations, fear of meeting anyone new, preference for being alone, blushing, verbal hesitation and awkwardness, inhibition, reluctance to join conversations and holding back from joining social groupings. There are large differences among people in their manifestation of shyness, ranging from the brash, highly assured individual to someone who is almost crippled by the condition. When markedly present it is regarded as a considerable handicap, though as we saw in chapter 2 (p. 32), there are large cultural differences in the value attached to such a characteristic.

Shyness is evident in quite young children, and by and large takes the same form as in adults. Does that mean that individual differences in this propensity are present from the start and then remain with the individual as a permanent feature? An impressive body of research has been devoted to this question (see Crozier, 2000), and there are now quite a lot of indications that shyness has (probably quite complex) genetic roots. Thus, in our discussion of temperament earlier in this chapter (pp. 306–7), we found mention made in each of the different schemes outlined there of a characteristic related to shyness: Thomas and Chess (1977) listed a group of babies best characterized as 'slow to warm up'; Buss and Plomin (1984) included sociability as one of the continua for which there is good evidence of a genetic basis, with shyness at one extreme of the continuum; and likewise

Rothbart et al. (2001) mentioned extraversion as an inherited characteristic similar in meaning to sociability.

However, the fact that a personality attribute has a genetic basis does not mean that it remains rigidly fixed and constant throughout life – like, say, eye colour. From the various longitudinal studies that have been conducted on children, there are a good many indications that, to some extent at least, the degree of shyness in individuals can vary over time. Changes are most likely at life transition points when children encounter new settings and new people: when, for example, they first enter school, or change school, or go to university (Asendorpf, 2000). Where the transition is particularly demanding on the individual's general sociability and adaptation to strangers and is not successfully mastered, there can be lasting changes towards greater shyness, but likewise certain confidence-boosting experiences may well bring about change in the opposite direction.

The fullest account of shyness and its developmental origins is to be found in a series of reports by Jerome Kagan and his colleagues (e.g. Kagan, Reznick & Snidman, 1988; Kagan, Snidman & Arcus, 1998), presenting the findings of a longitudinal study of a group of children followed up from infancy on and periodically investigated in a range of assessment situations. The findings convinced Kagan that shyness is part of a broader spectrum, identified by him as *inhibition* – a term that designates an initial reaction of anxiety, distress or wariness shown to all unfamiliar or challenging situations as well as people. Shy children, according to these findings, are not only anxious in the presence of strange people; they are reluctant to approach anything new, reacting as though inhibited and becoming anxious and distressed when unable to avoid the unknown. As early as 4 months inhibited and uninhibited children can already be differentiated: thus inhibited children (about 20 per cent of most samples) tend to become quiet and subdued when first confronted by something unknown, becoming increasingly agitated if the stimulation persists, whereas uninhibited children (about 40 per cent) give every indication of being at ease in the same situation and are likely to approach rather than avoid the unfamiliar stimulus. As physiological investigations indicate, it appears that some variation in the threshold of brain arousal is responsible for such differences among individuals, and it seems likely that this variation is of an inherited nature. As results from assessments in later childhood show (summarized in table 10.5), at all subsequent age points that the children in Kagan's study were assessed differences in responsiveness to unfamiliar events could be found: inhibited children tended to be wary, fearful and unsociable, whereas uninhibited children were at ease and interested in all new experiences. However, only a minority remained *consistently* inhibited or uninhibited throughout the follow-up period. These were the children at the two extremes, the highly inhibited and the very uninhibited: for them it was already possible to predict from their behaviour in infancy what their future status would be. Shyness as a persistent, stable trait could therefore only be found in children classified as extremely shy, and even there Kagan has conjectured that some environmental stress is required to maintain this style of behaviour, such as the death of a parent, marital conflict or mental illness in the family. In the rest

Table 10.5 Behaviour of inhibited and uninhibited children at various ages

Age	Procedure	Children's reactions
4 months	Presented with unfamiliar stimuli, e.g. balloon popping	*Inhibited children:* crying, vigorous motor activity *Uninhibited children:* no distress, little motor activity
2nd year	Confronted by a stranger; given novel objects	*Inhibited children:* signs of anxiety, withdraw *Uninhibited children:* fearless, showing interest
4 years	Meets unfamiliar adult; plays with unfamiliar children	*Inhibited children:* Subdued, avoids *Uninhibited children:* Outgoing, sociable
7 years	Parental questionnaire; interview with teachers; laboratory assessments	*Inhibited children:* Acquired range of anxiety symptoms *Uninhibited children:* Relatively free of anxiety symptoms

of the sample some degree of discontinuity prevailed, children moving in one direction or the other in line with whatever relevant influences they encountered in their social environment.

We can conclude that change appears to be the rule rather than the exception as far as shyness in childhood is concerned. Prediction with any degree of certainty is only possible with extreme groups: it is thus most probable that the very shy, quiet and restrained toddler will become an adolescent who is quiet, cautious and reluctant to mix in social settings; equally, the very sociable and spontaneous preschooler is highly likely to show similar characteristics in later childhood. Yet even with these children it would be unwise to assume that any one is immune to environmental influence; even here stability is a matter of probability rather than of certainty.

2 Aggression

Do aggressive children become aggressive adults? Or, to put it the other way round, were aggressive adults also aggressive children? The question has obvious practical significance; given the amount of violence in society, it would be most useful if one could predict from their early behaviour that certain kinds of children are likely to turn into violent adults. Much research has gone into attempts to provide answers.

One of the most ambitious studies was carried out by Huesmann and his colleagues (1984), taking the form of a 22-year follow-up of 600 individuals, with data also gathered about their parents and about their children. First seen at the age of 8, each child's aggressiveness was assessed by means of a peer-nomination index, derived from ratings of classmates of the child's behaviour in various situations. About 400 of these children were traced at the age of 30, when their aggressiveness was measured by means of self-ratings on a widely used personality inventory. In addition, ratings were obtained from the individual's spouse of any violent behaviour in the home, and official records were searched for information about convictions for crimes involving violence. The results indicate a substantial degree of stability of aggressiveness over the 22-year period. The most aggressive 8-year-olds were also the most aggressive at age 30 – a finding that applied rather more to males than to females, suggesting that a high level of aggressiveness in boys has a reasonable chance of turning into severe antisocial aggressiveness in the young adult. What is more, there were also indications of stability across generations: data collected on the aggressiveness of the individual's parents and (where available) on their children showed a distinct three-generation trend for aggressive parents to have aggressive children. Aggression, according to these results, appears to be a trait of considerable persistence.

A number of other studies have confirmed this general picture of continuity (e.g. Cairns, Cairns, Neckerman, Ferguson & Gariepy, 1989; Farrington, 1991; White, Moffitt, Earls, Robins & Silva, 1990), leading to the belief that disruptive or troublesome behaviour in childhood by males is one of the best predictors of adolescent and adult criminality, especially that involving violence. However, more recent studies have found things to be rather less clear-cut and drawn attention to a number of complications:

- Aggression is an umbrella term covering a range of different forms, and what applies to one may not apply to another. As pointed out by Tremblay (2002) in his survey of aggression research over the last century, one of the lessons we have had to learn is not to assume that a given form of aggressive behaviour at one time (e.g. disobedience in class) will accurately predict another form of aggressive behaviour at another point of time (e.g. arrests for physical violence).
- It is also necessary to avoid generalizations across sex. Boys mostly favour physical aggression, girls indirect aggression, and according to some findings (e.g. Cairns et al., 1989) the latter kind of behaviour is less likely to remain stable over age than the former.
- A distinction must be made between forward-looking and backward-looking methods of gathering data about age changes, for they will yield different kinds of findings. The former method, where children are followed up into adulthood, tells us that only a proportion of children displaying antisocial (including aggressive) behaviour will become antisocial adults; the latter method, where data about adults' childhood is gathered retrospectively, shows that virtually all antisocial adults were also antisocial children (Robins, 1966). Both statements are, of course, valuable but, being different, need to be considered together.
- Although stability over age in the relative level of aggressiveness has frequently been found, the degree of stability is mostly only moderate. Changes do occur;

while some children remain constant, others become either more or less
aggressive than their peers. Prediction is thus possible in only some cases; in
others the course of aggression from childhood to maturity follows a diversity
of paths.

   Much of recent research has picked up on this last point and attempted to
identify groups of children in whom the development of aggression takes distinct
courses. Various suggestions as to the nature of these groups have been made. For
example, according to one proposal (Moffitt, Caspi, Dickson, Silva & Stanton, 1996),
a distinction needs to be made between 'life-course persistent' and 'adolescence-
limited' children: the former are those who show consistently high levels of aggression from the early years on, having failed to learn to inhibit their emotional impulses
at that period; in the latter, on the other hand, aggressiveness is a passing phase,
manifesting itself mainly in late childhood and adolescence and initiated usually
by temporary social influences such as peer pressure. Another proposal (Brame,
Nagin & Tremblay, 2001) lists as many as seven subtypes, distinguished by a combination of level of aggression and the kind of changes that occur in this level from
childhood to adolescence. Again, a key finding here is that children with high-level
aggression early on are also likely to be adolescents with high-level aggression. Still
another line of research has focused on the social concomitants of aggressiveness
as a meaningful way of distinguishing children (Rutter & Rutter, 1993): those who
are not only aggressive but also come from dysfunctional families, where they
witness conflict and get little effective discipline or supervision, are more likely to
remain aggressive than children without such social handicaps.
   The outcome of this line of research remains to be settled; what is apparent is
that the developmental course of aggressiveness takes many diverse forms – an essential point to take into account if appropriate help is to be given to individuals with
differing characteristics and differing requirements. Such diversity makes prediction
from early behaviour no straightforward matter – a conclusion to which research
on the stability of shyness and of other personality attributes (e.g. emotionality,
self-esteem, helpfulness, impulsivity and various forms of psychopathology) also points.
In all these cases, whatever predispositions are to be found in the early years can
usually be modified to some extent by subsequent experience; *dis*continuities are
thus common. It is only at the extremes of the distribution, such as with the very
shy or the highly aggressive, that prediction over the years is likely to be successful. In these individuals inborn factors continue to play a predominant role; those
of more moderate predispositions, on the other hand, remain more open to environmental influences emanating from sources such as home, school and peer group.
For such individuals (and they make up the great majority), the general conclusion
is that the nature of individual attributes in the first few years bears only a weak
relationship to the nature of personality in maturity.
   There have been claims that prediction will be more successful if based on
combinations of attributes rather than on children's *single* attributes. In an account
of a highly ambitious research project, involving the follow-up of a cohort of over

Table 10.6 Continuity of personality style from early childhood to adulthood

Style	*Manifestation at age 3*	*Manifestation at ages 18–21*
Undercontrolled	Impulsive, emotionally volatile, irritable, impatient, restless, distractible	Impulsive, aggressive, thrill-seeking, unreliable, antisocial, reckless
Inhibited	Socially ill-at-ease, fearful, easily upset by strangers, shy	Overcontrolled, cautious, non-assertive, socially isolated, depressed
Well adjusted	Self-confident, friendly after initial wariness, tolerant of frustration, self-controlled	Normal, average, mentally healthy

Source: Based on Caspi (2000)

1,000 children in New Zealand from age 3 to 21 (the 'Dunedin study'), Caspi (2000) summarized the evidence of continuities found when the children were classified into three groups according to a constellation of temperament qualities observed at age 3. When assessed at various subsequent ages up to young adulthood, the groups continued to show distinctive characteristics throughout this period (see table 10.6 for details). The possibility arises therefore that considering isolated personality traits such as aggression and shyness gives a misleading picture, and that what has come to be called a *typological* approach is more meaningful because it does justice to the organizational nature of personality. However, let us note that here too the continuity found was far from complete; here too prediction could only be stated in terms of probabilities and not certainties: members of each group were more *likely* to develop according to a specific pattern, with still plenty of room for change. Once again, we find that discontinuity prevailed as well as a certain amount of continuity.

Predicting from early experience

Another way of attempting to trace developmental continuities is by starting from children's early experiences rather than from their early behaviour patterns. Such a course is based on the assumption that children are highly malleable in the very early stages of life and that the experiences they then absorb are of a foundational nature, determining the course of personality growth once and for all. If that is so, one should be able to predict outcome in maturity by knowing what happened at the beginning of life.

The assumption that early experience has unique significance is a common one, and writers as diverse as J. B. Watson and Sigmund Freud, from the perspectives of behaviourism and psychoanalysis respectively, have espoused it. As Watson (1925), in a much-quoted passage, put it:

Give me a dozen healthy infants, well-formed and my own special world to bring them
up in and I'll guarantee to take any one at random and train him to become any type
of specialist I might select – doctor, lawyer, artist, merchant-chief and, yes, even
beggar-man and thief – regardless of his talents, penchants, tendencies, abilities and
vocation and race of his ancestors.

And similarly Freud (1949):

Analytic experience has convinced us of the complete truth of the common assertion
that the child is psychologically father of the man and that the events of its first years
are of paramount importance for its whole subsequent life.

Very young children, according to these views, are considered to be highly impressionable and more receptive than at any later period, so that whatever experiences
they encounter then will have permanent consequences. The clues to later personality formation are therefore thought to lie in those first encounters of the child
with the environment.

A large body of empirical research is now available to evaluate these claims (for
detailed discussion see Clarke & Clarke, 2000, and Schaffer, 2002). Much of this
work concerns the effects of 'infantile trauma' – experiences of an aberrant and
stressful nature in the early years, such as being brought up in grossly depriving
institutions, where personal care and general stimulation are lacking to an extreme
degree. Take a study by Wayne Dennis (1973) of children reared for the first few
years of their lives in a Middle Eastern orphanage (referred to as the Creche), where
children were subjected to a regime of gross neglect involving a minimum of individual care and a general absence of virtually all forms of stimulation. As a result,
Dennis observed progressive deterioration in the children's developmental status
– from a mean developmental quotient of 100 at the beginning of the first year
(indicating average functioning) to a mere 53 at the end of the first year (i.e.
12-month-old children were performing at the level of 6-month-olds). This severe
retardation continued throughout the stay in the Creche: for example, more than
half the children were still not able to sit up at 21 months of age and fewer than
15 per cent were able to walk by the age of 3. Children of apparently good potential had thus become retarded to an extreme degree as a result of their treatment
in early childhood. Indeed, the retardation was such that no one doubted that it
was of a permanent nature, whatever the children's subsequent fate.

However, a number of years later, when the children were in their teens, Dennis
managed to trace his original group and reassess them. At the age of 6 most had
been transferred from the Creche to institutions more suitable for older children
– the girls to one and the boys to another. The remainder had been adopted straight
from the Creche. All were given intelligence tests; the IQs are given in figure 10.4.
These show that the girls continued to function at a grossly retarded level; the boys,
on the other hand, though below average, nevertheless performed well within
the normal range. This applied also to the adopted children, especially to those

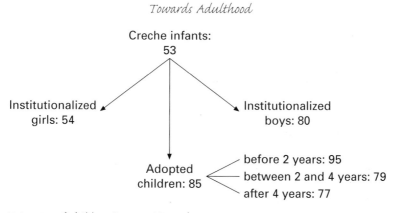

Figure 10.4 *IQs of children in Dennis's study.*

adopted before the age of 2. Why the difference between the institutionalized girls and the others? The answer lies in the kind of environment in which the children lived after the age of 6. The girls' institution was every bit as barren as the Creche; their deprivation simply continued. The boys' institution was very much more stimulating; it was better staffed, had more recreational and educational facilities and the children received much more individual attention. This applied, of course, even more so to the adopted children who lived normal family lives. Thus the effects of a grossly damaging experience, even one continued for 6 years, did not prove to be permanent; the damage seen at the time could be reversed and the children could be helped to achieve more typical intellectual functioning.

More recent work has both confirmed and extended these findings. Thus Rutter et al. (1998) followed up a large group of Romanian orphans, reared from birth in institutions under quite appalling conditions but brought to the UK before the age of 2 and placed there in adoptive families. At the time of transfer the children were severely impaired in their development, as seen in both their physical growth and their cognitive level, in comparison with a group of within-UK adoptees. Yet, when assessed at the age of 4, the children showed a remarkable degree of catch-up (see table 10.7); when reassessed at age 6 (O'Connor et al., 2000), they

Table 10.7 Cognitive test results obtained from 4-year-old children adopted from Romanian orphanages

| | Romanian adoptees | | Within-UK adoptees |
	Entry before 6 months	*Entry after 6 months*	
Tested:			
At entry to UK	76.5	46.1	–
At age 4 years	115.7	96.7	117.7

Source: Based on Rutter et al. (1998).

were found to have maintained their progress, though there was no evidence of further recovery. The catch-up was particularly impressive in those children who were adopted before the age of 6 months, but also notable for children placed at later ages. Further studies of Romanian orphans have similarly demonstrated their ability to catch up on social retardation too (Chisholm, 1998; Chisholm et al., 1995): even after spending several years with only minimal contact with caretakers, these children were able to form attachments to adoptive parents. Being kept emotionally 'on ice' did not prevent subsequent development of social bonds, albeit at the cost of a greater incidence of insecurity in the attachments formed than one would normally expect (see box 4.3, pp. 103–4). Age at the time of the move from adverse to beneficial environment is clearly an important consideration and sets limits to the extent of recovery. Nevertheless, the pattern of these findings as a whole underlines the remarkable resilience of development that is possible after early and severe deprivation.

Other studies, not only of the effects of early deprivation but also of other traumatic experiences, have produced similar results. They have demonstrated that the effects left by such events are not necessarily permanent, however early and however severe they may be; ill effects can be reversed by a drastic change in children's life experience, at least if brought about in time. We cannot be certain what 'in time' amounts to; as shown by the tragic story of Genie (described in box 9.2, pp. 285–6), a child brought up under highly depriving conditions for as long as the first 11 years of her life appears to have little chance of attaining normality. What is apparent is that personality development cannot be predicted on the basis of early experience alone; the connection between *early* and *late* is very much more complex, in that subsequent experiences can, under some conditions at least, reverse earlier effects and must also be taken into consideration when explaining the final product. We thus arrive at a much more optimistic picture of development than that presented by Freud and Watson: we are not inevitably victims of our past; what happens in the early years is important, but so is what happens in the later years of childhood. To understand outcome in maturity, it is therefore necessary to consider the whole sequence of development.

Tracing developmental trajectories

Developmental trajectories are the particular paths through life that individuals follow, distinguished by the degree of continuity/discontinuity characterizing each.

Instead of jumping straight from *early* to *late*, from experiences at the beginning of life to the point at which outcome is to be assessed, it has become clear that the early experience needs to be seen in the context of individual children's life paths, and that instead of expecting some particular trauma uniformly to lead to pathological outcomes it is necessary to recognize the modifying role of intervening events. Recognition has to be given, that is, to the fact that the **developmental trajectories** leading from early adversity to later personality functioning can take diverse forms in different individuals. Let us illustrate.

Table 10.8 Depression rates (%) among women according to childhood loss and adequacy of subsequent care

Type of loss	Adequate care	Inadequate care
Death of mother	10	34
Separation from mother	4	36
No loss of a parent	3	13

Source: Based on Harris, Brown & Bifulco (1986).

In a series of studies, Brown and his colleagues (e.g. Brown, 1988; Brown, Harris & Bifulco, 1986) investigated the link between loss of a parent in childhood and the development of depression in adult women. Such a link had previously been proposed on theoretical grounds, yet empirical investigations that attempted directly to associate the one with the other had come up with inconclusive results. However, by taking into account other, intervening experiences, Brown was able to demonstrate that the link occurred under certain conditions only, namely, where the death of the parent resulted in a lack of adequate parental care (see table 10.8). Thus when one compares women who had lost their mothers through death or separation but subsequently experienced adequate care with women who had undergone a similar loss but were then brought up under inadequate care arrangements, the rate of depression among the former was found to be much less than among the latter – indeed, only slightly higher than that among women who had never experienced loss of a parent. For that matter, unsatisfactory care arrangements in turn often led subsequently to other unfortunate experiences, such as premarital pregnancy and an unsatisfactory marriage, each of which contributed to the final outcome, i.e. the development of clinical depression. It appears therefore that the specific event originally experienced by the child, the loss of the parent, obtained its *long-term* significance primarily from the chain reaction it set up. The pathway from childhood experience to adult outcome may thus involve a whole sequence of steps, each of which is made more likely by what preceded it – a procedure that may well result in some children being put on a conveyor belt of ever-greater adversity.

Yet there is nothing inevitable about a chain reaction, even where the sequence is well under way. Periodically, individuals come to **turning points** where a choice has to be made among alternative courses: to stay on at school or leave; to obtain an unskilled job or to undertake further study or training; to marry a particular partner or not – these are some of the decisions to be made by young people. Whether their choice is free or not, the course taken may well reinforce or, on the contrary, help to minimize the consequences of previous experience. Take a study by Rutter, Quinton and Hill (1990), the goal of which was to establish whether children deprived of adequate parenting in turn

Turning points (also known as transition points) refer to the occasions when individuals are confronted with crucial choices as to the future course of their life.

become depriving parents. The girls investigated had spent a major part of their early years in institutions, and as adults were found to be less sensitive, less supportive and not as warm in their relationships with their own children as mothers brought up under typical circumstances. Yet by no means all the women from a deprived background showed these deficiencies: behind the group averages there was considerable variability in outcome, and this could be accounted for by tracing individual children's developmental trajectories leading from childhood experience to adult behaviour. For example, positive school experience was found to counteract some of the adverse effects of the children's home experiences, leading to enhanced self-esteem, and this in turn increased the chances of obtaining a job at the end of adolescence that was satisfying and fulfilling. Above all, finding a marriage partner who was supportive and not socially deviant enabled the women to function well generally and in particular to establish sound relationships with their children. Turning points take many forms (Caspi, 1998): as we saw in the study by Wayne Dennis above (pp. 336–7), transfer to a different institution can be one such transition, adoption another – both holding out the possibility (not always confirmed) of the child being diverted along a different pathway. Turning points are thus an essential part of any explanation of the connection between childhood events and adult behaviour; they can modify the effects of past experience even in adulthood, and help to account for the considerable variety of outcomes that follow identical events in early life.

We can conclude that the widely held belief, that the keys to the present lie solely in the distant past, is simplistic. The notion that early experiences are important just because they are early cannot be sustained. There is no straightforward correlation between age and sensitivity to experience. Consider the impact of parental divorce on children of different ages: no sweeping generalization linking age to vulnerability can be upheld (Hetherington & Stanley-Hagan, 1999); a more likely conclusion is that reactions vary among younger and older children in kind rather than in severity. The picture of the highly vulnerable infant and preschooler, who gradually grows into a mentally much more sturdy schoolchild and adolescent, cannot be borne out. Particular experiences have an impact depending on whatever mental organization exists at that particular developmental stage; it is the nature of that organization and not age as such that determines how the child responds. Timing matters, but not in terms of a simple 'the earlier the greater the effect' type of generalization. All depends on the kind of experience and the child's ability to interpret and incorporate it. Where there is developmental continuity, where for instance early maladjustment leads to later maladjustment, the explanation could well be found in environmental continuity. Thus children subjected to unfavourable upbringing in their first years are likely also to experience unfavourable upbringing in later childhood – either because the child remains in the same adverse rearing environment or because of the tendency for one misfortune to lead to another (the 'conveyor-belt' phenomenon). It is the cumulative effect of all links in the chain rather than the first link on its own that will then be responsible for any long-term damage.

Summary

One of the main developmental tasks for children concerns the process of *individuation*, i.e. the formation of a personal, unique identity. From birth on children already have an individuality, based on a set of characteristics generally referred to as *temperament*. These characteristics are almost certainly genetically determined and continue to play a role in influencing an individual's behaviour; they are thus likely to be the forerunners of what subsequently comes to be referred to as *personality*.

The *self* is the focus of personality, and much of childhood is devoted to finding an answer to the question 'Who am I?' In studying the self, it is useful to distinguish three constituents: self-awareness, self-concept and self-esteem. Self-awareness generally emerges in the second year; after that the self-concept comes to be fleshed out and increasingly refined – a process that continues right into adulthood. Self-esteem also undergoes developmental changes throughout the school years, becoming gradually more consistent and more realistic.

During adolescence children's ideas about themselves are often subjected to extensive modification, in keeping with the changes in their physical appearance and with the increase in introspectiveness referred to as the *identity crisis*. According to Erik Erikson, it is at this period of life above all that children need to resolve the question of their identity; only if they can cope with this particular developmental task will they be able successfully to proceed to adulthood and not continue to be bewildered by confusion as to their role in life.

How children think of themselves depends both on their cognitive development and on their social experience, especially on the expectations and attitudes of other people. This is most evident in cases of maltreatment, which can have marked implications for a child's development of self. The family is no doubt the cradle of children's sense of self; increasingly, however, the peer group also becomes a force in this respect, as seen in the effects that rejection and bullying have on victims' self-esteem.

One further aspect of self-development concerns children's acquisition of a sense of gender. This is a protracted process, involving the development of gender identity, gender stability and gender consistency. Psychological differences between the sexes have turned out to be surprisingly few; however, the phenomenon of gender segregation, found from the third year on and still evident in adolescence and maturity, can have marked effects on the respective interactive styles developed by the two sexes.

The extent to which there is continuity in our personal qualities from early childhood into adulthood, and hence whether it is possible to predict adult personality from behaviour in the first years, remains a lively topic of investigation. Two approaches have been taken, the first of which traces particular psychological attributes throughout development in order to determine their stability. Taking the examples of shyness and aggression, it must be concluded that stability tends to be confined to the extremes, such as the very shy or the highly aggressive, as a result of inborn influences remaining predominant. Amongst those of more moderate predisposition, however, change is the rule rather than the exception. These individuals are more open to influences in the environment, making fluctuations in personal qualities more likely.

The second approach concerns efforts to predict later outcome from early experience. This is based on the assumption that children at the beginning of life are so impressionable that traumatic experiences such as deprivation will mark them for life, irrespective of subsequent experience. This has been shown not to be the case: even children severely damaged in grossly neglecting institutions have been found to recover, given suitable conditions. The developmental course, one must conclude, is not set once and for all by particular experiences, however early and however severe. Subsequent events must also be taken into account, including the turning points which individuals have to negotiate while following their particular developmental trajectories.

FURTHER READING

Caspi, A. (1998). Personality development across the life course. In W. Damon (ed.), N. Eisenberg (vol. ed.), *Handbook of Child Psychology* (Vol. 3). New York: Wiley. Primarily concerned with the nature of personality differences and their origin in childhood, but includes a scholarly summary of the study of continuity and change in personality traits.

Clarke, A., & Clarke, A. (2000). *Early Experience and the Life Path.* London: Jessica Kingsley. An update of a very influential book (*Early Experience: Myth and Evidence*) published in 1976. Provides a useful account of the latest evidence concerning the effects of early experience.

Golombok, S., & Fivush, R. (1994). *Gender Development.* Cambridge: Cambridge University Press. Traces gender development from conception to adulthood, illustrating its role in such diverse areas as play, social relationships, moral development, school and work, and providing a useful account of the multiplicity of hormonal, cognitive, parental and peer influences on the course of development.

Harter, S. (1999). *The Construction of the Self: A Developmental Perspective.* New York: Guilford Press. A detailed, scholarly account of our current state of knowledge of the self and its development from the preschool years to late adolescence, as seen by one of the most productive contributors to the literature.

Maccoby, E. E. (1998). *The Two Sexes: Growing up Apart, Coming Together.* Cambridge, MA: Harvard University Press. One of the most important books on gender published in recent years. Focuses on the role that gender segregation plays both in childhood and in adulthood, but covers a great deal else relevant to gender development.

Glossary

Cross-references to further definitions in the glossary are given in **bold**.

Accommodation is the term used in Piaget's theory for the modification of mental structures to incorporate new information. The complementary process is **assimilation**.

Adult Attachment Interview (AAI) is a semi-structured procedure for eliciting adults' childhood experiences with attachment figures. It is used to assign individuals to various categories summarizing their state of mind with respect to close relationships.

Anoxia. The condition where the brain is deprived of essential supplies of oxygen, resulting in both physical and mental retardation if severe.

Apgar score. A measure of a newborn baby's condition, derived from a rating scale assessing a range of essential functions.

Assimilation is Piaget's term for the taking in of information by using already existing mental structures. The complementary process is **accommodation**.

Autobiographical memory system. The store of memories referring to the individual's past history, the function of which is to provide a sense of personal continuity and which is therefore essential for children's acquisition of a self-concept.

Behavioural genetics is the science investigating the hereditary basis of human and animal behaviour.

Chromosomes are tiny rod-shaped structures found in the nucleus of every cell in the body, housing the DNA of which the genes are composed.

Collectivist cultures are those societies which emphasize the mutual dependence of its members, and which accordingly bring up their children to value social conformity before individual goals (contrast with **individualistic cultures**).

Concepts are mental categories for the classification of diverse objects that share some particular characteristic.

Conservation is Piaget's name for the understanding that certain basic characteristics of an object, such as its weight and volume, remain constant even when its appearance is perceptually transformed.

Critical periods are those times in the course of development when an individual must be exposed to certain experiences in order to acquire a particular skill (see **sensitive periods**).

Cross-sectional research designs. Different groups of children varying in age are compared on some specific measure in order to assess how particular functions change in the course of development (contrast with **longitudinal research designs**).

Cultural tools are the objects and skills which each society has perfected to carry on its traditions and which must therefore be handed down from one generation to the next.

Developmental task. According to some writers such as Erik Erikson, childhood can be divided into a series of stages, each one of which presents the individual with some major challenge that must be met in order successfully to continue to the next stage.

Developmental trajectories are the particular paths through life that individuals follow, distinguished by the degree of continuity/discontinuity characterizing each.

Disequilibrium. In Piagetian theory the mental state when the individual encounters new information for which no mental structures exist as yet. See **equilibrium**.

Display rules refer to the cultural norms for the overt expression of emotion, including both the kind of emotions displayed and the circumstances under which they can be displayed.

Domain-specific, domain-general. Terms used to describe whether developmental processes apply only to certain mental functions or to all.

Emergent literacy refers to the very first stage of becoming literate, namely, the realization that written language is meaningful and interesting.

Emotional competence is the term used to designate individuals' abilities to cope both with their own emotions and with those of other people. It is the emotional equivalent of 'intelligence' as used for cognitive functions.

Equilibrium. In Piagetian theory this is the state reached through **assimilation** and **accommodation** when the individual has absorbed and made sense of new information. See **disequilibrium**.

Externalizing problems refer to 'acting out' behaviour disorders, such as aggression, violence and delinquency (as contrasted with **internalizing problems**).

Gender role knowledge is the awareness by children that certain kinds of behaviour are considered as 'right' for boys while others are 'right' for girls.

Genes are the units of hereditary transmission. They are made up of DNA and are found in particular locations on **chromosomes**.

Goal-corrected partnerships is the term used in John Bowlby's attachment theory to denote mature relationships. They are characterized by the ability of both partners to plan their actions in the light of their own goals and simultaneously to take account of the goals of the other person.

Guided participation is the procedure whereby adults help children to acquire knowledge through collaboration in problem-solving situations.

Identity crisis. Associated primarily with the writings of Erik Erikson, this term denotes the period of confusion and low self-esteem that is (controversially) said to be typical of adolescence.

Individualistic cultures are those societies where the independence of the individual is valued above all, and where children are therefore brought up to be self-reliant and self-assertive (contrast with **collectivist cultures**).

Individuation is the umbrella term for all the processes employed in children's acquisition of a personal identity (see **social identity**).

Infantile amnesia is the inability to remember events occurring in the first few years of life.

Internal working models are the mental structures which John Bowlby hypothesized as carrying forward into adulthood the attachment-related experiences encountered in early childhood.

Internalizing problems are disorders manifested through inward-turned symptoms, such as anxiety and depression (contrast with **externalizing problems**).

Joint attention episodes are those situations in which an adult and a child simultaneously focus upon some object and together carry out actions upon it.

Language acquisition device (LAD). According to Noam Chomsky, this is an inborn mental structure that enables children to acquire knowledge of the complexities of grammar with remarkable speed.

Language acquisition support system (LASS). Jerome Bruner proposed this term as a counter to Chomsky's reliance on inborn knowledge, to draw attention to the collection of strategies adults employ to help and support children's acquisition of language.

Longitudinal research designs. The same group of children is followed up and tested at different ages in order to trace change in the course of development (contrast with **cross-sectional research designs**).

Metacognition denotes the awareness and knowledge individuals have of their cognitive processes. It includes, for instance, metamemory and metacommunication.

Motherese. A particular style of adult-to-child talk (hence also referred to as A-to-C talk), in which adults modify their usual speech in order to make it more comprehensible and attention-worthy to the child being addressed.

Niche-picking. The process whereby individuals actively select those environments that fit in with their genetic predisposition.

Non-REM sleep. The quiet and deepest periods of sleep when brain activity is at its lowest (contrast with **REM sleep**).

Object permanence is Piaget's term for the realization that objects are independent entities that continue to exist even when the individual is not aware of them.

Operant conditioning refers to the procedure whereby an individual acquires a particular behaviour pattern as a result of being rewarded for performing it or punished for not performing it.

Operation in Piagetian theory is any procedure for mentally acting on objects.

Personal identity refers to those aspects of an individual's personality that distinguish him or her from other individuals (see **social identity**).

Phonology is the study of the sound systems that make up languages.

Pragmatics is the study of the rules that determine how we use language for practical purposes.

Recessive gene disorders appear when both parents supply the same recessive gene, with no dominant gene present to override its effects.

Reliability. Refers to the confidence we can have in a measuring instrument. Usually assessed by comparing results obtained at different times or from different testers.

REM sleep. This denotes the period of sleep when the brain is in a relatively active state, resulting in various bodily movements including rapid eye movements (REMs). Alternates with **non-REM sleep**.

Scaffolding is the process whereby adults offer help to a child in problem solving, and adjust both the kind and the amount of help to the child's level of performance.

Scripts are mental representations of particular everyday events and the behaviour and emotions appropriate to them.

Self-awareness is the very first step in the formation of a self and refers to the realization by children that they are distinct beings with an existence of their own.

Self-concept refers to the image that children build up of themselves, providing an answer to the question 'Who am I?'

Self-esteem concerns the value that children attach to their personal qualities, answering the question 'How good am I?' and ranging from very positive to very negative.

Semantics is the branch of linguistics concerned with the meaning of words and how we acquire them.

Sensitive periods are the times during development when an individual is more likely to acquire some particular skill than at other times (see **critical periods**).

Sex cells (also known as gametes) are the eggs of a female and the sperm of a male that combine during fertilization. Unlike other cells, they contain only 23 chromosomes instead of 46.

Social constructivism is the position adopted by Vygotsky and others that children's learning is based on active striving to make sense of the world rather than on passive acquisition, and that they do so most effectively in conjunction with others.

Social identity refers to an individual's sense of belonging to particular social categories like gender and ethnicity (see **personal identity**).

Socialization is the umbrella term for all those processes whereby children are helped to acquire the behaviour patterns and values required to live in their particular society.

Sociometric techniques take a variety of forms, all designed to provide quantitative indices of individuals' standing within a group (e.g. their popularity).

Strange Situation is the procedure whereby the quality of young children's attachment is assessed. It consists of a series of episodes stressful enough to activate attachment behaviour, and is used to assign children to various categories denoting the security of their attachments.

Syntax refers to the grammar of language, i.e. the rules whereby words are combined to make up meaningful sentences.

Systems theory is a particular way of describing organizations such as families. These are seen both as complex wholes and as made up of subsystems that, for certain purposes, can also be treated as independent units.

Temperament refers to the set of inborn characteristics that distinguish one person from another in the behavioural style they manifest.

Teratogens are substances like alcohol or cocaine that cross the maternal placenta and interfere with the development of the foetus.

Theory of mind (ToM) is the knowledge acquired in childhood that other people have an internal world of thoughts and feelings and that these are independent of one's own mental states.

Turning points (also known as transition points) refer to the occasions when individuals are confronted with crucial choices as to the future course of their life.

Universal grammar denotes those rules of language formation that are found in all possible human languages.

Validity. The extent to which a particular measuring instrument really reflects what it purports to measure. Usually assessed by comparing the result with other indices.

X and Y chromosomes are the bundles of DNA that determine an individual's sex.

Zone of proximal development. According to Vygotsky, this is the gap between what children already know and what they are capable of learning under guidance.

References

Adams, M. J. (1990). *Learning to Read: Thinking and Learning about Print*. Cambridge, MA: MIT Press.

Ainsworth, M. D. S., Blehar, M. C., Waters, E., & Wahls, S. (1978). *Patterns of Attachment*. Hillsdale, NJ: Erlbaum.

Amato, P. R., & Booth, A. (1996). A prospective study of divorce and parent–child relationships. *Journal of Marriage and the Family*, 58, 356–65.

Amato, P. R., & Keith, B. (1991). Parental divorce and the well-being of children: A meta-analysis. *Psychological Bulletin*, 110, 26–46.

Ariès, P. (1962). *Centuries of Childhood*. Harmondsworth: Penguin.

Asendorpf, J. B. (2000). Shyness and adaptation to the social world of university. In W. R. Crozier (ed.), *Shyness: Development, Consolidation and Change*. London: Routledge.

Aslin, R. N., Jusczyk, P. W., & Pisconi, D. B. (1998). Speech and auditory processing during infancy: Constraints on and precursors to language. In W. Damon (ed.), D. Kuhn & R. S. Siegler (vol. eds), *Handbook of Child Psychology* (Vol. 2). New York: Wiley.

Atkinson, R. C., & Shiffrin, R. M. (1968). Human memory: A proposed system and its control processes. In K. W. Spence & J. T. Spence (eds), *Advances in the Psychology of Learning and Motivation* (Vol. 2). New York: Academic Press.

Attie, I., & Brooks-Gunn, J. (1989). Development of eating problems in adolescent girls: A longitudinal study. *Developmental Psychology*, 25, 70–9.

Banks, M. S., Aslin, R. N., & Letson, R. D. (1975). Sensitive period for the development of binocular vision. *Science*, 190, 675–7.

Barnett, D., Ganiban, J., & Cicchetti, D. (1999). Maltreatment, negative expressivity, and the development of type D attachments from 12 to 24 months of age. In J. I. Vondra & D. Barnett (eds), Atypical attachment in infancy and early childhood among children at developmental risk. *Monographs of the Society for Research in Child Development*, 64 (3, Serial No. 258).

Baron-Cohen, S. (1995). *Mindblindness: An Essay on Autism and Theory of Mind*. Cambridge, MA: MIT Press.

Barrett, M. (1986). Early semantic representations and early semantic development. In S. A. Kuczaj & M. Barrett (eds), *The Development of Word Meaning*. New York: Springer.

Bartsch, K., & Wellman, H. M. (1995). *Children Talk About the Mind*. Oxford: Oxford University Press.

Bates, E. (1990). Language about me and you: Pronominal reference and the emerging concept of self. In E. Cicchetti & M. Beeghly (eds), *Self in Transition: Infancy to Childhood*. Chicago: University of Chicago Press.

Bateson, G., & Mead, M. (1940). *Balinese Character*. New York: Academy of Sciences.

Belsky, J. (1981). Early human experience: A family perspective. *Developmental Psychology*, 17, 3–23.

Belsky, J., & Most, R. K. (1981). From exploration to play: A cross-sectional study of infant and free play behavior. *Developmental Psychology*, 17, 630–9.

Benoit, D., & Parker, K. C. H. (1994). Stability and transmission of attachment among three generations. *Child Development*, 65, 1444–56.

Bettes, B. A. (1988). Maternal depression and motherese: Temporal and intonational features. *Child Development*, 59, 1089–96.

Bishop, D., & Mogford, K. (eds) (1993). *Language Development in Exceptional Circumstances*. Hove: Erlbaum.

Bivens, J. A., & Berk, L. A. (1990). A longitudinal study of the development of elementary school children's private speech. *Merrill-Palmer Quarterly*, 36, 443–63.

Bjorklund, D. F. (2000). *Children's Thinking: Developmental Function and Individual Differences* (3rd edn). Belmont, CA: Wadsworth.

Bloom, L. (1973). *One Word at a Time: The Use of Single-word Utterances before Syntax*. The Hague: Mouton.

Bloom, L., & Tinker, E. (2001). The intentionality model and language acquisition: Engagement, effort and the essential tension in development. *Monographs of the Society for Research in Child Development*, 66 (4, Serial No. 267).

Boden, M. (1988). *Computer Models of Mind*. Cambridge: Cambridge University Press.

Bolger, K. E., Patterson, J., & Kupersmidt, J. B. (1998). Peer relationships and self-esteem among children who have been maltreated. *Child Development*, 69, 1171–97.

Borke, H. (1971). Interpersonal perception of young children: Egocentrism or empathy? *Developmental Psychology*, 5, 263–9.

Bornstein, M. H., Tal, J., & Tamis-LeMonda, C. S. (1991). Parenting in cross-cultural perspective: The United States, France and Japan. In M. H. Bornstein (ed.), *Cultural Approaches to Parenting*. Hillsdale, NJ: Erlbaum.

Boulton, M. J., & Smith, P. K. (1994). Bully/victim problems in middle-school children: Stability, self-perceived competence, peer perceptions and peer acceptance. *British Journal of Developmental Psychology*, 12, 315–29.

Bower, T. G. R. (1974). *Development in Infancy*. San Francisco: W. H. Freeman.

Bowlby, J. (1969/1982). *Attachment and Loss*. Vol. 1: *Attachment* (1st and 2nd edns). London: Hogarth Press.

Bowlby, J. (1973). *Attachment and Loss*. Vol. 2: *Separation: Anxiety and Anger*. London: Hogarth Press.

Bowlby, J. (1980). *Attachment and Loss*. Vol. 3: *Loss, Sadness and Depression*. London: Hogarth Press.

Brame, B., Nagin, D. S., & Tremblay, R. E. (2001). Developmental trajectories of physical aggression from school entry to late adolescence. *Journal of Child Psychology and Psychiatry*, 42, 503–12.

Bretherton, I., & Beeghly, M. (1982). Talking about internal states: The acquisition of an explicit theory of mind. *Developmental Psychology*, 18, 906–21.

Briggs, J. L. (1970). *Never in Anger*. Cambridge, MA: Harvard University Press.

Bronfenbrenner, U. (1989). Ecological systems theory. In R. Vastra (ed.), *Annals of Child Development*. Vol. 6: *Six Theories of Child Development*. Greenwich, CT: JAI Press.

Brown, G. (1988). Causal paths, chains and strands. In M. Rutter (ed.), *Studies of Psychosocial Risk: The Power of Longitudinal Data*. Cambridge: Cambridge University Press.

Brown, G. W., Harris, T. O., & Bifulco, A. (1986). The long-term effects of early loss of parent. In M. Rutter, C. E. Izard & P. B. Read (eds), *Depression in Young People*. New York: Guilford Press.

Brown, R. (1965). *Social Psychology*. New York: Free Press.

Brown, R. (1973). *A First Language: The Early Stages*. Cambridge: Cambridge University Press.

Bruck, M., & Ceci, S. J. (1999). The suggestibility of children's memory. *Annual Review of Psychology*, 50, 419–39.

Bruner, J. S. (1983). *Child's Talk*. Cambridge: Cambridge University Press.

Buchsbaum, H., Toth, S., Clyman, R., Cicchetti, D., & Emde, R. (1992). The use of a narrative story stem technique with maltreated children: Implications for theory and practice. *Development and Psychopathology*, 4, 603–25.

Bullock, M., & Lutkenhaus, P. (1990). Who am I? Self-understanding in toddlers. *Merrill-Palmer Quarterly*, 36, 217–38.

Buss, A. H., & Plomin, R. (1984). *Temperament: Early Developing Personality Traits*. Hillsdale, NJ: Erlbaum.

Cairns, R. B., Cairns, B. D., Neckerman, H. J., Ferguson, L., & Gariepy, J. L. (1989). Growth and aggression: 1. Childhood to adolescence. *Developmental Psychology*, 25, 320–30.

Calkins, S. D. (1994). Origins and outcomes of individual differences in emotion regulation. In N. A. Fox (ed.), The development of emotion regulation: Biological and behavioural considerations. *Monographs of the Society for Research in Child Development*, 59 (2–3, Serial No. 240).

Calkins, S. D., Gill, K. L., Johnson, M. C., & Smith, C. L. (1999). Emotional reactivity and emotion regulation strategies as predictors of social behavior with peers during toddlerhood. *Social Development*, 8, 310–34.

Carey, S. (1978). The child as word learner. In M. Halle, J. Bresnan & G. A. Miller (eds), *Linguistic Theory and Psychological Reality*. Cambridge, MA: MIT Press.

Carpenter, M., Nagell, K., & Tomasello, M. (1998). Social cognition, joint attention and communicative competence from 9 to 15 months of age. *Monographs of the Society for Research in Child Development* (4, Serial No. 255).

Caspi, A. (1998). Personality development across the life course. In W. Damon (ed.), N. Eisenberg (vol. ed.), *Handbook of Child Psychology* (Vol. 3). New York: Wiley.

Caspi, A. (2000). The child is father of the man: Personality continuities from childhood to adulthood. *Journal of Personality and Social Psychology*, 78, 158–72.

Cassidy, J. (1994). Emotion regulation: Influences of attachment regulation. In N. A. Fox (ed.), The development of emotion regulation: Biological and behavioural considerations. *Monographs of the Society for Research in Child Development*, 59 (2–3, Serial No. 240).

Ceci, S. J., & Bruck, M. (1995). *Jeopardy in the Courtroom: A Scientific Analysis of Children's Testimony*. Washington, DC: American Psychological Association.

Chagnon, N. A. (1968). *Yanomamo: The Fierce People*. New York: Holt, Rinehart & Winston.

Chan, R. W., Raboy, B., & Patterson, C. J. (1998). Psychosocial adjustment among children conceived via donor insemination among children by lesbian and heterosexual mothers. *Child Development*, 69, 443–57.

Chase-Lonsdale, P. L., Cherlin, A. J., & Kiernan, K. E. (1995). The long-term effects of parental divorce on the mental health of young adults: A developmental perspective. *Child Development*, 66, 1614–34.

Chen, X., Hastings, P., Rubin, K., Chen, H., Cen, G., & Stewart, S. L. (1998). Child-rearing attitudes and behavioural inhibition in Chinese and Canadian toddlers: A cross-cultural study. *Developmental Psychology*, 34, 677–86.

Chi, M. T. H. (1978). Knowledge structures and memory development. In R. S. Siegler (ed.), *Children's Thinking: What Develops?* Hillsdale, NJ: Erlbaum.

Chisholm, K. (1998). A three-year follow-up of attachment and indiscriminate friendliness in children adopted from Romanian orphanages. *Child Development*, 69, 1092–106.

Chisholm, K., Carter, M. C., Ames, E. W., & Morison, S. J. (1995). Attachment security and indiscriminately friendly behavior in children adopted from Romanian orphanages. *Development and Psychopathology*, 7, 283–94.

Chomsky, N. (1986). *Knowledge of Language: Its Nature, Origins and Use*. New York: Praeger.

Cicchetti, D., & Barnett, D. (1991). Attachment organization in maltreated preschoolers. *Development and Psychopathology*, 4, 397–411.

Cicchetti, D., Ganiban, J., & Barnett, D. (1991). Contributions from the study of high-risk populations to understanding the development of emotion regulation. In J. Garber & K. A. Dodge (eds), *The Development of Emotion Regulation and Dysregulation*. Cambridge: Cambridge University Press.

Clark, E. V. (1982). The young word-maker: A case study of innovation in the child's lexicon. In E. Wanner & L. R. Gleitman (eds), *Language Acquisition: The State of the Art*. Cambridge: Cambridge University Press.

Clarke, A., & Clarke, A. (2000). *Early Experience and the Life Path*. London: Jessica Kingsley.

Clarke-Stewart, K. A., Goossens, F. A., & Allhusen, V. D. (2001). Measuring infant–mother attachment: Is the Strange Situation enough? *Social Development*, 10, 143–69.

Cohn, J. F., & Tronick, E. Z. (1983). Three-month-old infants' reactions to simulated maternal depression. *Child Development*, 54, 183–93.

Cole, M., & Cole, S. R. (2001). *The Development of Children* (4th edn). New York: W. H. Freeman.

Cole, P. M., Michel, M. K., & Teti, L. O. (1994). The development of emotion regulation and dysregulation: A clinical perspective. In N. A. Fox (ed.), The development of emotion regulation: Biological and behavioural considerations. *Monographs of the Society for Research in Child Development*, 59 (2–3, Serial No. 240).

Condry, J., & Condry, S. (1976). Sex differences: A study of the eye of the beholder. *Child Development*, 47, 812–19.

Cooley, C. H. (1902). *Human Nature and Social Order*. New York: Charles Scribner.

Coopersmith, S. (1967). *The Antecedents of Self-esteem*. San Francisco: W. H. Freeman.

Cox, M. (1992). *Children's Drawings*. London: Penguin.

Cox, M. (1997). *Drawings of People by the Under-5s*. London: Falmer Press.

Crain, W. (1999). *Theories of Development: Concepts and Applications* (4th edn). Englewood Cliffs, NJ: Prentice-Hall.

Crittenden, P. M. (1988). Relationships at risk. In J. Belsky & T. Nesworski (eds), *Clinical Implications of Attachment*. Hillsdale, NJ: Erlbaum.

Crook, C. K. (1994). *Computers and the Collaborative Experience of Learning*. London: Routledge.

Crowell, J. A., & Treboux, D. (1995). A review of adult attachment measures: Implications for theory and research. *Social Development*, 4, 294–327.

Crozier, W. R. (2000). *Shyness: Development, Consolidation and Change*. London: Routledge.

Cummings, E. M. (1994). Marital conflict and children's functioning. *Social Development*, 3, 16–36.

Cummings, E. M., & Davies, P. (1994a). Maternal depression and child development. *Journal of Child Psychology and Psychiatry*, 35, 73–112.

Cummings, E. M., & Davies, P. (1994b). *Children and Marital Conflict: The Impact of Family Disruption and Resolution.* New York: Guilford Press.

Curtiss, S. (1977). *Genie: A Psycholinguistic Study of a Modern-day 'Wild Child'.* London: Academic Press.

Damon, W. (1983). *Social and Personality Development.* London: W. W. Norton.

Darwin, C. (1872). *The Expression of the Emotions in Man and Animals.* London: Murray.

Dasen, P. R. (1974). The influence of culture and European contact on cognitive development in Australian Aborigines. In J. W. Berry & P. R. Dasen (eds), *Culture and Cognition: Readings in Cross-cultural Psychology.* London: Methuen.

Dasen, P. R. (ed.) (1977). *Piagetian Psychology: Cross-cultural Contributions.* New York: Gardner.

DeCasper, A. J., & Fifer, W. P. (1980). Of human bonding: Newborns prefer their mothers' voices. *Science*, 208, 1174–6.

DeCasper, A. J., & Prescott, P. A. (1984). Human newborns' perception of male voices. *Developmental Psychobiology*, 17, 481–91.

DeCasper, A. J., & Spence, M. J. (1986). Prenatal maternal speech influences newborns' perception of speech sounds. *Infant Behavior and Development*, 9, 133–50.

DeLoache, J. (1987). Rapid change in the symbolic functioning of very young children. *Science*, 238, 1556–7.

DeMause, L. (ed.) (1974). *The History of Childhood.* New York: Psychohistory Press.

Dempster, F. N. (1981). Memory span: Sources of individual and developmental differences. *Psychological Bulletin*, 89, 63–100.

Denham, S. (1998). *Emotional Development in Young Children.* New York: Guilford Press.

Dennis, W. (1973). *Children of the Creche.* New York: Appleton-Century-Crofts.

DeWolff, M. S., & van IJzendoorn, M. H. (1997). Sensitivity and attachment: A meta-analysis on parental antecedents of infant attachment. *Child Development*, 68, 571–91.

Diamond, J. (1990). War babies. Reprinted in S. J. Ceci & W. M. Williams (eds) (1999), *The Nature–Nurture Debate: The Essential Readings.* Oxford: Blackwell.

Diamond, M., & Sigmundson, H. K. (1997). Sex reassignment at birth. *Pediatric and Adolescent Medicine*, 151, 298–304.

Donaldson, M. (1978). *Children's Minds.* London: Fontana.

Dunn, J. (1988). *The Beginnings of Social Understanding.* Oxford: Blackwell.

Dunn, J., Bretherton, I., & Munn, P. (1987). Conversations about feeling states between mothers and their young children. *Developmental Psychology*, 23, 132–9.

Dunn, J., & Brown, J. R. (1994). Affect expression in the family: Children's understanding of emotions and their interactions with others. *Merrill-Palmer Quarterly*, 40, 120–37.

Dunn, J., Brown, J., & Beardall, L. (1991). Family talk about feeling states and children's later understanding of others' emotions. *Developmental Psychology*, 27, 448–55.

Dunn, J., Deater-Deckard, K., Pickering, K., Golding, J., & the ALSPAC Study Team (1999). Siblings, parents and partners: Family relationships within a longitudinal community study. *Journal of Child Psychology and Psychiatry*, 40, 1025–37.

Dunn, J., & Hughes, C. (1998). Young children's understanding of emotions within close relationships. *Cognition and Emotion*, 12, 171–90.

Durkin, K., Shire, B., Crowther, R. D., & Rutter, D. (1986). The social and linguistic context of early number word use. *British Journal of Developmental Psychology*, 4, 269–88.

Eaton, W. O., & Yu, A. P. (1989). Are sex differences in child motor activity level a function of sex differences in maturational status? *Child Development*, 60, 1005–11.

Eckerman, C. O., & Oehler, J. M. (1992). Very-low-birthweight newborns and parents as early social partners. In S. L. Friedman & M. D. Sigman (eds), *The Psychological Development of Low Birthweight Children*. Norwood, NJ: Ablex.

Egan, S. K., & Perry, D. G. (1998). Does low self-regard invite victimization? *Developmental Psychology*, 34, 299–309.

Eibl-Eibesfeldt, I. (1973). The expressive behavior of the deaf-and-blind-born. In M. von Cranach & I. Vine (eds), *Social Communication and Movement*. New York: Academic Press.

Eimas, P. D., Siqueland, E. R., Jusczyk, P., & Vigorito, J. (1971). Speech perception in infants. *Science*, 171, 303–6.

Eisenberg, A. R. (1992). Conflicts between mothers and their young children. *Merrill-Palmer Quarterly*, 38, 21–43.

Ekman, P. (1980). *The Face of Man*. New York: Garland.

Ekman, P., & Friesen, W. (1978). *Facial Action Coding System*. Palo Alto, CA: Consulting Psychologists Press.

Ekman, P., Sorenson, E. R., & Friesen, W. V. (1969). Pan-cultural elements in the facial display of emotions. *Science*, 164, 86–8.

Elder, G. H. (1974). *Children of the Great Depression*. Chicago: University of Chicago Press.

Elder, G. H., & Caspi, A. (1988). Economic stress in lives: Developmental perspectives. *Journal of Social Issues*, 44, 25–45.

Ellis, S., Rogoff, B., & Cromer, C. C. (1981). Age segregation in children's social interaction. *Developmental Psychology*, 17, 399–407.

Erel, O., & Burman, B. (1995). Inter-relatedness of marital relations and parent–child relations: A meta-analytic review. *Psychological Bulletin*, 118, 108–32.

Erikson, E. (1965). *Childhood and Society*. Harmondsworth: Penguin.

Erikson, E. (1968). *Identity: Youth and Crisis*. London: Faber.

Fabes, R. A., & Eisenberg, N. (1992). Young children's coping with interpersonal anger. *Child Development*, 63, 116–28.

Fabes, R. A., Eisenberg, N., Nyman, M., & Michaelieu, Q. (1991). Young children's appraisal of others' spontaneous emotional reactions. *Developmental Psychology*, 27, 858–66.

Fagot, B. I. (1978). The influence of sex of child on parental reactions to toddler children. *Child Development*, 49, 459–65.

Fagot, B. I., & Hagan, R. (1991). Observations of parent reactions to sex-stereotyped behaviors: Age and sex effects. *Child Development*, 62, 617–28.

Fagot, B. I., & Leinbach, M. D. (1987). Socialization of sex roles within the family. In D. B. Carter (ed.), *Current Conceptions of Sex Roles and Sex Typing*. New York: Praeger.

Fantz, R. (1956). A method for studying early visual development. *Perceptual and Motor Skills*, 6, 13–15.

Farrington, D. P. (1991). Childhood aggression and adult violence: Early precursors and later-life outcomes. In D. J. Pepler and K. H. Rubin (eds), *The Development and Treatment of Childhood Aggression*. Hillsdale, NJ: Erlbaum.

Farver, J. A. M., & Howes, C. (1993). Cultural differences in American and Mexican mother–child pretend play. *Merrill-Palmer Quarterly*, 39, 344–58.

Fergusson, D. M., Horwood, L. J., & Lynskey, M. T. (1992). Family change, parental discord and early offending. *Journal of Child Psychology and Psychiatry*, 33, 1059–76.

Fernald, A., & Morikawa, H. (1993). Common themes and cultural variations in Japanese and American mothers' speech to infants. *Child Development*, 64, 637–56.

Field, T. (1994). The effects of mother's physical and emotional unavailability on emotion regulation. In N. A. Fox (ed.), The development of emotion regulation: Biological and behavioural regulation. *Monographs of the Society for Research in Child Development*, 59 (2–3, Serial No. 240).

Fivush, R. (1987). Scripts and categories: Interrelationships in development. In U. Neisser (ed.), *Concepts and Conceptual Development*. Cambridge: Cambridge University Press.

Flavell, J. H. (2002). Development of children's knowledge about the mental world. In W. W. Hartup & R. K. Silbereisen (eds), *Growing Points in Developmental Science*. Hove: Psychology Press.

Flavell, J. H., Green, F. L., & Flavell, E. R. (1995). Young children's knowledge about thinking. *Monographs of the Society for Research in Child Development*, 60 (1, Serial No. 243).

Flavell, J. H., Miller, P. H., & Miller, S. A. (1993). *Cognitive Development* (3rd edn). Englewood Cliffs, NJ: Prentice-Hall.

Fogel, A., & Melson, G. F. (1988). *Child Development*. St. Paul, MN: West Publishing.

Foot, H., & Howe, C. (1998). The psycho-educational basis of peer-assisted learning. In K. Topping & S. Ehly (eds), *Peer-assisted Learning*. Mahwah, NJ: Erlbaum.

Foot, H., Morgan, M. J., & Shute, R. H. (1990). *Children Helping Children*. Chichester: Wiley.

Freud, S. (1949). *An Outline of Psycho-Analysis*. London: Hogarth Press.

Freund, L. S. (1990). Maternal regulation of children's problem-solving behavior and its impact on children's performance. *Child Development*, 61, 113–26.

Fridlund, A. J. (1994). *Human Facial Expression: An Evolutionary View*. San Diego, CA: Academic Press.

Frijda, N. H. (1986). *The Emotions*. Cambridge: Cambridge University Press.

Frith, U. (1989). *Autism: Explaining the Enigma*. Oxford: Blackwell.

Furrow, D. (1984). Social and private speech at two years. *Child Development*, 55, 355–62.

Furth, H., & Kane, S. R. (1992). Children constructing society: A new perspective on children at play. In H. McGurk (ed.), *Childhood Social Development: Contemporary Perspectives*. Hove: Erlbaum.

Gallimore, R., Weisner, T., Kaufman, S., & Bernheimer, L. (1989). The social construction of ecocultural niches: Family accommodation of developmentally delayed children. *American Journal of Mental Retardation*, 94, 216–30.

Gardner, B. T., & Gardner, R. A. (1971). Two-way communication with an infant chimpanzee. In A. M. Schrier & F. Stollnitz (eds), *Behavior of Non-human Primates* (Vol. 4). New York: Academic Press.

Garner, P. W., Jones, D. C., & Miner, J. L. (1994). Social competence among low-income preschoolers: Emotion socialization practices and social cognitive correlates. *Child Development*, 65, 622–37.

Garner, P. W., & Spears, F. M. (2000). Emotion regulation in low-income preschoolers. *Social Development*, 9, 246–64.

Garvey, C. (1990). *Play*. London: Fontana.

Gathercole, S. E. (1998). The development of memory. *Journal of Child Psychology and Psychiatry*, 39, 3–28.

Gelman, R., & Gallistel, C. R. (1978). *The Child's Understanding of Number*. Cambridge, MA: Harvard University Press.

Goldberg, S. (2000). *Attachment and Development*. London: Arnold.

Goldfield, B. A., & Reznick, J. S. (1990). Early lexical acquisition: Rate, content and the vocabulary spurt. *Journal of Child Language*, 17, 171–83.

Goldin-Meadow, S., & Morford, M. (1985). Gesture in early child language: Studies of deaf and hearing children. *Merrill-Palmer Quarterly*, 31, 145–76.

Goleman, D. (1995). *Emotional Intelligence*. London: Bloomsbury.

Golombok, S. (2000). *Parenting: What Really Counts?* London: Routledge.

Golombok, S., Cook, R., Bish, A., & Murray, C. (1995). Families created by the new reproductive technologies: Quality of parenting and social and emotional development of the children. *Child Development*, 66, 285–9.

Golombok, S., & Fivush, R. (1994). *Gender Development*. Cambridge: Cambridge University Press.

Golombok, S., MacCallum, F., & Goodman, E. (2001). The 'test tube' generation: Parent–child relationships and the psychological well-being of *in vitro* fertilization children at adolescence. *Child Development*, 72, 599–608.

Golombok, S., Murray, C., Brinsden, P., & Abdalla, H. (1999). Social versus biological parenting: Family functioning and socioemotional development of children conceived by egg or sperm donation. *Journal of Child Psychology and Psychiatry*, 40, 519–27.

Goodman, R. (1991). Developmental disorders and structural brain development. In M. Rutter & P. Casaer (eds), *Biological Risk Factors for Psychosocial Disorders*. Cambridge: Cambridge University Press.

Gopnik, A., & Sobel, D. (2000). Detecting blickets: How young children use information about novel causal powers in categorization and induction. *Child Development*, 71, 1205–22.

Gottfried, A. E., Gottfried, A. W., & Bathurst, K. (2002). Maternal and dual-earner employment status and parenting. In M. H. Bornstein (ed.), *Handbook of Parenting* (Vol. 2, 2nd edn). Mahwah, NJ: Erlbaum.

Graham, S., & Juvonen, J. (1998). Self-blame and peer victimization in middle school: An attributional analysis. *Developmental Psychology*, 34, 587–99.

Greenfield, P. (ed.) (1994). Effects of interactive entertainment technologies on development. *Developmental Psychology* (Special Issue), 15 (1).

Greenough, W. T., Black, J. E., & Wallace, C. S. (1987). Experience and brain development. *Child Development*, 58, 539–59.

Grice, H. P. (1975). Logic and conversation. In P. Cole & J. Morgan (eds), *Speech Acts: Syntax and Semantics* (Vol. 3). New York: Academic Press.

Haden, C. A., Ornstein, P. A., Eckerman, C. O., & Didow, S. M. (2001). Mother–child conversational interactions as events unfold: Linkages to subsequent remembering. *Child Development*, 72, 1016–31.

Hainline, L. (1998). The development of bias visual abilities. In A. Slater (ed.), *Perceptual Development: Visual, Auditory and Speech Perception in Infancy*. Hove: Psychology Press.

Haith, M. M. (1980). *Rules that Babies Look By*. Hillsdale, NJ: Erlbaum.

Halberstadt, A. G., Denham, S. A., & Dunsmore, J. C. (2001). Affective social competence. *Social Development*, 10, 79–119.

Harkness, S., & Super, C. M. (1992). Parental ethnotheories in action. In I. E. Sigel, A. V. McGillicuddy-DeLisi & J. J. Goodnow (eds), *Parental Belief Systems: The Psychological Consequences for Children* (2nd edn). Hillsdale, NJ: Erlbaum.

Harris, J. R. (1998). *The Nurture Assumption: Why Children Turn Out the Way They Do*. New York: Free Press.

Harris, M., & Hatano, G. (eds) (1999). *Learning to Read and Write: A Cross-linguistic Perspective*. Cambridge: Cambridge University Press.

Harris, P. (1989). *Children and Emotion*. Oxford: Blackwell.

Harris, P. (2000). *The Work of the Imagination.* Oxford: Blackwell.

Harris, T., Brown, G., & Bifulco, A. (1986). Loss of parent in childhood and adult psychiatric disorder: The role of lack of adequate parental care. *Psychological Medicine*, 16, 641–59.

Harter, S. (1987). The determinants and mediational role of global self-worth in children. In N. Eisenberg (ed.), *Contemporary Topics in Developmental Psychology.* New York: Wiley.

Harter, S. (1998). The development of self-representations. In W. Damon (ed.), N. Eisenberg (vol. ed.), *Handbook of Child Psychology* (Vol. 3). New York: Wiley.

Harter, S. (1999). *The Construction of the Self: A Developmental Perspective.* New York: Guilford Press.

Hartup, W. W. (1989). Social relationships and their developmental significance. *American Psychologist*, 44, 120–6.

Hawker, D. J. S., & Boulton, M. J. (2000). Twenty years' research on peer victimization and psychosocial maladjustment: A meta-analytic review of cross-sectional studies. *Journal of Child Psychology and Psychiatry*, 41, 441–55.

Heinicke, C. M. (2002). The transition to parenting. In M. H. Bornstein (ed.), *Handbook of Parenting* (Vol. 3, 2nd edn). Mahwah, NJ: Erlbaum.

Hetherington, E. M. (ed.) (1999). *Coping with Divorce, Single Parenting and Remarriage: A Risk and Resiliency Perspective.* Mahwah, NJ: Erlbaum.

Hetherington, E. M., & Stanley-Hagan, M. (1999). The adjustment of children with divorced parents: A risk and resiliency perspective. *Journal of Child Psychology and Psychiatry*, 40, 129–40.

Hinde, R. A. (1979). *Towards Understanding Relationships.* London: Academic Press.

Hinde, R. A. (1992). Human social development: An ethological/relationship perspective. In H. McGurk (ed.), *Childhood Social Development: Contemporary Perspectives.* Hillsdale, NJ: Erlbaum.

Hinde, R. A. (1997). *Relationships: A Dialectical Perspective.* Hove: Psychology Press.

Hoddap, R. M. (2002). Parenting children with mental retardation. In M. H. Bornstein (ed.), *Handbook of Parenting* (Vol. 1, 2nd edn). Mahwah, NJ: Erlbaum.

Hodges, J., & Tizard, B. (1989). Social and family relationships of ex-institutional adolescents. *Journal of Child Psychology and Psychiatry*, 30, 77–98.

Holloway, S. D., & Machida, S. (1992). Maternal child-rearing beliefs and coping strategies: Consequences for divorced mothers and their children. In I. E. Sigel, A. V. McGillicuddy-DeLisi & J. J. Goodnow (eds), *Parental Belief Systems: The Psychological Consequences for Children* (2nd edn). Hillsdale, NJ: Erlbaum.

Howe, C. (1993). Peer interaction and knowledge acquisition. *Social Development* (Special Issue), 2 (3).

Hudson, J. A. (1990). The emergence of autobiographical memory in mother–child conversations. In R. Fivush & J. A. Hudson (eds), *Knowing and Remembering in Young Children.* New York: Cambridge University Press.

Huesmann, L. R., Eron, L. D., & Lefkowitz, M. M. (1984). Stability of aggression over time and generations. *Developmental Psychology*, 20, 1120–34.

Hughes, C., & Leekam, S. (in press). What are the links between theory of mind and social relations? Review, reflections and new directions for studies of typical and atypical development. *Social Development.*

Hytten, F. E. (1976). Metabolic adaptation of pregnancy in the prevention of handicap through antenatal care. In A. C. Turnbull & F. P. Woodford (eds), *Review of Research Practice 18.* Amsterdam: Elsevier.

Inagaki, K., & Hatano, G. (1996). Young children's recognition of commonalities between animals and plants. *Child Development*, 67, 2823–4.

Izard, C. E. (1979). *The Maximally Discriminative Facial Movement Coding System (MAX)*. Newark, DE: University of Delaware Press.

Johnson, J. S., & Newport, E. L. (1989). Critical period effects in second language learning: The influence of instructional state on the acquisition of English as a second language. *Cognitive Psychology*, 21, 60–99.

Johnson, M. H., & Morton, J. (1991). *Biology and Cognitive Development: The Case of Face Recognition*. Oxford: Blackwell.

Kagan, J., Reznick, J. S., & Snidman, N. (1988). Biological bases of childhood shyness. *Science*, 240, 167–71.

Kagan, J., Snidman, N., & Arcus, D. (1998). Childhood derivatives of high and low reactivity in infancy. *Child Development*, 69, 1483–93.

Kearins, J. M. (1981). Visual spatial memory in Australian Aboriginal children of desert regions. *Cognitive Psychology*, 13, 434–60.

Kearins, J. M. (1986). Visual spatial memory in Aboriginal and white Australian children. *Australian Journal of Psychology*, 38, 203–14.

Keenan, E. O. (1974). Conversational competence in children. *Journal of Child Language*, 1, 163–83.

Kessen, W. (1965). *The Child*. New York: Wiley.

Klahr, D., & MacWhinney, B. (1998). Information processing. In W. Damon (ed.), D. Kuhn & R. S. Siegler (vol. eds), *Handbook of Child Psychology* (Vol. 2). New York: Wiley.

Kleinfeld, J. (1971). Visual memory in village Eskimos and urban Caucasian children. *Arctic*, 24, 132–7.

Klima, E., & Bellugi, U. (1979). *The Signs of Language*. Cambridge, MA: Harvard University Press.

Kohlberg, L. (1966). A cognitive developmental analysis of children's sex-role concepts and attitudes. In E. E. Maccoby (ed.), *The Development of Sex Differences*. Stanford, CA: Stanford University Press.

Kontos, S., & Nicholas, J. G. (1986). Independent problem solving in the development of metacognition. *Journal of Genetic Psychology*, 147, 481–95.

Kuczaj, S. A. (1978). Why do children fail to overregularize the progressive inflection? *Journal of Child Language*, 5, 167–71.

Kuebli, J., Butler, S., & Fivush, R. (1995). Mother–child talk about past emotions: Relations of maternal language and child gender over time. *Cognition and Emotion*, 9, 265–83.

Kuhn, D. (2000). Does memory belong to an endangered topic list? *Child Development*, 71, 21–5.

Ladd, G. W. (1992). Themes and theories: Perspectives on processes in family–peer relationships. In R. D. Parke & G. W. Ladd (eds), *Family–Peer Relationships: Modes of Linkage*. Hillsdale, NJ: Erlbaum.

LaFreniere, P., Strayer, F. F., & Gaulthier, R. (1984). The emergence of same-sex affiliative preferences among preschool peers: A developmental/etiological perspective. *Child Development*, 55, 1958–65.

Landry, S. H., & Chapieski, M. L. (1989). Joint attention and infant toy exploration: Effects of Down syndrome and prematurity. *Child Development*, 60, 103–18.

Landry, S. H., Smith, K. E., Swank, P. R., & Miller-Loncar, C. L. (2000). Early maternal and child influences on children's later independent cognitive and social functioning. *Child Development*, 71, 358–75.

Lazar, A., & Torney-Purta, J. (1991). The development of the subconcepts of death in young children. *Child Development*, 62, 1321–33.

Leaper, C. (1994). Exploring the consequences of gender segregation on social relationships. In C. Leaper (ed.), *Childhood Gender Segregation: Causes and Consequences*. San Francisco: Jossey-Bass.

Lecanuet, J.-P. (1998). Foetal responses to auditory and speech stimuli. In A. Slater (ed.), *Perceptual Development: Visual, Auditory and Speech Perception in Infancy*. Hove: Psychology Press.

Lempers, J. D., Flavell, E. R., & Flavell, J. H. (1977). The development in very young children of tacit knowledge concerning visual perception. *Genetic Psychology Monographs*, 95, 3–53.

Lenneberg, E. H. (1967). *Biological Foundations of Language*. New York: Wiley.

LeVine, R., Dixon, S., LeVine, S., Richman, A., Leiderman, P. H., Keefer, C. H., & Brazelton, T. B. (1994). *Child Care and Culture: Lessons from Africa*. Cambridge: Cambridge University Press.

Lewis, M. (1992). *Shame: The Exposed Self*. New York: Free Press.

Lewis, M., Alessandri, S. M., & Sullivan, M. W. (1990). Violations of expectancy, loss of control and anger expressions in young infants. *Developmental Psychology*, 26, 745–51.

Lewis, M., Alessandri, S. M., & Sullivan, M. W. (1992). Differences in shame and pride as a function of children's gender and task difficulty. *Child Development*, 63, 630–8.

Lewis, M., & Brooks-Gunn, J. (1979). *Social Cognition and the Acquisition of Self*. New York: Plenum.

Light, P. (1997). Computers for learning: Psychological perspectives. *Journal of Child Psychology and Psychiatry*, 38, 497–504.

Littleton, K., & Light, P. (eds) (1998). *Learning with Computers: Analysing Productive Interaction*. London: Routledge.

Livesley, W. J., & Bromley, D. B. (1973). *Person Perception in Childhood and Adolescence*. London: Wiley.

Locke, J. L. (1993). *The Child's Path to Spoken Language*. Cambridge, MA: Harvard University Press.

Loehlin, J. C. (1992). *Genes and Environment in Personality Development*. Newbury Park, CA: Sage.

Lukeman, D., & Melvin, D. (1993). The preterm infant: Psychological issues in childhood. *Journal of Child Psychology and Psychiatry*, 34, 837–50.

Luquet, G. H. (1927). *Le Dessin Enfantin*. Paris: Aléan.

Luria, A. R. (1961). *The Role of Speech in the Regulation of Normal and Abnormal Behavior*. New York: Liveright.

Lutz, C. (1987). Goals, events and understanding in Ifaluk emotion theory. In D. Holland & N. Quinn (eds), *Cultural Models in Language and Thought*. Cambridge: Cambridge University Press.

McCall, R. B., & Carriger, M. S. (1993). A meta-analysis of infant habituation and recognition memory performance as predictors of later IQ. *Child Development*, 64, 57–79.

Maccoby, E. E. (1990). Gender and relationships. *American Psychologist*, 45, 513–20.

Maccoby, E. E. (1998). *The Two Sexes: Growing up Apart, Coming Together*. Cambridge, MA: Harvard University Press.

Maccoby, E. E., & Jacklin, C. N. (1974). *The Psychology of Sex Differences*. Stanford, CA: Stanford University Press.

McFarlane, A. H., Bellissimo, A., & Norman, G. R. (1995). Family structure, family functioning and adolescent well-being: The transcendent influence of parental style. *Journal of Child Psychology and Psychiatry*, 36, 847–64.

McGarrigle, J., & Donaldson, M. (1974). Conservation accidents. *Cognition*, 3, 341–50.

McLane, J. B., & McNamee, G. D. (1990). *Early Literacy.* London: Fontana; Cambridge, MA: Harvard University Press.

McLaughlin, M. M. (1974). Survivors and surrogates: Children and parents from the ninth to the thirteenth century. In L. DeMause (ed.), *The History of Childhood.* New York: Psychohistory Press.

McShane, J. (1991). *Cognitive Development.* Oxford: Blackwell.

Magnusson, D., & Bergman, L. R. (1990). A pattern approach to the study of pathways from childhood to adulthood. In L. N. Robins & M. Rutter (eds), *Straight and Devious Pathways from Childhood to Adulthood.* Cambridge: Cambridge University Press.

Main, M., Kaplan, N., & Cassidy, J. (1985). Security in infancy, childhood and adulthood: A move to the level of representation. In I. Bretherton & E. Waters (eds), Growing points of attachment theory and research. *Monographs of the Society for Research in Child Development,* 50 (1–2, Serial No. 209).

Malatesta, C. Z., Culver, C., Tesman, J. R., & Shepard, B. (1989). The development of emotion expression during the first two years of life. *Monographs of the Society for Research in Child Development,* 54 (1–2, Serial No. 219).

Marfo, K. (1988). *Parent–Child Interaction and Developmental Disabilities.* New York: Praeger.

Markman, E. M. (1989). *Categorization and Naming in Children: Problems of Induction.* Cambridge: Cambridge University Press.

Marsh, H. W., Craven, R., & Debus, R. (1998). Structure, stability and development of young children's self-concepts: A multicohort, multioccasion study. *Child Development,* 69, 1030–53.

Martin, C. A., & Johnson, J. E. (1992). Children's self-perceptions and mothers' beliefs about development and competences. In I. E. Sigel, A. V. McGillicuddy-DeLisi & J. J. Goodnow (eds), *Parental Belief Systems: The Psychological Consequences for Children* (2nd edn). Hillsdale, NJ: Erlbaum.

Masataka, N. (1993). Motherese is a signed language. *Infant Behavior and Development,* 15, 453–60.

Mead, M. (1935). *Sex and Temperament in Three Primitive Societies.* New York: William Morrow.

Mead, M., & Newton, N. (1967). Cultural patterning of perinatal behaviour. In S. A. Richardson & A. F. Guttmacher (eds), *Childbearing: Its Social and Psychological Aspects.* New York: Williams & Wilkins.

Mesquita, B., & Frijda, N. H. (1992). Cultural variations in emotions: A review. *Psychological Bulletin,* 112, 179–204.

Messer, D. J. (1994). *The Development of Communication: From Social Interaction to Language.* Chichester: Wiley.

Millar, S. (1975). Visual experience or translation rules? Drawing the human figure by blind and sighted children. *Perception,* 4, 363–71.

Miller, P. H. (2002). *Theories of Developmental Psychology* (4th edn). New York: W. H. Freeman.

Miller, P. H., & Aloise, P. A. (1989). Young children's understanding of the psychological causes of behavior: A review. *Child Development,* 60, 257–85.

Miller, S. A. (1998). *Developmental Research Methods* (2nd edn). Englewood Cliffs, NJ: Prentice-Hall.

Minushin, P. (1988). Relationships within the family: A systems perspective on development. In R. A. Hinde & J. Stevenson-Hinde (eds), *Relationships Within Families.* Oxford: Clarendon Press.

Moffitt, T. E., Caspi, A., Dickson, N., Silva, P. S., & Stanton, W. (1996). Childhood-onset versus adolescent-onset antisocial conduct problems in males: Natural history from ages 3 to 18 years. *Development and Psychopathology,* 8, 399–424.

Molfese, V. J., & Molfese, D. L. (eds) (2000). *Temperament and Personality Development across the Life Span*. Mahwah, NJ: Erlbaum.

Money, J., & Ehrhardt, A. A. (1972). *Man and Woman/Boy and Girl*. Baltimore: Johns Hopkins University Press.

Moon, C., & Fifer, W. P. (1990). Newborns prefer a prenatal version of mother's voice. *Infant Behavior and Development*, 13, 530.

Moon, C., Panneton-Cooper, R. P., & Fifer, W. P. (1993). Two-day-olds prefer their native language. *Infant Behavior and Development*, 495–500.

Moore, C., & Dunham, P. (eds) (1995). *Joint Attention: Its Origins and Role in Development*. Mahwah, NJ: Erlbaum.

Moore, C., & Lemmon, K. (eds) (2001). *The Self in Time: Developmental Perspectives*. Mahwah, NJ: Erlbaum.

Moss, E., Gosselin, C., Parent, S., Rousseau, D., & Dumont, M. (1997). Attachment and joint problem-solving experiences during the preschool period. *Social Development*, 6, 1–17.

Murphy, B., & Eisenberg, N. (1997). Young children's emotionality, regulation and social functioning and their responses when they are targets of a peer's anger. *Social Development*, 6, 18–36.

Murphy, C. M. (1978). Pointing in the context of a shared activity. *Child Development*, 49, 371–80.

Murray, L., Hipwell, A., Hooper, R., Stein, A., & Cooper, P. J. (1996). The cognitive development of 5-year-old children of postnatally depressed mothers. *Journal of Child Psychology and Psychiatry*, 37, 927–35.

Murray, L., Sinclair, D., Cooper, P., Ducournau, P., Turner, P., & Stein, A. (1999). The socio-emotional development of 5-year-old children of postnatally depressed mothers. *Journal of Child Psychology and Psychiatry*, 40, 1259–72.

Nelson, C. A., & Bloom, F. E. (1997). Child development and neuroscience. *Child Development*, 68, 970–87.

Nelson, K. (1978). How children represent knowledge of their world in and out of language. In R. S. Siegler (ed.), *Children's Thinking: What Develops?* Hillsdale, NJ: Erlbaum.

Nelson, K. (ed.) (1986). *Event Knowledge: Structure and Function in Development*. Hillsdale, NJ: Erlbaum.

Nelson, K. (1989). *Narratives from the Crib*. Cambridge, MA: Harvard University Press.

Nelson, K. (1993). The psychological and social origins of autobiographical memory. *Psychological Science*, 4, 7–14.

Nelson, K. (2000). Socialization of memory. In E. Tulving & F. I. M. Craik (eds), *The Oxford Handbook of Memory*. Oxford: Oxford University Press.

Nelson, K., & Gruendel, J. (1981). Generalized event representations: Basic building blocks of cognitive development. In M. E. Lamb & A. L. Brown (eds), *Advances in Developmental Psychology* (Vol. 1). Hillsdale, NJ: Erlbaum.

Newport, E. L. (1990). Maturational constraints on language learning. *Cognitive Science*, 14, 11–28.

Newson, J., & Newson, E. (1974). Cultural aspects of childrearing in the English-speaking world. In M. P. M. Richards (ed.), *The Integration of a Child into a Social World*. Cambridge: Cambridge University Press.

Newton, M. (2002). *Savage Girls and Wild Boys: A History of Feral Children*. London: Faber.

Nicolich, L. M. (1977). Beyond sensori-motor intelligence: Assessment of symbolic maturity through analysis of pretend play. *Merrill-Palmer Quarterly*, 23, 89–100.

Nunes, T., & Bryant, P. (1996). *Children Doing Mathematics*. Oxford: Blackwell.

Oakhill, J. (1995). Development in reading. In V. Lee & P. D. Gupta (eds), *Children's Cognitive and Language Development*. Milton Keynes: Open University Press.

Oates, J. (1994). *Foundations of Child Development*. Oxford: Blackwell.

Ochs, E. (1982). Talking to children in Western Samoa. *Language in Society*, 11, 77–104.

Ochs, E., & Schieffelin, B. B. (1984). Language acquisition and socialization: Three developmental stories and their implications. In R. Shweder & R. LeVine (eds), *Culture Theory*. Cambridge: Cambridge University Press.

O'Connor, T. G., & the English and Romanian Adoptees Study Team (2000). The effects of global and severe privation on cognitive competence: Extension and longitudinal follow-up. *Child Development*, 71, 376–90.

O'Connor, T. G., Thorpe, K., Dunn, J., & the ALSPAC Study Team (1999). Parental divorce and adjustment in adulthood: Findings from a community sample. *Journal of Child Psychology and Psychiatry*, 40, 777–90.

Olson, H. C., Streissguth, A. P., Sampson, P. D., Barr, H. M., Bookstein, F. L., & Thiede, K. (1997). Association of prenatal alcohol exposure with behavioral and learning problems in early adolescence. *Journal of the American Academy of Child and Adolescent Psychiatry*, 36, 1187–94.

Parke, R. D. (2002). Fathers and families. In M. H. Bornstein (ed.), *Handbook of Parenting* (Vol. 3, 2nd edn). Mahwah, NJ: Erlbaum.

Parke, R. D., & Ladd, G. W. (eds) (1992). *Family–Peer Relationships: Modes of Linkage*. Hillsdale, NJ: Erlbaum.

Pederson, N. L., Plomin, R., Nesselroade, J. R., & McClearn, G. E. (1992). A quantitative genetic analysis of cognitive ability during the second half of the life span. *Psychological Science*, 3, 346–53.

Perry, D. G., Perry, L. C., & Kennedy, E. (1992). Conflict and the development of antisocial behavior. In C. U. Shantz & W. W. Hartup (eds), *Conflict in Child and Adolescent Development*. Cambridge: Cambridge University Press.

Piaget, J. (1926). *Judgment and Reasoning in the Child*. New York: Harcourt Brace Jovanovich.

Piaget, J. (1929). *The Child's Conception of the World*. New York: Harcourt Brace Jovanovich.

Piaget, J. (1951). *Play, Dreams, and Imitation in Childhood*. London: Routledge & Kegan Paul.

Piaget, J. (1953). *The Origins of Intelligence in the Child*. London: Routledge & Kegan Paul.

Piaget, J. (1954). *The Construction of Reality in the Child*. New York: Basic Books.

Pinker, S. (1994). *The Language Instinct: The New Science of Language and Mind*. London: Allen Lane.

Pinker, S. (2002). *The Blank Slate: The Modern Denial of Human Nature*. London: Allen Lane.

Plomin, R. (1990). *Nature and Nurture: An Introduction to Human Behavioral Genetics*. Pacific Grove, CA: Brooks/Cole.

Plomin, R., DeFries, J. C., McClearn, G. E., & Rutter, M. (1997). *Behavioral Genetics* (3rd edn). New York: W. H. Freeman.

Price-Williams, D., Gordon, W., & Ramirez, M. (1969). Skill and conservation: A study of pottery-making children. *Developmental Psychology*, 16, 769.

Putnam, S. P., Sanson, A. V., & Rothbart, M. K. (2002). In M. H. Bornstein (ed.), *Handbook of Parenting* (Vol. 1, 2nd edn). Mahwah, NJ: Erlbaum.

Pye, C. (1986). Quiche Mayan speech to children. *Journal of Child Language*, 13, 85–100.

Quinn, P. C., & Eimas, P. D. (1996). Perceptual organization and categorization in young infants. In C. Rovee-Collier & L. P. Lipsitt (eds), *Advances in Infancy Research* (Vol. 10). Norwood, NJ: Ablex.

Quinn, P. C., Slater, A. M., Brown, E., & Hayes, R. A. (2001). Developmental change in form categorization in early infancy. *British Journal of Developmental Psychology*, 19, 207–18.

Radke-Yarrow, M. (1998). *Children of Depressed Mothers: From Early Childhood to Maturity*. Cambridge: Cambridge University Press.

Rank, O. (1929). *The Trauma of Birth*. New York: Harcourt Brace.

Ratner, N. B. (1996). From 'signal to syntax': But what is the nature of the signal? In J. L. Morgan & K. Demuth (eds), *Signals to Syntax: Bootstrapping from Speech to Grammar in Early Acquisition*. Mahwah, NJ: Erlbaum.

Reese, E. (2002). Autobiographical memory development: The state of the art. *Social Development*, 11, 124–42.

Robins, L. N. (1966). *Deviant Children Grown Up*. Baltimore: Williams & Wilkins.

Rodgers, B., Power, C., & Hope, S. (1997). Parental divorce and adult psychological distress: Evidence from a national birth cohort. *Journal of Child Psychology and Psychiatry*, 38, 867–72.

Rogoff, B. (1990). *Apprenticeship in Thinking: Cognitive Development in Social Context*. New York: Oxford University Press.

Rogoff, B., Mistry, J., Goncu, A., & Mosier, C. (1993). Guided participation in cultural activity by toddlers and caregivers. *Monographs of the Society for Research in Child Development*, 58 (8, Serial No. 236).

Rollins, P., & Snow, C. (1999). Shared attention and grammatical development in typical children and children with autism. *Journal of Child Language*, 25, 653–74.

Rosch, E., Mervis, C. B., Gray, W. D., Johnson, D. M., & Boyes-Braem, P. (1976). Basic objects in natural categories. *Cognitive Psychology*, 8, 382–439.

Rosengren, K. S., Gelman, S. A., Kalish, C. W., & McCormick, M. (1991). As time goes by: Children's early understanding of growth in animals. *Child Development*, 62, 1302–20.

Rothbart, M. K., Ahadi, S. A., Hershey, K. L., & Fisher, P. (2001). Investigations of temperament at three to seven years: The children's behavior questionnaire. *Child Development*, 72, 1394–408.

Rothbart, M. K., & Bates, J. E. (1998). Temperament. In W. Damon (ed.), N. Eisenberg (vol. ed.), *Handbook of Child Psychology* (Vol. 3). New York: Wiley.

Rowe, D. C. (1993). Genetic perspectives on personality. In R. Plomin & G. E. McClearn (eds), *Nature, Nurture and Psychology*. Washington, DC: American Psychological Association.

Rubin, J. S., Provenza, F. J., & Luria, Z. (1974). The eye of the beholder: Parents' views on sex of newborns. *American Journal of Orthopsychiatry*, 5, 353–63.

Rubin, K. H. (guest ed.) (1994). From family to peer group: Relations between relationship systems. *Social Development* (Special Issue), 3 (3).

Rubin, K. H. (1998). Social and emotional development from a cultural perspective. *Developmental Psychology*, 34, 611–15.

Rubin, K. H., Bukowski, W. M., & Parker, J. G. (1998). Peer interactions, relationships, and groups. In W. Damon (ed.), N. Eisenberg (vol. ed.), *Handbook of Child Psychology* (Vol. 3). New York: Wiley.

Rubin, K. H., Fein, G. G., & Vandenberg, B. (1983). Play. In E. M. Hetherington (ed.), *Child Psychology* (Vol. 4). New York: Wiley.

Ruble, D. N., & Martin, C. L. (1998). Gender development. In W. Damon (ed.), N. Eisenberg (vol. ed.), *Handbook of Child Psychology* (Vol. 3). New York: Wiley.

Russell, J. A. (1994). Is there universal recognition of emotion from facial expression? A review of methods and studies. *Psychological Bulletin*, 115, 102–41.

Rutter, M. (1999). Autism: A two-way interplay between research and clinical work. *Journal of Child Psychology and Psychiatry*, 40, 169–88.

Rutter, M. (2002). Nature, nurture and development: From evangelism through science toward policy and practice. *Child Development*, 73, 1–21.

Rutter, M., & the English and Romanian Adoptees Study Team (1998). Developmental catch-up and deficit following adoption after severe global early privation. *Journal of Child Psychology and Psychiatry*, 39, 465–76.

Rutter, M., Giller, H., & Hagel, A. (1999). *Antisocial Behaviour by Young People*. Cambridge: Cambridge University Press.

Rutter, M., Quinton, D., & Hill, J. (1990). Adult outcome of institution-reared children: Males and females compared. In L. N. Robins & M. Rutter (eds), *Straight and Devious Pathways from Childhood to Adulthood*. Cambridge: Cambridge University Press.

Rutter, M., & Rutter, M. (1993). *Developing Minds*. London: Penguin.

Rutter, M., Silberg, J., O'Connor, T., & Simonoff, E. (1999). Genetics and child psychiatry: I. Advances in quantitative and molecular genetics. *Journal of Child Psychology and Psychiatry*, 40, 3–18.

Rymer, R. (1994). *Genie: A Scientific Tragedy*. London: Penguin.

Saarni, C. (1984). An observational study of children's attempts to monitor their expressive behavior. *Child Development*, 55, 1504–31.

Saarni, C. (1999). *The Development of Emotional Competence*. New York: Guilford Press.

Sameroff, A. J., & Chandler, M. J. (1975). Reproductive risk and the continuum of care-taking casualty. In F. D. Horowitz (ed.), *Review of Child Development Research* (Vol. 4). Chicago: University of Chicago Press.

Sander, L. W., Stechler, G., Burns, P., & Lee, A. (1979). Change in infant and caregiver variables over the first two months of life. In E. B. Thomas (ed.), *Origins of the Infant's Social Responsiveness*. Hillsdale, NJ: Erlbaum.

Savage-Rumbaugh, E. S., Murphy, J., Sevcik, R. A., Brakke, K. E., Williams, S. L., & Rumbaugh, D. M. (1993). Language comprehension in ape and child. *Monographs of the Society for Research in Child Development*, 58 (3–4, Serial No. 233).

Saxe, G. B., Guberman, S. R., & Gearhart, M. (1987). Social processes in early number development. *Monographs of the Society for Research in Child Development*, 52 (2, Serial No. 216).

Schaffer, H. R. (1974). Cognitive components of the infant's response to strangers. In M. Lewis & L. A. Rosenblum (eds), *The Origins of Fear*. New York: Wiley.

Schaffer, H. R. (1984). *The Child's Entry into a Social World*. London: Academic Press.

Schaffer, H. R. (1998). *Making Decisions about Children: Psychological Questions and Answers* (2nd edn). Oxford: Blackwell.

Schaffer, H. R. (2002). The early experience assumption: Past, present and future. In W. Hartup & R. Silbereisen (eds), *Growing Points in Developmental Science: An Introduction*. Hove: Psychology Press.

Schieffelin, B. B., & Ochs, E. (1983). A cultural perspective on the transition from prelinguistic to linguistic communication. In R. M. Golinkoff (ed.), *The Transition from Prelinguistic to Linguistic Communication*. Hillsdale, NJ: Erlbaum.

Scollon, R. (1976). *Conversations with a One-year-old*. Honolulu: University Press of Hawaii.

Searle, J. R. (1984). *Minds, Brains and Science*. London: Penguin.

Selman, R. (1980). *The Growth of Interpersonal Understanding*. New York: Academic Press.

Senechal, M., & LeFevre, J.-A. (2002). Parental involvement in the development of children's reading skills: A five-year longitudinal study. *Child Development*, 73, 445–60.

Shatz, M., & Gelman, R. (1973). The development of communication skills: Modifications in the speech of young children as a function of listener. *Monographs of the Society for Research in Child Development*, 38 (5, Serial No. 152).

Shimizu, H., & LeVine, R. A. (eds) (2001). *Japanese Frames of Mind: Cultural Perspectives on Human Development*. Cambridge: Cambridge University Press.

Shirley, M. M. (1933). *The First Two Years: A Study of Twenty-five Babies*. Vol. 2: *Intellectual Development*. Minneapolis: University of Minnesota Press.

Shostak, M. (1981). *Nissa: The Life and Words of a !Kung Woman*. Cambridge, MA: Harvard University Press.

Siegler, R. S. (1998). *Children's Thinking* (3rd edn). Upper Saddle River, NJ: Prentice-Hall.

Sigel, I. E., & McGillicuddy-DeLisi, A. V. (2002). Parental beliefs and cognitions. In M. H. Bornstein (ed.), *Handbook of Parenting* (Vol. 3, 2nd edn). Mahwah, NJ: Erlbaum.

Sinclair, D., & Murray, L. (1998). Effects of postnatal depression on children's adjustment to school: Teachers' reports. *British Journal of Psychiatry*, 172, 58–63.

Skinner, B. F. (1957). *Verbal Behavior*. New York: Appleton-Century-Crofts.

Slater, A., Carrick, R., Bell, C., & Roberts, E. (1999). Can measures of infant information processing predict later intellectual ability? In A. Slater & D. Muir (eds), *The Blackwell Reader in Developmental Psychology*. Oxford: Blackwell.

Slee, P. T., & Rigby, K. (eds) (1998). *Children's Peer Relations*. London: Routledge.

Slobin, D. I. (1986). Cross-linguistic evidence for the language-making capacity. In D. I. Slobin (ed.), *The Cross-linguistic Study of Language Acquisition*. Hillsdale, NJ: Erlbaum.

Snow, C. (1977). The development of conversation between mothers and babies. *Journal of Child Language*, 4, 1–22.

Snow, C. (1989). Understanding social interaction and language acquisition: Sentences are not enough. In M. H. Bornstein & J. S. Bruner (eds), *Interaction in Human Development*. Hillsdale, NJ: Erlbaum.

Snow, C., & Ferguson, C. A. (1977). *Talking to Children: Language Input and Acquisition*. Cambridge: Cambridge University Press.

Snow, C., & Ninio, A. (1986). The contracts of literacy: What children learn from learning to read books. In W. H. Teale & E. Sulzby (eds), *Emergent Literacy: Writing and Reading*. Norwood, NJ: Ablex.

Snow, M. E., Jacklin, C. N., & Maccoby, E. E. (1983). Sex-of-child differences in father–child interaction at one year of age. *Child Development*, 54, 227–52.

Sollie, D., & Miller, B. (1980). The transition to parenthood at a critical time for building family strengths. In N. Stinnet & P. Knaub (eds), *Family Strengths: Positive Models of Family Life*. Lincoln: University of Nebraska Press.

Spock, B. (1948). *Baby and Child Care*. New York: Duell, Sloan & Pearce.

Sroufe, A. (1979). The coherence of individual development. *American Psychologist*, 34, 834–41.

Sroufe, L. A. (1996). *Emotional Development*. Cambridge: Cambridge University Press.

Sroufe, L. A., Egeland, B., & Carlson, E. A. (1999). One social world: The integrated development of parent–child and peer relationships. In W. A. Collins & B. Laursen (eds), *Relationships as Developmental Contexts. Minnesota Symposia on Child Psychology* (Vol. 30). Mahwah, NJ: Erlbaum.

Stern, M., & Karraker, K. H. (1989). Sex stereotyping of infants: A review of gender labelling studies. *Sex Roles*, 20, 501–22.

Stipek, D., Recchia, S., & McClintic, S. (1992). Self-evaluation in young children. *Monographs of the Society for Research in Child Development*, 57 (1, Serial No. 226).

Streissguth, A. P., Barr, M. H., & Sampson, P. D. (1990). Moderate prenatal alcohol exposure: Effects on child IQ and learning problems at age 7.5 years. *Alcoholism: Clinical and Experimental Research*, 14, 662–9.

Tamis-LeMonda, C. S., Bornstein, M. H., & Baumwell, L. (2001). Maternal responsiveness and children's achievements of language milestones. *Child Development*, 72, 748–67.

Tanner, J. M. (1962). *Growth at Adolescence*. Oxford: Blackwell.

Tardiff, T. (1996). Nouns are not always learned before verbs: Evidence from Mandarin speakers' early vocabulary. *Developmental Psychology*, 32, 492–504.

Tessler, M., & Nelson, K. (1994). Making memories: The influence of joint encoding on later recall by young children. *Consciousness and Cognition*, 3, 307–26.

Tharp, R., & Gallimore, R. (1988). *Rousing Minds to Life: Teaching, Learning and Schooling in Social Context*. Cambridge: Cambridge University Press.

Thomas, A., & Chess, S. (1977). *Temperament and Development*. New York: Bremner/Mazel.

Thompson, R. A. (2000). The legacy of early attachments. *Child Development*, 71, 145–52.

Tizard, B. (1977). *Adoption: A Second Chance*. London: Open Books.

Tobin, J. J., Wu, Y. H., & Davidson, D. H. (1989). *Preschool in Three Cultures: Japan, China, and the United States*. New Haven, CT: Yale University Press.

Tomasello, M., Manule, S., & Kruger, A. C. (1986). Linguistic environment of one- to two-year-old twins. *Developmental Psychology*, 22, 169–76.

Tomasello, M., & Todd, J. (1983). Joint attention and lexical acquisition style. *First Language*, 4, 197–212.

Tremblay, R. E. (2002). The development of aggressive behaviour during childhood: What have we learned in the past century? In W. W. Hartup & R. K. Silbereisen (eds), *Growing Points in Developmental Science*. Hove: Psychology Press.

Triandis, H. C. (1995). *Individualism and Collectivism*. Boulder, CO: Westview Press.

Tronick, E. Z., Als, H., Adamson, L., Wise, S., & Brazelton, T. B. (1978). The infant's response to entrapment between contradictory messages in face-to-face interaction. *Journal of the American Academy of Child Psychiatry*, 17, 1–13.

Truby King, F. (1924). *The Expectant Mother and Baby's First Month, for Parents and Nurses*. London: Macmillan.

Tudge, J., & Winterhoff, P. (1993). Can young children benefit from collaborative problem solving? Tracing the effects of partner competence and feedback. *Social Development*, 2, 242–59.

Tulving, E., & Craik, F. I. M. (eds) (2000). *The Oxford Handbook of Memory*. Oxford: Oxford University Press.

van der Molen, M. W., & Ridderinkoff, K. R. (1998). The growing and aging brain: Life-span changes in brain and cognitive functioning. In A. Demetriou, W. Doise & C. F. M. van Lieshout (eds), *Life-span Developmental Psychology*. Chichester: Wiley.

van der Veer, R., & van IJzendoorn, M. H. (1988). Early childhood attachment and later problem solving: A Vygotskian perspective. In J. Valsiner (ed.), *Child Development within Culturally Structured Environments* (Vol. 1). Norwood, NJ: Ablex.

Vygotsky, L. S. (1956). *Selected Psychological Investigations*. Moscow: Izdatel'stvo Academii Pedagogicheskikh Nauk.

Vygotsky, L. S. (1962). *Thought and Language*. Cambridge, MA: MIT Press.

Vygotsky, L. S. (1978). *Mind in Society: The Development of Higher Psychological Processes*. Cambridge, MA: Harvard University Press.

Vygotsky, L. S. (1981a). The genesis of higher mental functions. In J. V. Wertsch (ed.), *The Concept of Activity in Soviet Psychology*. Armonk, NY: Sharpe.

Vygotsky, L. S. (1981b). The instrumental method in psychology. In J. V. Wertsch (ed.), *The Concept of Activity in Soviet Psychology*. Armonk, NY: Sharpe.

Vygotsky, L. S. (1987). Thinking and speech. In R. W. Rieber & A. S. Carton (eds), *The Collected Works of L. S. Vygotsky*. New York: Plenum.

Waldinger, R. J., Toth, S. L., & Gerber, A. (2001). Maltreatment and internal representations of relationships: Core relationship themes in the narratives of abused and neglected preschoolers. *Social Development*, 10, 41–58.

Warren, A. R., & Tate, C. S. (1992). Egocentrism in children's telephone conversations. In R. M. Diaz & L. E. Berk (eds), *Private Speech: From Social Interaction to Self-regulation*. Hillsdale, NJ: Erlbaum.

Waters, E., Merrick, S., Treboux, D., Crowell, J., & Albersheim, L. (2000). Attachment security in infancy and early adulthood: A twenty-year longitudinal study. *Child Development*, 71, 684–9.

Watson, J. B. (1925). *Behaviorism*. New York: People's Institute Publishing Company.

Weinraub, M., Hornath, D. L., & Gringlas, M. B. (2002). Single parenthood. In M. H. Bornstein (ed.), *Handbook of Parenting* (Vol. 3, 2nd edn). Mahwah, NJ: Erlbaum.

Wellman, H., Cross, D., & Watson, J. (2001). Meta-analysis of theory-of-mind development: The truth about false belief. *Child Development*, 72, 655–84.

Wellman, H., & Estes, D. (1986). Early understanding of mental entities: A re-examination of childhood realism. *Child Development*, 57, 910–23.

Wells, G. (1985). *Language Development in the Preschool Years*. Cambridge: Cambridge University Press.

Wertsch, J. V. (1979). From social interaction to higher psychological processes: A clarification and application of Vygotsky's theory. *Human Development*, 22, 1–22.

White, J. L., Moffitt, T. E., Earls, F., Robins, L., & Silva, P. A. (1990). How early can we tell? Predictors of childhood conduct disorder and adolescent delinquency. *Criminology*, 28, 507–33.

White, L., & Brinkerhoff, D. (1981). The sexual division of labor: Evidence from childhood. *Social Forces*, 60, 170–81.

Whitehurst, G. J., & Lonigan, C. J. (1998). Child development and emergent literacy. *Child Development*, 69, 848–72.

Wood, D. (1998). *How Children Think and Learn* (2nd edn). Oxford: Blackwell.

Wood, D., Bruner, J. S., & Ross, G. (1976). The role of tutoring in problem solving. *Journal of Child Psychology and Psychiatry*, 17, 89–100.

Wood, D., & Wood, H. (1996). Vygotsky, tutoring and learning. *Oxford Review of Education*, 22, 5–16.

Woolley, J. D. (1997). Thinking about fantasy: Are children fundamentally different thinkers and believers from adults? *Child Development*, 68, 991–1011.

Yuill, N. (1993). Understanding of personality and dispositions. In M. Bennett (ed.), *The Child as Psychologist*. Hemel Hempstead: Harvester Wheatsheaf.

Name Index

Subject Index